Courtesy of the author

About the Author

HERBERT W. WARDEN III is the editor of *In Praise of Sailors: A Nautical Anthology of Art, Poetry, and Prose*. A graduate of Princeton University, Mr. Warden served in the Marine Corps in World War II and in the Korean War.

AMERICAN COURAGE

AMERICAN
COURAGE

Remarkable True Stories

Exhibiting the Bravery That Has Made

Our Country Great

★ ★ ★

Edited by

HERBERT W. WARDEN III

★ ★ ★

Harper

An Imprint of HarperCollins*Publishers*

Pages 377–379 constitute an extension of this copyright page.

A hardcover edition of this book was published in 2005 by William Morrow, an imprint of HarperCollins Publishers.

HarperCollins books may be purchased for educational, business, or sales promotional use. For information please write: Special Markets Department, HarperCollins Publishers, 10 East 53rd Street, New York, NY 10022.

FIRST HARPER PAPERBACK PUBLISHED 2006.

The Library of Congress has catalogued the hardcover edition as follows:

American courage : remarkable true stories exhibiting the bravery that has made our country great / [edited by] Herbert W. Warden.— 1st ed.
   p.   cm.
   Includes bibliographical references.
   ISBN 0-06-078239-0 (alk. paper)
   1. United States—History—Anecdotes. 2. United States—Biography—Anecdotes. 3. Courage—United States—Anecdotes.
4. National characteristics, American—Anecdotes. I. Warden, Herbert W.

E178.6.A393   2005
920.073—dc22
[B]   2004063570

ISBN-10: 0-06-078240-4 (pbk.)
ISBN-13: 978-0-06-078240-5 (pbk.)

06 07 08 09 10 ❖/RRD 10 9 8 7 6 5 4 3 2 1

TO

Nancy Warden and Bert Warden

Polly & Herb Taylor

Anne & Mark Sinkinson

★

Heather, Charlotte & Hudson Taylor

Libby & Fordy Sinkinson

Contents

THE CIVIL WAR

THE WAYS OF THE WEST

THE AMERICAN CENTURY

Preface

THEODORE ROOSEVELT proclaimed that the true hallmarks of the American character were "courage, vitality, perseverance, clean living, sturdy good sense, and an inflexible rectitude of soul." All of this is true, but the president's first word—*courage*—seems to capture the enduring quality of Americans that has been expressed throughout our history, whether fighting for liberty or seeking a better life in the face of physical hardship. It signals an indomitable spirit that has allowed us as a nation to stand tall when challenged, without fear or trepidation. Indeed, courage is not just the absence of fear; on the contrary, it is the ability to act in the face of one's fears.

The stories in *American Courage,* which span almost four centuries, represent the best that Americans can be in times of crisis or when confronted with adversity. I began collecting these stories thirty years ago, and I still marvel that these splendid examples of courage are fact, not fiction. I have taken the selections from autobiographies, eyewitness reports, and historical accounts; each is a good story well told, be it by the participant or a historian. At times I have edited the prose; each chapter has an introduction to set the scene historically. Though the collection does not aspire to be comprehensive, the writings are the voice of America's remarkable history, marking our passage in world history as we fought, sometimes with ourselves, to build a free nation from scratch.

Many of the episodes in this book were decisive turning points in American history. After the landing of the Pilgrims at Plymouth, Massachusetts, in December 1620, the Mayflower Compact, signed by forty-one adults, became a seeds-of-democracy landmark. The Pilgrims formed a "civil body politic" to frame "just and equal laws" and submit to the will of the majority in whatever regulations of government were agreed upon. Out of the 104 *Mayflower* passengers, only 50 survived that initial deadly winter. Yet these first settlers led the way for shipload after shipload of immigrants to follow them. William Bradford, the Pilgrims' leader for thirty years, wrote with just pride, "May not, and ought not, the children of these fathers rightly say: 'Our fathers were Englishmen who came over this great ocean, and were ready to perish in this Wilderness.' "

The fifty-six signers of the Declaration of Independence created a new nation—the United States of America. Each signer pledged his life, his fortune, and his sacred honor. He was committing treason, and he was subject to death by hanging. In speaking of the prospect of hanging, heavyset, great-bellied Benjamin Harrison of Virginia wryly twitted tiny, wiry Elbridge Gerry of Massachusetts: "With me it will be all over in a minute, but you, you will be dancing on air an hour after I am gone." The jest captures the confidence with which these early patriots approached their deadly serious actions.

The Declaration was followed by Washington crossing the ice-choked Delaware River on Christmas night, 1776, in the most daring exploit of the Revolution. His password that night was "Victory or Death." A snowstorm with near zero visibility shielded Washington's movements, as he launched a two-prong surprise attack on Trenton, New Jersey. During the battle he rode up alone on horseback to a major and his troops, and called out, "March on, my brave fellows, after me!" while he spun his horse toward the enemy. His victory at Trenton, and a few days later at Princeton, where he whipped the British, turned the tide of the Revolutionary War.

Lesser-known episodes had historic consequences too. George Rogers Clark's forced winter march to capture Vincennes (1779) from the British delivered the southern end of the Old Northwest territory (now Ohio, Indiana, and Illinois) into American hands. Sam Houston with his seven hundred men and famous war cry "Remember the Alamo!" surprised and routed Santa Anna at San Jacinto. This battle won Texas its independence and set the stage for the Mexican War (1846–1848), whereafter Mexico relinquished all claims to Texas above the Rio Grande, and ceded New Mexico and California.

American Courage also includes breathtaking accounts of men and women whose daring and hardihood gave bone and sinew to our country—from Davy Crockett's report from the Alamo and the chronicle of a slave escaping to freedom to the story of the D-Day invasion and the resolve of the passengers of Flight 93 on September 11, 2001. As the old-time cowboys said of the brave, "He had bones in his spinal column, and knew how to die standin' up." When twenty-five-year-old Charles Lindbergh first flew the Atlantic nonstop to Paris, Ambassador Herrick welcomed him with a speech fathering this thought: "A nation which breeds such boys need never fear for its future."

*

The birth of American independence began with the courage to emigrate. The men and women who set foot on a gangplank and sailed across the Atlantic to face the unknown literally abandoned their parental roots. By a process of self-selection, our forefathers left behind the indecisive and timorous. Once here, after Father Time produced new generations, and as the frontier slowly moved west, the daring still went first. Early Texas pioneers said it with pith and punch:

> *Cowards never started.*
> *Weaklings never got here.*
> *And the unfit don't stay.*

And in Thomas Jefferson's impassioned words: "There is not a single crowned head in Europe whose talents or merits would entitle him to be elected a vestryman by the people of any parish in America."

The turbulent frontier was the crucible for the new American breed. The historian Frederick Jackson Turner observed: "The wilderness masters the colonist. It finds him a European in dress, industries, tools, modes of travel, and thought. It takes him from the railroad car and puts him in a birch canoe. It strips off the garments of civilization and arrays him in the hunting shirt and the moccasin. It puts him in a log cabin of the Cherokee and Iroquois and runs an Indian palisade around him. In short, at first the environment is too strong for the man. He must accept the conditions which it furnishes, or perish."

Behind the explorers came the fur trappers and hunters and then the pioneer settlers. In the land of the plains came the cattlemen, followed by the farmers who tilled the soil and fenced the land. People congregated in towns, and manufacturers arrived to recruit workers. Each group had its place in time, and its own frontier to master.

Looking back, this nation seems to have been perpetually at war during any given individual's lifetime. Ours is a fighting nation, symbolized by an early American flag with a coiled rattlesnake, emblazoned with the words "Don't tread on me." Today our material conditions have changed, but what it means to be an American has not. We currently are engaged in a war on terror not of our own making. It seems that America will always be challenged and that our courageous national character will always be required. Take heart from these stories. Remember, "eternal vigilance is the price of liberty"; expect no surcease. As the old-time cowboys said, "Keep your craw full of sand and fightin' tallow."

—HWW III

THE EARLY YEARS

The Pilgrims' Farewell

(from William Bradford,
Of Plymouth Plantation 1620–1647)

HENRY VIII, *king of England, broke with the Roman Catholic pope in 1532–33 over his divorce. He stopped all types of payments and appeals to Rome, claimed jurisdiction over all spiritual matters, and required from the clergy an oath of allegiance to the Crown. In 1559, under Queen Elizabeth I, an Act of Supremacy was passed declaring that the sovereign was the supreme head of the Anglican Church and* The Book of Common Prayer *was the proper guidebook to the Almighty.*

During the reigns of Elizabeth I (1558–1603) and James I (1603–1625), small independent bands of breakaway worshippers sprang up. Those called Puritans distinguished themselves from the Anglicans in matters of organization and independence. They held that each individual could communicate directly with God without an intermediary hierarchy of bishop, pope, or king. They believed that each congregation had the right to choose its own leaders, hold simple services in simple places, and eschew the vestments, hauteur, pageantry, and protocols of the Anglican church. However, under the Acts of Uniformity, such religious independence by the Puritans constituted disobedience to the Crown.

The Anglican clergy pressed the authorities to enforce the law on religious conformity. Puritan meetings were sporadically spied upon, forcing them underground. In 1571 and in 1586 two Puritan groups were arrested, but members continued to hold their services in prison. On one occasion, sixteen out of fifty who were imprisoned died of jail fever. Two Puritan leaders, John Greenwood and Henry Barrowe, were imprisoned in 1587 and later sentenced to death for "devising and circulating seditious books." They were hung in 1593. The situation left the Puritans with but three options—to stay underground, to conform to the Anglican religion, or to emigrate from England.

Seeking freedom of worship in Holland, the first band of Pilgrims, as we now know the Puritans, sold their homes and possessions. Since it was then illegal to emigrate, they secretly chartered and boarded a sailing ship. The treacherous captain trapped them belowdecks, stole their goods and money, and betrayed them to the authorities, who seized and imprisoned them. The second contingent, secretly organized by William Brewster, rowed only the men out to their chartered ship to inspect it for safety and avoid another case of chicanery. Left ashore, the women and children with their baggage were discovered, intercepted by "horse and foot," and rounded up, leaving only the men to sail, forlorn and destitute, across the sea to Holland. These women and children were shifted from one inadequate prison to another for months on end, without trial, sufficient food, or shelter. Their final, successful exodus took place in 1608.

A group of about one hundred Pilgrims landed in Amsterdam and soon migrated to Leyden, where they lived and worked. After twelve years, the congregation, having increased to three hundred, found the work hard and their incomes small. They also feared that they lacked sufficient civil autonomy and were apprehensive of their children being "Dutchified." In the winter of 1616–17 they decided that America would be a freer, more secluded place to independently lead their lives and practice their beliefs.

Selected from his Of Plymouth Plantation, *here is William Bradford's story of the Pilgrims' farewell as they boarded the ship* Speedwell *for*

England. The Speedwell *sailed them across the English Channel, to England, but once it left England, in company with the larger* Mayflower, *leaks in the hull forced it to turn back. Only the* Mayflower *made it to America.*

* * *

A T LENGTH, the provisions were collected and everything was ready. A small ship [the *Speedwell*] was brought to Holland to help in transportation, and to stay in the New World for fishing and such other affairs as might be for the good and benefit of the colony. Another vessel, the *Mayflower,* was hired at London.

So being ready to depart from Leyden, the day was spent in solemn humiliation, their pastor taking his text, from Ezra vii.21: "And there at the river, by Ahava, I proclaimed a fast, that we might humble ourselves before our God, and seek of Him a right way for us, and for our children, and for all our substance." The rest of the time was spent in pouring out prayers to the Lord with great fervency, mixed with an abundance of tears. And the time of being come that they must depart, they were accompanied with most of their brethren out of the city, unto a town sundry miles off called Delftshaven, where the ship lay ready to receive them. So they left the goodly and pleasant city of Leyden which had been their resting place for nearly twelve years; but they knew they were pilgrims, and looked not much on those things, but lifted up their eyes to the heavens, their dearest country, and quieted their spirits.

When they came to Delftshaven they found the ship and all things ready. Their friends who could not come with them followed after them, and sundry also came from Amsterdam to see them board ship and take leave of them. That night was spent with little sleep by the most, but with friendly entertainment and Christian discourse and other expressions of true Christian love. The next day (the wind being fair) they went aboard and their friends with them, where truly doleful was the sight of that sad and mournful parting to see what sighs and sobs did sound amongst them, what tears did gush from every eye, and pithy speeches pierced each heart, that sundry of the Dutch strangers that stood on the quay as spectators could not refrain from tears. Yet comfortable and sweet it was to see such lively and true expressions of dear and unfeigned love.

But the tide, which stays for no man, calling them away that were thus loath to depart, their reverend pastor falling down on his knees (and they all with him) with watery cheeks commended them with most fervent prayers to the Lord and His blessing. And then with mutual embraces and many tears they took their leaves one of another, which proved to be the last leave to many of them.

★ 2 ★

The Decimation and Survival
of Plymouth Colony

(from William Bradford,
Of Plymouth Plantation 1620–1647)

T HE MAYFLOWER *was a three-masted, bark-rigged ship of
180 tons, with a speed of two and a half knots. It sailed from England on September 16, 1620. While aboard ship the Pilgrims
signed an extraordinary document called the Mayflower Compact, in
which they agreed to self-government. Not until November 21, 1620, did
they sight Cape Cod, their first glimpse of the New World, and anchor
in what would one day be Provincetown Harbor. Ashore they collected
wood and water and explored the countryside, spotting signs of native
inhabitants—cultivation and a grave. After a short march they were
attacked by "Indians" with bows and arrows, fired back, and returned
to the* Mayflower. *They sailed across the bay to land at Plymouth, where
they began to build log houses and a stockade. Again from his book*
Of Plymouth Plantation, *here is William Bradford's account of the
hardships faced by the young colony.*

* * *

B EING THUS ARRIVED in a good harbor, and brought safe to land, they fell upon their knees and blessed the God of Heaven who had brought them over the vast and furious ocean, and delivered them from all perils and miseries thereof, again to set their feet on the firm and stable earth, their proper element.

But here I cannot but stay and make a pause, and stand half amazed at this poor people's present condition. And so I think the reader will, too, when he well considers the same. Being thus passed the vast ocean . . . they had now no friends to welcome them, nor inns to entertain or refresh their weatherbeaten bodies; no houses or much less towns to repair to, to seek for succour . . . For the season was winter, and they that know the winters of that country know them to be sharp and violent, and subject to cruel and fierce storms, dangerous to travel to known places, much more to search an unknown coast. Besides, what could they see but a hideous and desolate wilderness, full of wild beasts and wild men—and what multitudes there might be of them they knew not. Which ever way they turned their eyes (save upward to the heavens) they could have little solace or content in respect to any outward objects.

Summer was gone. The whole country, full of woods and thickets, represented a wild and savage hue. If they looked behind them, there was the mighty ocean which they had passed and which now was a bar and gulf to separate them from all the civilized parts of the world. What could now sustain them but the Spirit of God and His grace?

May not and ought not the children of these fathers rightly say: "Our fathers were Englishmen who came over this great ocean, and were ready to perish in this wilderness; but they cried unto the Lord, and He heard their voice and looked on their adversity." On the 15th of December they arrived and resolved where to pitch their dwelling; and on the 25th began to erect the first house for common use to receive them and their goods. After they had provided a place for their goods, and begun some small cottages for their habitation, as time would admit, they met and consulted of laws and orders, both for their civil and military government.

In these hard and difficult beginnings they found some discontents and murmurings arise amongst them, and some gave mutinous speeches, but they were soon quelled and overcome by the wisdom, patience, and just and equal carriage of things by Governor John Carver, and the better part, which clave faithfully together in the main. But that which was most sad and lamentable was, that in two or three months' time half their company had died, especially in January and February, being the depth of winter, and wanting houses and other comforts; being inflicted with scurvy and other diseases which this long voyage and their inaccommodate condition had brought upon them.

So as they died sometimes two or three a day during these months, that of the 100 odd persons from the *Mayflower*, scarcely fifty remained. And of these in the time of most distress, there was but six or seven persons who to their great commendations, be it spoken, spared no pains night nor day, but with abundance of toil and hazard of their own health, fetched them wood, made them fires, dressed them meat, made their beds, washed their loathsome clothes, clothed and unclothed them. In a word, did all the homely and necessary offices for them which dainty and queasy stomachs cannot endure to hear named; and all this willingly and cheerfully, without any grudging in the least, showing herein their true love unto their friends and brethren; a rare example and worthy to be remembered.

Two of these seven were Mr. William Brewster, their reverend Elder, and Miles Standish, their Captain and military commander, unto whom myself and many others were much beholden in our low and sick condition. And yet the Lord so upheld these persons as in this general calamity they were not at all infected either with sickness or lameness. And what I have said of these I may say of many others who died in this general visitation, and others yet living; that whilst they had health, yea, or any strength continuing, they were not wanting to help any that had need of them. And I doubt not but their recompense is with the Lord.

Mrs. Rowlandson's Captivity

(from Mary Rowlandson,
The Soveraignty & Goodness of God, Being a
Narrative of the Captivity and Restauration of
Mrs. Mary Rowlandson, 1682)

AFTER THE FOUNDING *of Plymouth and the Bay Colony, two major wars were fought with the Indians. The first, the Pequot War (1636–37), was waged along the Connecticut shoreline. The second was called King Philip's War (1675–76) after the Indian chief who raided an arc of villages twenty to forty miles north, west, and south of Boston. It was the fiercest of New England's wars, and pivotal for the survival of the colonists.*

As the settlers moved inland from the seacoast, speculators purchased land from the Indians. But the Indians' concept of owning land was communal, while the colonists' was proprietary. To live, a hunting Indian needed twenty times more land than a farmer did. When the Indians deeded land to the colonists, they thought the unused land was to be shared, not vacated; their hunting and fishing rights to be continued, not abrogated. Over time, the pioneer settlements moved within ten to forty miles of the Indian villages. This was near enough to heighten the Indians' fear of encroachment, near enough for trading, and near enough for attack.

Upon the death of Massasoit, chief sachem of the Wampanoag tribe, who were the original friends of the Pilgrims, the tribe elected his son, King Philip, as his successor. Philip dressed with the flourish of a king, ran up bills in Boston, and sold land to pay for his debts. For nine years he watched and plotted as his hunting lands slowly shrank. In 1671 he was forced to acknowledge the English king, observe the king's laws, pay tribute, and follow the advice of Plymouth in matters of war and the disposal of Indian lands. Silent and sullen, he faced a simple choice: total subjugation or total war, for which he would need the help of neighboring tribes. Philip brought into his league the Narragansetts (southwest of Providence) and the Nipmucks (around Sturbridge, Massachusetts), who were squeezed between the western settlements of the Bay Colony and those on the Connecticut River.

In June 1675 King Philip struck his first blow. From his base near Bristol, Rhode Island, he attacked Swansea (near Fall River), Massachusetts, then turned on Dartmouth (near Bedford). Escaping north, Philip had aroused the fear, wrath, and military union of Plymouth, the Bay Colony, and Connecticut.

The tempo quickened. The Indians struck Mendon, Massachusetts, in July, Lancaster and Brookfield in August, then, between September and December, the towns along the Connecticut River—Northfield, Deerfield, Hadley, Hatfield, and Springfield. In December attacks began against the arc of towns outside Boston, first Worcester and then Concord. In February 1676 it was Medfield and Lancaster, where Mrs. Rowlandson's story begins. The raids continued through June, against Plymouth, Weymouth, Scituate, Chelmsford, and Groton. All told, the Indians assaulted thirty-nine towns and destroyed sixteen.

The settlers defended their villages from selected strong houses. At the first alarm, the townspeople would run to these garrisoned forts to fight. Thus surprise coupled with hit-and-run tactics was essential to the Indians' success.

Mary Rowlandson was the wife of the minister in Lancaster during King Philip's War. She writes, in this excerpt from a 1682 edition of her autobiographical narrative, The Soveraignty & Goodness of God, Being a Narrative of the Captivity and Restauration of Mrs. Mary Rowlandson, *of the sack of Lancaster and her first ten days as a captive in three "removes," or camps. After eighty-two days of captivity, she was ransomed for twenty pounds. Following the ordeal, she and her surviving son and daughter returned to Boston to be reunited with her husband.*

* * *

ON THE TENTH of February, 1676, about sunrise, the Indians attacked Lancaster. Hearing the noise of some guns, we looked out. Several houses were burning, and the smoke ascending to heaven. There were five persons taken in one house. The father, the mother, and a suckling child they tomahawked. The other two they took and carried away alive. There were two others, who were set upon outside of their garrison. One was tomahawked, the other escaped. Another, running along, was shot and wounded, and fell down. He begged of them his life, promising them money, but they would not hearken to him, but tomahawked him and stripped him naked, and split open his bowels. Another, seeing many of the Indians about his barn, ventured and went out, but was quickly shot down. There were three others belonging to the same garrison who were killed. The Indians getting up upon the roof of the barn, had the advantage to shoot down upon them over their fortification. Thus these murderous wretches went on burning and destroying all before them.

At length they came and beset our own house, and quickly it was the dolefulest day that ever mine eyes saw. The house stood upon the edge of a hill. Some of the Indians got behind the hill, others into the barn, and others behind any thing that would shelter them. From all which places they shot against the house, so that the bullets seemed to fly like hail. They wounded one man among us, then another, and then a third. After two hours, they brought flax and hemp to set the house afire. They fired it once and one of our men ventured out and quenched it. But they quickly fired it again, and it took.

Now came the dreadful hour. Some in our house were fighting for their lives, others wallowing in their blood. The house on fire over our heads, and the bloody heathen ready to tomahawk us if we stirred out. Now might we hear mothers and children crying out for themselves, and one another, Lord, what shall we do? Then I took my children (and one of my sisters her's) to go forth and leave the house. But as soon as we came to the door, and appeared, the Indians shot so thick, that the bullets rattled against the house, as if one had taken a handful of stones and threw them, so that we were fain to fall back.

But out we must go. The fire increasing, and coming along behind us, roaring, and the Indians gaping before us with their guns, spears, and hatchets, to devour us. No sooner were we out of the house, but my brother-in-law (being wounded in the throat, defending the house), fell down dead. Whereat the Indians scornfully shouted, and hallooed, and were presently upon him, stripping off his clothes. The bullets were flying thick, one went through my side, and the same (as it would seem) through the bowels and hand of my dear child in my arms, only six years old. One of my elder sister's children, named William, had then his leg broken, which the Indians perceiving, they tomahawked him. Thus were we butchered by those merciless heathens, standing amazed, with blood running down to our heels.

My elder sister being yet in the house, and seeing those woeful sights, the infidels hauling mothers one way, and children another, and some wallowing in their blood, and her eldest son telling her that her son William was dead, and myself was wounded, she said, And, Lord let me die with them: which was no sooner said, but she was struck with a bullet, and fell down dead over the threshold. The Indians laid hold of us, pulling me one way, and the children another, and said, "Come, go along with us." I told them they could kill me. They answered, if I were willing to go along with them, they would not hurt me.

Oh, the doleful sight that now was to behold at this house! Come, behold the works of the Lord, what desolations he has made in the earth. Of thirty-seven persons who were in this one house, none escaped either present death, or a bitter captivity, save only one, who might say as in Job i.15: And I only am escaped to tell the news. There were twelve killed, some shot, some stabbed with their spears, some tomahawked. When we are in prosperity, oh, the little that we think of such dreadful sights, and to see our dear friends and relations lie bleeding out their heart's blood upon the ground. There was one who was chopped into the head with a hatchet, and stripped naked, and yet was crawling up and down. It is a solemn sight to see so many Christians lying in their blood, some here, and some there, like a company of sheep torn by wolves. All of them stripped naked by a company of hell-hounds, roaring, singing, ranting and insulting, as if they would have torn our very hearts out; yet the Lord by his almighty power preserved a number of us from death, for there were twenty-four of us taken alive and carried captive.

I had often before this said, that if the Indians should come, I should choose rather to be killed by them, than taken alive; but when it came to the trial, my mind changed; their glittering weapons so daunted my spirit, that I chose rather to go along with those (as I may say) ravenous bears, than that moment to end my days. And that I may better declare what happened to me during that grievous captivity, I shall particularly speak of the several Removes we had up and down the wilderness.

THE FIRST REMOVE

Now away we must go with those barbarous creatures, with our bodies wounded and bleeding, and our hearts no less than our bodies. About a mile we went that night, up upon a hill within sight of our town, where they intended to lodge.

This was the dolefulest night that ever my eyes saw. Oh the roaring and singing and dancing and yelling of those black creatures in the night, which made the place a lively resemblance of hell; and as miserable was the waste that was there made, of horses, cattle, sheep, swine, calves, lambs, roasting pigs, and fowl, (which they had plundered in the town), some roasting, some lying and burning, and some boiling, to feed our merciless enemies, who were joyful enough, though we were disconsolate.

To add to the dolefulness of the former day, and the dismalness of the present night, my thoughts ran upon my losses and sad bereaved condition. All was gone, my husband gone (at least separated from me, he being in the Bay; and to add to my grief, the Indians told me they would kill him as he came homeward); my children gone, my relations and friends gone, our house and home and all our comforts within door and without, all was gone, except my life, and I knew not but the next moment that it might go too. There remained nothing to me but one poor wounded babe and it seemed at present worse than death, that it was in such a pitiful condition, bespeaking compassion and I had no refreshing for it, nor suitable things to revive it.

THE SECOND REMOVE

But now, the next morning, I must turn my back upon the town, and travel with them into the vast and desolate wilderness, I knew not whither. It is not my tongue nor pen can express the sorrows of my heart, and bitterness of my spirit, that I had at this departure: but God was with me in a wonderful manner, carrying me along, and bearing up my spirit, that it did not quite fail.

One of the Indians carried my poor wounded babe upon a horse; it went moaning all along: "I shall die, I shall die." I went on foot after it, with sorrow that cannot be expressed. At length I took it off the horse and carried it in my arms till my strength failed, and I fell down with it. Then they set me upon a horse with my wounded child in my lap, and there being no furniture upon the horse's back, as we went down a steep hill, we both fell over the horse's head at which they like inhuman creatures laughed, and rejoiced to see it, though I thought we should there have ended our days, overcome with so many difficulties. But the Lord renewed my strength still, and carried me along that I might see more of his power.

After this it quickly began to snow and when night came on they stopped. And now I must sit down in the snow before a little fire, and a few boughs behind me, with my sick child in my lap, and calling much for water, being now (through the wound) fallen into a violent fever. My own wound was also growing so stiff that I could scarce sit down or rise up; yet so it must be that I must sit all this cold winter night upon the cold snowy ground, with my sick child in my arms looking that every hour would be the last of its life, and having no Christian friend near me, either to comfort or help me. Oh, I may see the wonderful power of God, that my spirit did not utterly sink under my afflictions; still the Lord upheld me with his gracious and merciful spirit, and we were both alive to see the light of morning.

THE THIRD REMOVE

The morning being come, they prepared to go on their way. One of the Indians got up on a horse and they set me up behind him with my poor sick babe in my lap. A very wearisome and tedious day I had of it; what with my own wound, and my child being so exceedingly sick, and in a lamentable condition with her wound. It may be easily judged what a poor feeble condition we were in, there being not the least crumb of refreshment that came within either of our mouths from Wednesday night to Saturday night, except only a little cold water. This day in the afternoon, about an hour by sun, we came to an Indian town called Wenimesset. When we were come, oh the number of pagans (our merciless enemies) that there came about me! I might say, as David, Psal. xxvii.13. I had fainted, unless I had believed, etc. The next day was the Sabbath. I then remembered how careless I had been of God's holy time; how many Sabbaths I had lost and misspent, and how evilly I had walked in God's sight; which lay so closely upon my spirit, that it was easy for me to see how righteous it was with God to cut off the thread of my life, and cast me out of his presence forever. Yet the Lord still showed mercy to me, and upheld me; and as he wounded me with one hand, so he healed me with the other. Then I took oak leaves and laid to my side, and with the blessing of God it cured me also; yet before the cure was wrought, I may say, as it is in Psal.xxxviii. 5, 6. My wounds stick and are corrupt, I am troubled, I am bowed down greatly, I go mourning all the day long. I sat much alone with my poor wounded child in my lap, which moaned night and day, having nothing to revive the body, or cheer the spirits of her; but instead of that, sometimes one Indian would come and tell me one hour, that your master will tomahawk her, and then a second and then a third, your master will quickly knock your child in the head.

This was all the comfort I had from them, miserable comforters are ye all, as he said. Thus nine days I sat upon my knees with my babe upon my lap, till my flesh was raw again. My child being even ready to depart this sorrowful world, they bade me carry it out to another wigwam (I suppose because they would not be troubled with such spectacles), whither I went with a very heavy heart, and down I sat with the picture of death in my lap. About two hours in the night my sweet babe, like a lamb, departed this life, on February 18, 1675, it being about six years and five months old. It was about nine days from the first wounding in this miserable condition, without any refreshing of one nature or another, except a little cold water. I cannot but take notice, how at another time I could not bear to be in the room where any dead person was, but now the case is changed; I must, and can lie down by my dead babe, side by side, all the night after. I have thought since of the wonderful goodness of God to me, in preserving me in the use of my reason and sense in that distressed time, that I did not use wicked and violent means to end my own life. In the morning when they understood that my child was dead, they sent for me home to my master's wigwam (by my master in this writing must be understood Quanopin, who was a Sagamore, and married King Philip's wife's sister; not that he first took me, but I was sold to him by another Narragansett Indian, who took me when first I came out of the garrison). I went to take up my dead child in my arms to carry it with me, but they bid me let it alone: there was no resisting, but go I must and leave it. When I had been awhile at my master's wigwam, I took the first opportunity I could to go look after my dead child. When I came I asked them what they had done with it. Then they told me it was upon the hill,—then they went and showed me where it was, where I saw the ground was newly digged, and there they told me they had buried it. There I left that child in the wilderness, and must commit it, and myself also, in this wilderness condition to Him who is above all.

★ 4 ★

Ben Franklin—On the Lam
at Age 17, Homeless, Jobless,
and Nigh Penniless

(from Benjamin Franklin,
The Autobiography of Benjamin Franklin, 1789)

B ENJAMIN FRANKLIN *snatched lightning from the sky and the scepter from tyrants. "In any age, in any place," wrote Mark Van Doren, "Franklin would have been great. Mind and will, talent and art, strength and ease, wit and grace met in him as if Nature had been lavish and happy when he was shaped." He poured commonsense observations and moral maxims into* Poor Richard's Almanack, *which became an annual best seller. As a scientist he was lionized in Europe, and elected to the Royal Society of London and the Royal Academy of Sciences in Paris. He invented bifocal eyeglasses, the Franklin stove, and the lightning rod. Flying a kite with a key during a thunderstorm, he proved that lightning was electricity. In Philadelphia he installed the city police and street lighting, organized the American Philosophical Society, founded the University of Pennsylvania, and launched the first circulating library in the United States. He signed the Declaration of Independence and presided as president of the Continental Congress, which placed Washing-*

ton in command, issued the first continental currency, and assumed responsibility to fight the war against England. Finally, with John Adams and John Jay, he nailed down favorable terms for the United States in the 1783 Treaty of Paris, ending the Revolutionary War.

The youngest of thirteen children, he was the son of a candlemaker known for his wisdom—friends sought his counsel, and he arbitrated many disputes. Ben inherited his genes.

Like Lincoln, Franklin was self-educated. He could never remember when he could not read. As a youth he borrowed all the books he could and bought as many as he could afford: Plutarch, John Bunyan, Robert Burton, Daniel Defoe, Cotton Mather, Joseph Addison, Richard Steele, and John Locke. At night he trained himself to rephrase what others wrote, seeking to express the same thoughts more briefly, more clearly, and more colorfully. He loved to debate justice and politics. At first he argued declaratively. Then he switched to the Socratean method of stepping-stone inquiries to entrap an opponent. Ultimately he adopted his own style—deft and logical, self-effacing, and never combative. "Men should be taught as if you taught them not," he wrote.

Like George Washington, he deliberately trained his character. He practiced the manners of polite society and their courteous regard for others. He entertained the men and women he conversed with, mixing humor with wisdom and common sense. He played the violin, guitar, and harp. His personal charm, self-reliance, and hard work turned chance into opportunity.

When Franklin was fourteen his father apprenticed him to his half-brother, a Boston printer, as an indentured servant for a term of four years. In time his brother turned on him and beat him. So Ben broke his contract, for which he could have been arrested, and ran away to Philadelphia at seventeen. There he soon launched a successful printing firm and began one of the most remarkable careers in American history.

With this selection from The Autobiography of Benjamin Franklin, join runaway Ben Franklin at age seventeen, as he flees from his humble beginnings in Boston headed for New York—aimless and penniless, armed only with brains, charm, guts, and gumption.

* * *

A T LENGTH, a fresh difference arising between my brother and me, I took it upon me to assert my freedom, presuming that he would not venture to produce the new indentures. It was not fair in me to take this advantage, and this I therefore reckon one of the first errata of my life; but the unfairness of it weighted little with me, when under the impressions of resentment for the blows his passion too often urged him to bestow upon me, though he was otherwise not an ill-natur'd man: perhaps I was too saucy and provoking.

When he found I would leave him, he took care to prevent my getting employment in any other printing-house of the town, by going round and speaking to every master, who accordingly refus'd to give me work. I then thought of going to New York, as the nearest place where there was a printer; and I was rather inclin'd to leave Boston when I reflected that I had already made myself a little obnoxious to the governing part, and, from the arbitrary proceedings of the Assembly in my brother's case, it was likely it might, if I stay'd, soon bring myself into scrapes; and farther, that my indiscreet disputations about religion began to make me pointed at with horror by good people as an infidel or atheist. I determin'd on the point, but my father now siding with my brother, I was sensible that, if I attempted to go openly, means would be used to prevent me. My friend Collins, therefore, undertook to manage a little for me. He agreed with the captain of a New York sloop for my passage, under the notion of my being a young acquaintance of his that had got a naughty girl with child, whose friends would compel me to marry her, and therefore I could not appear or come away publicly. So I sold some of my books to raise a little money, was taken on board privately, and as we had a fair wind, in three days I found myself in New York, near 300 miles from home, a boy of but 17, without the least recommendation to or knowledge of, any person in the place, and with very little money in my pocket.

My inclinations for the sea were by this time worne out, or I might now have gratify'd them. But, having a trade, and supposing myself a pretty good workman, I offer'd my service to the printer in the place, old Mr. William Bradford, who had been the first printer in Pennsylvania, but removed from thence upon the quarrel of George Keith. He could give me no employment, having little to do, and help enough already; but says he: "My son at Philadelphia has lately lost his principal hand, Aquila Rose, by death; if you go thither, I believe he may employ you." Philadelphia was 100 miles farther; I set out, however, in a boat for Amboy, leaving my chest and things to follow me round by sea.

In crossing the bay, we met with a squall that tore our rotten sails to pieces, prevented our getting into the Kill and drove us upon Long Island. In our way, a drunken Dutchman, who was a passenger too, fell overboard; when he was sinking, I drew him up, so that we got him in again. His ducking sobered him a little, and he went to sleep, taking first out of his pocket a book, which he desir'd I would dry for him. It proved to be my old favorite author, Bunyan's *Pilgrim's Progress* in Dutch, finely printed, on good paper, with copper cuts, a dress better than I had ever seen it wear in its own language. I have since found that it has been translated into most of the languages of Europe, and suppose it has been more generally read than any other book, except perhaps the Bible. Honest John was the first that I know of who mix'd narration and dialogue, a method of writing very engaging to the reader, who, in the most interesting parts, finds himself, as it were, brought into the company, and present at the discourse. Defoe, in his *Crusoe*, his *Moll Flanders, Religious Courtship, Family Instructor,* and other pieces, has imitated it with success, and Richardson has done the same in his *Pamela*, etc.

When we drew near the island, we found it was at a place where there could be no landing, there being a great surf on the stony beach. So we dropt anchor and swung round towards the shore. Some people came down to the water edge and hallow'd to us, as we did to them, but the wind was so high, and the surf so loud, that we could not hear so as to understand each other. There were canoes on the shore, and we made signs and hallow'd that they should fetch us, but they either did not understand us, or thought it impracticable, so they went away, and night coming on, we had no remedy but to wait till the wind should abate; and, in the meantime, the boatman and I concluded to sleep, if we could; and so crowded into the scuttle, with the Dutchman, who was still wet, and the spray beating over the head of our boat, leak'd thro' to us, so that we were soon almost as wet as he. In this manner we lay all night with very little rest; but, the wind abating the next day, we made a shift to reach Amboy before night, having been thirty hours on the water, without victuals, or any drink but a bottle of filthy rum, the water we sailed on being salt.

In the evening I found myself very feverish, and went in to bed; but, having read somewhere that cold water drank plentifully was good for a fever, I follow'd the prescription, sweat plentifully most of the night, my fever left me, and in the morning, crossing the ferry, I proceeded on my journey on foot, having fifty miles to Burlington, where I was told I should find boats that would carry me the rest of the way to Philadelphia.

It rained very hard all the day; I was thoroughly soak'd, and by noon a good deal tired; so I stopt at a poor inn, where I staid all night, beginning now to wish that I had never left home. I cut so miserable a figure, too, that I found, by the questions ask'd me, I was suspected to be some runaway servant, and in danger of being taken up on that suspicion. However, I proceeded the next day, and got in the evening to an inn, within eight or ten miles of Burlington, kept by one Dr. Brown. He entered into conversation with me while I took some refreshment, and, finding I had read a little, became very sociable and friendly. Our acquaintance continu'd as long as he liv'd. He had been, I imagine, an itinerant doctor, for there was no town in England, or country in Europe, of which he could not give a very particular account. He had some letters, and was ingenious, but much of an unbeliever, and wickedly undertook, some years after, to travestie the Bible in doggrel verse, as Cotton had done Virgil. By this means he set many of the facts in a very ridiculous light, and might have hurt weak minds if his work had been published; but it never was.

At his house I lay that night, and the next morning reach'd Burlington, but had the mortification to find that the regular boats were gone a little before my coming, and no other expected to go before Tuesday, this being Saturday; wherefore I returned to an old woman in the town, of whom I had bought gingerbread to eat on the water, and I ask'd her advice. She invited me to lodge at her house till a passage by water should offer; and being tired with my foot travelling, I accepted the invitation. She understanding I was a printer, would have had me stay at that town and follow my business, being ignorant of the stock necessary to begin with. She was very hospitable, gave me a dinner of ox-cheek with great good will, accepting only a pot of ale in return; and I thought myself fixed till Tuesday should come. However, walking in the evening by the side of the river, a boat came by, which I found was going towards Philadelphia, with several people in her. They took me in, and, as there was no wind, we row'd all the way; and about midnight, not having yet seen the city, some of the company were confident we must have passed it, and would row no farther; the others knew not where we were; so we put toward the shore, got into a creek, landed near an old fence, with the rails of which we made a fire, the night being cold, in October, and there we remained till daylight. Then one of the company knew the place to be Cooper's Creek, a little above Philadelphia, which we saw as soon as we got out of the creek, and arriv'd there about eight or nine o'clock on the Sunday morning, and landed at the Market-street wharf.

I have been the more particular in this description of my journey, and shall be so of my first entry into that city, that you may in your mind compare such unlikely beginnings with the figure I have since made there. I was in my working dress, my best clothes being to come round by sea. I was dirty from my journey; my pockets were stuff'd out with shirts and stockings, and I knew no soul nor where to look for lodging. I was fatigued with travelling, rowing, and want of rest; I was very hungry; and my whole stock of cash consisted of a Dutch dollar, and about a shilling in copper. The latter I gave the people of the boat for my passage, who at first refus'd it, on account of my rowing; but I insisted on their taking it. A man being sometimes more generous when he has but a little money than when he has plenty, perhaps thro' fear of being thought to have but little.

Then I walked up the street, gazing about till near the market-house I met a boy with bread. I had made many a meal on bread, and, inquiring where he got it, I went immediately to the baker's he directed me to, in Second-street, and ask'd for bisket, intending such as we had in Boston; but they, it seems, were not made in Philadelphia. Then I asked for a three-penny loaf, and was told they had none such. So not considering or knowing the difference of money, and the greater cheapness nor the names of his bread, I bade him give me three-penny worth of any sort. He gave me, accordingly, three great puffy rolls. I was surpriz'd at the quantity, but took it, and, having no room in my pockets, walk'd off with a roll under each arm, and eating the other. Thus I went up Market-street as far as Fourth-street, passing by the door of Mr. Read, my future wife's father; when she, standing at the door, saw me, and thought I made, as I certainly did, a most awkward, ridiculous appearance. Then I turned and went down Chestnut-street and part of Walnut-street, eating my roll all the way, and, coming round, found myself again at Market-street wharf, near the boat I came in, to which I went for a draught of the river water; and, being filled with one of my rolls, gave the other two to a woman and her child that came down the river in the boat with us, and were waiting to go farther.

Thus refreshed, I walked again up the street, which by this time had many clean-dressed people in it, who were all walking the same way. I joined them, and thereby was led into the great meeting-house of the Quakers near the market. I sat down among them, and, after looking round awhile and hearing nothing said, being very drowsy thro' labor and want of rest the preceding night, I fell fast asleep, and continu'd so till the meeting broke up, when one was kind enough to rouse me. This was, therefore, the first house I was in, or slept in, in Philadelphia.

Walking down again toward the river, and looking in the faces of people, I met a young Quaker man whose countenance I lik'd, and accosting him, requested would he tell me where a stranger could get lodging. We were then near the sign of the Three Mariners. "Here," says he, "is one place that entertains strangers, but it is not a reputable house; if thee wilt walk with me, I'll show thee a better." He brought me to the Crooked Billet in Water-street. Here I got a dinner, and, while I was eating it, several sly questions were asked me, as it seemed to be suspected, from my youth and appearance, that I might be some runaway.

After dinner, my sleepiness return'd, and, being shown to a bed, I lay down without undressing, and slept till six in the evening; was call'd to supper, went to bed again very early, and slept soundly till next morning. Then I made myself as tidy as I could, and went to Andrew

Bradford the printer's. I found in the shop the old man, his father, whom I had seen in New York, and who, travelling on horseback, had got to Philadelphia before me. He introduc'd me to his son, who receiv'd me civilly, gave me a breakfast, but told me he did not at present want a hand, being lately suppli'd with one; but there was another printer in town, lately set up, one Keimer, who, perhaps, might employ me; if not, I should be welcome to lodge at his house, and he would give me a little work to do now and then till fuller business should offer.

The old gentleman said he would go with me to the new printer; and when we found him, "Neighbor," says Bradford, "I have brought to see you a young man of your business; perhaps you may want such a one." He ask'd me a few questions, put a composing stick in my hand to see how I work'd, and then said he would employ me soon, though he had just then nothing for me to do; and taking old Bradford, whom he had never seen before, to be one of the town's people that had a good will for him, enter'd into a conversation on his present undertaking and prospects; while Bradford, not discovering that he was the other printer's father, on Keimer's saying he expected soon to get the greatest part of the business into his own hands, drew him on by artful questions and starting little doubts, to explain all his views, what interest he reli'd on, and in what manner he intended to proceed. I, who stood by and heard all, saw immediately that one of them was a crafty old sophister, and the other a mere novice. Bradford left me with Keimer, who was greatly surpris'd when I told him who the old man was.

Keimer's printing-house, I found, consisted of an old shatter'd press, and one small, worn-out font of English, which he was then using himself, composing an *Elegy on Aquila Rose*, before mentioned, an ingenious young man, of excellent character, much respected in the town, clerk of the Assembly, and a pretty poet. Keimer made verses too, but very indifferently. He could not be said to write them, for his manner was to compose them in the types directly out of his head. So there being no copy, but one pair of cases, and the *Elegy* likely to require all the "letter," no one could help him. I endeavor'd to put his press (which he had not yet us'd, and of which he understood nothing) into order fit to be work'd with; and, promising to come and print off his *Elegy* as soon as he should have got it ready, I return'd to Bradford's,

who gave me a little job to do for the present, and there I lodged and di-
eted. A few days after, Keimer sent for me to print off the *Elegy*. And
now he had got another pair of cases, and a pamphlet to reprint, on
which he set me to work.

These two printers I found poorly qualified for their business. Bradford had not been bred to it, and was very illiterate; and Keimer, tho'
something of a scholar, was a mere compositor, knowing nothing of
presswork. He had been one of the French prophets, and could act their
enthusiastic agitations. At this time he did not profess any particular religion, but something of all on occasion; was very ignorant of the
world, and had, as I afterward found, a good deal of the knave in his
composition. He did not like my lodging at Bradford's while I work'd
with him. He had a house, indeed, but without furniture, so he could
not lodge me; but he got me a lodging at Mr. Read's, before mentioned, who was the owner of his house; and, my chest and clothes
being come by this time, I made rather a more respectable appearance
in the eyes of Miss Read than I had done when she first happen'd to see
me eating my roll in the street.

I began now to have some acquaintance among the young people of
the town, that were lovers of reading, with whom I spent my evenings
very pleasantly; and gaining money by my industry and frugality, I lived
very agreeably, forgetting Boston as much as I could, and not desiring
that any there should know where I resided, except my friend Collins,
who was in my secret, and kept it when I wrote to him. At length, an incident happened that sent me back again much sooner than I had intended. I had a brother-in-law, Robert Holmes, master of a sloop that
traded between Boston and Delaware. He being at Newcaster, forty
miles below Philadelphia, heard there of me, and wrote me a letter
mentioning the concern of my friends in Boston at my abrupt departure, assuring me of their good will to me, and that everything would
be accommodated to my mind if I would return, to which he exhorted
me very earnestly. I wrote an answer to his letter, thank'd him for his advice, but stated my reasons for quitting Boston fully and in such a light
as to convince him I was not so wrong as he had apprehended.

Sir William Keith, governor of the province, was then at Newcastle,
and Captain Holmes, happening to be in company with him when my

letter came to hand, spoke to him of me, and sho'd him the letter. The governor read it, and seem'd surpris'd when he was told my age. He said I appear'd a young man of promising parts, and therefore should be encouraged; the printers at Philadelphia were wretched ones; and, if I would set up there, he made no doubt I should succeed; for his part, he would procure me the public business, and do me every other service in his power. This my brother-in-law afterwards told me in Boston, but I knew as yet nothing of it; when, one day, Keimer and I being at work together near the window, we saw the governor and another gentleman (which proved to be Colonel French, of Newcastle), finely dress'd, come directly across the street to our house; and heard them at the door.

Keimer ran down immediately, thinking it a visit to him, but the Governor enquir'd for me, came up and with a condescension and politeness I had been quite unus'd to, made me many compliments, desired to be acquainted with me, blam'd me kindly for not having made myself known to him when I first came to the place, and would have me away with him to the tavern where he was going with Col. French to taste as he said some excellent madeira. I was not a little surpriz'd, and Keimer star'd like a pig poison'd. I went however with the Governor and Col. French to a tavern on the corner of Third Street, and over the madeira he proposed my setting up my business, laid before me the probabilities of success, and both he and Col. French assur'd me I should have their interest and influence in procuring the public business of both governments.

★ 5 ★

George Washington's Winter
Journey to Warn the French

(from George Washington,
The Journal of Major George Washington, 1754)

OVERNOR DINWIDDIE *of Virginia made an extraordinary choice when he selected his man to warn the French, thrust-
ing south from Canada, against building forts in British
territory. He picked George Washington, then only twenty-one years old.
Fort Duquesne (on the site of present-day Pittsburgh) was the most strategic of all these forts, planned or actual. A French fort there would effectively block the "Gateway to the West" for Virginia and Pennsylvania.
France's grand strategy was to develop a series of forts along the Allegheny
and Ohio Rivers, then down the Mississippi to Louisiana, confining the
British to the eastern seaboard.*

*On November 14, 1753, Washington set out with horses, baggage, four
hostlers and orderlies, the frontiersman Christopher Gist, and a Dutch soldier who said he could speak French. The trip was arduous and dangerous. The trail was through forests and along waterways harboring
friendly and hostile Indians. Winter was closing upon them. On December 4 Washington rode into Venango, Pennsylvania. The French received*

*him courteously and sent him on to meet their senior officer, Legardeur de
St. Pierre, at Fort LeBoeuf on French Creek near Erie. St. Pierre rejected
Dunwoodie's demands. "He told me that the country belonged [to the
French]," reported Washington, "that no Englishman has the right to
trade upon these waters; and that he had orders to make every person pris-
oner who attempted it on the Ohio, or the waters of it."*

*To make the trip, young Washington had to be physically tough and
frontier-wise. Psychologically, he must have had a certain gravitas to be
chosen to represent the authorities of Virginia to the French and reinforce
the impression that the British just might back up their warning by force of
arms. In fact they did. Six months later Washington returned to attack the
French at Great Meadows—the first engagement of the French and Indian War (1754–1763).*

*Washington left Fort LeBoeuf on December 16 carrying St. Pierre's
written rebuff. At Venango, where he had left his horses, he found them too
fatigued to rely on, states his report—which was published in 1754 under
the title* The Journal of Major George Washington: Sent by the Honorable Robert Dinwiddie, Esq., His Majesty's Lieutenant-Governor,
and Commander in Chief of Virginia, to the Commandant of the
French Forces on [the] Ohio.

*   *   *

OUR HORSES were now so weak and feeble, and the baggage so
heavy (as we obliged to provide all the necessaries which the journey would require) that we doubted much their performing it. Therefore, myself and others (except the drivers who were obliged to ride)
gave up our horses for packs, to assist along with the baggage. I put myself in an Indian walking dress, and continued with them for three days,
until I found there was no probability of their getting home in any rea-
sonable time. The cold increased very fast, and the roads were becoming much worse by a deep snow, continually freezing. Therefore, I was
uneasy to get back to make a report of my proceedings to His Honor
the Governor, I determined to prosecute my journey the nearest way
through the woods on foot . . .

I took my necessary papers, pulled off my clothes, and tied my self up in a match coat. Then with gun in hand and pack at my back, in which there were my papers and provisions, I set out with Mr. Gist, fitted in the same manner.

On Wednesday, the following day, December 26th, just after we had passed a place called Murdering-Town (where we intended to quit the path, and steer across the country for Shannapins town) when we fell-in with a party of French Indians, who had lain in wait for us.

One of them had fired at Mr. Gist or me, not 15 steps off, but fortunately missed. We took this fellow into custody, and kept him until about nine o'clock that night. Then we let him go, and walked all the remaining part of the night without making any stop . . . that we might get the start, so far as to be out of the reach of their pursuit the next day, since we were well assured that they would follow our track as soon as it was light. The next day we continued traveling until quite dark, and got to the river about two miles above Shannapins.

We expected to have found the river frozen, but it was not—only about 50 yards from each shore. The ice, I suppose, had broken up above, for it was drifting in vast quantities.

There was no way for getting over, but on a raft. Which we set about making, with but one poor hatchet, and finished just after sun setting. This was a whole day's work. We got it launched, and went on board it. Then set off.

But before we were half way over, we were jammed in the ice, in such a manner that we expected every moment that our raft to sink, and ourselves to perish. I put out my setting pole to try to stop the raft, so that the ice might pass by. The rapidity of the stream threw the raft with so much violence against the pole, that it jerked me out into ten feet of water. But fortunately I saved myself by catching hold of one of the raft's logs.

Notwithstanding all our efforts we could not get the raft to either shore, but were obliged, as we were near an island, to quit our raft and make for it.

The cold was so extremely severe, that Mr. Gist had all his fingers and some of his toes frozen. The water was frozen so hard, that we found no difficulty the next morning of getting off the island on the ice, and we went to Mr. Frazier's. . . .

As we intend to take horses here, and it required some time to find them, I went up about three miles to the mouth of the Yaughyaughane to visit Queen Alliquippa, who had expressed great concern that we'd passed her in going to the Fort. I made her a present of a match coat and a bottle of rum, which latter was thought much the better present of the two.

Tuesday, the 1st day of January, we left Mr. Frazier's house, and arrived at Mr. Gist's at Monongahela on the 2nd.

NOTE:—Murdering Town was on a tributary of the Connoquenessing in what is now the southwestern part of Butler County. Shannapins was an Indian village on the Allegheny, near the foot of Thirty-third Street, Pittsburgh. The island was Wainwright's, which is now part of the mainland.

6

Daniel Boone Discovers Kentucky
and Incessant Warfare

(from Daniel Boone, "The Adventures of Daniel Boone"
in *The Discovery, Settlement and Present State of Kentucke*
by John Filson, 1784)

NUMEROUS INDIAN ATTACKS *on frontier settlements were fomented and supplied by the British during the Revolutionary War. The Kentucky region, in particular, became known as "the Dark and Bloody Ground." After the war, when land was put up for sale, John Filson published* The Discovery, Settlement and Present State of Kentucke *to improve the morbid image and encourage settlement. When the popular book came out in 1784 the trans-Appalachian movement had begun. In the book was an appendix containing an autobiography by Daniel Boone (1734–1820), the legendary frontiersman who had spent years exploring the region. "The Adventures of Daniel Boon" did much to secure his subsequent reputation; it was a paean to Kentucky, as well as a personal history of continuous warfare with the Indians from 1769 to 1782. Here are Boone's adventures in their entirety.*

* * *

I T WAS ON THE 1ST OF MAY, 1769, that I resigned my domestic
happiness, and left my family and peaceful habitation on the Yadkin-
River, in North-Carolina, to wander through the wilderness of America, in quest of the country of Kentucky, in company with John Finley,
John Stuart, Joseph Holden, James Money, and William Cool. On the
7th of June, after traveling through a mountainous wilderness, in a
western direction, we found ourselves on Red-River, where John Finley
had formerly been trading with the Indians; and from the top of an em-
inence saw with pleasure the beautiful level of Kentucky. For some time
we had experienced the most uncomfortable weather. We now en-
camped, made a shelter to defend us from the inclement season, and
began to hunt and reconnoiter the country. We found an abundance of
wild beasts in this vast forest. The buffaloes were more numerous than
cattle on other settlements, browsing upon the leaves of the cane, or
cropping the herbage of these extensive plains. We saw hundreds in a
drove, and the numbers about the salt springs were amazing. In this
forest, the habitation of beasts of every American kind, we hunted with
success until December.

On the 22d of December, John Stuart and I had a pleasing ramble;
but fortune changed the day at the close of it. We had passed through a
great forest, in which stood myriads of trees, some gay with blossoms,
others rich with fruits. Nature had here a series of wonders and a fund
of delights. Here she displayed her ingenuity and industry in a variety of
flowers and fruits, beautifully coloured, elegantly shaped, and charm-
ingly flavoured; and we were diverted with numberless animals present-
ing themselves perpetually to our view.

In the decline of the day, near the Kentucky-River, as we descended
the brow of a small hill, a number of Indians rushed out of a thick
cane-brake and made us prisoners. They plundered us, and kept us in
confinement seven days. During this time, we discovered no uneasiness
or desire to escape, which made them less suspicious; but in the dead
of night, as we lay by a large fire in a thick cane-brake, when sleep
had locked up their senses, my situation not disposing me to rest, I gen-

tly awoke my companion. We seized this favourable opportunity and departed, directing our course towards our old camp; but found it plundered, and our companions dispersed or gone home. About this time my brother, Squire Boone, with another adventurer, who came to explore the country shortly after us, was wandering through the forest, and accidentally found our camp. Notwithstanding our unfortunate circumstances, and our dangerous situation, surrounded by hostile savages, our meeting fortunately in the wilderness gave us the most sensible satisfaction.

Soon after this, my companion in captivity, John Stuart, was killed by the savages; and the man that came with my brother returned home by himself. We were then in a dangerous, helpless situation, exposed daily to perils and deaths among savages and wild beasts, not a white man in the country but ourselves. Thus, many hundred miles from our families, in the howling wilderness, we did not continue in a state of indolence, but hunted every day, and prepared a little cottage to protect us from the winter storms. We met with no disturbance during the winter.

On the first May, 1770, my brother returned home by himself for a new recruit of horses and ammunition, leaving me alone without bread, salt, or sugar, or even a horse or dog. I passed a few days uncomfortably. The idea of a beloved wife and family, and their anxiety on my account, would have exposed me to melancholy, if I had further indulged the thought.

One day I undertook a tour through the country, when the diversity and beauties of nature I met with in this charming season, expelled every gloomy thought. Just at the close of the day, the gentle gales ceased; a profound calm ensued; not a breath shook the tremulous leaf. I had gained the summit of a commanding ridge, and looking round with astonishment and delight, beheld the ample plains and beauteous tracts below. On one hand, the famous Ohio, rolling in silent dignity, and marking the western boundary of Kentucky with inconceivable grandeur. At a vast distance I beheld the mountains lift their venerable brows and penetrate the clouds. All things were still. I kindled a fire near a fountain of sweet water, and feasted on the loin of a buck, which a few hours before I had killed. The shades of night soon overspread the hemisphere, and the earth seemed to gasp after the hovering moisture. My excursion had fatigued my body and amused my mind. I laid me down to sleep, and awoke not until the sun had chased away the night.

I continued this tour, and in a few days explored a great part of the country, each day equally pleased as the first; after which I returned to my old camp, which had not been disturbed in my absence. I did not confine my lodging to it, but often reposed in thick cane-brakes, to avoid the savages, who, I believe, often visited my camp, but fortunately during my absence. No populous city, with all the varieties of commerce and stately structures, could afford so much pleasure to my mind as the beauties of nature I found in this country. Until the 24th of July, I spent the time in an uninterrupted scene of sylvan pleasures, when my brother, to my great felicity, met me, according to appointment, at our old camp. Soon after we left the place, and proceeded to Cumberland River, reconnoitering that part of the country, and giving names to the different rivers.

In March, 1771, I returned home to my family, being determined to bring them as soon as possible, at the risk of my life and fortune, to reside in Kentucky, which I esteemed a second paradise. On my return, I found my family in happy circumstances. I sold my farm at Yadkin, and what goods we could not carry with us; and on the 25th of September, 1773, we bade farewell to our friends, and proceeded on our journey to Kentucky, in company with five more families, and forty men that joined us in Powell's Valley, which is one hundred and fifty miles from the now settled parts of Kentucky; but this promising beginning was soon overcast with a cloud of adversity.

On the 10th of October, the rear of our company was attacked by a number of Indians, who killed six and wounded one man. Of these, my eldest son was one that fell in the action. Though we repulsed the enemy, yet this unhappy affair scattered our cattle, brought us into extreme difficulty, and so discouraged the whole company, that we retreated forty miles to Clench River.

We had passed over two mountains, Powell's and Walden's, and were approaching Cumberland Mountain when this adverse fortune overtook us. These mountains are in the wilderness, in passing from the old settlements in Virginia to Kentucky, are ranged in a S.W. and

N.E. direction, are of great length and breadth, and not far distant from each other. Over them nature has formed passes, less difficult than might be expected from the view of such huge piles. The aspect of these cliffs is so wild and horrid, that it is impossible to behold them without terror.

Until the 6th of June, 1774, I remained with my family on the Clench, when I and Michael Stoner were solicited by Governor Dunmore, of Virginia, to conduct a number of surveyors to the falls of Ohio. This was a tour of near eight hundred miles, and took us sixty-two days. On my return, Governor Dunmore gave me the command of three garrisons, during the campaign against the Shawanese.

In March, 1775, at the solicitation of a number of gentlemen of North-Carolina, I attended their treaty at Wataga with the Cherokee Indians, to purchase the lands on the south side of Kentucky River. After this I undertook to mark out a road in the best passage from the settlements, through the wilderness, to Kentucky. Having collected a number of enterprising men, well armed, I soon began this work. We proceeded until we came within fifteen miles of where Boonsborough now stands, where the Indians attacked us, and killed two, and wounded two more. This was the 20th of March, 1775. Three days after they attacked us again; we had two killed and three wounded. After this we proceeded on the Kentucky River without opposition.

On the first of April we began to erect the fort of Boonsborough, at a salt-lick, sixty yards from the river, on the south side. On the 4th, they killed one of our men. On the 14th of June, having finished the fort, I returned to my family on the Clench. Soon after I removed my family to this fort: we arrived safe; my wife and daughters being the first white women that stood on the banks of Kentucky River. December 24th, the Indians killed one man and wounded another, seeming determined to persecute us for erecting this fort.

July 14th, 1776, two of Colonel Colway's daughters, and one of mine, were taken prisoners near the fort. I immediately pursued the Indians with only eighteen men. On the 16th I overtook them, killed two of them, and recovered the girls. The Indians had divided themselves into several parties, and attacked, on the same day, all our settlement and forts, doing a great deal of mischief. The husbandman was shot dead in the field, and most of the cattle were destroyed. They continued their hostilities until the 15th of April, 1777, when a party of one hundred of them attacked Boonsborough, and killed one man and wounded four. July 4th, they attacked it again with two hundred men, and killed one of us and wounded two. They remained forty-eight hours, during which we killed seven of them. All the settlements were attacked at the same time.

July 19th, Colonel Logan's fort was besieged by two hundred Indians. They did much mischief: there were only fifteen men in the fort; they killed two, and wounded four of them. Indians' loss unknown.

July 25th, twenty-five men came from Carolina. About August 20th, Colonel Bowman arrived with one hundred men from Virginia. Now we began to strengthen, and had skirmishes with the Indians almost every day. The savages now learned the superiority of the *long-knife*, as they called the Virginians, being out-generalled almost in every battle. Our affairs began to wear a new aspect; the enemy did not now venture open war, but practised secret mischief.

January 1st, 1778, I went with thirty men to the Blue Licks, on Licking River, to make salt for the different garrisons. February 7th, hunting by myself to procure meat for the company, I met a party of one hundred and two Indians, and two Frenchmen, marching against Boonsborough. They pursued and took me. The next day I capitulated for my men, knowing they could not escape. They were twenty-seven in number, three having gone home with salt. The Indians, according to the capitulation, used us generously. They carried us to Old Chillicothe, the principal Indian town on the Little Miami.

On the 18th of February, we arrived there, after an uncomfortable journey, in very severe weather. On the 10th of March, I and ten of my men were conducted to Detroit. On the 30th we arrived there, and were treated by Governor Hamilton, the British commander at that post, with great humanity.

The Indians had such an affection for me, that they refused one hundred pounds sterling offered them by the governor, if they would leave me with the others, on purpose that he might send me home on my parole. Several English gentlemen there, sensible of my adverse fortune, and touched with sympathy; generously offered to supply my wants, which I declined with many thanks, adding, that I never expected it would be in my power to recompense such unmerited generosity.

On the 10th of April, they brought me towards Old Chillicothe, where we arrived on the 25th day of the same month. This was a long and fatiguing march through an exceeding fertile country, remarkable for fine springs and streams of water. At Chillicothe I spent my time as comfortably as I could expect; was adopted, according to their custom, into a family, where I became a son, and had a great share in the affections of my new parents, brothers, sisters, and friends.

I was exceedingly familiar and friendly with them, always appearing as cheerful and satisfied as possible, and they put great confidence in me. I often went a hunting with them, and frequently gained their applause for my activity. At our shooting matches, I was careful not to exceed many of them in shooting; for no people are more envious than they are in this sport. I could observe in their countenances and gestures the greatest expressions of joy when they exceeded me, and when the reverse happened, of envy.

The Shawanese king took great notice of me, treated me with profound respect and entire friendship, and often intrusted me to hunt at my liberty. I frequently returned with the spoils of the woods, and as often presented some of what I had taken to him, expressive of my duty to my sovereign. My food and lodging were in common with them; not so good, indeed, as I could desire, but necessity made every thing acceptable. I now began to meditate an escape, but carefully avoided giving suspicion. Until the 1st of June, I continued at Old Chillicothe, and then was taken to the salt springs on the Sciota, and kept there ten days making salt. During this time I hunted with them, and found the land, for a great extent about this river, to exceed the soil of Kentucky, if possible, and remarkably well watered.

On my return to Chillicothe, four hundred and fifty of the choicest Indian warriors were ready to march against Boonsborough, painted and armed in a dreadful manner. This alarmed me, and I determined to escape.

On the 16th of June, before sunrise, I went off secretly, and reached Boonsborough on the 20th, a journey of one hundred and sixty miles, during which I had only one meal. I found our fortress in a bad state; but we immediately repaired our flanks, gates, posterns, and formed double bastions, which we completed in ten days. One of my fellow-prisoners escaped after me, and brought advice that on account of my flight the Indians had put off the expedition for three weeks.

About August 1st, I set out with nineteen men to surprise Point-Creek-Town, on Sciota. Within four miles we fell in with thirty Indians, going against Boonsborough. We fought, and the enemy gave way. We suffered no loss. The enemy had one killed and two wounded. We took three horses, and all their baggage. The Indians having evacuated their town, and gone altogether against Boonsborough, we returned, passed them on the 6th day, and on the 7th arrived safe at Boonsborough. On the 8th the Indian army, four hundred and forty-four in number, commanded by Captain Dugnesne, and eleven other Frenchmen, and their own chiefs, came and summoned the fort. I requested two days consideration, which they granted. During this, we brought in, through the posterns, all the horses and other cattle we could collect. On the 9th, in the evening, I informed their commander that we were determined to defend the fort while a man was living.

They then proposed a treaty, and said, if we sent out nine men to conclude it, they would withdraw. The treaty was held within sixty yards of the fort, as we suspected the savages. The articles were agreed to and signed; when the Indians told us it was their custom for two Indians to shake hands with every white man, as an evidence of friendship. We agreed to this also. They immediately grappled us to take us prisoners; but we cleared ourselves of them, though surrounded by hundreds, and gained the fort safely, except one that was wounded by a heavy fire from their army. On this they began to undermine the fort, beginning at the water-mark of Kentucky River, which is sixty yards from the fort. We discovered this by the water being made muddy with the clay, and countermined them by cutting a trench across their subterranean passage. The enemy, discovering this by the clay we threw out of the fort, desisted. On the 20th of August they raised the siege. During this dreadful siege, we had two men killed and four wounded. We lost a number of cattle. We killed thirty-seven of the enemy, and wounded a great number. We picked up one hundred and twenty-five pounds of their bullets, besides what stuck in the logs of the fort. Soon after this I went into the settlement, and nothing worthy of notice passed for some time.

In July, 1779, during my absence, Colonel Bowman, with one hundred and sixty men, went against the Shawanese at Old Chillicothe. He arrived undiscovered; a battle ensued, which lasted till ten in the morning, when Colonel Bowman retreated thirty miles. The Indians collected all their strength and pursued him, when another engagement ensued for two hours, not to Colonel Bowman's advantage. Colonel Harrod proposed to mount a number of horses and break the enemy's line, who at this time fought with remarkable fury. This desperate measure had a happy effect, and the savages fled on all sides. In these two battles we had nine men killed and one wounded. The enemy's loss was uncertain, only two scalps being taken.

June 22d, 1780, about six hundred Indians and Canadians, under Colonel Bird, attacked Riddle's and Martin's Stations, and the forts of Licking River, with six pieces of artillery: they took all the inhabitants captive, and killed one man and two women, and loaded the others with the heavy baggage, and such as failed in the journey were tomahawked. The hostile disposition of the savages caused General Clark, the commandant at the Falls of Ohio, to march with his regiment and the armed force of the country against Peccaway, the principal town of the Shawanese, on a branch of the Great Miami, which he finished with great success, took seventeen scalps, and burned the town to ashes, with the loss of seventeen men.

About this time I returned to Kentucky with my family; for during my captivity, my wife, who despaired of ever seeing me again, expecting the Indians had put a period to my life, oppressed with the distresses of the country, and bereaved of me, her only happiness, had, before I returned, transported my family and goods, on horses, through the wilderness, amidst a multitude of dangers, to her father's house, in North Carolina.

Shortly after the troubles at Boonsborough, I went to them, and lived peaceably there until this time. The history of my going home, and returning with my family, forms a series of difficulties, an account of which would swell a volume, and being foreign to my purpose, I shall purposely omit them.

I settled my family in Boonsborough once more; and shortly after, on the sixth day of October, 1780, I went in company with my brother to the Blue Licks; and, on our return home, we were fired upon by a party of Indians. They shot him, and pursued me, by the scent of their dog, three miles; but I killed the dog, and escaped. The Winter soon came on, and was very severe, which confined the Indians to their wigwams.

The severity of this Winter caused great difficulties in Kentucky. The enemy had destroyed most of the corn, the Summer before. This necessary article was scarce, and dear; and the inhabitants lived chiefly on the flesh of buffaloes. The circumstances of many were very lamentable: However, being a hardy race of people, and accustomed to difficulties and necessities, they were wonderfully supported through all their sufferings, until the ensuing Fall, when we received abundance from the fertile soil.

Towards Spring, we were frequently harassed by Indians; and, in May, 1782, a party assaulted Ashton's station, killed one man, and took a Negro prisoner. Capt. Ashton, with twenty-five men, pursued, and overtook the savages, and a smart fight ensued, which lasted two hours; but they being superior in number, obliged Captain Ashton's party to retreat, with the loss of eight killed, and four mortally wounded; their brave commander himself being numbered among the dead.

The Indians continued their hostilities; and, about the tenth of August following, two boys were taken from Major Hoy's station. This part was pursued by Capt. Holder and seventeen men, who were also defeated, with the loss of four men killed, and one wounded. Our affairs became more and more alarming. Several stations which had lately been erected in the country were continually infested with savages, stealing their horses and killing the men at every opportunity. In a field, near Lexington, an Indian shot a man, and running to scalp him, was himself shot from the fort, and fell dead upon his enemy.

Every day we experienced recent mischiefs. The barbarous savage nations of Shawanese, Cherokees, Wyandots, Tawas, Delawares, and several others near Detroit, united in a war against us and assembled their choicest warriors at old Chelicothe, to go on the expedition, in order to destroy us, and entirely depopulate the country. Their savage minds were inflamed to mischief by two abandoned men, Captains McKee and Girty. These led them to execute every diabolical scheme; and, and the fifteenth day of August, commanded a party of Indians and Canadians, of about five hundred in number, against Briant's station, five miles from Lexington. Without demanding a surrender, they furiously assaulted the garrison, which was happily prepared to oppose them; and, after they had expended much ammunition in vain, and killed the cattle round the fort, not being likely to make themselves masters of this place, they raised the siege, and departed in the morning of the third day after they came, with the loss of about thirty killed, and the number of wounded uncertain. Of the garrison four were killed, and three wounded.

On the eighteenth day Col. Todd, Col. Trigg, Major Harland, and myself, speedily collected one hundred and seventy-six men, well armed, and pursued the savages. They had marched beyond the Blue Licks to a remarkable bend of the main fork of Licking River, about forty-three miles from Lexington, as it is particularly represented in the map, where we overtook them on the nineteenth day. The savages observing us, gave way; and we, being ignorant of their numbers, passed the river. When the enemy saw our proceedings, having greatly the advantage of us in [our] situation, they formed the line of battle, as represented in the map, from one bend of Licking to the other, about a mile from the Blue Licks. An exceedingly fierce battle immediately began, for about fifteen minutes, when we, being over-powered by numbers, were obliged to retreat, with the loss of sixty-seven men; seven of whom were taken prisoners. The brave and much lamented Colonels Todd and Trigg, Major Harland and my second son, were among the dead. We were informed that the Indians, numbering their dead, found they had four killed more than we; and therefore, four of the prisoners they had taken, were, by general consent, ordered to be killed, in a most barbarous manner, by the young warriors, in order to train them up to cruelty; and then they proceeded to their towns.

On our retreat we were met by Col. Logan, hastening to join us, with a number of well-armed men. This powerful assistance we unfortunately wanted in the battle; for, notwithstanding the enemy's superiority of numbers, they acknowledged that, if they had received one more fire from us, they should undoubtedly have given way. So valiantly did our small party fight, that, to the memory of those who unfortunately fell in the battle, enough of honour cannot be said. Had Col. Logan and his party been with us, it is highly probable we should have given the savages a total defeat.

I cannot reflect upon this dreadful scene, but sorrow fills my heart. A zeal for the defence of their country led these heroes to the scene of action, though with a few men to attack a powerful army of experienced warriors. When we gave way, they pursued us with the utmost eagerness, and in every quarter spread destruction. The river was difficult to cross, and many were killed in the flight, some just entering the river, some in the water, others after crossing in ascending the cliffs. Some escaped on horse-back, a few on foot; and, being dispersed every where, in a few hours, brought the melancholy news of this unfortunate battle to Lexington. Many widows were now made. The reader may guess what sorrow filled the hearts of the inhabitants, exceeding any thing that I am able to describe. Being reinforced, we returned to bury the dead, and found their bodies strewed every where, cut and mangled in a dreadful manner. This mournful scene exhibited a horror almost unparalleled: Some torn and eaten by wild beasts; those in the river eaten by fishes; all in such a putrified condition, that no one could be distinguished from another.

As soon as General Clark, then at the Falls of the Ohio, who was ever our ready friend, and merits the love and gratitude of all his countrymen, understood the circumstances of this unfortunate action, he ordered an expedition, with all possible haste, to pursue the savages, which was so expeditiously effected, that we overtook them within two miles of their towns, and probably might have obtained a great victory, had not two of their number met us about two hundred poles before we come up. These returned quick as lightning to their camp with the alarming news of a might army in view. The savages fled in the utmost disorder, evacuated their towns, and reluctantly left their territory to our mercy. We immediately took possession of Old Chelicothe without opposition, being deserted by its inhabitants. We continued our pursuit through five towns on the Miami rivers, Old Chelicothe, Pecaway, New Chelicothe, Will's Towns, and Chelicothe, burnt them all to ashes, entirely destroyed their corn, and other fruits, and every where spread a scene of desolation in the country. In this expedition we took seven prisoners and five scalps, with the loss of only four men, two of whom were accidentally killed by our own army.

This campaign in some measure dampened the spirits of the Indians, and made them sensible of our superiority. Their connections were dissolved, their armies scattered, and a future invasion put entirely out of their power; yet they continued to practice mischief secretly upon the inhabitants, in the exposed parts of the country.

In October following, a party made an excursion into that district called the Crab Orchard, and one of them, being advanced some distance before the others, boldly entered the house of a poor defenceless family, in which was only a Negro man, a woman and her children, terrified with the apprehensions of immediate death. The savage, perceiving their defenceless situation, without offering violence to the family attempted to captivate the Negro, who, happily proved an over-match for him, threw him on the ground, and, in the struggle, the mother of the children drew an ax from a corner of the cottage, and cut his head off, while her little daughter shut the door. The savages instantly appeared, and applied their tomahawks to the door. An old rusty gun-barrel, without a lock, lay in a corner, which the mother put through a small crevice, and the savages, perceiving it, fled. In the mean time, the alarm spread through the neighbourhood; the armed men collected immediately, and pursued the savages into the wilderness. Thus Providence, by the means of this Negro, saved the whole of the poor family from destruction. From that time, until the happy return of peace between the United States and Great Britain, the Indians did us no mischief. Finding the great king beyond the water disappointed in his expectations, and conscious of the importance of the Long Knife, and their own wretchedness, some of the nations immediately desired peace; to which, at present, they seem universally disposed, and are sending ambassadors to General Clark, at the Falls of the Ohio, with the minutes of their Councils; a specimen of which, in the minutes of the Piankashaw Council, is subjoined.

To conclude, I can now say that I have verified the saying of an old Indian who signed Col. Henderson's deed. Taking me by the hand, at the delivery thereof, Brother, says he, we have given you a fine land, but I believe you will have much trouble in settling it.—My footsteps have often been marked with blood, and therefore I can truly subscribe to its original name. Two darling sons, and a brother, have I lost by savage hands, which have also taken from me forty valuable horses, and abundance of cattle. Many dark and sleepless nights have I been a companion for owls, separated from the cheerful society of men, scorched by the Summer's sun, and pinched by the Winter's cold, an instrument ordained to settle the wilderness. But now the scene is changed: Peace crowns the sylvan shade.

What thanks, what ardent and ceaseless thanks are due to that all-superintending Providence which has turned a cruel war into peace, brought order out of confusion, made the fierce savages placid, and turned away their hostile weapons from our country! May the same Almighty Goodness banish the accursed monster, war, from all lands, with her hated associates, rapine and insatiable ambition. Let peace, descending from her native heaven, bid her olives spring amidst the joyful nations; and plenty, in league with commerce, scatter blessings from her copious hand.

This account of my adventures will inform the reader of the most remarkable events of this country.—I now live in peace and safety, enjoying the sweets of liberty, and the bounties of Providence, with my once fellow-sufferers, in this delightful country, which I have seen purchased with a vast expense of blood and treasure, delighting in the prospect of its being, in a short time, one of the most opulent and powerful states on the continent of North America; which, with the love and gratitude of my country-men, I esteem a sufficient reward for all my toil and dangers.

THE REVOLUTIONARY WAR

7

The Boston Tea Party

(from George Hewes, eyewitness account in
Yankee Life by Those Who Lived It
edited by June Barrows Mussey)

O N THE NIGHT *of December 16, 1773, American patriots, dis-guised as Indians, jettisoned 342 chests of British tea owned by the East India Company into Boston Harbor. Its London ware-houses bulging with seventeen million pounds of unsold tea, the company resolved to unload its cargoes already docked at Boston Harbor, by force if necessary. Parliament had enacted a law that gave the East India Com-pany the exclusive right to import tea into England duty-free, then ship it across the Atlantic to the East Coast. If the tea was unloaded as planned on December 17, the American colony would bear the burden of three pence a pound customs duty. Politically that was taxation without repre-sentation. Economically the Yankees preferred to smuggle in their tea.*

From the British perspective, the destruction of 342 giant chests of East India Company tea was neither vandalism nor theft—it was treason. After the Boston Tea Party's defiance, Parliament cracked down with harsher laws. Boston was to be blockaded until she paid for the lost tea. Judges, marshals, and sheriffs were no longer to be elected; rather they would be appointed by the royal governor. The governor was empowered to commandeer private houses in any town to quarter his redcoat soldiers. Meetings to debate citizen rights were forbidden. Committees of correspondence—which coordinated their political activities with their counterpart committees in other towns and colonies—were outlawed. With a finality bordering on sadness, King George III wrote: "The dye is now cast. The colonies must either submit or triumph." Paul Revere, the principal express rider for the Boston Committee of Safety, carried the news of the Boston Tea Party to New York.

Sixteen months later, Revere received the famous "one if by land, two if by sea" signal from a lantern atop Boston's North Church. He rowed across the Charles River with muffled oars, mounted his horse, and galloped to Lexington to warn John Adams and John Hancock that eight hundred British soldiers were on their way to arrest them and seize the patriots and their caches of arms and gunpowder. The next day at Lexington and Concord, "the embattled farmers stood, and fired the shot heard round the world." Critics claimed in those days that "Bostonians were better at resolving what to do, than doing what they had resolved." The Boston Tea Party, followed by the uprising of the minutemen at Concord, dispelled that illusion.

George Hewes was one of the "Indians" at the Boston Tea Party. He knew the risks and consequences. To avoid recognition he and his fellows smeared their faces with war paint and dressed like Mohawk Indians. Here is Hewes's eyewitness report.

* * *

I NEVER KNEW who proposed we destroy the tea in Boston Harbor. Only by a friend's allusions to the participation of certain people in whom I had confidence, together with the knowledge I had of the spirit of the times, gave me confidence that a sufficient number of associates would accompany me in this enterprise. The tea was contained in three ships, laying near each other, at what was called at that time Griffin's wharf. They were surrounded by armed ships of war. The commanders of these men-of-war had publicly declared that if the rebels (as they were pleased to style the Bostonians) should not withdraw their opposition to the landing of the tea before a certain day—the 17th day of December, 1773—they should on that day force it on shore under cover of their cannons. On the day preceding the seventeenth, we held a meeting of the citizens of the county of Suffolk, convened at Old South Church in Boston, for the purpose of consulting on what measures might be considered expedient to prevent the landing of the tea, or secure the people from having to pay the duty. At that meeting a committee was appointed to call on Governor Hutchinson, and request him to inform them whether he would take any measures to satisfy the people on the object of the meeting. When this committee first visited the governor, he told them he would give them a definite answer by five o'clock in the afternoon. At the hour appointed, the committee again repaired to the governor's house. On inquiry they found he had gone to his country seat at Milton, a distance of about six miles. When the committee returned and informed the meeting of the absence of the governor, there was a confused murmur among the members, and the meeting was immediate dissolved. Samuel Adams declared: "This meeting can do no more to save the country." Others cried out, "Let every man do his duty, and be true to his country." And there was a general huzzah for Griffin's wharf. It was now evening. I immediately dressed myself in the costume of an Indian. I carried a small hatchet (which I and my associates denominated a tomahawk) and a club. In the shop of a blacksmith I painted my face and hands with coal dust. I then repaired to Griffin's wharf, where the ships lay that contained the tea. When I first appeared on the streets, after being thus disguised, I fell in with many who were dressed, equipped and painted as I was. We joined forces and marched in order to the place of our destination. When we arrived at the wharf, there were three of our number who assumed an authority to direct our operations, to which we readily submitted. They divided us into three parties for the purpose of boarding the three tea ships at the same time. The name of him who commanded the division to which I was assigned, was Leonard Pitt. The names of the other commanders I never knew. We were immediately ordered by the respective commanders to board all ships at the same time, which we promptly obeyed. The commander of the division to which I belonged, as soon as we were on board the ship, appointed me boatswain, and ordered me to go to the captain and demand of him the keys to the hatches and a dozen candles. I made the demand accordingly, and the captain promptly replied and delivered the articles; but he requested me at the same time to do no damage to the ship or rigging. We were then ordered by our commander to open the hatches and take out all the chests of tea and throw them overboard. We immediately proceeded to execute his orders. We cut and split the tea chests with our tomahawks, in order to expose them to the effects of the water. As we were throwing the tea overboard, there were several attempts made by some of the citizens of Boston and its vicinity, to carry off small quantities of it for their family use. To effect that object, they would watch for an opportunity to snatch up a handful from the deck, where it had became plentifully scattered, and put it into their pockets. One Captain O'Conner, whom I well knew, came on board for that purpose, and when he supposed he was not noticed, filled his pockets, and also the lining of his coat. But I detected him, and gave information to the captain of what he was doing. We were ordered to take him into custody. Just as he was stepping from the vessel, I seized him by the skirt of his coat, and in attempting to pull him back, I tore it off, but springing forward, by a rapid effort, he made his escape. He had however to run a gauntlet through the crowd upon the wharf. Each one as he passed gave him a kick or a stroke. The next day we nailed the skirt of his coat, which I had pulled off, to the whipping post in Charlestown, the place of his residence, with a label upon it, commemorative of the occasion which had thus subjected its owner to our popular indignation. Another attempt was made to save a little tea from the ruins of the cargo, by a tall aged man, who wore a large cocked hat and white wig, which was fashionable at that time. He had slightly slipped a little into his pocket, but being detected they seized him. Taking his hat and wig from his head, they threw them, together with the tea they had emptied from his pockets, into the water. In consideration of his advanced age, he was permitted to escape, with now and then a slight kick. In about three hours from the time we went on board, we had broken and thrown overboard every tea chest to be found in the ship. Those in the other ships were disposing of the tea in the same way, at the same time. We were surrounded by armed British ships, but no attempt was made to resist us. We then quietly retired to our several places of residence, without having any conversation with each other, or taking any measure to discover who our associates were. Nor do I recollect having had the knowledge of the name of a single individual concerned in that affair, except that of Leonard Pitt, the commander of my division, who I have mentioned. There appeared to be an understanding that each individual should volunteer his services, keep his own secret, and risk the consequences for himself. No disorder took place during that transaction, and it was observed at that time, that the stillest night ensued that Boston had enjoyed for many months. The next morning, after we had cleared the ships of the tea, it was discovered that very considerable quantities of it were still floating upon the surface of the water around the harbor. To prevent the possibility of any of it being saved for use, a number of small boats were manned by sailors and citizens, who rowed out into those parts of the harbor wherever the tea was visible, and by beating it with oars and paddles, so thoroughly drenched it, as to render its entire destruction inevitable.

★ 8 ★

Surrender—
"In the Name of the Great Jehovah
and the Continental Congress"

(from Ethan Allen,

A Narrative of Col. Ethan Allen's Captivity, 1779)

E THAN ALLEN SHOUTED *these famous words in anger and exas-peration. He and his Green Mountain Boys had just stormed Fort Ticonderoga before dawn on May 10, 1775. He caught the British commander inside the fort in the act of putting on his pants. The commander asked Allen by what authority he demanded surrender.*

"In the name of the Great Jehovah and the Continental Congress," came Allen's inspired answer.

Ethan Allen was a tall man of Herculean strength. Stories had it that in an altercation with a New York sheriff and his six deputies, Ethan single-handedly knocked all seven unconscious. And that in a dispute with two land surveyors, he grabbed the pair, one in each arm, lifted them off the ground, and banged their heads together. He also had a sense of humor. When the British sought to arrest him and offered a twenty-pound bounty, he rode to Albany and tacked up his own poster offering a twenty-pound bounty for the arrest of the governor.

As a boy he read the Bible and every other available book in Cornwall,

Connecticut. At age nine he wrote down his thoughts, which so impressed his father that Ethan was sent away to school in Salisbury, to prepare for college. But his father died when Ethan was in his teens, and he had to return to the farm to support his family.

After successfully operating a furnace to produce potash, he sold it and moved to Vermont, which at that time was part of the New Hampshire Land Grants. New York considered this land under its jurisdiction and tried to add a second settler's fee on top of New Hampshire's. Those who refused this double taxation would face eviction. This galvanized armed opposition which evolved into the Green Mountain Boys—some three hundred men led by Ethan Allen.

The Connecticut Assembly financed Allen to mobilize his Green Mountain Boys to seize Fort Ticonderoga at the southern end of Lake Champlain. On the night of May 9, 1775, 350 armed men rendezvoused at Hand's Cove on the east side of the lake. Boats were scarce. What few there were had to ferry the men across, then return for others. Before dawn only eighty-three men and officers had reached the other side. Rather than wait for more men and lose the advantage of surprise, Allen decided to strike with the force he had. His report follows, as published in his 1779 memoir, A Narrative of Colonel Ethan Allen's Captivity.

* * *

I LANDED EIGHTY-THREE MEN near the garrison, and sent the boats back for the rear guard, commanded by Seth Warner. But the day began at dawn, and I found myself under the necessity to attack the fort before the rear could cross the lake. As the attack was viewed hazardous, I harangued the officers and soldiers in the manner following:

> "Friends and fellow soldiers! You have for a number of years past, been a scourge and terror to arbitrary power. Your valor has been famed abroad, and acknowledged, as appears by the advice and orders sent to me (from the General Assembly of Connecticut) to surprise and take the garrison now before us.
>
> "I now propose to advance before you in person and conduct

you through the wicker-gate. For we must this morning either quit our pretensions to valor, or possess ourselves of this fortress in a few minutes. And, in as much as it is a desperate attempt (which none but the bravest of men dare undertake), I do not urge it on any contrary to his will.

"You that will undertake voluntarily—poise your firelocks!"

The men being (at this time) drawn up in three ranks, each poised his firelock. I ordered them to face to the right, and, at the head of the center file, I marched them immediately to the wicker-gate aforesaid, where I found a sentry posted. He instantly snapped his fuse at me. I ran immediately toward him, and he retreated into the parade ground within the garrison, gave a halloo, and ran under a bomb-proof.

My party, who had followed me into the fort, I formed on the parade ground in such a manner as to face the two barracks, which faced each other. The garrison being asleep (except for the sentries), we gave three huzzahs, which greatly surprised them.

One of the sentries made a pass at one of my officers. My first thought was to kill him with my sword, but, in an instant, I altered the design and fury of the blow to a slight cut on the side of the head, upon which he dropped his gun, and asked quarter, which I readily granted him. I demanded of him the place where the commanding officer slept. He showed me a pair of stairs in the front of a barrack, on the west part of the garrison, which led up to a second story in said barrack, to which I immediately repaired. I ordered the commander (Capt. Delaplace) to come forth instantly, or we would sacrifice the whole garrison. The captain came immediately with his britches in his hand.

I ordered him to deliver to me the Fort instantly. He asked me by what authority I demanded it. I answered: "In the name of the Great Jehovah and the Continental Congress" (the authority of the Congress being very little known at that time).

He began to speak again, but I interrupted him, and with my drawn sword over his head, I again demanded an immediate surrender of the garrison, to which he immediately complied.

He ordered his men to be forthwith paraded without arms, as he had given up the garrison.

In the meantime some of my officers had given orders, and consequence thereof, sundry of the barrack door were beat down, and about
one third of the garrison imprisoned—which consisted of the said commander, Lt. Feltham, a conductor of artillery, a gunner, two sergeants,
and forty-four rank and file; about one hundred pieces of cannon, one
13 inch mortar, and a number of swivels. This surprise was carried into
execution in the gray of the morning on the 10th day of May, 1775.
The sun seemed to rise that morning with a superior luster; and Ticonderoga and its dependencies smiled on its conquerors, who passed
about the flowing bowl, and wished success to Congress, and liberty
and freedom of America.

★ 9 ★

The Declaration of Independence—
"We Must All Hang Together,
or Assuredly We Shall All
Hang Separately"

(from the Reverend Charles A. Goodrich,
*Lives of the Signers of the Declaration of
Independence*, 1832)

O N JULY 3, 1776, John Adams wrote to his wife, Abigail, from
the Second Continental Congress in Philadelphia: *"Yesterday
the greatest question was decided, which ever was debated in
America, and a greater, perhaps never was nor will be decided among
men. A resolution was passed without one dissenting colony, 'that these
United Colonies are, and of right ought to be, free and independent
States . . . Britain has been filled with folly, and America with wisdom.'"*
After the Declaration was signed, Adams reported, *"I am well aware of
the toil, and blood, and treasure that it will cost us to maintain the declaration, and support and defend these States. Yet, through all the gloom, I
can see the rays of ravishing light and glory. I can see the end is worth more
than all the means, and that posterity will triumph in that day's transaction, even although we should rue it, which I trust in God we shall not."*

Fifty-six brave men proudly signed this pivotal document, which dissolved their tie to Britain and declared the United Colonies free and independent states. What happened to the men who signed and committed

treason to the Crown? All became targets for British retribution, and for some their lives were fraught with risk and deprivations—as evidenced in this 1832 account from Charles Goodrich's Lives of the Signers of the Declaration of Independence.

★ ★ ★

THOMAS JEFFERSON—VIRGINIA

M R. JEFFERSON RETIRED to Monticello, when intelligence was received, two days after, that a body of troops under command of General Tarlton were rapidly approaching Charlottesville, for the purpose of surprising and capturing members of the assembly. They had only time, after the alarm was given, to adjourn to meet at Staunton, and to disperse, before the enemy entered the village. Another party had diverted their course to Monticello to capture the ex-governor. Fortunately an express messenger hastened from Charlottesville, to convey intelligence to Mr. Jefferson of their approach. Scarcely had the family time to make arrangements to effect their escape, before the enemy was seen ascending the hill leading to the mansion-house. Mr. Jefferson himself, mounting his horse, narrowly escaped, by taking a course through the woods.

GEORGE CLYMER—PENNSYLVANIA

During the fall of 1777 the family of Mr. Clymer resided in the county of Chester, about twenty-five miles from Philadelphia, and suffered severely, in consequence of an attack by a band of British soldiers, who thirsted for revenge. The furniture of the house was destroyed, and a large stock of liquors shared a similar fate. Fortunately, the family made their escape.

FRANCIS LEWIS—NEW YORK

In the autumn of 1776, Lewis's house was plundered by a party of British light horse. His extensive library and valuable papers were wantonly destroyed. Nor were they content with the ruin of his property.

Unfortunately Mrs. Lewis fell into their power, and was retained a prisoner for several months. During her captivity she was closely confined, without even the comfort of a bed to lie upon, or a change of clothes. Mrs. Lewis was at length released, but her sufferings during her confinement had so much impaired her constitution, that in the course of a year or two, she sunk into the grave.

WILLIAM FLOYD—NEW YORK

While at Philadelphia attending Congress, the American troops evacuated Long Island, which was taken possession of by the British Army. The family of Mr. Floyd were obliged to flee for safety across Long Island sound to Connecticut. His house was occupied by a company of horsemen for the remainder of the war. Thus, for nearly seven years, Mr. Floyd and his family were refugees from their habitation, nor did he, during this long period, derive any benefit from his landed estate.

LEWIS MORRIS—NEW YORK

When Mr. Morris gave his vote for the Declaration of Independence, he exhibited a patriotism which few had it in their power to display. He was at this time in possession of an extensive domain within a few miles of the city of New York. The British army soon spread desolation over the beautiful and fertile manor of Morrisania. His track of woodland of more than a thousand acres in extent and of incalculable value, was destroyed; his house was greatly injured; his fences ruined; his stock driven away; his family obliged to live in a state of exile. Few men during the Revolution were called upon to make greater sacrifices than Mr. Morris. None made them more cheerfully.

JOHN HART—NEW JERSEY

During the latter part of the year 1776, New Jersey became the theater of war. The people were distressed, and there was wanton destruction of property, including Mr. Hart's, by the enemy. His children were obliged to flee, his farm was pillaged, and great exertions were made to secure him as a prisoner. The situation of Mrs. Hart was at the same time distressing. She was afflicted with a disease, which prevented her removal to a place of safety, and eventually caused her death. Mr. Hart continued at her side, until the enemy had nearly reached the house, when he made his escape, his wife being safer alone than if he were present. For some time he was hunted and pursued with the utmost zeal. He was scarcely able to elude his enemies, was often in great want of food, and sometimes destitute of a comfortable lodging for the night. In one instance he was obliged to conceal himself during the night in the usual resting place of a large dog who was his companion for the time.

RICHARD STOCKTON—NEW JERSEY

On the thirtieth of November, 1776, he was unfortunately taken prisoner by a party of refugee royalists. He was dragged from his bed at night, and carried to New York where he was treated with the greatest indignity. In New York he was placed in the common prison where he was in want of even the common necessaries of life. Mr. Stockton was at length released, but his confinement had been so strict, and his sufferings so severe that his constitution never after recovered from the shock. His fortune, which had been ample, was greatly reduced. His lands were devastated, his papers and library were burned, his implements of husbandry destroyed, and his stock seized and driven away. His health began to fail him. He continued to languish for several years and died in 1781, in the fifty third year of his age.

WILLIAM MORRIS—PENNSYLVANIA

Mr. Morris received a letter from Gen. Washington, then with his army on the Delaware opposite Trenton, who was in need of $10,000 to obtain intelligence on the movement and position of the enemy. Mr. Morris ran across a Quaker friend and reported Washington's situation, and the immediate necessity of $10,000. "Sir," said Mr. Morris, "you must let me have it. My note and my honor will be your only security." The Quaker hesitated for a moment, but at length replied,

"Robert, thou shalt have it," whereby Washington gained a signal victory over the Hessians at Trenton, animating the drooping spirits of patriotism.

In 1779 or 1780 Washington's army was in distressing need of lead. Fortunately at this juncture a privateer belonging to Mr. Morris arrived at the wharf with ninety tons of lead as ballast. Half of this lead was immediately given by Mr. Morris, and the other half, purchased by Mr. Peters, was also given with Mr. Morris becoming security for all the debt. On another occasion Morris supplied the army with four or five thousand barrels of flour upon his own private credit. It is certain that Robert Morris provided Washington with the funds to move his army south and corner Cornwallis in Yorktown, the decisive battle which terminated the war.

The latter part of Morris's life was rendered unhappy, by an unfortunate scheme of land speculation, in which he engaged, and by which his pecuniary affairs became exceeding embarrassed [including debtor's prison], yet amidst his severest trials, he maintained a firmness and independence of character, which in similar circumstances belong to but few.

Thomas Heyward, Jr., Arthur Middleton, and Edward Rutledge—South Carolina

In the spring of 1780, the City of Charleston was besieged by the British under General Clinton, and taken into possession by him. On the reduction of the place Heyward, Middleton and Rutledge became prisoners of war. They were transported to St. Augustine, Florida. During his absence Heyward suffered greatly in respect to his property—his plantation being much injured by a party of marauders, and all of his slaves seized and carried away.

Abraham Clark—New Jersey

Two or three sons of Mr. Clark were officers in the army, during the revolutionary struggle. Unfortunately they were captured by the enemy. During a part of their captivity, their sufferings were extreme, being confined to the notorious prison ship *Jersey* in the New York harbor. Painful as the condition of his sons was, Mr. Clark scrupulously avoided calling the attention of Congress to the subject, except in a single instance. One of his sons, a captain of artillery, had been cast into a dungeon, where he received no other food than that which was conveyed to him through a keyhole by his fellow prisoners. On a representation of these facts to Congress, that body immediately directed a course of retaliation in respect to a British officer. This had the desired effect, and Captain Clark's condition was improved.

★ 10 ★

Washington Crosses the Delaware—
"Victory or Death"

(from Henry Cabot Lodge,
American Statesmen: George Washington, 1890)

I**N ALL** *of George Washington's illustrious career as father of our nation, his singular, most crucial stroke of genius was when he crossed the Delaware River on the night of December 25, 1776, and launched his surprise attack on Trenton. That night his password was "victory or death." His decision to lead that successful attack saved the American Revolution and breathed new life into the Patriot cause.*

The years 1775 and 1776 saw a cascade of events: the battles of Lexington and Concord (1775) were followed by the capture of Fort Ticonderoga. Then came the battle of Bunker Hill, which was lost, after which Washington assumed command of the continental forces. In 1776 the British evacuated Boston and the Declaration of Independence was proclaimed. General Richard Howe invaded Long Island and captured New York. Washington retreated across New Jersey into Pennsylvania, pursued by the British. Congress fled Philadelphia to relocate in Baltimore, as the patriot cause looked hopeless before the overwhelming might of the British. Morale disintegrated as enlistments were due to expire on December 31, which would have emasculated Washington's little army. Then came Washington's two bold historic strikes—the victorious battles of Trenton and Princeton, whereby the patriot cause was preserved and the spirit of '76 prevailed.

The Washington we see today on the one-dollar bill, bewigged and puff-cheeked, gives us no clue of George Washington the warrior, the man of action, the leader who saved, sustained, and won the American Revolution.

Washington encountered his first battle experience in 1755 when he set out with General Edward Braddock to attack Fort Duquesne (on the site of today's Pittsburgh). The French and the Indians ambushed Braddock, mortally wounding him. Amid the smoke and slaughter, Lieutenant Colonel Washington dashed to rally his Virginia troops, trying to stay the tide of disaster. He had two horses shot from under him, and four bullets pierced his coat.

"Washington laid Braddock in his grave four days after the defeat, and read over the dead the solemn words of the English service. Wise, sensible, and active in the advance, splendidly reckless on the day of the battle, cool and collected on the retreat, Washington alone emerged from that history of disaster with added glory."

Washington's midlife was one of constant fighting—for the Revolution would last six and a half years. From Henry Cabot Lodge's nineteenth-century American Statesmen biography, George Washington, *we turn now to Washington in Pennsylvania during December 1776. Cakes of ice are beginning to float down the Delaware, and Washington has commandeered all boats for miles up and down the river, and kept them on the Pennsylvania side.*

★ ★ ★

B Y THE MIDDLE of December Howe felt satisfied that the American army would soon dissolve, and leaving strong detachments in various posts he withdrew to New York. His premises were sound, and his conclusions logical, but he make his usual mistake of overlooking and underestimating the American general. No sooner was it known that he was on his way to New York than Washington, at the head of his dissolving army, resolved to take the offensive and strike an outlying post. In a letter of December 14th, the day after Howe began to move, we catch the first glimpse of Trenton. It was a bold spirit that, in the dead of winter, with a broken army, no prospect of reinforcements, and in the midst of a terror-stricken people, could thus resolve with some four thousand men to attack an army thoroughly appointed, and numbering in all its divisions twenty-five thousand soldiers.

This is the dreary winter Washington was planning and devising and sending hither and thither for men, and never ceased through it all to write urgent and ever sharper letters and keep a wary eye upon the future. He not only wrote strongly, but he pledged his own estate and exceeded his powers in desperate efforts to raise money and men. On the 20th he wrote Congress: "It may be thought that I am going a good deal out of the line of my duty to adopt these measures, or to advise thus freely. A character to lose, an estate to forfeit, the inestimable blessings of liberty at stake, and a life devoted, must be my excuse." Even now across the centuries these words come with a grave solemnity to our ears, and we can feel as he felt when he alone saw that he stood on the brink of a great crisis. It is an awful thing to know that the life of a nation is at stake, and this thought throbs in his words, measured and quiet as usual, but deeply fraught with much meaning to him and to the world.

By Christmas all was ready, and when the Christian world was rejoicing and feasting, and the British officers in New York and in the New Jersey towns were reveling and laughing, Washington prepared to strike. His whole force, broken into various detachments, was less than six thousand men. To each division was assigned, with provident forethought, its exact part. Nothing was overlooked, nothing omitted; and then every division commander failed, for good reason or bad, to do his duty. Gates was to march from Bristol with two thousand men, Eking was to cross at Trenton, Patna was to come up from Philadelphia, Griffin was to make a diversion against Donop. When the moment came, Gates, disapproving the scheme, was on his way to Congress, and Wilkinson, with his message, found his way to headquarters by following the bloody tracks of the barefooted soldiers. Griffin abandoned New Jersey and fled before Donop. Patna would not even attempt to leave Philadelphia, and Eking made no effort to cross at Trenton. Cad-walader, indeed, came down from Bristol, but after looking at the river and the floating ice, gave it up as desperate.

But there was one man who did not hesitate nor give up, nor halt on account of floating ice. With twenty-four hundred hardy veterans, Washington crossed the Delaware. The night was bitter cold and the passage difficult. When they landed, and began their march of nine miles to Trenton, a fierce storm of sleet drove in their faces. Sullivan, marching by the river, sent word that the arms of his men were wet. "Then tell your general," said Washington, "to use the bayonet, for the town must be taken." In broad daylight they came to the town. Washington, at the front and on the right of the line, swept down the Pennington road, and as he drove in the pickets he heard the shouts of Sullivan's men, as, with Stark leading the van, they charged in from the river. A company of yagers and the light dragoons slipped away, there was a little confused fighting in the streets. Colonel Johann Rall fell, mortally wounded, his Hessians threw down their arms, and all was over. The battle had been fought and won, and the Revolution was saved.

Taking his thousand prisoners with him, Washington crossed the Delaware to his old position. Had all done their duty, as he had planned, the British hold on New Jersey would have been shattered. As it was, it was only loosened. Congress, aroused at last, had invested Washington with almost dictatorial powers; but the time for action was short. The army was again melting away, and only by urgent appeals were some veterans retained, and enough new men gathered to make a force of five thousand men. With this army Washington prepared to finish what he had begun.

Trenton struck alarm and dismay into the British, and Cornwallis, with seven thousand of the best troops, started from New York to redeem what had been lost. Leaving three regiments at Princeton, he pushed hotly after Washington, who fell back behind the Assunpink River, skirmishing heavily and successfully. When Cornwallis reached the river he found the American army drawn up on the other side awaiting him. An attack on the bridge was repulsed, and the prospect looked uninviting. Some officers urged an immediate assault; but night was

falling, and Cornwallis, sure of the game, decided to wait till the morrow. He, too, forgot that he was facing an enemy who never overlooked
a mistake, and never waited an hour. With quick decision Washington
left his camp-fires burning on the river bank, and taking roundabout
roads, which he had already reconnoitered, marched on Princeton. By
sunrise he was in the outskirts of the town. Mercer, detached from
Washington with some three hundred men, fell in with Maxhood's regiment, and a sharp action ensued. Mercer was mortally wounded, and
his men gave way just as Washington's main army came upon the field.
The British charged, and as the raw Pennsylvania troops in the van wavered, Washington rode to the front, and reining his horse within thirty
yards of the British, ordered his men to advance. The volleys of musketry left him unscathed, the men stood firm, the other divisions came
rapidly into action, and the enemy gave way in all directions. The two
other British regiments were driven through the town and routed. Had
there been cavalry they would have been entirely cut off. As it was,
they were completely broken, and in this short but bloody motion they
lost five hundred men in killed, wounded, and prisoners. It was too late
to strike the magazines at Brunswick, as Washington had intended, and
so he withdrew once more with his army to the high lands to rest
and recruit.

His work was done, however. The country, which had been supine,
and even hostile, rose now, and the British were attacked, and suppressed, and cut off in all directions, until at last they were shut up
in the immediate vicinity of New York. The tide had been turned; and
Washington had won the precious breathing time which was all he
required.

Frederick the Great is reported to have said that this was the most
brilliant campaign of the century. It certainly showed all the characteristics of the highest strategy and most consummate generalship. With a
force numerically insignificant as compared with that opposed to him,
Washington won two decisive victories, striking the enemy suddenly
with superior numbers at each point of attack. The Trenton campaign
has all the quality of some of the last battles fought by Napoleon in
France before his retirement to Elba. Moreover, these battles show not
only generalship of the first order but great statesmanship. They display

that prescient knowledge which recognizes the supreme moment when all must be risked to save the state. By Trenton and Princeton Washington inflicted deadly blows upon the enemy, but he did far more by reviving the patriotic spirit of the country fainting under the bitter experience of defeat, and by sending fresh life and hope and courage throughout the whole people.

It was the decisive moment of the war. Sooner or later the American colonies were sure to part from the mother-country, either peaceably or violently. But there was nothing inevitable in the Revolution of 1776, nor was its end at all certain. It was in the last extremities when the British overran New Jersey, and if it had not been for Washington that particular revolution would have most surely failed. Its fate lay in the hands of the general and his army; and to the strong brain growing ever keener and quicker as the pressure became more intense, to the iron will gathering a more relentless force as defeat thickened, to the high unbending character, and to the passionate and fighting temper of Washington, we owe the brilliant campaign which in the darkest hour turned the tide and saved the cause of the Revolution.

★ 11 ★

Clark's Secret March
on Vincennes, 1778

(from Walter Havighurst, *George Rogers Clark—
Soldier in the West*)

LIKE GEORGE WASHINGTON, *George Rogers Clark was recognized in his early manhood as a leader. Tall and rugged with red hair and high cheekbones, Clark won fame in Lord Dunmore's War (1774) and later as an Indian fighter. His prowess earned him the Indian sobriquet "the first man living, the great and invincible Long Knife."*

He was also the great persuader. In 1776, at age twenty-four, he called a meeting of the frontier forts in Harrodsburg, Kentucky. Wanting recognition and protection as a county, he was elected to lead a delegation to Virginia to seek a more definitive connection between Kentucky and Virginia. Patrick Henry, governor of Virginia, and his executive council granted Clark five hundred pounds of gunpowder to defend Kentucky, and the General Assembly made Kentucky a county of Virginia.

The year 1777 was known as the "Bloody '77." The western settlements were attacked continuously. The British lieutenant governor Henry Hamilton, the "Hair-buyer," was paying hefty prices for American scalps and prisoners. In response, Clark was made lieutenant colonel in charge of a force of 370 men divided into seven companies. Relying on intelligence from two spies, Clark decided to attack Kaskaskia, a fortified Virginia outpost on the Mississippi along the water routes that led to Detroit, the supply depot for the Indians. In June 1778 Clark with 175 men marched over land for six days and, without firing a shot, took the fort by surprise. He persuaded the French there and in neighboring towns to join forces with him. He then summoned Indian tribes from as far away as five hundred miles. In a speech he offered the Indians a red belt of war or the white belt of peace, and thereby persuaded them to remain neutral during the coming campaign.

Hamilton moved down from Detroit with his men via the Maumee and Wabash Rivers, to block Clark at Vincennes, Illinois. Clark realized he could not maintain his foothold if, in the spring, Hamilton was resupplied and reinforced by Indians. He decided to attack Vincennes in "the depth of winter," writing Patrick Henry that if he failed, "this country and also Kentucky is lost."

From historian Walter Havighurst, George Rogers Clark—Soldier in the West, *this is the story of Clark's extraordinary march. A bullet through the breast of a British soldier announced Clark's arrival. Clark's sharpshooters peppered the fort. Behind a slight hill, Clark paraded a few of his men carrying flags. Back and forth they marched. All Hamilton could see were the moving flags, and hear the shouts. Clark's ruse made 172 men look like 600. Within thirty-six hours Hamilton surrendered.*

Clark's superhuman swamp march, his willpower, his inspiring leadership, his contagious spirit of invincibility, his oratory, his strategic thinking, and his deft bluff-and-bully tactics delivered huge chunks of the southern portion of the Old Northwest Territory (Ohio, Indiana, Illinois, Wisconsin, Michigan, and Minnesota) into American hands. Clark's conquests helped establish the Great Lakes as the northern boundary of the United States.

★ ★ ★

A DESPERATE SITUATION *needs desperate resolution*—there was no alternative. The more George Rogers Clark thought of it the more inevitable his plan became.

That night he called his captains and told them. They were silent, doubtful, fearful. He talked a little more, acknowledging the hardships and dangers of the march. But the season being so hostile, no enemy would suppose that an attack could come over an impassable country. An enemy off guard is an enemy half beaten; surprise is stronger than an arsenal. Slowly the doubting captains began to speak. "Yes, we took Kaskaskia by surprise." . . . "Yes, the time is favorable." "Yes, we can capture the 'Hair-buyer'!"

Boldness is a strong contagion. Now all Kaskaskia came to life with courage and resolve. French volunteers offered to join the desperate march. Citizens brought provisions, blankets, boots, caps, mufflers, mittens. Clark would need stores of ammunition for his attack and a cannon to breach the heavy walls of the fort. With funds borrowed from Merchant Vigo, he bought a Mississippi flatboat, mounted six small cannon on the deck, and loaded the cabin with supplies. This was the *Willing*, the first gunboat on the western rivers. Aboard it marched Captain John Rogers, Clark's cousin, and forty men, mostly from Cahokia. On the gray fourth day of February, shortly after noon, they pushed into the current of the swollen Kaskaskia River. They would go down the Mississippi, up the Ohio, up the Wabash. Below Vincennes they would hide in the river thickets, waiting the arrival of Clark's regiment across the prairies.

While the *Willing* disappeared around a bend of the river, Clark sat in his office writing a message to Governor Patrick Henry: "... *I know the case is desperate; but Sir, we must either quit the country or attack. . . . Great things have been effected by a few men well conducted. Perhaps we may be fortunate.*"

It was a hazardous, perilous plan, against enormous odds. That night George Rogers Clark sat late beside the fire. *Perhaps we may be fortunate* . . .

On the fifth day of February, 1779, while drums rolled in the fort yard, the citizens of Kaskaskia lined the street below. In the stockade Father Gibault raised his hand; the drums ceased and the priest said a simple heartfelt blessing. As the drums rolled again, Clark's regiment filed out the fort gate in a thin cold rain. It was midafternoon; all morning the captains had been busy, inspecting the men's clothing, ammunition, and provisions, tallying the pack ponies and their loads of tents, baggage, and supplies. Now in mingled French and English the townsfolk cried out their last farewells.

The men marched steadily, followed by the plodding pack train. Soon they were on the empty prairie. Behind them, in the cold seep of the rain, lay the huddled houses of Kaskaskia; behind was Merchant Vigo who had counted out money for the campaign, the old men who had given rifle balls and powder, the women who had stitched twenty flags for their soldiers to raise from the roofs and bastions of Vincennes. Behind was the warmth of familiar hearth fires; ahead lay 200 miles of soaking prairie and drowned bottom land, and at the end a superior enemy waited in a massive fort. Hour after hour they tramped on. Some remembered what was behind them, some thought of what was ahead. Some, perhaps, just marched. Long-striding Virginians and Kentuckians in deerskin jackets, dark-eyed French-Americans in match coats and mackinaws, they marched together in the rain. In all they were 130 men.

Six miles out on the prairie the winter dusk came down. They made their camp on desolate ground; they ate a cold supper washed down with smoking tea. They huddled over reluctant fires, trying to dry their boots and mackinaws. They rolled in their blankets and slept on sodden earth; before daylight they were on their way again. Hour after hour they slogged through mud and mire under a sky the color of wet ashes. A file of stubborn, plodding men, they made twenty-seven miles before they pitched their square camp in the winter dusk, baggage in the middle, sentries posted all around. The third day brought great flat plains of standing water, and the rain kept falling. With a kind of incredulity the men remembered when sunlight washed a green and fragrant prairie; now they gave up thought of warmth and dryness. They splashed on toward a watery horizon.

But the commander kept their spirits burning. Each day he sent out mounted hunters at the sign of game. They came back with quarters of venison and buffalo, and at the end of the day's march one of the four companies gave a feast. They ate like a war party on a triumphant raid. Tearing juicy flesh from bones, grinning with greasy, bearded faces, gulping down their burning whisky ration, they feasted together.

Clark passed from one supper fire to another, a hulking, mud-smeared man with a gruff humor, sampling the joints of smoking meat and nodding approval of the cooking. He was a commander with a kind of triumph in him, not seeming to think of the hardships, the hazards, the desperate test ahead. So, feasting and laughing, singing rowdy songs and whooping like savages, the men forgot the misery of the march. The hot food roused their blood, and the whooping raised their courage. They were young men, in a wild new country, on a mission of daring.

During the day's march, Clark often gave his horse to the hunters and fell in with the men. Sometimes he swung along in silence, his big feet sloshing up and down. But he was mysteriously aware of the army's spirit. He knew when the men were grim with weariness and when their thoughts went ahead with uncertainty and fear. At those times his ragged voice lifted a song or raised a war whoop, and gradually the other voices took it up until the whole wretched regiment sang and shouted under the desolate sky. At weary stretches of mud he set out on a lumbering run, challenging them all to a footrace. At the edge of swollen creeks he held his rifle high and lunged into the water with a savage war cry. So he kept them going; they took fire, like wet faggots, from his own nerve and will. They finished the day's march and devoured their food like a gaunt wolf pack in the firelight. They held numb and swollen hands to the blaze; the leather steamed and stiffened on their feet. They slept in sodden blankets and they did not complain.

On February 13, a week away from Kaskaskia, they reached the Little Wabash. That small river was now a vast flood, five miles across, with the drowned bottoms of the Embarrass River and the swollen Wabash beyond. They were sixty-three forbidding miles from Vincennes. From that camp Clark stared at the gray water, knee-deep, waist-deep, sometimes shoulder-deep. Now a third of his men were shaking with chills and fever. It was five miles to the hills on the opposite shore, and over all that plain of water the cold rain kept falling. Clark ordered his strongest men to take axes, to fell poplar logs, to hollow out canoes. In the first crude craft he sent a party ahead to build a landing platform on the distant shore. Into other canoes they loaded their sick and their baggage. Then they were ready to march.

Clark took the lead, plunging into waist-deep water, lifting his long rifle overhead. The men splashed after him. In that numbing water he kept their courage alive. Time after time he promised land ahead; when the water rose about his waist, he broke into the strains of "A Soldier's Life" or "Billy of the Wild Woods" or "A Man Who Wouldn't Hoe Corn." At last they reached the wooded shore. They landed their baggage and helped their sick ashore. Provisions were short, but Clark was more concerned with secrecy than hunger. He ordered short rations and no firing of guns.

They made a cheerful camp, laughing over their nightmare march, repeating a dozen times how in deep water the drummer boy had crawled onto his drum and floated on it like a raft. Strengthened by hardship, made bold by difficulty, they thought nothing could stop them. Now they spoke of the formidable Wabash, as a creek; they would find a way to cross it. And when they reached Vincennes— Before the fires died down, there was talk of marching on Detroit.

That night, lying sleepless in a wet blanket, Clark had his own grim realization. They were now in the enemy's country, a flooded valley behind them, their horses abandoned with no possibility of retreat. He wondered about the Wabash; could the *Willing* ascend a flooded river in time to keep their rendezvous below Vincennes.

Next day they marched through endless swamps and creek bottoms. Hour after hour they stumbled through freezing mud and splashed through ice-skimmed water. It was long after dark before they stumbled on dry ground and made their desolate camp. The day that followed, and the day that followed that, were the same. At night they gnawed a handful of parched corn and slept with exhaustion.

On the evening of February 17 they reached the Embarrass River at a point nine miles from Vincennes. Those nine miles were a vast drowned bottom, broken by islanded hills and ridges. Gaunt with fatigue and hunger they marched along the Embarrass to its juncture with the Wabash. They marched grimly. Clark and his captains shouted, but the men slogged on in silence. Mud, mud, mud, mud . . . water, water, water, water . . . cold, cold, cold, cold . . . war, war, war, war. . . . In a weary, aching trance they kept moving, one foot lifting, then another, one stride more.

So they reached the Wabash. Now Vincennes was upstream, still nine miles away, across the swollen channel and the drowned bottom lands. They had no rations left—not even a rind of bacon or a handful of corn. Here they were to meet the *Willing;* but the flooded Wabash lay empty between the wooded hills.

"Camp Hunger" the men called it. Clark promptly had a pair of axmen hollowing out a log, and in that canoe he sent a party down-stream to find the *Willing.* The rest waited, remembering the bushels of corn and the stacks of dried buffalo meat they had loaded on the gunboat. They watched in silence while the canoe came back, and the gaunt faces of the paddlers told the news before they voiced it. The *Willing* had not arrived. (The gunboat had been delayed by floodwater and was now at the mouth of the Wabash, 100 miles away.)

It was a hungry night. In the cold gray daybreak they heard a boom of a cannon—the morning gun from the frowning fort at Vincennes. At that moment General Hamilton was sitting down to a hot and hearty breakfast, but Clark gave his men no time to think of food. He kept them chopping trees and lacing logs together with fox vines from the branches; on those makeshift rafts he sent men toward Vincennes to steal boats. They poled the rafts away, and too soon they returned. A mile away they had found a camp of Indians around four large camp-fires; they dared not go farther for fear of being discovered. Again Clark sent men down river, to look for the *Willing.* He paced the muddy shore while his gaunt troops chewed the bark of slippery elm to quiet their stomach pains. They had not tasted food for two days.

Weak as they were, Clark kept his axmen hollowing on wet poplar logs. At noon the river sentries brought in a captured boat, and five astonished Frenchmen were led to the commander. They answered Clark's questions readily, declaring that no one in Vincennes suspected the presence of American troops in the Wabash country. That evening a hunter came in with fresh-killed venison. One deer for 130 men— it made their hunger violent.

Next morning in the leaden dawn they ferried the Wabash, and still they were cut off from the town by miles of flooded lowland. With a muttered "March!" Clark plunged into knee-deep water. The men waded after him. All day the gray rain fell, all day they foundered on, pushing their canoes through drowned timber and across desolate bays of flood. The five Frenchmen from Vincennes were amazed at this march; they had told Clark it was impossible to reach Vincennes without a fleet of boats. When Clark asked the location of the nearest dry land, they described a sugar camp, a grove of maple trees on a rounded hill. A canoe went ahead through submerged thickets, but it could not find a passage. Then Clark went forward, wading into the deepening stream. It was cold as ice.

Waist-deep in sullen water, he turned to his men. They watched him in silence, eyes fearful and beaten, faces gaunt and hollow. Some were shaking with chills, some were dazed with fever; in all of them hunger was gnawing like an animal. Suddenly Clark raised his powder horn. He poured a pinch of precious gunpowder into his wet hand and smeared the black mixture on his face. His voice went up in a frenzied, yowling war whoop; in it sounded hunger, grimness, desperation, but it ended in a fierce defiance. He turned then and lunged into the stream. For a moment the men stared blankly, eyes dead as cinders in their famished faces. Then one man blacked his own cheeks and plunged in. Another followed, and another; the gaunt regiment was moving. Ahead of them Clark lifted his rifle. His ragged voice began a song, and behind him, in a thin and growing chorus, the men joined in. They were a wretched, starving, and exhausted army—singing.

At last they felt firm ground beneath their feet. They followed it through a chaos of brush and bending willow branches. It led to a half acre of mounded land, covered with bare maple trees. They made their camp in the sugar grove. It was a cold night but they slept like dead.

In the morning the Frenchmen from Vincennes pointed to the broad Horseshoe Plain—not a plain now but a gray sea covering a great sickle bend of the Wabash. The sky had cleared in the night and a yellow sun rose over the woodlands. Clark stood among his silent men. This was the final march, he told them. In two hours they would see the roofs of Vincennes. There could be no weakness now.

He stationed Major Bowman in the rear with orders to shoot any man who faltered or turned back. Then he led the way. Out in the desolate Horseshoe Plain there were no half-drowned bushes to grasp at, no trees to cling to.

Clark ordered canoes to carry the weakest men, to land them on the far shore, and to return for others. The rest struggled on, arms around each other's shoulders, floundering toward the land. There was no singing now. Even the commander kept silent, but he kept advancing. When at last they reached a brushy ridge, they would have sunk down, numb and exhausted, but Clark kept them on their feet. They chopped branches and started fires. The strong men dragged the weak around and around the burning embers until their clothing had dried and the blood was brisk in their veins.

When a sentry reported a craft on the water, Clark sent a party after it. They captured a large canoe paddled by Indian women; in it were buffalo meat, corn, tallow, and a nest of blackened kettles. Hungry eyes glittered while the kettles warmed on the fire. Broth was fed to the weak and fevered men; all of them had a ration of corn. It was not a feast, but it quickened sluggish blood and put strength into exhausted muscles. With new spirit they pushed on.

In canoes and afoot they crossed another mile of flood land and came to the brushy knob of Warrior's Island, with sunlight slanting through its winter trees. From there Clark gazed across two miles of flat and open country to Post Vincennes—the houses scattered along the river, the timbered church and the long stockade of the fort with its five frowning blockhouses catching the rays of the sinking sun. Around him stood his men, staring at the goal of their impossible march.

A NEW NATION

12

A Pioneer Settler's Hardships

(from Mr. Hubbell, public document, 1824)

BENEATH THE GREEN MANTLES *of Vermont's mountains lies a rocky subsurface. During the Ice Age glaciers covered the land, gouged out its valleys and littered them with a myriad of granite stones and boulders. Ever since, Vermonters have been clearing their land, removing rocks, and wrestling with meager farm soil. This scratch farming taught Vermonters to sweat for their living, to improvise, and not to count on Lady Luck. Vermonters like to say that they go it alone except for barn raising, maple sugaring, and square dancing.*

Mastering the wilderness in order to live was hard, rough, dangerous work. Only the strongest in body and spirit prevailed. One such group was the Hubbell family, and Mr. Hubbell's personal account of the early settlement of Vermont near the Canadian border follows. His story was so remarkable that four separate justices of the peace who knew him confirmed the truth of his experiences and signed their names at the end of this testimony.

* * *

IN THE LATTER PART of February, 1789, I set out from the town of
Norwalk, in Connecticut, on my journey for Wolcott, Vermont, to
commence a settlement and make that my residence; family consisting
of my wife and five children, they all being girls, the eldest nine or ten
years old. My team was a yoke of oxen and a horse. After I had proceeded on my journey to within about one hundred miles of Wolcott,
one of my oxen failed, but I however kept him yoked with the other till
about noon each day; then turned him before, and took his end of the
yoke myself, and proceeded on in that manner with my load to about
fourteen miles of my journey's end, when I could get the sick ox no further, and was forced to leave him with Thomas W. Connel, in Johnson;
but he had neither hay nor grain for him. I then proceeded on with
some help to Esq. McDaniel's in Hydepark: this brought me to about
eight miles of Wolcott, and to the end of the road. It was now about the
20th of March; the snow not far from four feet deep; no hay to be had
for my team, and no way for them to subsist but by browse. As my
sick ox at Connel's could not be kept on browse, I interceded with a
man in Cambridge for a little hay to keep him alive, which I backed, a
bundle at a time, five miles, for about ten days, when the ox died. On
the 6th of April I set out from Esq. McDaniel's, his being the last house,
for my intended residence in Wolcott, with my wife and two eldest
children. We had eight miles to travel on snow-shoes, by marked
trees—no road being cut: my wife had to try this new mode of travelling, and she performed the journey remarkable well. The path had
been so trodden by snow-shoes as to bear up the children. Esq. Taylor,
with his wife and two small children, who moved on with me, had gone
on the day before. We were the first families in Wolcott: in Hydepark
there had two families wintered the year before. To the east of us it was
eighteen mile to inhabitants, and no road but marked trees: to the
south, about twenty, where there was infant settlement, but no communication with us; and to the north, it was almost indefinite, or to
the regions of Canada.

I had now got to the end of my journey, and I may say almost to
end of my property, for I had not a mouthful of meat or kernel of grain

for my family, nor had I a cent of money left to buy with, or property that I could apply to that purpose. I however had the good luck to catch a sable. The skin I carried fifty miles, and exchanged for half a bushel of wheat, and backed it home. We had now lived three weeks without bread; though in the time I had bought a moose of an Indian, and backed the meat five miles, which answered to subsist upon. I would here remark that it was my fate to move on my family at that memorable time called the "scarce season," which was generally felt through the state, especially in the northern parts in the infant settlements: no grain or provision of any kind, of consequence, was to be had on the river Lamoille. I had to go into New Hampshire, sixty miles, for the little I had for my family, till harvest, and this was so scanty a pittance that we were under the painful necessity of allowancing the children till we had a supply. The three remaining children that I left in Hydepark, I brought one at a time on my back on snow-shoes, as also the whole of my goods.

I moved from Connecticut with the expectation of having fifty acres of land given me when I came on, but this I was disappointed of, and was under the necessity soon after I came on of selling a yoke of oxen and a horse to buy the land I now live on, which reduced my stock to but one cow; and this I had the misfortune to lose the next winter. That left me wholly destitute of a single creature: of course the second summer I had to support my family without a cow. I would here notice that I spent the summer before I moved, in Wolcott, in making preparation for a settlement, which, however, was of no avail to me, and I lost the summer; and to forward my intended preparation, I brought on a yoke of oxen, and left them, when I returned in the fall, with a man in Johnson, to keep through the winter, on certain conditions; but when I came on in the spring, one of them was dead, and this yoke of oxen that I put off for my land was made of the two surviving ones.

But to proceed, in the fall I had the good fortune to purchase another cow; but misfortunes still continued, for the June following she was killed by a singular accident. Again I was left without a cow, and here I was again frustrated in my calculations: this last cow left a fine heifer calf that in the next fall I lost by being choked. Soon after I arrived, I took two cows to double in four years. I had one of my own besides, which died in calving. In June following, one of those taken to double, was killed while fighting: the other was found dead in the yard; both of which I had to replace. In the same spring, one of my neighbor's oxen hooked a bull of two years old, which caused his death soon after. Here I was left destitute—no money to buy, or article to traffic for one: but there was a door opened. I was informed that a merchant in Haverhill was buying snakeroot and sicily. This was a new kind of traffic that I had no great faith in; but I thought to improve every means or semblance of means in my power. Accordingly, with the help of my two oldest girls, I dug and dried a horse-load, and carried this new commodity to the merchant; but his was like most hearsay reports of fine markets, always a little way ahead, for he knew nothing about this strange article, and would not even venture to make an offer; but after a long conference I importuned with the good merchant to give me a three year old heifer for my roots, on certain conditions too tedious to mention. I drove her home, and with joy she was welcomed to my habitation, and it has been my good fortune to have a cow ever since. Though my faith was weak; yet being vigilant and persevering, I obtained the object, and the wilderness produced me a cow.

When I came into Wolcott, my farming tools consisted of one axe and an old hoe. The first year I cleared about two acres, wholly without any team, and being short of provision was obliged to work the chief of the time till harvest with scarce a sufficiency to support nature. My work was chiefly by the river. When too faint to labor, for want of food, I use to take a fish from the river, broil it on the coals, and eat it without bread or salt, and then to my work again. This was my common practice the first year till harvest. I could not get a single potato to plant the first season, so scarce was this article. I then thought if I could but get enough of this valuable production to eat I would never complain. I rarely see this article cooked, but the thought strikes my mind; in fact to this day I have a great veneration for this precious root. I planted that which I cleared in season with corn; and an early frost ruined the crop, so that I raised nothing the first year: had again to buy my provision. My seed corn, about eight quarts, cost me two and a half yards of whitened linen, yard wide, and this I had to go twenty miles after.

Though this may be called extortion, it was a solitary instance of the kind; all were friendly and ready to assist me in my known distress, as far as they had ability. An uncommon degree of sympathy pervaded all the new settlers, and I believe this man heartily repented the act, for he was by no means indigent, and was many times reminded of it by way of reproof.

My scanty supply of bread-corn made it necessary to improve the first fruits of harvest at Lake Champlain, to alleviate our distress, it being earlier than with us. Accordingly, on the last days of July or first of August, I took my sickle, and set out for the Lake, a distance of better than forty miles. When I had got there, I found their grain was not ripe enough to begin upon; but was informed that on the Grand Isle they had begun their harvest. I was determined to go on, but had nothing to pay my passage. I finally hired a man to carry me over from Georgia for the small compensation of a case and two lances that I happened to have with me; but when I had to go on to the Island, I found I was still too early. There was no grain ripe here, but I found the most forward I could, plead my necessity, and stayed by the owner till I got one and a half bushel of wheat, and worked for him to pay for it: it was quite green; I dried it and set out for home; but my haste to get back prevented my drying it sufficiently. I found a boat bound for Mansfield's mills, on the river Lamoille, and got my grain on board, and had it brought there free from expense. I got it ground, or rather mashed, for it was too damp to make meal. I here hired my meal carried on to Cambridge borough for my sickle, and there got it ground the second time, but it was still far from good meal. From the Borough I was so fortunate as to get it home on a horse. I was a fortnight on this tour. My wife was fearful some accident had happened, and sent a man in pursuit of me, who met me on my way home. I left my family without bread or meal, and was welcomed home with tears: my wife baked a cake, and my children again tasted bread.

I had the good fortune to buy on trust, the winter after I lost my corn, of a man in Cambridge, twenty four miles from home, twelve bushels of corn, and one of wheat. This, by the assistance of some kind friends, I got to Esq. McDaniel's. I also procured by digging on shares in Hydepark, twelve or thirteen bushels of potatoes. This grain and potatoes I carried eight miles on my back. My common practice was one half bushel of meal, and one half bushel of potatoes at a load.

The singular incidents that took place in getting this grain on, though tedious to mention, may be worthy of notice. Soon after I set out from home, sometime in the month of March, it began to rain, and was a very rainy day and night. The Lamoille was raised—the ice became rotten and dangerous crossing—many of the small streams were broken up. The man of who I purchased the grain was so good as to take his team and carry it to the mill. The owner of the mill asked me how I expected to get my meal home. I answered him as the case really was, that I knew not. The feeling man then offered me his oxen and sled to carry it to the Park, and I thankfully accepted his kind offer. He then turned to the miller, and directed him to grind my grist toll free. While at the mill a man requested me to bring a half hogshead tub on my sled up to Johnson. By permission of the owner of the oxen, he put the tub on the sled, and it was a Providential circumstance; for when I came to Brewster's branch, a wild stream, I found it broken up, run rapid and deep. At first I was perplexed what to do. To go across with my bags on the sled would ruin my meal; I soon thought of the tub; this held about half of my bags; the other half I left on the shore, and proceeded into the branch and crossed with safety. Though I was wet nearly to my middle, I unloaded the tub and returned into the branch, holding the tub on the sled, but the stream was so rapid, the tub being empty that in spite of all my exertions I was washed off the sled and carried down the stream, holding on to the tub, for this I know was my only alternative to get across my load. At length I succeeded in getting the tub to the shore, though I was washed down the stream more than twenty rods, sometimes up to my armpits in the water, and how I kept the tub from filling in this hasty struggle, I know not, but so it was. The oxen, though turned toward home, happily for me, when they had to go across the stream, stopt in the path, till I came up with the tub. I then put in the other half of my load, and succeeded in getting the whole across the branch, and traveled on about three miles and put up for the night. Wet as I was, and at that season of the year, it is easy to conceive my uncomfortable situation, for the thaw was over, and it was chilly and cold. In the morning I proceeded home—came to the river; not being sensible how weak the ice was, I attempted to cross, but here a scene ensued that I can never forget. When about half across the river, I perceived the ice settling under my oxen. I jumped on to the tongue of my sled, and hastened to the oxen's heads and pulled out the pin that held the yoke. By this time the oxen were sunk to their knees in water. I then sprang to the sled, and drawed it back to the shore, without the least difficulty, notwithstanding the load, and returned to my oxen. By this time they had broken a considerable path in the ice, and were struggling to get out. I could do nothing but stand and see them swim round—sometimes they would be nearly out of sight, nothing scarcely but their horns to be seen—they would then rise and struggle to extricate themselves from their perilous situation. I called for help in vain; and to fly for assistance would have been imprudent and fatal. Notwithstanding my unhappy situation, and the manner by which I came by the oxen, etc. I was not terrified in the least—I felt calm and composed;—at length the oxen swam up to where I stood and laid their heads on the ice at my feet. I immediately took the yoke from off their necks; they lay still till the act was performed, and then returned to swimming as before. By this time they had made an opening in the ice as much as two roads across. One of them finally swam to the down stream side, and in an instant, as if lifted out of the water, he was on his side on the ice, and got up and walked off; the other swam to the same place and was out in the same way. I stood on the opposite side of the opening, and saw with astonishment every movement. I then thought, and the impression is still on my mind, that they were helped out by supernatural means; most certainly no natural cause could produce an effect like this: that a heavy ox six and a half feet in girth, can of his own natural strength heave himself out of the water on his side on the ice, is too extraordinary to reconcile to a natural cause:—that in the course of divine Providence events do take place out of the common course of nature, that our strongest reasoning cannot comprehend, is impious to deny; though we acknowledge the many chimeras of superstition, ignorance and barbarism in the world; and when we are eye witnesses to such events, it is not for us to doubt, but to believe and tremble. Others have a right to doubt my testimony: but in this instance, for me to doubt would be perjury to my own conscience, and I may add ingratitude to my Divine Benefactor. In fact a signal Providence seemed to direct that path for me to pursue to procure this grain. Though I was doomed to encounter perils, to suffer fatigue and toil, there was a way provided for me to obtain the object in view. In the first onset I accidentally fell in with the man of whom I purchased at the Park. I found he had grain to sell. I requested of him this small supply on trust: we were strangers to each other—a peculiar friend of mine, happening to be by, volunteered his word for the pay. I knew not where nor how to get the money, but necessity drove me to make the purchase, and in the course of the winter I was so fortunate as to catch sable enough to pay the debt by the time it was due. Though I hazarded my word, it was in a good cause—it was for the relief of my family, and so it terminated. But to return.

I had now gone to the extent of my abilities for bread corn, but was destitute of meat; and beef and pork were scarcer in those times. Accordingly I had to have recourse to wild meat for a substitute, and had the good luck to purchase moose of a hunter; and the meat of two more I brought in on shares—had the one for bringing in the other. These two were uncommonly large—were judged to weight seven hundred weight each. The meat of these three moose I brought in on my back, together with the large bones and heads. I backed them five or six miles over rough land, cut up by sharp ridges and deep hollows, and interspersed with underbrush and windfalls, which made it impracticable to pass with a hand sled, which, could I have used, would have much eased my labour. A more laborious task was this than that of bringing my meal, &c. from the Park.

My practice was to carry my load in a bag, to tie the ends of the bag so nigh that I could but comfortable get my head through, so that the weight of my load would rest on my shoulders. I often had to encounter this hardship in the time of a thaw, which made the task more severe, especially in the winter and for part of the spring, when the snow became coarse and harsh, and will not so readily support the snow-shoe. My hold would often fail without any precious notice to guard against— perhaps slide under a log or catch in a bush and pitch me into the snow with my load about my neck. I have repeatedly had to struggle in this situation for some time to extricate myself from my load, it being impossible to get up with my load on. Those who are acquainted with this kind of burden may form an idea of what I had to encounter—the great difficulty of carrying a load on snow-shoes in the time of a thaw, is one of those kinds of fatigue that it is hard to describe, nor can be conceived but by experience. It is wearisome at such times to travel without a load but with one, especially at this late season, it is intolerable: but thaw or freeze, my necessities obliged me to be at my task, and still to keep up my burden. I had to draw my firewood through the winter on a hand sled: in fact, my snow-shoes were constantly hung to my feet.

Being destitute of team for four or five years, and without farming tools, I had to labor under great embarrassments: my grain I hoed in the three first years. After I raised sufficiency for my family, I had to carry it twelve miles to mill on my back, for the three first years: this I had constantly to do once a week. My common load was one bushel, and generally carried it eight miles before I stopped to rest. My family necessities once obliged me to carry a moose hide thirty miles on my back, and sell it for a bushel of corn, and bring that home in the same way.

For a specimen of the hardships those have often to encounter who move into the wilderness, I will give the following, that took place the winter after I came on: we had a remarkable snow, the first, of consequence, that fell; it was full two feet deep. Our communication was with the inhabitants of Hydepark, and it was necessary for us to keep the road, or rather path, so that we could travel; we were apprehensive of danger, if we did not immediately tread a path through this snow. I was about out of meal, and had previously left a bushel at a deserted house about five miles on the way. I agree with Esq. Taylor, he being the only inhabitant with me, to start the next day on the proposed tour. We accordingly started before sunrise; the snow was light, and we sunk deep into it. By the middle of the day it give some, which made it still worse; our snow-shoes loaded at every step: we had to use nearly our whole strength to extricate the loaded shoe from its hold. It seemed that our hip joints would be drawn from their sockets. We were soon worried—could go but a few steps without stopping; our fatigue and toil became almost insupportable—were obliged often to sit down and rest, and were several times on the point of giving up the pursuit, and stop for the night, but this must have been fatal, as we had no axe to cut wood for a fire; our blood was heated and we must have chilled. We finally, at about dusk, reached the deserted house, but were in effect exhausted. It seemed we could not have reached this house had it been twenty rods further: so terrible is the toil to travel through deep snow, that no one can have a sense of it till taught by experience. This day's journey is often on my mind; in my many hard struggles it was one of the severest. We struck up a fire and gathered some fuel that lay about the house, and after we had recovered strength, I baked a cake of my meal, we then lay down on some hewn planks, and slept sound till morning. It froze at night; the track we had made rendered it quite feasible traveling. The next day I returned home with my bushel of meal.

Another perilous tour I will mention, that occurred this winter. It was time to bring on another load of meal from Esq. McDaniel's. I proposed in my mind to go early the next morning. There had been a thaw, and in the time of the thaw a man had driven a yoke of oxen from Cabot, and went down on my path, and trod it up. The night was clear—the moon shone bright, and it was remarkably cold. I woke, supposing it nearly day, and set out, not being sensible of the cold, and being thinly clad I soon found I was in danger of freezing, and began to run, jump, and thrash my hands, &c. The path being full of holes, and a light snow had just fallen that filled them up, I often fell, and was in danger of breaking my limbs, &c. The cold seemed to increase, and I was forced to exert my utmost strength to keep from freezing: my limbs became numb before I got through, though I ran about every step of the eight miles, and when I got to McDaniel's the cocks crowed for day. I was surprised upon coming to the fire to find that the bottoms of my moccasins and stocking were cut and worn through, the bottoms of my feet being entirely bare, having cut them by the holes in the path, but notwithstanding the severity of the frost, I was preserved, not being frozen in any part. Had I broken a limb, or but slightly spraint a joint, which I was in imminent danger of doing, I must have perished on the way, as a few minutes of respite must have been fatal.

In the early part of my residence in Wolcott, by some means I obtained knowledge of their being beaver on a small stream in Hardwick;

and desirous to improve every means in my power for the support of my family, and to retrieve my circumstances, I determined on a tour to try my fortune at beaver hunting. Accordingly, late in the fall, I set out in company with my neighbor Taylor on the intended enterprise. We took what was called the Coos road, which was nothing more than marked trees; in about seven miles we reached the stream, and proceeded up it about three miles farther, and searched for beaver, but were soon convinced that they had left the ground. We, however, set a few traps. Soon after we started it began to rain, and before night the rain turned to a moist snow that melted on us as fast as it fell. Before we reached the hunting ground, we were wet to our skins; night soon came on—we found it necessary to camp (as the hunters use the term); with difficulty we struck up a fire; but our fuel was poor, chiefly green timber—the storm increased—the snow continued moist; our bad accommodations grew worse and worse; our fire was not sufficient to warm us and much less to dry us. We dared not attempt to lay down, but continued on our feet through the night, feeding our fire and endeavoring to warm our shivering limbs. This is a memorable night to me—the most distressing I ever experienced; we anxiously looked for day. At length the dawn appeared, but it was a dismal and a dreary scene. The moist snow had adhered to every thing in its way; the trees and underwood were remarkably loaded, were completely hid from sight—nothing to be seen but snow, and nothing to be heard but the cracking of the bended boughs under the enormous weight, we could scarcely see a rod at noon day. When light enough to travel, we set out for home, and finding it not safe to leave the stream for fear of getting bewildered and lost, we followed it back; it was lined the chief of the way with beaver meadow, covered with a thick growth of alders; we had no way to get through them but for one to go forward and beat off the snow with a heavy stick. We thus proceeded, though very slowly, down the stream to the Coos road, and worried through the ten miles home at the dusk of the evening, nearly exhausted by fatigue, wet and cold, for it began to freeze in the morning; our clothes were frozen stiff on our backs; when I pulled off my great coat it was so stiff as to stand up on the floor. In order to save our traps we had to make another trip, and one solitary muskrat made up our compensation for this hunting tour.

A painful circumstance respecting my family I must here mention: In the year 1806 we were visited with sickness that was uncommonly distressing, five being taken down at the same time, and several dangerously ill. In this sickness I lost my wife, the partner of my darkest days, who bore her share of our misfortunes with becoming fortitude. I also lost a daughter at the same time, and another was bedrid about six months, and unable to perform the least labour for more than a year. This grievous calamity involved me in debts that terminated in the loss of my farm, my little all; but by the indulgence of feeling relatives I am still permitted to stay on it. Though I have been doomed to hard misfortune I have been blest with a numerous offspring; have had by my two wives seventeen children, thirteen of the daughters have had forty-seven grand-children, and six great grand-children, making my posterity seventy souls.

I have here given but a sketch of my most important sufferings. The experienced farmer will readily discover, that under the many embarrassments I had to encounter, I must make but slow progress in clearing land; no soul to help me, no funds to go to: raw and inexperienced in this kink of labor, though future wants pressed the necessity of constant application to this business, a great portion of my time was unavoidably taken up in pursuit of sustenance for my family; however reluctant to leave my labor, the support of nature must be attended to, the calls of hunger cannot be dispensed with. I have now to remark, that at this present time, my almost three score years and ten, I feel the want of those forced exertions of bodily strength that were spent in those perils and fatigues, and have worn down my constitution, to support my decaying nature.

When I reflect on those past events, the fatigue and toil I had to encounter, the dark scenes I had to pass through, I am struck with wonder and astonishment at the fortitude and presence of mind that I then had to bear me up under them. Not once was I discouraged or disheartened: I exercised all my powers of body and mind to do the best I could, and left the effect for future events to decide, without embarrassing my mind with imaginary evils, I could lay down at night, forgetting my troubles, and sleep composed and calm as a child; I did in reality experience the just proverb of the wise man, that "the sleep of the laboring man is sweet, whether he eat little or much." Nor can I close my tale of sufferings without rendering my feeble tribute of thanks and praise to my benign Benefactor, who supplies the wants of the needy, and relieves the distressed, that in his wise Providence has assisted my natural strength both of body and of mind to endure those scenes of distress and toil.

County of Orleans, Nov'r. 1824.

The undersigned, having read in manuscript the foregoing narrative, and having lived in habits of intimacy with, and in the neighborhood of Mr. Hubbell at the time of his sufferings, we are free to inform the public, that we have no doubt but his statements are, in substance, correct. Many of the circumstances therein narrated we were at the time personally knowing to, and are sensible more might be added without exaggeration, in many instances wherein he suffered.

Thomas Taylor, *Justice of Peace*
Darius Fitch, *J. of Peace*
John McDaniel, *J. P.*
Jesse Whitney, *J. P.*

13

William Cooper Saves a Town

(from William Cooper, *A Guide in the Wilderness:*
Or the History of the First Settlement in the
Western Counties of New York, 1810)

FROM 1776 TO 1785 *the pioneer movement exploded. The Scotch-*
Irish sprang across the mountains of North Carolina and Virginia to
settle eastern Tennessee. Using the Cumberland Gap, they crossed into
Kentucky. Settlers moved into the Shenandoah and Susquehanna Valleys.
They pushed up the Monongahela to Fort Pitt and thence down the Ohio
River. General "Mad Anthony" Wayne finally secured that area with his
1794 victory at the battle of Fallen Timbers and the Treaty of Greenville.

William Cooper, father of the novelist James Fenimore Cooper, ac-
quired a land patent for forty thousand acres in 1785 at the headwaters of
the Susquehanna River. There, on the shores of beautiful Lake Otsego, New
York, he founded Cooperstown, where "if you don't like the weather, wait
ten minutes." His family was large, his capital small. He raised some
money, purchased the land, and resold all of it to prospective settlers on fair
terms with time payments. By 1806, Cooper could boast that he had "set-
tled more acres than any man in America," and the families within his
land patent were happy and prosperous.

His wisdom lay in locating settlers close enough, sixty together, so that one neighbor's surplus and skill could satisfy another's needs. His success lay in a sense of duty to his landowners, timely improvisations, hard work, and persuasive leadership. "Let me be clearly understood," wrote Judge Cooper about developing land on the frontier, "that no man who does not possess a steady mind, a sober judgment, fortitude, perseverance, and above all, common sense, can expect to reap the reward, which to him who possesses these qualifications, is almost certain." From his Guide in the Wilderness: Or the History of the First Settlement in the Western Counties of New York, *here is William Cooper's 1810 account of the struggle, survival, and prosperity of his settlement.*

* * *

IN 1785 I visited the rough and hilly country of Otsego, where there existed not an inhabitant, nor any trace of a road; I was alone three hundred miles from home, without bread, meat, or food of any kind; fire and fishing tackle were my only means of subsistence. I caught trout in the brook, and roasted them on the ashes. My horse fed on the grass that grew by the edge of the waters. I laid me down to sleep in my watchcoat with nothing but the melancholy Wilderness around me. In this way I explored the country, formed my plans of future settlement, and meditated upon the spot where a place of trade or a village should afterwards be established. In May 1786 I opened the sales of 40,000 acres, which, in sixteen days, were all taken up by the poorest order of men. I soon after established a store, and went to live among them, and continued so to do till 1790, when I brought on my family. For the ensuing four years the scarcity of provisions was a serious calamity. The country was mountainous; there were neither roads nor bridges. But the greatest discouragement was in the extreme poverty of the people, none of whom had the means of clearing more than a small spot in the midst of the thick and lofty woods. Their grain grew chiefly in the shade. Their maize did not ripen. Their wheat was blasted, and the little they did gather they had no mill to grind within twenty miles distance. Not one in twenty had a horse, and the way lay through rapid streams, across swamps, or over bogs. They had neither provisions to take with them, nor money to purchase them. If the father of a family went abroad to labour for bread, it cost him three times its value before he could bring it home, and all the business on his farm stood still till his return.

I resided among them, and saw too clearly how bad their condition was. I erected a store-house, and during each winter filled it with large quantities of grain, purchased in distant places. I procured from my friend Henry Drinker a credit for a large quantity of sugar kettles; he also lent me some pot ash kettles, which we conveyed as best we could; sometimes by partial roads on sleighs, and sometimes over the ice. By this means I established pot ash works among the settlers, and made them debtor for their bread and labouring utensils. I also gave them credit for their maple sugar and pot ash, at a price that would bear transportation. In the first year after the adoption of this plan I collected in one mass forty-three hogsheads of sugar, and three hundred barrels of pot and pearl ash, worth about nine thousand dollars. This kept the people together and at home, and the country soon assumed a new face.

I had not funds of my own sufficient for the opening of new roads. So I collected the people at convenient seasons, and by joint efforts we were able to throw bridges over the deep streams, and to make, in the cheapest manner, such roads as suited our then humble purposes.

In the winter preceding the summer of 1789, grain rose in Albany to a price before unknown. The demand swept the whole granaries of the Mohawk country. The number of beginners who depended upon it for their bread greatly aggravated the evil, and a famine ensued, which will never be forgotten by those who, though now in the enjoyment of ease and comfort, were then afflicted with the cruelest of wants.

In the month of April I arrived amongst them with several loads of provisions, destined for my own use and that of the labourers I had brought with me for certain necessary operations. But in a few days all was gone, and there remained not one pound of salt meat nor a single biscuit. Many were reduced to such distress, as to live upon the roots of wild leeks; some more fortunate lived upon milk, whilst others supported nature by drinking a syrup made of maple sugar and water. The quantity of leeks they eat had such an effect upon their breath, that they could be smelled at many paces distance, and when they came together, it was like cattle that had pastured in a garlic field. A man of the name of Beets mistaking some poisonous herb for a leek, ate it, and died in consequence. Judge of my feelings at this epoch, with two hundred families about me, and not a morsel of bread.

A singular event seemed sent by a good Providence to our relief. It was reported to me that unusual shoals of fish were seen moving in the clear waters of the Susquehanna. I went and was surprised to find that they were herrings. We made something like a small net, by the interweaving of twigs, and by this rude and simple contrivance, we were able to take them in thousands. In less than ten days each family had an ample supply with plenty of salt. I also obtained from the Legislature, then in session, seventeen hundred bushels of corn. This we packed on horses backs, and on our arrival made a distribution among the families, in porportion to the number of individuals of which each was composed.

This was the first settlement I made, and the first attempted after the revolution. It was, of course, attended with the greatest difficulties. Nevertheless, to its success many others have owed their origin. It was besides the roughest land in all the state, and the most difficult of cultivation of all that has been settled; but for many years past it has produced every thing necessary to the support and comfort of man. It maintains at present eight thousand souls, with schools, academies, churches, meetinghouses, turnpike roads, and a market town. It annually yields to commerce large droves of fine oxen, great quantities of wheat and other grain, abundance of pork, pot ash in barrels, and other provisions. Merchants with large capitals, and all kinds of useful mechanics reside upon it. The waters are stocked with fish, the air is salubrious, and the country thriving and happy. When I contemplate all this, and above all, when I see these good old settlers meet together, and hear them talk of past hardships, of which I bore my share, and compare the misery they then endured with the comforts they now enjoy, my emotions border upon weakness, which manhood can scarcely avow.

⋆ 14 ⋆

The Hazards of Floating
Down the Ohio River

(from John M'Clung, *Sketches of Western Adventure,*
Containing an Account of the Most Interesting Incidents
Connected with the Settlement of the West from
1755–1794, 1832)

TODAY *if you move from New York City to the Midwest, you hitch
a U-Haul trailer to your car and head for the Pennsylvania
Turnpike at sixty-five miles per hour. After the Revolutionary
War, when land speculation was ablaze, life was different. You'd hitch
your horses to a wagon and head toward Pittsburgh, then an outpost of
376 souls. To cross the Alleghenies was not easy—wave after wave of
three-thousand-foot mountains extended from the Mohawk Valley to the
Tennessee River. Consider the following description of one family of twelve
who had decided to make the arduous trek:*

> *The man carried an ax and a gun on his shoulders—the wife, the rim
> of a spinning wheel in one hand and a loaf of bread in another. Sev-
> eral little boys and girls, each with a bundle according to their size.
> Two poor horses each heavily loaded with some poor necessaries. On top
> of the baggage of one was an infant, rocked to sleep in a kind of wicker
> cage, lashed securely to the horse. A cow formed one of the company,*

and she was destined to bear her proportion of service. A bed cord was wound around her horns, and a bag of meal on her back.

Once near Pittsburgh, westward-bound settlers could buy a flatboat— forty-two feet long, twelve feet wide, drawing two and a half feet of water. Steered by oars, these rafts were swept by a steady current down the Ohio River, southwest toward the Mississippi.

An earlier pioneer to such an adventure was Colonel Rufus Putnam from Massachusetts, one of the founders of the Ohio Company of Associates. In 1786 the Ohio Company ran newspaper advertisements asking Revolutionary War officers and soldiers to meet at the Bunch of Grapes Tavern in Boston. Only eleven men showed up. Yet at its peak the company obtained rights to 1,781,700 acres, "north-westerly of the Ohio River," an area slightly larger than the state of Delaware. In 1788, forty-eight armed men and boys from the Ohio Company floated down the river on homemade flatboats loaded with lumber and supplies and built from scratch the town of Marietta, Ohio. In those days two large flatboats were capable of carrying "twenty-nine whites, twenty-four negroes, nine dogs, twenty-three horses, cows, hogs, etc., besides provisions and furniture." Indians along the Ohio River waxed and waned as a threat to voyagers.

From John M'Clung's Sketches of Western Adventure, Containing an Account of the Most Interesting Incidents Connected with the Settlement of the West from 1755–1794, *here's a travel tale down the Ohio River in 1791.*

* * *

I N THE YEAR 1791, while the Indians were yet troublesome, especially on the banks of the Ohio, Captain William Hubbell, who had previously emigrated to Kentucky from the state of Vermont, and who, after having fixed his family in the neighborhood of Frankfort, then a frontier settlement, had been compelled to go to the eastward on business, was a second time on his way to this country. On one of the tributary streams of the river Monongahela, he procured a flat bottomed boat, and embarked in company with Mr. Daniel Light, and Mr. William Plascut and his family, consisting of a wife and eight children, destined for Limestone, Kentucky. On their progress down the river Ohio, and soon after passing Pittsburgh, they saw evident traces of Indians along the banks, and there is every reason to believe that a boat which they overtook, and which, through carelessness, was suffered to run aground on an island, became a prey to these merciless savages.

Though Captain Hubbell and his party stopped some time for it in a lower part of the river, it did not arrive, and it has never to their knowledge been heard of since. Before they reached the mouth of the Great Kenhawn, they had, by several successive additions, increased their number to twenty, consisting of nine men, three women, and eight children. The men, besides these mentioned above, were one John Stoner, an Irishman and a Dutchman (whose names are not recollected), Messrs. Ray and Tucker, and Mr. Kilpatrick, whose two daughters also were of the party. Information received at Gallipolis confirmed the expectation of a serious conflict with a large body of Indians. Every possible preparation was made for a formidable and successful resistance of the anticipated attack.

The nine men were divided into three watches for the night, which were alternately to continue awake and be on the lookout for two hours at a time. The arms on board, which consisted principally of old muskets much out of order, were collected, loaded, and put in the best possible condition for service. At about sunset on that day, the 23d of March, 1791, our party overtook a fleet of six boats descending the river in company, and intended to have continued with them, but as their passengers seemed to be more disposed to dancing than fighting, and as, soon after dark, notwithstanding the remonstrances of Captain Hubbell, they commenced fiddling and dancing instead of preparing their arms and taking the necessary rest preparatory to battle, it was wisely considered more hazardous to be in such company than to be alone.

It was therefore determined to proceed rapidly forward by aid of the oars, and to leave those thoughtless fellow-travelers behind. Captain Hubbell and his party proceeded steadily forward *alone*. Early in the night a canoe was dimly seen floating down the river, in which were probably Indians reconnoitering.

It was now agreed, that should the attack, as was probable, be deferred till morning, every man should be up before the dawn in order to make as great a show as possible of numbers and of strength; and that, whenever the action should take place, the women and children should lie down on the cabin floor and be protected as well as they could by the trunks and other baggage, which might be placed around them. In this perilous situation they continued during the night, and the captain, who had not slept more than one hour since he left Pittsburgh, was too deeply impressed with the imminent danger which surrounded him to obtain any rest at that time.

Just as daylight began to appear in the east, and before the men were up and at their posts agreeably to arrangement, a voice at some distance below them in a plaintive tone repeatedly solicited them to come on shore, as there were some white persons who wished to obtain a passage in their boat. This the captain very naturally and correctly concluded to be an Indian artifice, and its only effect was to rouse the men and place every one on his guard. The voice of entreaty was soon changed into the language of indignation and insult, and the sound of distant paddles announced the approach of the savage foe. At length three Indian canoes were seen through the mist of the morning rapidly advancing. With the utmost coolness the captain and his companions prepared to receive them. The chairs, tables, and other encumbrances were thrown into the river, in order to clear the deck for action.

Every man took his position, and was ordered not to fire till the savages had approached so near, that (to use the words of Captain Hubbell), "the flash from the guns might singe their eyebrows"; and a special caution was given, that the men should fire successively, so that there might be no interval. On the arrival of the canoes, they were found to contain about twenty-five or thirty Indians each. As soon as they had approached within the reach of musket shot, a general fire was given from one of them, which wounded Mr. Tucker through the hip so severely that his leg hung only by the flesh, and shot Mr. Light just below the ribs. The three canoes placed themselves at the bow, stern, and on the right side of the boat, so that they had an opportunity of raking in every direction. The fire now commenced from the boat, and had a powerful effect in checking the confidence and fury of the Indians.

The captain, after firing his own gun, took up that of one of the wounded men, raised it to his shoulder, and was about to discharge it, when a ball came and took away the lock; he coolly turned round, seized a brand of fire from the kettle which served for a caboose, and applying it to the pan, discharged the piece with effect. A very regular and constant fire was now kept up on both sides. The captain was just in the act of raising his gun a third time when a ball passed through his right arm, and for a moment disabled him. Scarcely had he recovered from the shock and re-acquired the use of his hand, which had been suddenly drawn up by the wound, when he observed the Indians in one of the canoes just about to board the boat in its bow, where the horses were placed belonging to the party. So near had they approached, that some of them had actually seized with their hands the side of the boat.

Severely wounded as he was, he caught up a pair of horsemen's pistols and rushed forward to repel the attempt at boarding. On his approach the Indians fell back, and he discharged a pistol with effect at the foremost man. After firing the second pistol, he found himself without arms, and was compelled to retreat; but stepping back upon a pile of small wood which had been prepared for burning in the kettle, the thought struck him, that it might be made use of in repelling the foe, and he continued for some time to strike them with it so forcibly and actively that they were unable to enter the boat, and at length he wounded one of them so severely that with a yell they suddenly gave way. All the canoes instantly discontinued the contest and directed their course to Captain Greathouse's boat, which was then in sight. Here a striking contrast was exhibited to the firmness and intrepidity which had been displayed.

Instead of resisting the attack, the people on board of this boat retired to the cabin in dismay. The Indians entered it without opposition, and rowed it to the shore, where they instantly killed the captain and a lad of about fourteen years of age. The women they placed in the center of their canoes, and manning them with fresh hands, again pursued Captain Hubbell and party. A melancholy alternative now presented itself to these brave but almost desponding men, either to fall a prey to the savages themselves, or to run the risk of shooting the women, who had been placed in the canoes in the hope of deriving protection from their presence. But "self preservation is the first law of nature," and the captain very justly remarked, there would not be much humanity in preserving their lives at such a sacrifice, merely that they might become victims of savage cruelty at some subsequent period.

There were now but four men left on board of Captain Hubbell's boat, capable of defending it, and the captain himself was severely wounded in two places. The second attack, however, was resisted with almost incredible firmness and vigor. Whenever the Indians would rise to fire, their opponents would commonly give them the first shot, which in almost every instance would prove fatal. Notwithstanding the disparity of numbers, and the exhausted condition of the defenders of the boat, the Indians at length appeared to despair of success, and the canoes successively retired to the shore. Just as the last one was departing, Captain Hubbell called to the Indian, who was standing in the stern, and on his turning round, discharged his piece at him. When the smoke, which for a moment obstructed the vision, was dissipated, he was seen lying on his back, and appeared to be severely, perhaps mortally wounded.

Unfortunately the boat now drifted near to the shore where the Indians were collected, probably between four and five hundred, were soon rushing down on the bank. Ray and Plascut, the only men remaining unhurt, were placed at the oars, and as the boat was not more than twenty yards from shore, it was deemed prudent for all to lie down in as safe a position as possible and attempt to push forward with the utmost practicable rapidity. While they continued in this situation, nine balls were shot into one oar, and ten into the other, without wounding the rowers, who were hidden from view and protected by the side of the boat and the blankets in its stern. During this dreadful exposure to the fire of the savages, which continued about twenty minutes, Mr. Kilpatrick observed a particular Indian, whom he thought a favorable mark for his rifle, and, notwithstanding the solemn warning of Captain Hubbell, rose to shoot him. He immediately received a ball in his mouth, which passed out at the back part of his head, and was almost at the same moment shot through the heart. He fell among the horses that about the same time were killed, and presented to his afflicted daughters and fellow travelers, who were witnesses of the awful oc-currence, a spectacle of horror which we need not further attempt to describe.

The boat was now providentially and suddenly carried out into the middle of the stream, and taken by the current beyond the reach of the enemy's balls. Our little band, reduced as they were in numbers, wounded, afflicted, and almost exhausted by fatigue, were still unsub-dued in spirit, and being assembled in all their strength, men, women, and children, with an appearance of triumph gave three hearty cheers, calling to the Indians to come on again if they were fond of the sport.

Thus ended this awful conflict, in which out of nine men, two only escaped unhurt. Tucker and Kilpatrick were killed on the spot, Stoner was mortally wounded and died on his arrival at Limestone, and all the rest, excepting Ray and Plascut, were severely wounded. The women and children were all uninjured, excepting a little son of Mr. Plascut, who, after the battle was over, came to the captain and with great cool-ness requested him to take a ball out of his head. On examination it ap-peared that a bullet which had passed through the side of the boat had penetrated the forehead of this little hero, and remained under the skin. The captain took it out, and the youth, observing, "That is not all," raised his arm, and exhibited a piece of bone at the point of his elbow, which had been shot off and hung only by the skin. His mother ex-claimed, "Why did you not tell me of this?"

"Because," he coolly replied, "the captain directed us to be silent during the action, and I thought you would be likely to make a noise if I told you."

The boat made the best of its way down the river, and the object was to reach Limestone that night. The captain's arm had bled profusely, and he was compelled to close the sleeve of his coat in order to retain the blood and stop its effusion. In this situation, tormented by excruci-ating pain and faint through loss of blood, he was under the necessity of steering the boat with his left arm, till about ten o'clock that night, when he was relieved by Mr. William Brooks, who resided on the bank of the river, and who was induced by the calls of the suffering party to come out to their assistance. By his aid and that of some other persons who were in the same manner brought to their relief, they were enabled to reach Limestone about twelve o'clock that night.

Crowds of people, as might be expected, came to witness the boat which had been the scene of so much heroism, and such horrid carnage, and to visit the resolute little band by whom it had been so gallantly and perseveringly defended. On examination it was found that the sides of the boat were literally filled with bullets and with bullet holes. There was scarcely a space of two feet square in the part above water, which had not either a ball remaining in it or a hole through which a ball had passed. Some persons who had the curiosity to count the number of holes in the blankets which were hung up as curtains in the stern of the boat, affirmed that in the space of five feet square there were one hundred and twenty-two. Four horses out of five were killed, and the escape of the fifth amidst such a shower of balls appears almost miraculous.

★ 15 ★

American Privateer and
British Man-of-War Clash

(from A.B.C. Whipple,
Tall Ships and Great Captains)

ONE GENERATION *after the Revolutionary War, the United States grappled again with Great Britain in the War of 1812. As Wellington and Napoleon fought on the continent, "trading with the enemy" became an anathema for both sides. With England dominating the sea lanes, President James Madison recommended and a divided Congress declared war on England. Poorly prepared for war, the United States, with only sixteen ships of the line, rallied under the slogan: "Free Trade and Sailors Rights." The British interdiction of American shipping and the impressments of British-born sailors snatched off American ships were particularly galling. Furthermore, the British in Canada were suspected of supporting the Shawnee brothers, Tecumseh and The Prophet, and the 1811 Battle of Tippecanoe was perhaps a harbinger of things to come.*

The War of 1812 lasted for two years. It encompassed: several desultory attempts to invade Canada and cut the British supply lines; a number of successful sea battles (the Constitution *over the* Guerrière, *the* United

States *over the* Macedonian, *and the* Hornet *over the* Peacock *which gave heart to America; the step by step extension of a British blockade along the east coast that slowly strangled shipping; Commodore Perry's ferocious battle on Lake Erie ("We have met the enemy and they are ours"); and the British landing and burning of Washington, D.C., where Dolley Madison saved a portrait of George Washington moments before the British arrived to torch the White House. In the south Gen. Andrew Jackson waged a brilliant defense of New Orleans and later seized Pensacola, Florida. This foot-in-the-door helped persuade Spain to sell Florida to the United States in 1819 for five million dollars.*

In the beginning, the government issued a "letter of marque" to privateer businessmen who would arm their own ships. Any booty from English ships seized went to the owner, captain, and crew. The key to success for a privateer was a light, well armed, fast sailing ship that could overtake and capture merchant ships, and outrun, but not outgun, a British man-of-war.

One such privateer was the Prince de Neufchâtel *built in 1813 in New York, and owned by Mme. Flory Charretton, an American citizen. Her daring son-in-law, John Ordronoux, captained the* Prince.

One hundred and seven feet long at the waterline, twenty-six feet in breadth, eleven black gun ports on each side, her outstanding visual characteristics were her yellow sides and her sharply raked masts designed for lightning speed. She was chased seventeen times, but never caught. She was estimated to have reached twelve knots during one chase. She captured a score of ships in the English Channel and the Irish Sea. Before returning to America, she had earned almost three million dollars. Off Nantucket, Ordronoux spotted and pounced on the British merchantman Douglas *bound for Liverpool. We now experience the* Prince of Neufchâtel's *mortal combat with* H.M.S. Endymion, *a British frigate. The story is told by that great spinner of nautical yarns, A. B. C. Whipple in* Tall Ships and Great Captains.

* * *

SHE FIRST CAME into view off the island's south shore. From Mill Hill, the highest spot on Nantucket Island, they could see her as a speck, then slowly taking shape as the fading winds eased her toward the point. As she approached, the watchers on the hill could also make out the ship she had in tow. A little later they saw that she and her companion were being pursued.

The thing about her that most struck the watchers on the hill was the angle of her masts, raked back at almost seventy-five degrees. With these masts and her lean hull, low in the water, she looked fast. But she was not at the moment; with what must have been every sail in her locker, she was straining to make headway in the fleeting airs. She was what is called a hermaphrodite schooner—not quite a schooner, but almost. Like a schooner she carried fore-and-aft sails on both her main and fore masts. Like a brig she carried square sails on both masts too, the square top sails towering above the fore-and-aft sails below. She was very much like a brigantine as well; only the schooner's foresail made her different. On a curious little royal pole atop her mainmast and on her elongated bowsprit she carried clouds of canvas, conveying the impression of the speed she would carry under ordinary winds. Even now, with scarcely a ripple on the waters off Nantucket's south shore, she moved slowly ahead. Her lines, the American flag on her masthead, the thin line of her gun ports along her sides all identified her as a U.S. privateer. That meant that the second vessel, a small, square-rigged ship, under full sail but keeping pace only with the aid of the tow line, was the privateer's prize. And it meant that the third vessel, off to the south, was a British frigate.

The pursuer was only half a dozen miles away, but her bulk loomed on the horizon as she came down on her prey. The breezes that only flickered along the island's shore still held a bit more strongly farther out at sea. The frigate crowded on all sail while they lasted, before darkness gave the privateer a chance to escape.

On the hill the windmills had ceased creaking as the wind dropped. Across the moors between Mill Hill and the south shore the colors changed as the sun settled off to the right. Few, probably none, of the islanders who stood and watched the slow motion chase knew the name of the privateer or her prize. Some, though, were no doubt able to identify the frigate. She was the *H.M.S. Endymion,* on patrol duty off the Atlantic coast. She had been sent from her station off New York to

Halifax for repairs, and on her return had sighted the privateer and her prize. The *Endymion* had been in the waters before. The frigate's assignment was to patrol the coast, awe the "colonists," blockade their seaborne commerce and destroy privateers. This was her intent as she came ponderously down toward the schooner.

Presumably, in light airs, the privateer could get away, if the frigate did not catch a strong slant of wind first. But the privateer was working in toward the shifting sand bars where the water shoaled off to a few feet. If the privateer captain caught a breeze and tried to cut across the tip of the island, especially in the dark, he could get trapped in the narrow channel between Old Man Shoal and Miacomet Rip. It was partly to warn the privateer captain and partly to find out what ship she was, that one islander decided to launch a boat from the south shore and go out to her.

He was Charles Hilburn, a pilot who knew all the shoals and rip tides around the island. When Hilburn announced that he was going out to the schooner, three or four Nantucketers said they would join him. This was not an easy decision to make on Nantucket during the War of 1812.

Nantucket lies thirty miles out to sea, off the tip of the Massachusetts coast. Exposed, isolated, out of sight of the nearest land, the island's location helped mold the individualistic, independent character of its inhabitants. But in wartime Nantucket was defenseless. During the Revolution the islanders had been visited by British raiding parties and had asked the new U.S. government for protection, in vain. In the War of 1812 the pattern was repeated. The American Navy could not spare a patrol for one island, and Nantucket could hardly arm a navy of her own. So her people accepted the hard alternative; they had declared themselves neutral. The British admiral in command of the area, Sir Alexander Cochrane, had exacted a high price. On September, 1814, after nearly two years of delaying, Nantucket's selectmen had agreed to pay no taxes to the U.S. government, and the admiral had agreed to let the islanders go unhindered to the mainland for wood and to the Grand Banks for fish. That was one month before sails of the privateer and her British pursuer appeared off Nantucket's south shore.

So the islanders faced a dilemma. Most of them were Quakers. It was a violation of their religious principles to take part in the war. Those who did not agree on religious grounds felt that it was a breach of their neutrality agreement to go to the aid of an American privateer in the face of a British frigate. Even putting principles aside, what would the British retaliation be? This situation was not the same as a vessel in distress because of a storm or shipwreck. The privateer had made her own captures and in fact had one under tow. Capture by the British, in turn, was the chance her captain had accepted when he first set out. And if the frigate did overhaul the privateer what could the islanders do to help?

But there were others who took a less logical, more emotional attitude. Those were fellow Americans out there, and if they were not already in distress, they would soon be. If, as it appeared in the gathering dusk, a flat calm were settling on the sea for the next hour or so, an islander who knew the waters and currents could help the captain keep off the hidden shoals. And to some there must have been the furtive anticipation of striking a blow against the fleet that had harassed them for two years. So, despite the objections of some of the Quakers, Hilburn and three or four other islanders determined to go out to the privateer and lend whatever aid they could through the coming night. Climbing into their little horse-drawn carts, they bumped across the rutted road to the south shore.

By the time the boat was hauled down to the water from one of the fishing shacks along the shore, the sun was nearly down. A small crowd had tramped across the wide sand beach to watch. The privateer lay about half a mile out, her yellow sides turning reddish in the sunset. The last breeze had gone. The schooner's anchor was down. She rolled in the swells coming off the Atlantic. The prize has been cast loose and had anchored as well. To the south the frigate *Endymion* was barely moving. The cold dampness of the October evening seeped in off the sea. There were no demonstration from the huddled band on the beach as the boat crunched over the last bit of sand and slapped against the waves. There must, however, have been a few murmured good-byes from the wives and mothers who realized what the night had in store.

To the rhythmic slap-slap of bow against water and the thump of oars against tholepins, the islanders worked their way out to the schooner. She rose suddenly out of the dusk ahead of them, the current chirping around her anchor chain and bow, her raked masts lifting into the sky, her yellow hull splotched with powder stains at the gun ports. Because of her long, low design, her bulwarks were almost near enough to the water for the men to climb aboard from the boat. But first, softly in the quiet night, there was the hail and reply, and the islanders learned their identity.

She was the privateer *Prince de Neufchâtel*; John Ordronoux, master. Captain Ordronoux happily accepted the offer of Hilburn and his companions. The Nantucketers climbed aboard. When they looked around her disordered decks and saw what they had let themselves in for, some of them must have wished that they had stayed on shore.

The brutal wear and tear of many battles showed everywhere—in the chipped masts and spars, the patched sails, the spliced halyards. Out of an original crew that should have numbered 150, the *Prince de Neufchâtel* had fewer than forty men; the rest had gone to man the prizes that Ordronoux had sent into American or neutral port. But a more ominous price of the privateer's victories was evident in the sounds that came from below: the rumbling of thirty-seven prisoners who were confined in her hold and were growing restless at the preparations for battle.

Captain Ordronoux had no time for amenities at the moment. His reinforcements were quickly put to work readying the *Prince* for defense. The calm, if it held, meant that there would be no ship-to-ship engagement. That was just as well, since the *Endymion* mounted forty guns and the *Prince* eighteen. But the alternative prospect was little better: a battle that could be murderous under such conditions. The decision to launch this kind of battle was up to the captain of the *Endymion*. If there were no breeze, he could not come up close enough for the classic exchange of broadsides. He could, however, try an attack with his boats.

Nearly everything favored the attacker in such a maneuver. The privateer could be expected to have a skeleton crew. Even from a distance her shape would indicate her low bulwarks, making her easy to board. The *Endymion*'s captain could fill four or five boats with marines and send them down to slip along side the schooner, swarm onto her decks and overpower her defenses. All this was obvious to Captain

Ordronoux as it was to the British captain, and the privateer skipper hurried his defenses.

Every weapon that could be armed was readied. The gun ports were swung open. The guns were double-shotted and tilted to aim downward at approaching boats. Muskets by the dozens were loaded and stacked along the bulwarks. Baskets filled with loaded pistols were placed within easy reach. The schooner's sides were slushed with grease, to make it more difficult for attackers to climb aboard. Hammocks of netting were fashioned above the bulwarks, and cannon balls were suspended in them. One swipe of a cutlass would drop them into the boats when they came along side. More cannon balls were piled on deck, to be thrown over the side into the boats that those in the netting missed. Stations were allotted along the rail. Captain Ordronoux went about explaining each man's mission. By now all light had gone. In the hushed darkness of the night everyone took his station and waited.

The scene can be imagined. The dead calm lay heavily on the sea. Beyond the narrow, visible rim of water the island was lost, its presence revealed only by an occasional flickering light. The swells were slow and smooth, rocking the schooner gently at her anchor. Now and then there would be the creak of a mast as the schooner rolled, or the slap of a sail which has been brailed up out of the way of action but ready to be loosed at the first wisp of a breeze. From the island's shore would come the mew of a gull, the squawk of a fish hawk. All other sounds would be hushed—the men on the deck of the privateer treading quietly on their toes, conversing in whispers so as not to reveal the schooner's presence to the attackers they knew must come. And now, as they waited, . . . the signal sounded softly down the deck. The boats were coming.

At sea at night there is nearly always the sensation that the visibility is better than on land. There is always the contrast between the blackness along the water's surface and the lighter tone of the sky. The lookout at sea makes the most of this contrast. It was what the men aboard the privateer were doing that night. But apparently the first warning came to the ear rather than the eye, as someone heard the thump of a muffled oar.

God only knows how many boats there were out there. But gradually the dark, low shapes became visible on the water, moving silently and swiftly, bow-on to present the smallest target, straight for the sides of the *Prince de Neufchâtel.*

It was a few moments before everyone could hear the rubbing of the oars and the drip-drip of water as the boats were stroked toward the target. Their outlines could be made out plainly by now. Five boats were coming in at different angles, toward bow and stern quarters. The attackers themselves were huddled in poised tenseness. Waiting just as tensely at the rail of the *Prince,* the defenders studied the overwhelming numbers of marines and strained to catch the sound of the first boat thumping against the schooner's side, when the night exploded.

At Captain Ordronoux's orders a battery of the Prince's guns had opened fire on the boats. Evidently he had waited too long, and the boats had crept in under the guns' angle of fire, because the broadside missed. But Ordronoux had had the guns loaded with langrage too— iron bars, chain, spikes and other murderous short-range junk. The crashing explosions of the guns were followed by the shrill screams of the attackers as whistling shards of metal cut them up and whirring lengths of chain garroted them. Their cries were taken up in the other boats as they launched the attack.

From the deck of the *Prince* it looked like fireworks as the British muskets went off, and the toughest privateersmen must have been chilled by the battle cries of so many men. The boats now came thumping alongside the *Prince* and the marines made their first attempt to swarm aboard. But the defenders along the rail, not three feet away from the men reaching up from the boats, fought them off with desperation. Some who had waited, cradling heavy cannon balls in their aching arms, hefted them high and sent them hurtling into the boats below. There were crunching sounds of splintering wood, thundering splashes as the balls caromed off into the water, shrieks as skulls were fractured. Other defenders peered over the rail, gingerly to avoid getting picked in the eye by a rapier, and fired pistols into the milling masses below. In the flashes of gunfire the faces of the marines stood out, the whites of their teeth and eyes in contrast to their blackened faces. Other privateersmen swung their cutlasses in shimmering arcs, thwacking against the sides of the schooner as they chopped at reaching arms and sliced off grasping fingers. The ship and the boats became a tangled pandemonium of cursing, shouting and screaming as the attack reached battle pitch. And so far the privateersmen were beating off the first wave.

As the pulse of the battle mounted, so did the din. The shouting of the men along the rail was answered by the moans and yells coming up from the attackers in the boats. On deck there was the constant rattle of gunfire, the clatter of empty pistols and muskets being tossed aside and the scramble of powder boys reloading them. And from below decks came the echoing and re-echoing yells of the prisoners. As the battle churned above them, they stormed against the barred companionway and the hatch grating, trying to take advantage of the opportunity to break free. So the *Prince de Neufchâtel* was beset from all sides and from within as well. Straining at her anchor as the strong currents rushed passed, rocking under the weight of men surging from side to side, her sails lit by flashes of gunfire, her yards wreathed in smoke, she appeared like a hell ship on which hundreds of demons had run amuck.

Actually her decks were defended by less than forty men, some American, some French like her skipper, some Swedish like her first mate. Still they managed to keep 111 British marines from coming aboard. But they could not hold out much longer. They were firing their pistols and muskets much faster than the boys could reload them. Most of the cannon balls on deck had been dropped into the boats below, and apparently had only sunk one. The balls in the netting had mostly been cut away, with little more effect. The defenders at the rail were slipping in smears of blood. The rail itself was a jagged chunk of splinters where knives and cutlasses had chopped at the hands of marines trying to pull themselves aboard. One by one the privateersmen were dropping on the deck or toppling over the side. Captain Ordronoux, counting the forces and assessing the tide of battle, could see that it was finally going against him. In fact, at this point he could not count more than twenty privateersmen fighting. The rest were sprawled on deck or gone. Below him the uproar of the prisoners indicated that they were on the verge of smashing their way out. Then the marines from the boats under the bow came climbing over the rail and onto the forecastle deck.

Ordronoux was waiting for them with his last defense, a deck gun loaded and aimed toward the bow. He gave the prearranged signal for his men to scramble aft out of the line of fire, but he could not wait for them all. The British marines were already swarming down the deck toward him. Ordronoux fired.

The gun was loaded with canister shot and bags of musket balls. Like a huge spray of buckshot it swept the deck. The marines went down like mowed grass.

But so did most of Ordronoux's crew. Now all the remaining marines had to do was launch one more attack, from the waist or stern of the schooner. There were not enough privateersmen left to hold them off, even for a few moments while Ordronoux swung his deck gun into position. The next attack would be the last.

It never came. In the boats below, the plunging cannon balls, the musketry and the pistol fire had done their work, and the carnage on deck had finished the job. Not only were there no more boarding attempts, but faintly above the din came the cry of a boat commander: "Quarter! Quarter! Quarter!"

A few more shots and it was over. Looking about his deck, Ordronoux discovered that he had exactly eight crew members left. Peering over the bulwarks, he could make out only one of the five British boats; three (it turned out) had drifted away with not enough able-bodied men to propel them. The other had sunk. In the boat still alongside, only here and there did a man move. At least ninety British had been killed, and at least thirty privateersmen. The battle had lasted twenty minutes.

The contrast between the din of battle and the hush that followed was enough to make Ordronoux's ears ring. Now the only sounds were from the deck and from alongside, the thumping of the boat still made fast to the *Prince*'s side, the whimpering of a dying powder boy. Even the howling of the prisoners below had suddenly ceased, as they listened for a sign that would tell them who had won. The acrid smoke of gunpowder hung heavily in the air. And off to the south, the *Endymion* sent up rockets, signaling in vain for her boats to return.

Captain Ordronoux, alone on his quarterdeck binding his wounds, realized that in fact the battle was not yet won. Few British marines in the boat along side were able to move about, but there were more able-bodied men than he had left. His first mate was wounded. The pilot, Charles Hilburn, who had come out to offer his services, had kept his station at the schooner's helm despite several wounds; finally he had been killed. The *Prince*'s surgeon was injured. Ahead of Ordronoux and his eight remaining able-bodied men lay the job of tending the wounded and preparing the dead for later burial at sea. More important, it would not be long before the British survivors realized that they could still take the *Prince*.

Summoning his eight men, Ordronoux got the British boat hauled toward the bow of the schooner and tied up there. The boat's commander called up to him asking for help; some of his wounded men would not live until morning if they did not get medical help. Ordronoux replied that his surgeon was wounded and that he could not help. He was sorry, but the commander would have to make do with the dressings which Ordronoux would pass down. Ordronoux then set about making his own men as comfortable as he could until morning.

It was a long night. Men cried out as they were moved onto pallets. Others sobbed unceasingly. Once in a while the night was split by the scream of a man gone into delirium. Little by little the sounds tapered off, as some became unconscious and others died. When light blue dawn first streaked the sky out toward the Grand Banks, Ordronoux put into effect what he had planned through the night.

Just aft of the mainmast he had a sail strung across most of the schooner's deck. From his cabin he brought out a fife, and he put two of his remaining men into service. In time with the fife the two men pranced back and forth across the deck, stamping as heavily as they could. Ordronoux hoped that in the boat tied near the bow the British survivors would think that the privateer captain ran a taut ship, and still had enough men for a morning muster.

Off to the north the dim shape of the island slowly revealed the green hills, the brightly colored October moors, the south shore and a

knot of people who stood at the water's edge as if they had waited there
all night. Astern, dangerously near the shore the *Prince*'s prize lay at anchor. Outward toward Old Man Shoal, Ordronoux could make out
three British boats drifting helplessly, the arms of wounded or dead
marines hanging over the side. And off toward the south, her acres of
canvas still hanging in the windless air, sat the *Endymion*.

Ordronoux went forward and told the boat commander, a lieutenant named Ormond, that he could go ashore to get help for his
wounded. He expected a truce while some of his own wounded were
sent to the island for treatment. Ormond agreed. Slowly the barge
went off, rowed by a couple of men each, to pick up the three drifting
boats and head toward the island. They were followed shortly by a boat
from the *Prince,* carrying her most seriously wounded and taking the
one or two Nantucket survivors home. By the time they reached the
shore, the little group of islanders had increased to a crowd, and men
waded into the waves to help unload the sprawled bodies, of attacker
and defender alike.

All that day the British frigate and American privateer sat within
sight of each other. Though an occasional breeze ruffled her sails,
the *Endymion* made no move toward her quarry. Aboard the *Prince*
Captain Ordronoux worked to be ready to flee as soon as his boat
returned. Aboard the *Endymion* Captain Henry Hope wrote his account of the battle, adding that he had apparently lost more men in this
action against a schooner than he would have lost in action against another frigate. He did not so record, but Nantucketers claimed that he
did not even make the gesture of a chase when on the next morning
the privateer's boat returned, sail was loosed to a light breeze and the
Prince de Neufchâtel moved off, setting her course northeast to round
the tip of Cape Cod.

16

Davy Crockett Reports
from Inside the Alamo

(from Davy Crockett, *Col. Crockett's Exploits
and Adventures in Texas*, 1839)

THE MASSACRE at the Alamo, and its impact on Texas and the nation, is the key to understanding how the Southwest became part of the United States of America. That giant sweep of land, which today ranges from Texas to California, was once owned by Spain and governed through Mexico City. Three centuries passed before this Spanish colony dissolved. Napoleon was the catalyst; in 1807 he attacked Portugal and occupied Madrid, installing his brother on the Spanish throne. The duke of Wellington led the British in a counterattack through Portugal, setting off the seven-year Peninsular War, which distracted and weakened Spain while it emboldened Mexico.

In Mexico one revolt after another flared and failed. But finally by 1821 the Mexicans had overthrown the monarchists, declared independence, established a new government, seized church property, and forced the clergy to swear civil obedience or leave.

One of the first acts of this new Mexican government was to invite Americans to settle in Texas. Large land grants the size of Rhode Island *with guarantees of local autonomy were offered to colonizers such as Stephen Austin. Compared with the western territories where homesteaders could buy only 80 acres at $1.25 an acre, the land in Texas was cheap and a farmer could buy 277 acres. If he promised to raise cattle, he could secure an additional 4,338 acres. Bear in mind that at the time of the first land grants Texas was populated by about 15,000 hostile Indians, 5,000 friendly Indians, 4,000 Spaniards and Mexicans, and 1,500 Americans.*

Soon one flash-in-the-pan Mexican government succeeded another, and the offers of land grants to the Americans ceased. But the Americans had gained a toehold, and their immigration continued. Meanwhile, the military leaders in Mexico plotted and skirmished. By 1834 General Antonio López de Santa Anna had bullied and fought his way to the top to become dictator of Mexico. Calling himself "the Napoleon of the West," Santa Anna vowed to oust the Americans from Texas. He crossed the Rio Grande at the head of an elite army and swiftly thrust three hundred miles into Texas. Near San Antonio he bottled up the Americans in the Alamo and laid siege.

One of those inside the Alamo was frontiersman and former congressman from Tennessee Davy Crockett. Between the fighting he found time to write letters and personal recollections, before losing his life at the Alamo. The following passage is taken from his posthumously published memoir, Col. Crockett's Exploits and Adventures in Texas.

* * *

I WRITE THIS on the nineteenth of February, 1836, at San Antonio. We are all in high spirits, though we are rather short of provisions, for men who have appetites that could digest any thing but oppression; but no matter, we have a prospect of soon getting our bellies full of fighting, and that is victuals and drink to a true patriot any day. We had a little sort of convivial party last evening: just about a dozen of us set to work, most patriotically, to see whether we could not get rid of that curse of the land, whisky, and we made considerable progress; but my poor friend, Thimblerig, [Crockett had a penchant for giving his friends nicknames such as Thimblerig, Bee Hunter, etc.] got sewed up just about as tight as the eyelet-hole in a lady's corset, and a little tighter too, I reckon; for when we went to bed he called for a boot-jack, which was brought to him, and he bent down on his hands and knees, and very gravely pulled off his hat with it, for the darned critter was so thoroughly swiped that he didn't know his head from his heels. But this wasn't all the folly he committed: he pulled off his coat and laid it on the bed, and then hung himself over the back of a chair; and I wish I may be shot if he didn't go to sleep in that position, thinking every thing had been done according to Gunter's late scale. Seeing the poor fellow completely used up, I carried him to bed, though he did belong to the Temperance Society; and he knew nothing about what had occurred until I told him next morning. The Bee Hunter didn't join us in this blow-out. Indeed, he will seldom drink more than just enough to prevent his being called a total abstinence man. But then he is the most jovial fellow for a water drinker I ever did see.

This morning I saw a caravan of about fifty mules passing by Bexar, and bound for Santa Fé. They were loaded with different articles to such a degree that it was astonishing how they could travel at all, and they were nearly worn out by their labours. They were without bridle or halter, and yet proceeded with perfect regularity in a single line; and the owners of the caravan rode their mustangs with their enormous spurs, weighing at least a pound a piece, with rowels an inch and a half in length, and lever bits of the harshest description, able to break the jaws of their animals under a very gentle pressure. The men were dressed in the costume of Mexicans.

Colonel Travis sent out a guard to see that they were not laden with munitions of war for the enemy. I went out with the party. The poor mules were bending under a burden of more than three hundred pounds, without including the panniers, which were bound so tight as almost to stop the breath of the poor animal. Each of the sorrowful line came up, spontaneously, in turn to have his girth unbound and his load removed. They seemed scarcely able to keep upon their feet, and as they successively obtained relief, one after another heaved a long and deep sigh, which it was painful to hear, because it proved that the poor brutes had been worked beyond their strength. What a world of misery man inflicts upon the rest of creation in his brief passage through life!

Finding that the caravan contained nothing intended for the enemy, we assisted the owners to replace the heavy burdens on the backs of the patient but dejected mules, and allowed them to pursue their weary and lonely way. For a full two hours we could see them slowly winding along the narrow path, a faint line that ran like a thread through the extended prairie; and finally they were whittled down to the little end of nothing in the distance, and were blotted out from the horizon.

The caravan had no sooner disappeared than one of the hunters, who had been absent several days, came in. He was one of those gentlemen who don't pride themselves much upon their costume. He was dressed in five jackets, all of which failed to conceal his raggedness. He states that he had met some Indians on the banks of the Rio Frio, who informed him that Santa Anna, with a large force, had already crossed the Neuces, and might be expected to arrive before San Antonio in a few days. We immediately set about preparing to give him a warm reception, for we are all well aware, if our little band is overwhelmed by numbers, there is little mercy to be expected from the cowardly Mexicans—it is war to the knife.

I jocosely asked the ragged hunter, who was a smart, active young fellow, of the steamboat and alligator breed, whether he was a rhinoceros or a hyena, as he was so eager for a fight with the invaders.

"Neither the one, nor t'other, Colonel," says he, "but a whole menagerie in myself. I'm shaggy as a bear, wolfish about the head, active as a cougar, and can grin like a hyena, until the bark will curl off a gum log. There's a sprinkling of all sorts in me, from the lion down to the skunk; and before the war is over you'll pronounce me an entire zoological institute, or I miss a figure in my calculation. I promise to swallow Santa Anna without gagging, if you will only skewer back his ears and grease his head a little."

He told me that he was one in the fatal expedition fitted out from New Orleans, in November last, to join the contemplated attack upon Tampico by Mehia and Peraza. They were, in all, about one hundred and thirty men, who embarked as emigrants to Texas; and the terms agreed upon were, that it was optional whether the party took up arms in defence of Texas, or not, on landing. They were at full liberty to act as they pleased. But the truth was, Tampico was their destination, and an attack on that city the covet design, which was not made known before land was in sight.

The emigrants were landed, some fifty, who doubtless had a previous understanding, joined the standard of General Mehia, and the following day a formidable fort surrendered without an attack.

The whole party were now tendered arms and ammunition, which even those who had been decoyed accepted; and, the line being formed, they commenced the attack upon the city. The hunter continued: "On the 15th of November our little army, consisting of one hundred and fifty men, marched into Tampico, garrisoned by two thousand Mexicans, who were drawn up in battle array in the public square of the city. We charged them at the point of the bayonet, and although they so greatly outnumbered us, *in two minutes* we completely routed them; and they fled, taking refuge on the house tops, from which they poured a destructive fire upon our gallant little band. We fought them until daylight, when we found our number decreased to fifty or sixty broken down and disheartened men. Without ammunition, and deserted by the officers, twenty-eight immediately surrendered. But a few of us cut our way through, and fortunately escaped to the mouth of the river, where we got on board a vessel and sailed for Texas.

"The twenty-eight prisoners wished to be considered as prisoners of war; they made known the manner in which they had been deceived, but they were tried by a court-martial of Mexican soldiers, and condemned to be shot on the 14th day of December, 1835, which sentence was carried into execution."

After receiving this account from my new friend, the old pirate and the Indian hunter came up, and they went off to liquor together, and I went to see a wild Mexican hog, which one of the hunters had brought in. These animals have become scarce, which circumstance is not to be deplored, for their flesh is of little value; and there will still be hogs enough left in Mexico, from all I can learn, even though these should be extirpated.

February 22. The Mexicans, about sixteen hundred strong, with their President Santa Anna at their head, aided by Generals Almonte, Cos, Sesma, and Castrillon, are within two leagues of Bexar. General

Cos, it seems, has already forgot his parole of honour, and has come back to retrieve the credit he lost in this place in December last. If he is captured a second time, I don't think he can have the impudence to ask to go at large again without giving better bail than on the former occasion. Some of the scouts came in, and bring reports that Santa Anna has been endeavoring to excite the Indians to hostilities against the Texians, but so far without effect. The Comanches, in particular, entertain such hatred for the Mexicans, and at the same time hold them in such contempt, that they would rather turn their tomahawks against them, and drive them from the land, than lend a helping hand. We are up and doing, and as lively as Dutch cheese in the dog-days. The two hunters that I have already introduced to the reader left the town, this afternoon, for the purpose of reconnoitering.

February 23. Early this morning the enemy came in sight, marching in regular order, and displaying their strength to the greatest advantage, in order to strike us with terror. But that was no go; they'll find that they have to do with men who will never lay down their arms as long as they can stand on their legs. We held a short council of war, and, finding that we should be completely surrounded, and overwhelmed by numbers, if we remained in the town, we concluded to withdraw to the fortress of Alamo, and defend it to the last extremity. We accordingly filed off, in good order, having some days before placed all the surplus provisions, arms, and ammunition in the fortress. We have had a large national flag made; it is composed of thirteen stripes, red and white, alternately, on a blue ground with a large white star, of five points, in the centre, and between the points the letters TEXAS. As soon as all our little band, about one hundred and fifty in number, had entered and secured the fortress in the best possible manner, we set about raising our flag on the battlements; on which occasion there was no one more active than my young friend, the Bee Hunter. He had been all along sprightly, cheerful, and spirited, but now, notwithstanding the control that he usually maintained over himself, it was with difficulty that he kept his enthusiasm within bounds. As soon as we commenced raising the flag he burst forth, in a clear, full tone of voice, that made the blood tingle in the veins of all who heard him:

Up with your banner, Freedom,
Thy champions cling to thee;
They'll follow where'er you lead 'em,
To death, or victory;—
Up with your banner, Freedom.

Tyrants and slaves are rushing
To tread thee in the dust;
Their blood will soon be gushing,
And stain our knives with rust;—
But not thy banner, Freedom.

While stars and stripes are flying,
Our blood we'll freely shed;
No groan will 'scape the dying,
Seeing thee o'er his head;—
Up with your banner, Freedom.

This song was followed by three cheers from all within the fortress, and the drums and trumpets commenced playing. The enemy marched into Bexar, and took possession of the town, a blood-red flag flying at their head, to indicate that we need not expect quarters if we should fall into their clutches.

In the afternoon a messenger was sent from the enemy to Colonel Travis, demanding an unconditional and absolute surrender of the garrison, threatening to put every man to the sword in case of refusal. The only answer he received was a cannon shot, so the messenger left us with a flea in his ear, and the Mexicans commenced firing grenades at us, but without doing any mischief. At night Colonel Travis sent an express to Colonel Fanning at Goliad, about three or four days' march from this place, to let him know that we are besieged. The old pirate volunteered to go on this expedition, and accordingly left the fort after night fall.

February 24. Very early this morning the enemy commenced a new battery on the banks of the river, about three hundred and fifty yards from the fort, and by afternoon they amused themselves by firing at us from that quarter. Our Indian scout came in this evening, and with him a reinforcement of thirty men from Gonzales, who are just in the nick of time to reap a harvest of glory; but there is some prospect of sweating blood before we gather it in. An accident happened to my friend Thimblerig this afternoon. He was intent on his eternal game of thimbles, in a somewhat exposed position, while the enemy were bombarding us from the new redoubt. A three ounce ball glanced from the parapet and struck him on the breast, inflicting a painful but not dangerous wound. I extracted the ball, which was of lead, and recommended to him to drill a hole through it, and carry it for a watch seal. "No," he replied, with energy, "may I be shot six times if I do; that would be making a bauble for an idle boast. No, Colonel, lead is getting scarce, and I'll lend it out at compound interest.—Curse the thimbles!" he muttered, and went his way, and I saw no more of him that evening.

February 25. The firing commenced early this morning, but the Mexicans are poor engineers, for we haven't lost a single man, and our outworks have sustained no injury. Our sharp shooters have brought down a considerable number of stragglers at a long shot. I got up before the peep of day, hearing an occasional discharge of a rifle just over the place where I was sleeping, and I was somewhat amazed to see Thimblerig mounted alone on the battlement, no one being on duty at the time but the sentries. "What are you doing there?" says I. "Paying my debts," says he, "interest and all."

"And how do you make out?" says I.

"I've nearly got through," says he; "Stop a moment, Colonel, and I'll close the account." He clapped his rifle to his shoulder, and blazed away, then jumped down from his perch, and said, "That account's settled; them chaps will let me play out my game in quiet next time." I looked over the wall, and saw four Mexicans lying dead on the plain. I asked him to explain what he meant by paying his debts, and he told me that he had run the grape shot into four rifle balls, and that he had taken an early stand to have a chance of picking off stragglers. "Now, Colonel, let's go take our bitters," said he; and so we did.

The enemy have been busy during the night, and have thrown up

two batteries on the opposite side of the river. The battalion of Mata-
moros is posted there, and cavalry occupy the hills to the east and on
the road to Gonzales. They are determined to surround us, and cut us
off from reinforcement, or the possibility of escape by a sortie.—Well,
there's one thing they cannot prevent: we'll still go ahead, and sell our
lives at a high price.

February 26. Colonel Bowie has been taken sick from over exertion
and exposure. He did not leave his bed to-day until twelve o'clock. He
is worth a dozen common men in a situation like ours. The Bee Hunter
keeps the whole garrison in good heart with his songs and his jests, and
his daring and determined spirit. He is about the quickest on the trigger, and the best rifle shot we have in the fort. I have already seen him
bring down eleven of the enemy, and at such a distance that we all
thought it would be waste of ammunition to attempt it. His gun is first-
rate, quite equal to my Betsey, though she has not quite as many trin-
kets about her. This day a small party sallied out of the fort for wood
and water, and had a slight skirmish with three times their number from
the division under General Sesma. The Bee Hunter headed them, and
beat the enemy off, after killing three. On opening his Bible at night, of
which he always reads a portion before going to rest, he found a musket
ball in the middle of it. "See here, Colonel," said he, "how they have
treated the valued present of my dear little Kate of Nacogdoches."

"It has saved your life," said I.

"True," replied he, more seriously than usual, "and I am not the
first sinner whose life has been saved by this book." He prepared for
bed, and before retiring he prayed, and returned thanks for his providential escape; and I heard the name of Catherine mingled in his prayer.

February 27. The cannonading began early this morning, and ten
bombs were thrown into the fort, but fortunately exploded without
doing any mischief. So far it has been a sort of tempest in a teapot; not
unlike a pitched battle in the Hall of Congress, where the parties array
their forces, make fearful demonstrations on both sides, then fire away
with loud sounding speeches, which contain about as much meaning as
the report of a howitzer charged with a blank cartridge. Provisions are

becoming scarce, and the enemy are endeavouring to cut off our water. If they attempt to stop our grog in that manner, let them look out, for we shall become too wrathy for our shirts to hold us. We are not prepared to submit to an excise of that nature, and they'll find it out. This discovery has created considerable excitement in the fort.

February 28. Last night our hunters brought in some corn and hogs, and had a brush with a scout from the enemy beyond gun-shot of the fort. They put the scout to flight, and got in without injury. They bring accounts that the settlers are flying in all quarters, in dismay, leaving their possessions to the mercy of the ruthless invader, who is literally engaged in a war of extermination, more brutal than the untutored savage of the desert could be guilty of. Slaughter is indiscriminate, sparing neither sex, age, nor condition. Buildings have been burnt down, farms laid waste, and Santa Anna appears determined to verify his threat, and convert the blooming paradise into a howling wilderness. For just one fair crack at that rascal, even at a hundred yards distance, I would bargain to break my Betsey, and never pull the trigger again. My name's not Crockett if I wouldn't get glory enough to appease my stomach for the remainder of my life. The scouts report that a settler, by the name of Johnson, flying with his wife and three little children, when they reached the Colorado, left his family on the shore, and waded into the river to see whether it would be safe to ford with his wagon. When about the middle of the river he was seized by an alligator, and, after a struggle, was dragged under the water, and perished. The helpless woman and her babes were discovered, gazing in agony on the spot, by other fugitives who happily passed that way, and relieved them. Those who fight the battles experience but a small part of the privation, suffering, and anguish that follow in the train of ruthless war. The cannonading continued, at intervals, throughout the day, and all hands were kept up to their work. The enemy, somewhat imboldened, draws nigher to the fort. So much the better.—There was a move in General Sesma's division toward evening.

February 29. Before daybreak we saw General Sesma leave his camp with a large body of cavalry and infantry, and move off in the direction of Goliad. We think that he must have received news of Colonel Fanning's coming to our relief. We are all in high spirits at the prospect of being able to give the rascals a fair shake on the plain. This business of being shut up makes a man wolfish.

I had a little sport this morning before breakfast. The enemy had planted a piece of ordinance within gun-shot of the fort during the night, and the first thing in the morning they commenced a brisk cannonade, point-blank, against the spot where I was snoring. I turned out pretty smart, and mounted the rampart. The gun was charged again, a fellow stepped forth to touch her off, but before he could apply the match I let him have it, and he keeled over. A second stepped up, snatched the match from the hand of the dying man, but Thimblerig, who had followed me, handed me his rifle, and the next instant the Mexican was stretched on the earth beside the first. A third came up to the cannon, my companion handed me another gun, and I fixed him off in like manner. A fourth, then a fifth, seized the match, who both met with the same fate, and then the whole party gave it up as a bad job, and hurried off to the camp, leaving the cannon ready charged where they had planted it. I came down, took my bitters, and went to breakfast. Thimblerig told me that the place from which I had been firing was one of the snuggest stands in the whole fort, for he never failed picking off two or three stragglers before breakfast, when perched up there. And I recollect, now, having seen him there, ever since he was wounded, the first thing in the morning, and the last at night,—and at times thoughtlessly playing at his eternal game.

March 1. The enemy's forces have been increasing in numbers daily, notwithstanding they have already lost about three hundred men in the several assaults they have made upon us. I neglected to mention in the proper place, that when the enemy came in sight we had but three bushels of corn in the garrison, but have since found eighty bushels in a deserted house. Colonel Bowie's illness still continues, but he manages to crawl from his bed every day, that his comrades may see him. His presence alone is a tower of strength.—The enemy becomes more daring as his numbers increase.

March 2. This day the delegates meet in general convention, at the town of Washington, Texas, to frame our Declaration of Independence. That the sacred instrument may never be trampled on by the children of those who have freely shed their blood to establish it, is the sincere wish of David Crockett. Universal independence is an almighty idea, far too extensive for some brains to comprehend. It is a beautiful seed that germinates rapidly, and brings forth a large and vigorous tree, but like the deadly Upas, we sometimes find the smaller plants wither and die in its shades. Its blooming branches spread far and wide, offering a perch of safety to all alike, but even among its protecting branches we find the eagle, the kite, and the owl preying upon the helpless dove and sparrow. Beneath its shade myriads congregate in goodly fellowship, but the lamb and the fawn find but frail security from the lion and the jackal, though the tree of independence waves over them. Some imagine independence to be a natural charter, to exercise without restraint, and to their fullest extent, all the energies, both physical and mental, with which they have been endowed; and for their individual aggrandizement alone, without regard to the rights of others, provided they extend to all the same privilege and freedom of action. Such independence is the worst of tyranny.

March 3. We have given over all hopes of receiving assistance from Goliad or Refugio. Colonel Travis harangued the garrison, and concluded by exhorting them, in case the enemy should carry the fort, to fight to the last gasp, and render their victory even more serious to them than to us. This was followed by three cheers.

March 4. Shells have been falling into the fort like hail during the day, but without effect. About dusk, in the evening, we observed a man running toward the fort, pursued by about a dozen Mexican cavalry. The Bee Hunter immediately knew him to be the old pirate who had gone to Goliad, and, calling to the two hunters, he sallied out of the fort to the relief of the old man, who was hard pressed. I followed close after. Before we reached the spot the Mexicans were close on the heel of the old man, who stopped suddenly, turned short upon his pursuers, discharged his rifle, and one of the enemy fell from his horse. The chase was renewed, but finding that he would be overtaken and cut to pieces, he now turned again, and, to the amazement of the enemy, became the assailant in his turn. He clubbed his gun, and dashed among them like a wounded tiger, and they fled like sparrows. By this time we reached the spot, and, in the ardour of the moment, followed some distance before we saw that our retreat to the fort was cut off by another detachment of cavalry. Nothing was to be done but to fight our way through. We were all of the same mind. "Go ahead!" cried I, and they shouted, "Go ahead, Colonel!" We dashed among them, and a bloody conflict ensued. They were about twenty in number, and they stood their ground. After the fight had continued about five minutes, a detachment was seen issuing from the fort to our relief, and the Mexicans scampered off, leaving eight of their comrades dead upon the field. But we did not escape unscathed, for both the pirate and the Bee Hunter were mortally wounded, and I received a sabre cut across the forehead. The old man was speaking, as soon as we entered he bore my young friend to his bed, dressed his wounds, and I watched beside him. He lay, without complaint or manifesting pain, until about midnight, when he spoke, and I asked him if he wanted any thing. "Nothing," he replied, but drew a sigh that seemed to rend his heart, as he added, "Poor Kate of Nacogdoches!" His eyes were filled with tears, as he continued, "Her words were prophetic, Colonel"; and then he sang, in a low voice that resembled the sweet notes of his own devoted Kate,

> *But toom cam' the saddle, all bluidy to see,*
> *And hame cam' the steed, but hame never cam' he.*

He spoke no more, and, a few minutes after, died. Poor Kate, who will tell this to her!

March 5. Pop, pop, pop! Bom, bom, bom! throughout the day.—No time for memorandums now.—Go ahead!—Liberty and independence for ever!

[*Here ends Colonel Crockett's manuscript.*]

17

Sam Houston, with Seven Hundred Half-Fed, Half-Clad, Half-Armed Men, Declares, "We Go to Conquer" Texas!

(from General Sam Houston, speech before
U.S. Senate, February 28, 1859)

*S*ANTA ANNA'S PUNITIVE EXPEDITION, *advancing into Texas from Mexico, wiped out the 187 defenders of the Alamo, then at Goliad massacred the 300 men who had surrendered. The last hope for an independent Texas was Sam Houston with his 700 frontiersmen. Outnumbered two to one, Houston clashed with Santa Anna at the battle of San Jacinto on April 21, 1836. The fate of Texas hinged on this battle.*

Houston was born in Tennessee, on the edge of the Indian frontier. Though he had little formal schooling, he was known to have memorized Homer's Iliad *in full. He clerked at a trader's store as a teenager, ran away, and lived with the Cherokees for three years. He fought with General Andrew Jackson in the Creek War, where he was seriously wounded in a charge at Horseshoe Bend and earned Jackson's respect for his bravery.*

In 1818 Houston returned to Nashville to study law, and in 1823 he was elected to Congress. Later he became the governor of Tennessee. President Andrew Jackson sent him to Texas in 1832 to negotiate a treaty with the Indians. He was elected a delegate to the Texas constitutional convention seeking independence from Mexico, and at the outbreak of war he was named commander in chief.

Principled, truthful, fearless, and patriotic, Houston possessed a contagious enthusiasm that made him a charismatic leader of men. In battle he was a wily tactician. He recounts the battle of San Jacinto rather modestly in his official report, using the third person. Houston also refers to H. Yoakum's book History of Texas *and extols its accurate description of the battle. The following account of the battle of San Jacinto is Houston's story converted to the first person, with additional details of the battle gleaned by Yoakum from his interviews with the combatants.*

★ ★ ★

THE ALAMO in San Antonio was nothing more than a church, and derived its cognomen from the fact of its being surrounded by poplars or cottonwood trees. Since the Mexican revolution in 1812, the Alamo was known as a fortress.

As Commander-in-Chief I sent an order to Colonel Neill, who was in command of the Alamo, to blow up the place, and fall back to Gonzales, making that a defensive position, which was supposed to be the furthest boundary the enemy would ever reach.

This was on the 17th of January, 1836. My order was secretly superseded by the governing council. Colonel Travis, having relieved Colonel Neill, did not blow up the Alamo, nor retreat with such articles as were necessary for the defense of the country. Instead he remained in possession from the 17th of January until the last of February, when the Alamo was invested by the forces of Santa Anna. Surrounded inside the Alamo, and cut off from all succor, the consequence was that they were all destroyed. They fell victim to the ruthless feelings of Santa Anna, in contrivance with the Council, and in violation of my plans for the defense of the country.

On the day I left Washington, Texas (the 6th of March), the Alamo had fallen, as I had anticipated. On the way to Gonzales I met many fugitives. I arrived there on the 11th of March. In Gonzales I found 374 men—half fed, half clad, and half armed, and without organization. That was the nucleus on which I had to form an army and defend the country.

No sooner had I arrived, and was satisfied that the Alamo had fallen, I sent a dispatch to Colonel Fannin, fifty-eight miles away, which would reach him in thirty hours, to fall back, from Goliad, twenty-five miles to Victoria, on the Guadalupe River, thus placing him within striking distance of Gonzales. Thus he had only to march the twenty-five miles to be on the east side of the Colorado River, which was all the succor I could hope for. I received an answer from Colonel Fannin, stating *that he had received my order; had held a council of war; and that he had determined to defend the place, and called it Fort Defiance, and had taken the responsibility to disobey my order* . . .

Fannin, after disobeying my orders, attempted on the 19th of March to retreat. He had only 25 miles to reach Gonzales. His opinions of chivalry and honor were such that he would not avail himself of the night to do it in, although he had been admonished by the smoke of the enemy's encampment for eight days previous to attempting a retreat. He then attempted to retreat in open day light.

The Mexican cavalry surrounded him. He halted in a prairie, without water, and commenced to build a fortification. There he was further surrounded by the enemy, who, from the hill tops, shot down upon him.

Although the most gallant and spirited men were with him, he remained in that situation all that night and the next day, when he presented a flag of truce. He entered into a capitulation, and was taken to Goliad, on a promise to return to the United States with all associated with him. In less than eight days, he and his men were massacred. I believed some few did escape, and most who did joined my army.

I then moved back from the Colorado and took position on the Brazos River. But at San Felipe I found a spirit of dissatisfaction in the troops. For the provisional Government had removed east. It had left Washington, and gone to Harrisburg, Texas. The apprehension of the settlers had been awakened and increased, rather than decreased. The spirits of the men were bowed down. Hope seemed to have departed. Only with my little band alone remained anything like a consciousness of strength.

On the Brazos, the efficient force under my command amounted to five hundred and twenty men. At our encampment on the Brazos, we received for the first time our first pieces of artillery. But they were without munitions. Old horseshoes and all pieces of iron that could be procured were cut up. There were no cartridges and but few balls. Two small six-pounders, presented by the magnanimity of the people of Cincinnati, and subsequently called the "twin sisters," were the first pieces of artillery that were used in Texas. From thence the march continued at Donoho's, three miles from Groce's. It required several days to cross the Brazos with horses and wagons.

The march to Harrisburg was effected through the greatest possible difficulties. The prairies were quagmired. Not withstanding that, the remarkable success of the march brought the army in a little time to Harrisburg, opposite which we halted. I gave orders to immediately prepare rations for three days, and to be at an early hour in readiness to cross the watery bayou.

The next morning I addressed a note in pencil to Colonel Henry Raquet, of Nacogdoches, in these words:

Camp at Harrisburg, April 19, 1836

Sir: This morning we are in preparation to meet Santa Anna. It is the only chance of saving Texas. From time to time I have looked for reinforcements in vain. The Convention adjourning to Harrisburg, struck *panic* throughout the country. Texas could have started [raised] at least four thousand men. We will only have about seven hundred to march with, besides the camp guard. We go to conquer. It is wisdom growing out of necessity, to meet the enemy now. Every consideration enforces it. No previous occasion would justify it. The troops are in fine spirits, and now is the time for action.

We shall use our best efforts to fight the enemy to such advantage as will insure victory, though the odds are greatly against us. I leave the result in the hands of a wise God, and rely upon his Providence.

My country will do justice to those who serve her. The rights for which we fight will be secured, and Texas free.

A crossing of the bayou was effected by the evening, and the line of march was taken up for San Jacinto, for the purpose of cutting off Santa Anna below the junction of the San Jacinto and Buffalo bayou.

In the morning the sun had risen brightly, and I determined with this omen, "today the battle shall take place." After I dismissed my war council, I sent for Deaf Smith and his comrade, Reeves. They came mounted, and I gave them axes so as not to attract the attention of the troops. They placed their axes in their saddles, as Mexicans carry swords and weapons, and started swiftly for a bridge that was the only route of retreat for us and the Mexicans. I told Deaf Smith: "you will be speedy if you wish to return in time for the scenes that are about to be enacted here." They executed my order. When my troops and I were within sixty yards of charging the enemy's front, Deaf Smith returned and announced that the bridge was cut down.

It was announced to the army for the first time. For the idea that the bridge would be cut down was never thought of by any one except my-self, until I ordered it to be done, and then only known to Smith and his comrade. It would have made the army polemics if it had been known that Vince's bridge was to be destroyed, for it cut off all means of escape for either army. There was no alternative but victory or death.

★   ★   ★

The plan of battle is well described in the official report, to be found in Yoakum's History of Texas:

Shortly after the departure of Smith and Reeves to destroy the bridge, Lt. Col. Bennett was sent through the camp to ascertain the state of feeling among the troops. He reported them all enthusiastic and in fine spirits. It was now three o'clock in the afternoon. The Mexicans were dull and heavy, the higher class of them enjoying their siesta. Santa Anna admits he himself was asleep. Houston then ordered the troops parade, which they did with alacrity and spirit.

The locality of the Texas camp afforded ample opportunity to form in order of battle without being seen by the enemy. Burleson's regiment was placed in the center; Sherman's on the left wing; the artillery, under Hockey, on the right of Burleson; the infantry under Millard, on the right of the artillery; and the cavalry, under Lamar (whose gallant conduct the day before had won him this command), on the extreme right. The enemy's cavalry was on his left wing; his center, which was fortified, was composed of his infantry, with his artillery in an opening in the center of the breastwork. He had extended his extreme right to the river, so as to occupy a skirt of timber projecting out from it.

The Texas cavalry was first dispatched to the front of the enemy's horse, to draw attention; while the remainder of the army, which had advanced in column to the cluster of timber three or four hundred yards in front were deploying into line. The evolution was quickly preformed, and the whole force advanced rapidly and in good order. The secretary of war, at the request of Houston, took command of the left wing.

While the Texans were thus advancing, Deaf Smith rode at the top of his horse's speed to the front, and informed Houston that Vince's bridge was destroyed. The general announced it to the line. The "Twin Sisters" now advanced to within two hundred yards of the Mexican breastwork, and opened a destructive fire with grape and canister. Sherman's regiment commenced action upon the Texan left. The whole line, advancing in double quick time, cried, "Remember the Alamo!"—"Remember Goliad!"—and while approaching the enemy's works, received his fire, but withheld their own until within pistol shot. The effect of this fire on the enemy was terrible. But the Texans made no halt—onward they went. On the left they penetrated the woodland; the Mexicans fled. On the right the Texan cavalry charged that of the enemy; the latter fled. In the center the Texan artillery advanced within seventy yards of that of the Mexicans, but ceased to fire, for Burleson's regiment and Millard's infantry had stormed the breastwork and took the enemy's artillery, and were driving them back.

In fifteen minutes after the charge, the Mexicans gave way at all points, and the pursuit was general. Some of them fled to the river, some to the swamp in their rear, others toward Vince's bridge, but the largest portion perhaps to a clump of trees not far to the rear, where they surrendered. Such was their consternation, and so sudden their defeat, that their cannon was left loaded, and their precious movables untouched. Those who were asleep, awoke only in time to be overwhelmed. Those who were cooking their dinner, left it uneaten. Those who were playing monte, left the game unfinished.

The morass in the rear and right of the enemy's camp, and into which so many of the fugitives fled, presented an awful scene. Men and horses, dead and dying, formed a bridge for the furious pursuers. The Texans, having no time to load their guns, used them as clubs. So with their pistols—they then had recourse to their bowie-knives, and finally to the weapons of the fallen enemy. It is said that Deaf Smith, after announcing the news of the destruction of the bridge, threw himself into the midst of the enemy, and, after breaking his own sword, coolly took another from one he had slain, and continued the work of death. "Houston, the commander-in-chief," says the secretary of war in his report, "acted with great gallantry, encouraging the men to attack, and heroically charged, in front of the infantry, within a few yards of the enemy." It was here that he received a severe wound in his ankle, and had his horse shot two or three times.

At dark the pursuit of the enemy ceased.

The aggregate force of the Texan army in the battle was seven hundred and eighty three. That of the enemy was twice the number. The Mexicans lost six hundred and thirty killed, two hundred and eight wounded, and seven hundred and thirty prisoners. The Texan loss was only eight killed and twenty five wounded!

One prisoner dressed as a private, but with fine studs on the bosom of his shirt asked to be conducted to Sam Houston.

★　★　★

From Houston's story:

When he was brought into our camp and my interview with him took place, I was lying on the ground. Looking up, I saw Santa Anna, who announced to me in Spanish: "I am General Antonio Lopez de Santa Anna, President of the Republic of Mexico, and a prisoner at your disposition."

⋆ 18 ⋆

Andrew Jackson's
Duel to the Death

(from James Parton, *General Jackson*, 1892)

P ERHAPS THE MOST NOTORIOUS DUEL *in America was
in 1804 when Aaron Burr mortally wounded his political rival,
Alexander Hamilton, in a remote field across the Hudson River
from New York City, in Weehawken, New Jersey. Duels enabled men to respond to a verbal insult when the rule of law might not. Senators, congress-
men, and newspaper editors dueled to assuage their wounded honor. Even
Abe Lincoln came close to a duel with drawn cutlasses.*

*Duels were rampant in America between 1790 and 1810, especially in
the South. New Orleans, as late as 1834, had more duelists defending their
honor than there were days in the year: "fifteen on one Sunday morning;
one hundred and two between the 1st of January and the end of April."*

*Here Jackson's nineteenth-century biographer, James Parton, relates
the story of how General (and future president) Andrew Jackson and
Charles Dickinson, the best shot in Tennessee, got into an imbroglio and
ended up sighting along their pistol barrels and firing at each other's
heart.*

* * *

FOR THE AUTUMN HORSE RACES of 1805, a great match was arranged between General Jackson's Truxton and Captain Joseph Ervin's Plowboy. The stakes were two thousand dollars, payable on the day of the race in notes, which notes were to be then due; forfeit, eight hundred dollars. Six persons were interested in this race: on Truxton's side, General Jackson, Major W. P. Anderson, Major Verrell, and Captain Pryor; on the side of Plowboy, Captain Ervin and his son-in-law, Charles Dickinson. Before the day appointed for the race arrived Ervin and Dickinson decided to pay the forfeit and withdraw their horse, which was amicably done, and the affair was supposed to be at an end.

About this time a report reached General Jackson's ears that Charles Dickinson had uttered disparaging words of Mrs. Jackson, which was with Jackson the sin not to be pardoned. Dickinson was a lawyer by profession, but, like Jackson, speculated in produce, horses, and, it is said, in slaves. He was well connected, possessed considerable property, and had a large circle of friends. He is represented as a somewhat wild, dissipated young man, yet not unamiable, nor disposed wantonly to wound the feelings of others. When excited by drink, or by any other cause, he was prone to talk loosely and swear violently, as drunken men will. He had the reputation of being the best shot in Tennessee. Upon hearing this report, General Jackson called on Dickinson and asked him if he had used the language attributed to him. Dickinson replied that if he had, it must have been when he was drunk. Further explanations and denials removed all ill feeling from General Jackson's mind, and they separated in a friendly manner.

A second time, it is said Dickinson uttered offensive words respecting Mrs. Jackson in a tavern at Nashville, which were duly conveyed by some meddling parasite to General Jackson. Jackson, I am told, then went to Captain Ervin and advised him to exert his influence over his son-in-law, and induce him to restrain his tongue and comport himself like a gentleman in his cups. "I wish no quarrel with him," said Jackson; "he is used by my enemies in Nashville, who are urging him on to pick a quarrel with me. Advise him to stop in time." It appears, however, that enmity grew between these two men. In January, 1806, when the events occurred that are now to be related, there was the worst possible feeling between them.

Deadly enmity existing between Jackson and Dickinson; a very trivial event was sufficient to bring them into collision. A young lawyer of Nashville, named Swann, misled by false information, circulated a report that Jackson had accused the owners of Plowboy of paying their forfeit in notes other than those which had been agreed upon—notes less valuable because not due at the date of settling. General Jackson, in one of his letters to Mr. Swann, went out of his way to assail Charles Dickinson by name, calling him "a base poltroon and cowardly tale-bearer," requesting Swann to show Dickinson these offensive words, and offering to meet him in the field if he desired satisfaction for the same. Upon reading the letter, Dickinson published a card which contained these words: "I declare him, notwithstanding he is a major-general of the militia of Mero district, to be a worthless scoundrel, 'a poltroon and a coward'—a man who, by frivolous and evasive pretexts, avoided giving the satisfaction which was due to a gentleman whom he had injured. This has prevented me from calling on him in the manner I should otherwise have done, for I am well convinced that he is too great a coward to administer any of those anodynes he promised me in his letter to Mr. Swann."

Jackson instantly challenged Dickinson. The challenge was promptly accepted. Friday, May 30, 1806, was the day appointed for the meeting; the weapons, pistols; the place, a spot on the banks of the Red River, in Kentucky.

The place appointed for the meeting was a long day's ride from Nashville. Thursday morning, before the dawn of day, Dickinson stole from the side of his young and beautiful wife, and began silently to prepare for the journey.

He mounted his horse and repaired to the rendezvous where his second and half a dozen of the gay blades of Nashville were waiting to escort him on his journey. Away they rode, in the highest spirits, as though they were upon a party of pleasure. Indeed, they made a part of pleasure of it. When they stopped for rest or refreshment, Dickinson is said to have amused the company by displaying his wonderful skill with the pistol. Once, at a distance of twenty-four feet, he fired four balls, each at the word of command, into a space that could be covered by a silver dollar. Several times he cut a string with his bullet from the same distance. It is said that he left a severed string hanging near a tavern, and said to the landlord, as he rode away, "If General Jackson comes along this road, show him *that!*"

Very different was the demeanor of General Jackson and the party that accompanied him. His second, General Thomas Overton, an old Revolutionary soldier, versed in the science and familiar with the practice of dueling, had reflected deeply upon the conditions of the coming combat, with the view to conclude upon the tactics most likely to save his friend from Dickinson's unerring bullet. For this duel was not to be the amusing mockery that some modern duels have been. This duel was to be *real*. It was to be an affair in which each man was to strive with his utmost skill to effect the purpose of the occasion—disable his antagonist and save his own life. As the principal and the second rode apart from the rest, they discussed all the chances and probabilities with the single aim to decide upon a course which should result in the disabling of Dickinson and the saving of Jackson. The mode of fighting which had been agreed upon was somewhat peculiar. The pistols were to be held downward until the word was given to fire; then each man was to fire as soon as he pleased. With such an arrangement it was scarcely possible that both the pistols should be discharged at the same moment. There was a chance, even, that by extreme quickness of movement one man could bring down his antagonist without himself receiving a shot. The question anxiously discussed between Jackson and Overton was this: Shall we try to get the first shot, or shall we permit Dickinson to have it? They agreed, at length, that it would be decidedly better to *let* Dickinson fire first.

Jackson ate heartily at supper that night, conversing in a lively, pleasant manner, and smoked his evening pipe as usual. Jacob Smith remembers being exceedingly well pleased with his guest, and, on learning the cause of his visit, heartily wishing him a safe deliverance. Before breakfast on the next morning the whole party mounted and rode down the road that wound close along the picturesque banks of the stream. The horsemen rode about a mile along the river, then turned down toward the river to a point on the bank where they had expected to find a ferryman. No ferryman appearing Jackson spurred his horse into the stream and dashed across, followed by all his party. They rode into the poplar forest two hundred yards or less, to a spot near the center of a level platform or river bottom, then covered with forest, now smiling with cultivated fields. The horsemen halted and dismounted just before reaching the appointed place. Jackson, Overton, and a surgeon who had come with them from home walked on together, and the rest led their horses a short distance in an opposite direction.

"How do you feel about it now, General?" asked one of the party, as Jackson turned to go.

"Oh, all right," replied Jackson, gayly; "I shall wing him, never fear."

Dickinson's second won the choice of position, and Jackson's the office of giving the word. The astute Overton considered this giving of the word a matter of great importance, and he had already determined how he would give it if the lot fell to him. The eight paces were measured off and the men placed. Both were perfectly collected. All the politenesses of such occasions were very strictly and elegantly performed. Jackson was dressed in a loose frock-coat, buttoned carelessly over his chest and concealing in some degree the extreme slenderness of his figure. Dickinson was the younger and handsomer man of the two. But Jackson's tall, erect figure, and the intensity of his demeanor, it is said, gave him a most superior and commanding air, as he stood under the tall poplars on this bright May morning, silently awaiting the moment.

"Are you ready?" said Overton.

"I am ready," replied Dickinson.

"I am ready," said Jackson.

The words were no sooner pronounced than Overton, with a sudden shout, cried, using his old-country pronunciation:

"FERE!"

Dickinson raised his pistol quickly and fired. Overton, who was looking with anxiety and dread at Jackson, saw a puff of dust fly from the breast of his coat, and saw him raise his left arm and place it tightly across his chest. He is surely hit, thought Overton, and in a bad place, too. But no; he does not fall. He raised his pistol. Overton glanced at

Dickinson. Amazed at the unwonted failure of his aim, and apparently appalled at the awful figure and face before him, Dickinson had unconsciously recoiled a pace or two.

"Great God!" he faltered, "have I missed him?"

"Back to the MARK, sir!" shrieked Overton with his hand upon his pistol.

Dickinson recovered his composure, stepped forward to the peg, and stood with his eyes averted from his antagonist. All this was the work of a moment, though it requires many words to tell it.

General Jackson took deliberate aim and pulled the trigger. The pistol neither snapped nor went off. He looked at the trigger, and discovered that it had stopped at half-cock. He drew it back to its place and took aim a second time. He fired. Dickinson's face blanched; he reeled; his friends rushed toward him, caught him in their arms, and gently seated him on the ground, leaning against a bush. They stripped off his clothes. The blood was gushing from his side in a torrent. The ball had passed through the body, below the ribs. Such a wound could not but be fatal.

Overton went forward and learned the condition of the wounded man. Rejoining his principal, he said, "He won't want anything more of you, General," and conducted him from the ground. They had gone a hundred yards, Overton walking on one side of Jackson, the surgeon on the other, and neither speaking a word, when the surgeon observed that one of Jackson's shoes was full of blood.

"My God! General Jackson, are you hit?" he exclaimed, pointing to the blood.

"Oh! I believe," replied Jackson, "that he has pinked me a little. Let's look at it. But say nothing about it there," pointing to the house.

He opened his coat. Dickinson's aim had been perfect. He had sent the ball precisely where he supposed Jackson's heart was beating. But the thinness of his body and the looseness of his coat combining to deceive Dickinson, the ball had only broken a rib or two and raked the breast-bone. It was a somewhat painful, bad-looking wound, but neither severe nor dangerous, and he was able to ride to the tavern without much inconvenience. Upon approaching the house he went up to one of the negro women who was churning and asked her if the butter had come. She said it was just coming. He asked for some buttermilk. While she was getting it for him she observed him furtively open his coat and look within it. She saw that his shirt was soaked with blood, and she stood gazing in. She dipped out a quart measure full of buttermilk and gave it to him. He drank it off at a draught; then went in, took off his coat, and had his wound carefully examined and dressed. That done, he dispatched one of his retinue to Dr. Catlett, to inquire respecting the condition of Dickinson, and to say that the surgeon attending himself would be glad to contribute his aid toward Mr. Dickinson's relief. Polite reply was returned that Mr. Dickinson's case was past surgery. In the course of the day General Jackson sent a bottle of wine to Dr. Catlett for the use of his patient.

But there was one gratification which Jackson could not, even in such circumstances, grant him. A very old friend of General Jackson writes to me thus: "Although the general had been wounded, he did not desire it should be known until he had left the neighborhood, and had therefore concealed it at first from his own friends. His reason for this, as he once stated to me, was, that as Dickinson considered himself the best shot in the world, and was certain of killing him at the first fire, he did not want him to have the gratification even of knowing that he had touched him."

Poor Dickinson bled to death.

General Jackson's wound proved to be more severe and troublesome than was at first anticipated. It was nearly a month before he could move about without inconvenience, and when the wound healed it healed falsely; that is, some of the viscera were slightly displaced, and so remained. Twenty years after, this forgotten wound forced itself upon his remembrance, and kept itself there for many a year.

★ 19 ★

Fighting Belly to Belly with
a Grizzly Bear

(from George Ruxton, *Adventures in Mexico and
the Rocky Mountains*, 1847)

IN JANUARY 1803, *Thomas Jefferson asked Congress for $2,500 to
finance an expedition to explore up the Missouri River to its source
in the Rocky Mountains, thence down the nearest westward-flowing
waterway to the Pacific. Also in April of that year the great Louisiana
Purchase was negotiated with France for $11,250,000. It included New
Orleans, west Florida, and everything west of the Mississippi to the Rocky
Mountains and as far north as Montana. For fifty years after the Lewis
and Clark Expedition (1804–1806), the mountain men surfaced in western history. They were hunters, trappers, and traders with the Indians
at annual rendezvous. Beavers were their principal quarry. The under-
fur of the beaver was used to make felt hats, as well as coats, muffs, and lin-
ings. However, fashions change. By 1850, silk hats had replaced felt hats,
and overtrapping had exhausted the beaver supply.*

    *Wild and independent, these wilderness trappers later served as guides
to explorers, missionaries, and settlers, and as scouts for the army. They
were the true "Openers of the West."*

Trapper Thomas Fitzpatrick was called "White Hair." When he was only twenty-six, his hair turned white—the result of a harrowing, starving escape from Indians. He accompanied John Charles Frémont, and was a respected, peace-seeking Indian agent. "Old" Cabel Greenwood at age eighty-one led the first wagon train across the Sierra Nevada and, at eighty-four, with his son, helped rescue the stranded, snowbound Donner party. Jedediah Smith, once mauled by a grizzly bear, led the party that re-discovered the South Pass, the key to the central Overland Trail by which wagons could reach Oregon and California. He was the first American to cross the Southwest. The names roll on: William Ashley, who held the first rendezvous in 1825 and sailed down the dangerous Green River in buf-falo-skin boats, and his partner, Andrew Henry. The Sublette brothers, James Clyman, Etienne Provost, and William Williams were among the first to see Yosemite Valley. Jim Bridger was the first white man to discover the Great Salt Lake. He tasted the waters there and proclaimed: "Hell, we are on the shores of the Pacific."

There were wonderful tall tales about these mountain men. Typical was this description of Davy Crockett: "He took hail stones for "Life Pills" . . . picked his teeth with a pitchfork . . . fanned himself with a hurricane . . . could drink the Mississippi dry . . . and shoot six cords of bear in one day."

From the 1847 book Adventures in Mexico and the Rocky Mountains *by George Ruxton, here is the miracle story of John Glass, a man of "steel nerves and nine lives."*

* * *

THE GRIZZLY BEAR is the fiercest of the ferae naturae of the mountains. His great strength and wonderful tenacity of life render an encounter with him anything but desirable. Therefore it is a rule with the Indians and white hunters never to attack him unless backed by a strong party. Although, like every other wild animal, he usually flees from man, yet at certain seasons, when maddened by love or hunger, he not unfrequently charges at first sight of a foe. Then, un-less killed dead, a hug at close quarters is anything but a pleasant embrace. His strong hooked claws will strip the flesh from the bones as easily as a cook peels an onion. . . .

Some years ago a trapping party was on their way to the mountains, led, I believe, by old Sublette, a well-known captain of the West. Amongst the band was one John Glass, a trapper who had been all his life in the mountains, and had seen, probably, more exciting adventures, and had had more wonderful and hairbreadth escapes, than any of the rough and hardy fellows who make the West their home, and whose lives are spent in a succession of perils and privations.

On one of the streams running from the "Black Hills," a range of mountains northward of the Platte, Glass and a companion were one day setting their traps. On passing through a cherry-thicket which skirted the stream, Glass, who was in advance, descried a large grizzly bear quietly turning up the turf with his nose, searching for yampa-roots or pig-nuts. Glass immediately called his companion. Both, proceeding cautiously, crept to the skirt of the thicket, and, taking steady aim at the animal, whose broadside was fairly exposed at the distance of twenty yards, discharged their rifles at the same instant, both balls taking effect, but not inflicting a mortal wound.

The bear, giving a groan of pain, jumped with all four legs from the ground, and, seeing the wreaths of smoke hanging at the edge of the brush, charged at once in that direction, snorting with pain and fury. About a hundred yards from the thicket was a steep bluff, and between these points was a level piece of prairie; Glass saw that his only chance was to reach this bluff, and, shouting to his companion to make for it, they both broke from the cover and flew like lightning across the open space. When more than half way across, the bear being about fifty yards behind them, Glass, in the lead, tripped over a stone, and fell to the ground. Just as he rose to his feet, the beast, rising on his hind feet, confronted him. As he closed, Glass, never losing his presence of mind, cried to his companion to load up quickly, and Glass discharged his pistol full into the body of the animal. At the same moment the bear, with blood streaming from its nose and mouth, knocked the pistol from his hand with one blow of its paw and, fixing his claws deep into his flesh, rolled with him to the ground. The hunter, notwithstanding his hopeless situation, struggled manfully, drawing his knife and plunging it several times into the body of the beast, which, furious with pain, tore with tooth and claw the body of the wretched victim, actually baring the ribs of the flesh and exposing the very bones.

Weak with loss of blood, and with eyes blinded with the blood that streamed from his lacerated scalp, the knife at length fell from his hand, and Glass sank down insensible, and to all appearance dead. His companion, who, up to this moment, had watched the conflict, which, however, lasted but a few seconds, thinking that his turn would come next, and not having had presence of mind even to load his rifle, fled with might and main back to camp, where he narrated the miserable fate of poor Glass. The captain of the band of trappers, however, dispatched the man with a companion back to the spot where he lay, with instructions to remain by him if still alive, or to bury him if, as all supposed, he was defunct, promising them at the same time a sum of money for so doing.

On reaching the spot, which was red with blood, they found Glass still breathing, and the bear, dead and stiff, actually lying upon his body. Poor Glass presented a horrifying spectacle; the flesh was torn in strips from his chest and limbs, and large flaps strewed the ground; his scalp hung bleeding over his face, which was also lacerated in a shocking manner. The bear, besides the three bullets which had pierced its body, bore the marks of the fierce nature of Glass's final struggle, no less than twenty gaping wounds in the breast and belly testifying to the gallant defense of the mountaineer.

Imagining that, if not already dead, the poor fellow could not possibly survive more than a few moments, the men collected his arms, stripped him even of his hunting shirt and moccasins, and, merely pulling the dead bear off the body, mounted their horses, and slowly followed the remainder of the party, saying, when they reached it, that Glass was dead as probably they thought, and that they had buried him. In a few days the gloom which pervaded the trappers' camp, occasioned by the loss of a favorite companion, disappeared, and Glass's misfortune, although frequently mentioned over the camp-fire, at length was almost entirely forgotten in the excitement of the hunt and Indian perils which surrounded them.

Months elapsed, the hunt was over, and the party of trappers were on their way to the trading-fort with their packs of beaver. It was nearly sundown, and the round adobe bastions of the mud-built fort were just in sight, when a horseman was seen slowly approaching them along the banks of the river. When near enough to discern his figure, they saw a lank cadaverous form with a face so scarred and disfigured that scarcely a feature was discernible.

Approaching the leading horsemen, one of who happened to be the companion of the defunct Glass in his memorable bear scrape, the stranger, in a hollow voice, reining in his horse before them, exclaimed, "Hurraw, Bill, my boy! you thought I was 'gone under' that time, did you? but hand me over my horse and gun, my lad; I ain't dead yet by a damn sight!"

What was the astonishment of the whole party, and the genuine horror of Bill and his worthy companion in the burial story, to hear the well-known, though now much altered, voice of John Glass, who had been killed by a grizzly bear months before, and comfortably interred, as the two men had reported, and all had believed! There he was, however, and no mistake about it; and all crowded round to hear from his lips, how, after the lapse of he knew not how long, he had gradually recovered, and being without arms, or even a butcher's knife, he had fed upon the almost putrid carcass of the bear for several days, until he had regained sufficient strength to crawl, when, tearing off as much of the bear's-meat as he could carry in his enfeebled state, he crept down the river; and suffering excessive torture from his wounds, and hunger, and cold, he made the best of his way to the fort, which was some eighty or ninety miles from the place of his encounter with the bear, and, living the greater part of the way upon roots and berries, he after many, many days, arrived in a pitiable state, from which he had now recovered, and was, to use his own expression, "as slick as a peeled onion."

All Hell Broke Loose Right Under
the Parson's Nose

(from Reverend Peter Cartwright,
Autobiography of Peter Cartwright,
the Backwoods Preacher, 1857)

THE BIBLE LED *the way to America. First the Pilgrims came to Plymouth to escape English persecution. In turn, the Pilgrims ousted Roger Williams for his different beliefs. Williams traveled "fourteen weeks of bitter winter season without knowing what bread or bed did mean" to found Providence, Rhode Island. There, with thirteen followers, he created the first commonwealth in the world to guarantee religious freedom unequivocally. To the south, Lord Baltimore attracted Catholics to Maryland, and later William Penn beckoned Quakers to Philadelphia.*

Over the centuries, a number of charismatic leaders founded religious denominations. Mother Ann Lee started the Shakers. Joseph Smith's visions launched the Mormons, whom Brigham Young led to Salt Lake City. In Boston Mary Baker Eddy founded Christian Science. One preacher, William Young, persuaded tens of thousands that the second coming of Christ was imminent. He urged his followers to prepare for that final day by climbing up on their housetops and haystacks in order to shorten their ascent to heaven. He set the date for the second coming for October 22, 1843.

There have been uncanny times of a national spiritual quickening. In 1734, the first revival, known as the Great Awakening, was ignited by the intellect and sermons of Jonathan Edwards and culminated in 1740 with the fiery zeal of George Whitefield's evangelism. Thus was the American Methodist Church born.

A Second Great Awakening began in 1790. Peter Cartwright was a circuit-riding minister who fanned the flames of the revival, crisscrossing Illinois preaching fire, brimstone, and salvation.

Cartwright once had a "set-to" with a Herculean ferryman who defamed him—right in the middle of the Sangamon River. Cartwright hurled the ferryman overboard, then held him under water long enough to extract three gasping promises: (1) that he would say the Lord's Prayer each morning and evening; (2) that he would hear every preacher who came within five miles; and, (3) that he would forevermore so ferry across the river any Methodist minister, free of charge. Cartwright's constituents elected him to Congress. He later lost his seat to Abraham Lincoln. Here, in a passage from the Autobiography of Peter Cartwright, the Backwoods Preacher, *published in 1857, Cartwright relates how he managed his ministry when holy hell broke out.*

★　★　★

OUR LAST QUARTERLY-MEETING was a camp-meeting. We had a great many tents, and a large turnout for a new country, and, perhaps, there never was a greater collection of rabble and rowdies. They came drunk, and armed with dirks, clubs, knives, and horsewhips, and swore they would break up the meeting. After interrupting us very much on Saturday night, they collected early on Sunday morning, determined on a general riot.

At eight o'clock I was appointed to preach. About the time I was half through my discourse, two very fine-dressed young men marched into the congregation with loaded whips, and hats, and rose up and stood in the midst of the ladies, and began to laugh and talk. They were near the stand, and I requested them to desist and get off the seats;

but they cursed me, and told me to mind my own business, and said they would not get down.

I stopped trying to preach, and called for a magistrate. There were two at hand, but I saw they were both afraid. I ordered the magistrates to take these men into custody, but they said they could not do it. I told them, as I left the stand, to command me to take them, and I would do it at the risk of my life. I advanced toward the rowdies. They ordered me to stand off, but I advanced.

One of them made a pass at my head with his whip, but I closed in with him and jerked him off the seat. A regular scuffle ensued. The congregation by this time were all in a commotion. I heard the magistrate give general orders, commanding all friends of order to aid in suppressing the riot. In the scuffle I threw my prisoner down, and held him fast; he tried his best to get loose; I told him to be quiet, or I would pound his chest well.

The mob, who sided with the ruffians, rose, and rushed to the rescue of the two prisoners, for we had taken the other young man also. An old and drunken magistrate came up to me, and ordered me to let my prisoner go. I told him I should not. He swore if I did not, he would knock me down. I told him to crack away.

Then one of my friends, at my request, took hold of my prisoner, and the drunken justice made a pass at me; but I parried the stroke, and seized him by the collar and the hair of the head, and fetching him a sudden jerk forward, brought him to the ground, and jumped on him. I told him to be quiet, or I would pound him well.

The rowdy mob then rushed to the scene. They knocked down seven magistrates, and several preachers and others. I gave up my drunken prisoner to another, and threw myself in front of the friends of order. Just at this moment the ringleader of the mob and I met; he made three passes at me, intending to knock me down. The last time he struck at me, by the force of his own effort he threw the side of his face toward me. It seemed at that moment that I had not the power to resist temptation, and I struck a sudden blow in the burr of the ear and dropped him to the earth. Just at that moment the friends of order rushed by hundreds on the mob, knocking them down in every direction.

In a few minutes, the place became too strait for the mob, and they wheeled and fled in every direction; but we secured about thirty prisoners, marched them off to a vacant tent, and put them under guard till Monday morning, when they were tried, and every man was fined to the utmost limits of the law. The aggregate amount of fines and costs was near three hundred dollars. They fined my old drunken magistrate twenty dollars, and returned him to court, and he was cashiered at his office.

On Sunday, when we had vanquished the mob, the whole encampment was filled with mourning; and although there was no attempt to resume preaching till evening, yet, such was our confused state, that there was not then a single preacher on the ground willing to preach, from the presiding elder, John Sale, down. Seeing we had fallen on evil times, my spirit was stirred within me. I said to the elder, "I feel a clear conscience, for under the necessity of the circumstances we have done right, and now I ask to let me preach."

"Do," said the elder, "for there is no other man on the ground can do it."

The encampment was lighted up, the trumpet blown. I rose in the stand, and required every soul to leave the tents and come into the congregation. There was a general rush to the stand. I requested the brethren, if ever they prayed in all their lives, to pray now. My voice was strong and clear, and my preaching was more of an exhortation and encouragement than anything else. My text was, "The gates of hell shall not prevail."

In about thirty minutes the power of God fell on the congregation in such a manner as is seldom seen; the people fell in every direction, right and left, front and rear. It was supposed to be no less than three hundred fell like dead men in mighty battle; and there was no need of calling mourners, for they were strewed all over the camp-ground; loud wailings went up to heaven from sinners for mercy, and a general shout from Christians, so that the noise was heard afar off. Our meeting lasted all night, and Monday and Monday night; and when we closed on Tuesday, there were two hundred who had professed religion, and about that number joined the Church.

⋆ 21 ⋆

The Forty-niners: Broken Hearts
and Empty Pockets

(from Jim Nevins,
"Letter from J. M. Nevins to Russell Nevins
in Wisconsin, Sacramento City, Dec. 2, 1849")

G OLD WAS DISCOVERED *the morning of January 24, 1848,
by James W. Marshall, the foreman at Sutter's mill near Sacramento. As word crept out, the lust for gold set off a stampede of
prospectors. San Francisco and Monterey were soon drained of merchants,
blacksmiths, stevedores, clerks, and servants as they up and quit their jobs,
grabbed a pan and shovel, and hightailed it to the mountains.*

*"A frenzy seized my soul," confessed a novice prospector. "Piles of gold
rose up before me at every step. Thousands of slaves bowed to my beck and
call. Myriads of fair virgins contended for my love. In short, I had a violent attack of gold fever." Oh, the thrills of prospecting! The delirium of the
search, the euphoria of the find. "I crawled about the ground seizing bits of
stone, blowing the dust from them or rubbing them on my clothes, and then
peering at them with anxious hope. Presently I found a bright fragment
and my heart bounded! I hid behind a boulder—I polished it and scrutinized it with nervous eagerness and delight. The more I examined the
fragment the more I was convinced that I had found the door to fortune. I*

marked the spot and carried away my specimen. Of all the experiences of my life, this secret search was the nearest to unmarred ecstasy."

Within four months the gold fever infected the East and the exodus began. Some New England towns even banded together to form mining fraternities. The rich grubstaked the adventurous. They scrupulously signed contracts and swore to share their profits when they struck it rich. But when the men hit California running, it was every man for himself and devil take the hindmost.

Most forty-niners came by way of the Oregon Trail; others traveled via the Isthmus of Panama, where many died; and still others sailed around Cape Horn. By 1850, thirty-seven thousand miners worked the Feather, Yuba, Bear, and American Rivers. The average man's take was four to six dollars a day. By the time the gold rush was over, the gold bug had bitten 450,000 men.

Only a few unearthed a bonanza. In six days on the American River, Joe Smith found nuggets worth $8,000. Peter Bolas, panning the Sassafras River, garnered $18,000, in two weeks—$450,000 at today's gold prices.

Drawn by hope and then exhausted by disappointments, most prospectors eventually quit. Others were not as lucky. "The old crowd," wrote George McKinstry, Jr., to a colleague in 1851, "is scattered by death and disaster since you left. William Daylor by cholera; Jared Sheldon, shot in a row with miners; Perry McCoan by a fall from his horse; Sebastian Keyser drowned; Little Bill Johnson, who knows?; Captain Luce, missing in the mountains; old Thomas Hardy, rum; John Sinclain, cholera; William E. Shannon, cholera; old William Knight, rum as expected; Charley Heath, rum and missing; Bob Ridley, fever, I think. Old Kitnor, made a fortune and went bust; William A. Liedesdroff, dead; old Eliab Grimes, dead; Jack Fuller, ditto."

In this 1849 letter, included in Nobility in the Rough by David Boring, prospector Jim Nevins wrote home from Sacramento to tell his family of his challenging experiences.

* * *

SACRAMENTO CITY, December 2, 1849—My dear parents, wife, brother, Marilla, God bless her . . .

I now write you all for the first time from California. The golden land. To let you know I am alive and well. Hoping this will find you all in good health and good spirits, for I have not heard a word from you since the St. Joe letter.

I feel a little cross to think that you did not think of me enough to have a letter here for me when I got here, but hope you will now make up for lost time. Since I wrote you from Fort Laramie, fortune has used me rather roughly.

On the fourth of July we lost the off ox of the Hawks team. July 31 we lost the ox we bought in Missouri, Aug 22 we lost an ox and had to have our wagon and tools sold, as well as our provisions and what we could. Wooding very sick. We now joined another team from Illinois that had some cattle. We had three. All I saved was a two-bushel bag of some bedding. Before I go farther, I will tell you where we were when all this happened.

We had left the Humboldt river sixty miles from its sink, to take, as was told us, a much shorter route. This road against my advice. I cussed and swore enough to have carried a sawmill, but to no purpose. Chancey Wooding was as contrary as a D— h—. He never would agree with me in anything.

The road we took had 80 miles of desert and but one watering place, and not a spear of grass. The one I wanted had 50 miles of desert, but water in three places. Wooding grows worse until Sept 2 when Chancey Wooding ended his earthly career. He was buried on the Southern Oregon road about 120 miles from the Humboldt River.

Father I leave it to you to tell the relatives of his sad fate. I ought to have written to them but have not. His disorders were his old complaint. His liver and a new disease we had on the road called the Mountain fever. He was very obstinate. He would not take the doctors medicine (much less mine) for I believe as I am a living man, I could have saved him.

His property I have in my possession, and when I come home I will pay it to Helen Wooding, Milton's girls as he directed me, four days before his death.

We crossed the Sierra Nevadas Sept. 7 in the lowest spot in the whole ridge. 8 yoke cattle would pull up a wagon with 15 hundred in it.

The mountain was about as steep as a roof of a house, for one mile. Road very good. I was taken sick this morning, and my disorder was mountain fever. I was taken with a headache and back ache, and almost froze to death. After the coldness left me, then the fever. Gosh ninety! Didn't I catch it.

I felt a little scared too, because so many have died with this disorder. I took a big dose of the great Westerns, they operated gloriously and then I downed with quinine by the cart load, and got better.

We descended the west side of the mountain very fast. But I did not gain my health till about the first of Oct. We arrived at the Sacramento River at the mouth of deer creek Sept. 30 having lost every ox but old Brin and three weeks of time covering this northern route.

We were one hundred and fifty miles in Oregon, when we passed the ridge of the mountains. After resting three days we descended to the Feather River. We forded it. It is as large a stream as Rock River. I sold old Brin for 50 dollars.

Oct. 12 went to work, took a job. Made 17\frac{1}{2}$ per day, for two days. I worked in the mines $16\frac{1}{2}$ days and made in that time $215.00 and spent in that time $40.24. I had $135 left when I got to the mines. My pile is a good deal smaller now than when I started out, $280.00 all told.

I do not expect to earn more than my board this winter, although some that got into the mines before I did have four, five, six, and even ten thousand dollars.

It is very hard work in the mines. Use pans, cradles, quick silver, machine to work gold. The mines are as good as you hear them to be, but I would never advise the meanest dog in Christiandom to come to California.

Flour is worth in the mines 1.25 per pound, pork 1.50, sugar .50, coffee .50 per pound, brandy 50 cents drink, beef .30 and potatoes .40 per pound.

Oxen are worth 50 to 100 dollars per yoke. Mules 150. Horses 50 to 300 dollars each.

Medicine is plenty here. Quinine is 10 cents per ounce. Chalogogue 5 dollars per bottle. Doctors are plenty. One visit is 10 dollars.

Sacramento City contains at present about 20,000 inhabitants.

The houses are made of all kinds of material. Cloth, sheets, iron, wood, and sundried red bricks called doubas.

The Sacramento River is about a quarter of a mile wide. There are about fifty ships here in the river, used as store houses, and boarding houses. There are five steam boats on the river. Some go as high as Vernon, a small little town at the mouth of the Feather River.

The town is as big as Ft. Atkinson and only four months old. The American River city lots are selling from 1,000 to 30,000 dollars each.

My Father, that little book is still on the window sill before me. That goes when I go and death will part us. Father I had to throw away the note book, but saved one tune. Sing it Father and think of your unhappy son, thousands of miles away from home. I am not the only one who wishes himself home. Often do my thoughts wander back to the fireside of my family.

Oh my Mother, how I wish I had taken up with your advice and stayed at home. But I have nobody to blame but myself. Melvin when you eat your meals, think of your brother who has lived five days on beef and no salt at that. Would I be glad of the bread in the swill pail? I guess I would. I was hemmed in with high water on the Bear River.

My wife, kiss little Rilla for me and tell her that her father far away thinks of his child and home. If we were once more in that little brick house, happy I should be. What I called hard at home, was comfort compared to what I now get.

Give my respect to Ben and Louisa and the little one. To Uncle Tyler and Jason and Aunt Rosaline and all inquiring friends, if I have any.

My parents, I remain your respected son. My wife, your affectionate husband. My brother good by and God bless my child.

My dearest wife. It is going on seven long months since I have heard from you. Long seems separation. When shall we meet again? God only knows. Long years and months must pass before that time arrives, but keep up the good cheer, for let us once get home and nothing but death will separate us. My prospects are not very flattering at present, but I hope for better times. Luck must turn. I lost my all a getting here, but look for me next fall, if I live.

Jim Nevins

★ 22 ★

Mark Twain on the Daring
of a Mississippi Pilot

(from Mark Twain,
"Old Times on the Mississippi," 1875)

M ARK TWAIN (Samuel Clemens) might have been the most successful, charming, and engaging vagabond of his era. After his father's death in 1847 he started work in Missouri as a printer's apprentice with the Hannibal Courier. Yet he soon left to see New York, arriving with two to three dollars, and a ten-dollar bill sewn into his coat. After a short job stint, he left for Philadelphia, where he worked as a sub on the Inquirer and the Public Ledger. Next it was a "flying" trip to Washington, then out to St. Louis, "sitting up in a smoking car for two or three days and nights." Exhausted, he climbed aboard a steamboat destined for Muscatine, Iowa, and slept for thirty-six hours straight. Walking down the street in Keokuk, he saw a fifty-dollar bill blow by him, and he grabbed it: "the largest assembly of money I had ever seen in one spot." He advertised for its owner but kept it when no claimant showed. He bought a ticket to Cincinnati, where he worked in a printing office, then left aboard the Paul Jones for New Orleans, where he intended to sail for the Amazon River to make a bundle of money in coca speculation.

One of the ship's pilots was Horace Bixby. "Pretty soon I was doing a lot of steering for him in his daylight watches," Twain wrote. At New Orleans he inquired about the next boat to the Amazon and was told that "there probably wouldn't be any during that century." "So there I was," Twain mused. "I couldn't get to the Amazon. I had no friends in New Orleans, and no money to speak of. I went to Horace Bixby and asked him to make a pilot out of me. He said he would do it for five hundred dollars, one hundred dollars cash in advance." Twain managed to borrow this sum from a nice brother-in-law, and "within eighteen months I had become a competent pilot." The Civil War brought a halt to the paddle-wheel traffic on the Mississippi River and to Mark Twain's steamboat career. But there always was storytelling and writing left.

Twain found piloting exhilarating and enthralling. He wrote that a pilot "was the only unfettered human being that lived on the earth. Kings are but hampered servants of parliament and people; parliaments sit in chains forged by their constituency . . . but in the day I write of, the Mississippi pilot had none. The captain could stand upon the hurricane-deck, in the pomp of a very brief authority, and give him five or six orders while the vessel backed into the stream, and then the skipper's reign was over. The moment that boat was under way in the river, she was under the sole and unquestioned control of the pilot."

From his memoir, Old Times on the Mississippi, here is Mark Twain's account of his mentor Horace Bixby's skill and courage while at the wheel.

* * *

NEXT MORNING I felt pretty rusty and low-spirited. We went booming along, taking a good many chances, for we were anxious to "get out of the river" (as getting out to Cairo was called) before night should overtake us. But Mr. Bixby's partner, the other pilot, presently grounded the boat and we lost so much time getting her off that it was plain the darkness would overtake us a good long way above the mouth. This was a great misfortune, especially to certain of our visiting pilots, whose boats would have to wait for their return, no matter how long that might be. It sobered the pilot-house talk a good deal. Coming up-stream, pilots did not mind low water or any kind of darkness; nothing stopped them but fog. But down-stream work was different; a boat was too nearly helpless with a stiff current pushing behind her; so it was not customary to run down-stream at night in low water.

There seemed to be one small hope, however: if we could get through the intricate and dangerous Hat Island crossing before night, we could venture the rest; for we would have plainer sailing and better water. But it would be insanity to attempt Hat Island at night. So there was a good deal of looking at watches all the rest of the day and a constant ciphering upon the speed we were making; Hat Island was the eternal subject; sometimes hope was high and sometimes we were delayed in a bad crossing and down it went again. For hours all hands lay under the burden of this suppressed excitement; it was even communicated to me, and I got to feeling so solicitous about Hat Island, and under such an awful pressure of responsibility, that I wished I might have five minutes on shore to draw a good, full, relieving breath and start over again. We were standing no regular watches. Each of our pilots ran such portions of the river as he had run when coming upstream, because of his greater familiarity with it; but both remained in the pilot-house constantly.

An hour before sunset Mr. Bixby took the wheel and Mr. W. stepped aside. For the next thirty minutes every man held his watch in his hand and was restless, silent, and uneasy. At last somebody said, with a doomful sigh:

"Well, yonder's Hat Island—and we can't make it."

All the watches closed with a snap, everybody sighed and muttered something about its being "too bad, too bad—ah, if we could *only* have got here half an hour sooner!" and the place was thick with the atmosphere of disappointment. Some started to go out but loitered, hearing no bell-tap to land. The sun dipped behind the horizon, the boat went on. Inquiring looks passed from one guest to another, and one who had his hand on the door-knob and had turned it, waited, then presently took away his hand and let the knob turn back again. We bore steadily down the bend. More looks were exchanged and nods of surprised admiration—but no words. Insensibly the men drew together behind Mr. Bixby, as the sky darkened and one or two dim stars came out. The dead silence and sense of waiting became oppressive. Mr. Bixby pulled the cord and two deep, mellow notes from the big bell floated off on the night. Then a pause, and one more note was struck. The watchman's voice followed, from the hurricane-deck:

"Labboard lead, there! Stabboard lead!"

The cries of the leadsmen began to rise out of the distance and were gruffly repeated by the word-passers on the hurricane-deck.

"M-a-r-k three! M-a-r-k three! Quarter-less-three! Half twain! Quarter twain! M-a-r-k twain! Quarter less—"

Mr. Bixby pulled two bell-ropes, and was answered by faint jinglings far below in the engine-room, and our speed slackened. The steam began to whistle through the gauge-cocks. The cries of the leadsmen went on—and it is a weird sound, always, in the night. Every pilot in the lot was watching now, with fixed eyes, and talking under his breath. Nobody was calm and easy but Mr. Bixby. He would put his wheel down and stand on a spoke, and as the steamer swung into her (to me) utterly invisible marks—for we seemed to be in the midst of a wide and gloomy sea—he would meet and fasten her there. Out of the murmur of half-audible talk one caught a coherent sentence now and then—such as:

"There; she's over the first reef all right!"

After a pause, another subdued voice:

"Her stern's coming down just *exactly* right, by *George!* Now she's in the marks; over she goes!"

Somebody else muttered:

"Oh, it was done beautiful—*beautiful!*"

Now the engines were stopped altogether and we drifted with the current. Not that I could see the boat drift, for I could not, the stars being all gone by this time. This drifting was the dismalest work; it held one's heart still. Presently I discovered a blacker gloom than that which surrounded us. It was the head of the island. We were closing right down upon it. We entered its deeper shadow, and so imminent seemed the peril that I was likely to suffocate; and I had the strongest impulse to do *something,* anything, to save the vessel. But still Mr. Bixby stood by his wheel, silent, intent as a cat, and all the pilots stood shoulder to shoulder at his back.

"She'll not make it!" somebody whispered.

The water grew shoaler and shoaler by the leadsman's cries, till it was down to:

"Eight-and-a-half! E-i-g-h-t feet! E-i-g-h-t feet! Seven-and—"

Mr. Bixby said warningly through his speaking-tube to the engineer:

"Stand by, now!"

"Ay, ay, sir!"

"Seven-and-a-half! Seven feet! *Six*-and—"

We touched bottom! Instantly Mr. Bixby set a lot of bells ringing, shouted through the tube, "*Now*, let her have it—every ounce you've got!" then to his partner, "Put her hard down! Snatch her! Snatch her!" The boat rasped and ground her way through the sand, hung upon the apex of disaster a single tremendous instant, and then over she went! And such a shout as went up at Mr. Bixby's back never loosened the roof of a pilot-house before!

There was no more trouble after that. Mr. Bixby was a hero that night; and it was some little time, too, before his exploit ceased to be talked about by river-men.

Fully to realize the marvelous precision required in laying the great steamer in her marks in that murky waste of water, one should know that not only must she pick her intricate way through snags and blind reefs, and then shave the head of the island so closely as to brush the overhanging foliage with her stern, but at one place she must pass almost within arm's reach of a sunken and invisible wreck that would snatch the hull timbers from under her if she should strike it—and destroy a quarter of a million dollars' worth of steamboat and cargo in five minutes, and maybe a hundred and fifty human lives into the bargain.

The last remark I heard that night was a compliment to Mr. Bixby, uttered in soliloquy and with unction by one of our guests. He said:

"By the Shadow of Death, but he's a lightning pilot!"

A Fourteen-Year-Old Boy Rides
for the Pony Express

(from Gladys Shaw Erskine, *Broncho Charlie—*
A Saga of the Saddle)

B ETWEEN APRIL 1860 *and November 1861, the Pony Express*
carried letters from St. Joseph on the Missouri to San Francisco.
Using 190 relay stations spaced twenty-five to thirty-seven miles
apart, it passed through Kansas, by Fort Kearny, Nebraska, along the
Platte, to Fort Laramie, Wyoming, past the Buttes, over the mountains,
then Fort Bridger, Wyoming, Salt Lake City, Carson City, Nevada, Pla-
cerville, California, Sacramento, and finally San Francisco.

Only the fleetest and hardiest Indian-bred and army-hardened ponies
were used. The rider kept his pony on the full run—nineteen miles an
hour—switching horses at "swing" stations. When he reached a "home"
station—whatever the hour of day or night—another messenger, already
mounted and waiting, took the little mail pouch, struck spurs into his
steed, and with a whoop and holler was off like the wind. Away they
sped, rider and horse rising over grassy slopes, up to the snow, and down to
the sand. Two thousand miles in eight days!

Nature threw blizzards, dust storms, and floods in the path of the

*Pony Express rider. Indians attacked and killed the keepers of the out-
posts. In May 1860, Paiute warriors razed seven relay stations, killed sixteen employees, and drove off 150 horses. The Indians frequently harassed
the riders. "Pony Bob" Haslam finished his 120-mile run with an arm
riddled with bullets and a jawbone shattered by an arrow.*

*The average rider was twenty years old and weighed 125 pounds. He
was selected competitively for his strength, stamina, and sense of responsibility. Each man signed a pledge of loyalty to the company, promising sobriety, clean speech, and gentlemanly conduct "so help me, God." He was
then given a Bible.*

*Billy Tate carried the Pony Express mail between Camp Ruby and
Carson City, Nevada, armed only with a knife, a revolver, and an extra
cylinder of bullets. He must have been a natural rider, a crack shot, and
mature in his judgment to be hired at age fourteen. In this passage from*
Broncho Charlie—A Saga of the Saddle *by Gladys Shaw Erskine, a
friend and fellow Pony Express rider recounts Billy's last ride.*

* * *

BILLY WAS RIDIN' IN with the mail from Camp Ruby to Carson
City . . . that's a tough route. It's through valleys, and dry plains,
and then, all of a sudden, you're into the tablelands and the mountains,
and lots of places where there was rim rock, where your pony couldn't
get a foothold.

Well, Billy was comin' along there at a right good pace, sort of hum-
min' to himself, quiet-like, under his breath. Suddenly, an arrow
whizzed past his ear, and then another. Billy took one look and saw that
he was in for it sure. There was about thirteen Indians after him, on the
run . . . all yellin' like Billy-be-damned. Billy thought quick. He knew
that if he kept on the regular route they'd get him sure . . . for that was
across an open valley. So he turned his horse and headed up into the
tablelands and the rim rock . . . he thought he could slip in and out of
the gullies up there, and get away from the Indians.

Well, up he went, his horse's feet clatterin' and slippin' and the Indians after him and the arrows a-hissin'. Then his horse stumbled, and
Billy saw that he was wounded in the shoulder . . . then another arrow

struck the gallant pony in the flank . . . and on they went. They came to the gully, where Billy had thought he could get through . . . and his heart must have just about stood still, when he saw that it was a dead end gully . . . that it was a trap . . . and there he was, with his horse, the Pony Express pouch, his Bible, and his six shooter. So Billy, cool as you please, slid off his horse, and made a stand there . . . and shot it out with the Indians . . . Bannocks and Utes they was. And, by gad, he got seven of 'em before they got him. But the odds was too great . . . and they killed Billy Tate there, in the rim rock caves, defendin' the mail he carried. Fourteen-year-old Billy Tate, with his yellow hair soft as a child's, and his laughing blue eyes in a round childish face . . . but he died the death of a brave man.

And here's a queer thing. The Indians never touched his body. They didn't scalp him, and they left the horse, and even the pouch of the Pony Express with him there. Later, agents from the station traced where his horse had turned off the trail, with all the others in chase, and they guessed what had happened. Then they saw the blood on the trail, and then they came to the tablelands and the gully with only one opening . . . and there they found Billy, still clutchin' his gun, and his Bible beside him . . . and in the pass, seven dead Indians.

Some time later a Bannock told me all about it. He said: "Me no fight in tablelands. Me hear. Braves no could touch scalp of boy with hair like sun, and eyes like water. He brave. He go happy hunting ground with his horse. He be big brave there."

THE CIVIL WAR

⋆ 24 ⋆

The Escape of a
Female Slave

(from Harriet Jacobs,
Incidents in the Life of a Slave Girl, 1861)

THE FIRST SHIPLOAD OF *slaves landed in Virginia in 1619. Within two hundred years there were two million slaves in the South, accounting for one third of the population. Thomas Jefferson wrote about slavery, the institution in which he was himself complicit: "I tremble for my country, when I reflect that God is just; that his justice cannot sleep forever." By the middle of the nineteenth century, the expanding nation had set upon itself over the issue, particularly concerning the expansion of slavery into new states and territories. Perhaps the most famous arguments about slavery and the nation were made in the Lincoln-Douglas debates of 1859. Abraham Lincoln argued, "A house divided against itself cannot stand. I believe this government cannot endure, permanently half slave and half free. I do not expect the Union to be dissolved—I do not expect the house to fall—but I do expect it will cease to be divided. It will become all one thing, or all the other." Indeed the nation did divide over this conflict, and the Civil War proved to be the country's bloodiest conflict.*

From Incidents in the Life of a Slave Girl, *the following is a moving autobiographical narrative of Harriet Ann Jacobs's flight from slavery in an "undisclosed slave state" to freedom in Philadelphia. The book was published in 1861, several months before the outbreak of the Civil War, with Jacobs (1813–1897) using the nom de plume Linda Brent; in fact, she gave all the participants in her story false names to shield them.*

Linda (Jacobs) is a seventeen-year-old slave owned by Dr. Fisher (Dr. James Norcom), who lusts after her, telling her that she "was made for his use, made to obey his command in everything; that [she] was nothing but a slave, whose will must and should surrender to his." To block Fisher's advances, rather than succumb to him, she takes on a white lover, Mr. Sands (Samuel Tredway Sawyer), by whom she has two children—Ellen and Benny. Linda eventually escapes Dr. Fisher's continuing advances by hiding in a garret at her grandmother's cottage—a precarious position, for if discovered, she would be arrested and returned to her owner for punishment. In her own words, here is the story of her flight to a more secure freedom in Philadelphia.

* * *

I HARDLY EXPECT that the reader will credit me, when I affirm that I lived in that little dismal hole, almost deprived of light and air, and with no space to move my limbs, for nearly seven years. But it is a fact; and to me a sad one, even now; for my body still suffers from the effects of that long imprisonment, to say nothing of my soul.

Countless were the nights that I sat late at the little loophole scarcely large enough to give me a glimpse of one twinkling star. There, I heard the patrols and slave-hunters conferring together about the capture of runaways, well knowing how rejoiced they would be to catch me.

Season after season, year after year, I peeped at my children's faces, and heard their sweet voices, with a heart yearning all the while to say, "Your mother is here." At times, I was stupefied and listless; at other times I became very impatient to know when these dark years would end, and I should again be allowed to feel the sunshine, and breathe the pure air. Moreover, I was likely to be drowned out of my den, if I remained much longer; for the slight roof was getting badly out of repair, and uncle Phillip was afraid to remove the shingles, lest some one should get a glimpse of me. When storms occurred in the night, they spread mats and bits of carpet, which in the morning appeared to have been laid out to dry; but to cover the roof in the daytime might have attracted attention. Consequently, my clothes and bedding were often drenched.

I revolved various plans of escape in my mind, which I sometimes imparted to my grandmother, when she came to whisper with me at the trap-door. But whenever I alluded to the subject, she would groan out, "O, don't think of it, child. You'll break my heart," but my brother William and my children were continually beckoning me to the north.

And now I must go back a few months in my story. I have stated that the first of January was the time for selling slaves, or leasing them out to new masters. On the New Year's day preceding, one of my friends, named Fanny, was to be sold at auction, to pay her master's debts. My thoughts were with her during all the day, and at night I anxiously inquired what had been her fate. I was told that she had been sold to one master, and her four little girls to another master, far distant; that she had escaped from her purchaser, and was not to be found. Her mother was the old Aggie who lived in a small tenement belonging to my grandmother, and built on the same lot with her own house. Her dwelling was searched and watched, and that brought the patrols so near me. The hunters were somehow eluded, and not long afterwards, my son Benny accidentally caught sight of Fanny in her mother's hut. He told his grandmother, who charged him never to speak of it, explaining to him the frightful consequences; and he never betrayed the trust. My friend Fanny and I remained many weeks hidden within call of each other; but she was unconscious of the fact.

I had lived too long in bodily pain and anguish of spirit. Always I was in dread that by some accident, or some contrivance, slavery would succeed in snatching my children from me. This thought drove me nearly frantic, and I determined to steer for the North Star at all hazards. At this crisis, Providence opened an unexpected way for me to escape. My friend Peter came one evening, and asked to speak with me. "Your day has come, Linda," said he. "I have found a chance for you to

go to the Free States by sailing ship. You have a fortnight to decide."
The news seemed too good to be true; but Peter explained his arrangements, and told me all that was necessary was for me to say I would go.
I was going to answer him with a joyful yes, when the thought of Benny
came to my mind. I told him the temptation was exceedingly strong,
but I was terribly afraid of Dr. Flint's alleged power over my child, and
that I could not go and leave him behind. Peter remonstrated earnestly.
He said such a good chance might never occur again; that Benny was
free, and could be sent to me; and that for the sake of my children's wel-
fare I ought not to hesitate a moment.

   The anticipation of being a free woman proved almost too much for
my weak frame. The excitement stimulated me, and at the same time
bewildered me. I made busy preparations for my journey, and for my
son to follow me. I resolved to have an interview with him before I
went, that I might give him cautions and advice, and tell him how anxiously I should be waiting for him at the north. Grandmother stole up
to me as often as possible to whisper words of counsel. She insisted
upon my writing to Dr. Flint, as soon as I arrived in the Free States, and
asking him to sell me to her. She said she would sacrifice her house, and
all she had in the world, for the sake of having me safe with my children
in any part of the world. If she could only live to know *that* she could
die in peace. I promised the dear old faithful friend that I would write to
her as soon as I arrived, and put the letter in a safe way to reach her; but
in my own mind I resolved that not another cent of her hard earnings
should be spent to pay rapacious slaveholders for what they called their
property. And even if I had not been unwilling to buy what I had already a right to possess, common humanity would have prevented me
from accepting the generous offer, at the expense of turning my aged
relative out of house and home, when she was trembling on the brink
of the grave.

   I was to escape in a vessel; but I forbear to mention any further particulars. I was in readiness, but the vessel was unexpectedly detained
several days. Meantime, news came to town of a most horrible murder
committed on a fugitive slave named James. Charity, the mother of this
unfortunate young man, had been an old acquaintance of ours. I have
told the shocking particulars of his death, in my description of some

of the neighboring slaveholders. My grandmother, always nervously sensitive about runaways, was terribly frightened. She felt sure that a similar fate awaited me, if I did not desist from my enterprise. She sobbed, and groaned, and entreated me not to go. Her excessive fear was somewhat contagious, and my heart was not proof against her extreme agony. I was grievously disappointed, but I promised to relinquish my project.

When my friend Peter was apprised of this, he was both disappointed and vexed. He said, that judging from our past experience, it would be a long time before I had another such chance to throw away. I told him it need not be thrown away; that I had a friend concealed near by, who would be glad enough to take the place that had been provided for me. I told him about poor Fanny, and the kind-hearted, noble fellow, who never turned his back upon any body in distress, white or black, expressed his readiness to help her. Arrangements were made for Fanny to go on board the vessel the next night. They both supposed that I had long been at the north, therefore my name was not mentioned in the transaction. Fanny was carried on board at the appointed time, and stowed away in a very small cabin. This accommodation had been purchased at a price that would pay for a voyage to England. But when one proposes to go to fine old England, they stop to calculate whether they can afford the cost of the pleasure; while in making a bargain to escape from slavery, the trembling victim is ready to say, "Take all I have, only don't betray me!"

The next morning I peeped through my loophole, and saw that it was dark and cloudy. At night I received news that the wind was ahead, and the vessel had not sailed. I was exceedingly anxious about Fanny, and Peter too, who was running a tremendous risk at my instigation. Next day the wind and weather remained the same. Poor Fanny had been half dead with fright when they carried her on board, and I could readily imagine how she must be suffering now. Grandmother came often to my den, to say how thankful she was I did not go. On the third morning she rapped for me to come down to the storeroom. The poor old sufferer was breaking down under her weight of trouble. She was easily flurried now. I found her in a nervous, excited state, but I was not aware that she had forgotten to lock the door behind her, as usual. She was exceedingly worried about the detention of the vessel. She was afraid all would be discovered, and then Fanny, and Peter, and I, would all be tortured to death; and Phillip would be utterly ruined, and her house would be torn down. Poor Peter! If he should die such a horrible death as the poor slave James had lately done, and all for his kindness in trying to help me, how dreadful it would be for us all!

As she stood there, trembling and sobbing, a voice from the piazza called out, "Whar is you, Aunt Marthy?" Grandmother was startled, and in her agitation opened the door, without thinking of me. In stepped Jenny, "I's bin huntin ebery whar for you, Aunt Marthy," said she. "My missis wants you to send her some crackers." I had slunk down behind a barrel, which entirely screened me, but I imagined that Jenny was looking directly at the spot, and my heart beat violently. My grandmother immediately thought what she had done, and went out quickly with Jenny to count the crackers, locking the door after her. She returned to me, in a few minutes, the perfect picture of despair. "Poor child!" she exclaimed, "my carelessness has ruined you. The boat ain't gone yet. Get ready immediately, and go with Fanny. I ain't got another word to say against it now; for there's no telling what may happen this day."

Uncle Phillip was sent for, and he agreed with his mother in thinking that Jenny would inform Dr. Flint in less than twenty-four hours. He advised getting me on board the boat, if possible; if not, I had better keep very still in my den, where they could not find me without tearing the house down. He said it would not do for him to move in the matter, because suspicion would be immediately excited; but he promised to communicate with Peter. I felt reluctant to apply to him again, having implicated him too much already; but there seemed to be no alternative. Vexed as Peter had been by my indecision, he was true to his generous nature, and said at once that he would do his best to help me, trusting I should show myself a stronger woman this time.

He immediately proceeded to the wharf, and found that the wind had shifted, and the vessel was slowly beating down stream. On some pretext of urgent necessity, he offered two boatmen a dollar apiece to catch up with her. He was of lighter complexion than the boatman he hired, and when the captain saw them coming so rapidly, he thought officers were pursuing his vessel in search of the runaway slave he had on board. They hoisted sails, but the boat gained upon them, and the indefatigable Peter sprang on board.

The captain at once recognized him. Peter asked him to go below, to speak about a bad bill he had given him. When he told his errand, the captain replied, "Why, the woman's here already; and I've put her where you or the devil would have a tough job to find her."

"But it is another woman I want to bring," said Peter. "*She* is in great distress, too, and you shall be paid any thing within reason, if you'll stop and take her."

"What's her name?" inquired the captain.

"Linda," he replied.

"That's the name of the woman already here," rejoined the captain. "By George! I believe you mean to betray me."

"O!" exclaimed Peter, "God knows I wouldn't harm a hair of your head. I am too grateful to you. But there really *is* another woman in great danger. Do have the humanity to stop and take her!"

After a while they came to an understanding. Fanny, not dreaming I was any where about in that region, had assumed my name, though she called herself Johnson. "Linda is a common name," said Peter, "and the woman I want to bring is Linda Brent."

The captain agreed to wait at a certain place till evening, being handsomely paid for his detention.

Of course, the day was an anxious one for us all. But we concluded that if Jenny had seen me, she would be too wise to let her mistress know of it; and that she probably would not get a chance to see Dr. Flint's family till evening, for I knew very well what were the rules in that household. I afterwards believed that she did not see me; for nothing ever came of it, and she was one of those base characters that would have jumped to betray a suffering fellow being for the sake of thirty pieces of silver.

I made all my arrangements to go on board as soon as it was dusk. The intervening time I resolved to spend with my son. I had not spoken to him for seven years, though I had been under the same roof, and seen him every day, when I was well enough to sit at the loophole. I did not dare to venture beyond the storeroom; so they brought him there, and locked us up together, in a place concealed from the piazza door. It was an agitating interview for both of us. After we had talked and wept together for a little while, he said, "Mother, I'm glad you're going away. I wish I could go with you. I knew you was here; and I have been so afraid they would come and catch you!"

I was greatly surprised, and asked him how he had found it out.

He replied, "I was standing under the eaves, one day, before Ellen went away, and I heard somebody cough up over the wood shed. I don't know what made me think it was you, but I did think so. I missed Ellen, the night before she went away; and grandmother brought her back into the room in the night; and I thought maybe she'd been to see *you*, before she went, for I heard grandmother whisper to her, 'Now go to sleep; and remember never to tell.' "

I asked him if he ever mentioned his suspicions to his sister. He said he never did; but after he heard the cough, if he saw her playing with other children on that side of the house, he always tried to coax her round to the other side, for fear they would hear me cough, too. He said he had kept a close lookout for Dr. Flint, and if he saw him speak to a constable, or a patrol, he always told grandmother. I now recollected that I had seen him manifest uneasiness, when people were on that side of the house, and I had at the time been puzzled to conjecture a motive for his actions. Such prudence may seem extraordinary in a boy of twelve years, but slaves, being surrounded by mysteries, deceptions, and dangers, early learn to be suspicious and watchful, and prematurely cautious and cunning. He had never asked a question of grandmother, or Uncle Phillip, and I had often heard him chime in with other children, when they spoke of my being at the north.

I told him I was now really going to the Free States, and if he was a good, honest boy, and a loving child to his dear old grandmother, the Lord would bless him, and bring him to me, and we and Ellen would live together. He began to tell me that grandmother had not eaten any thing all day. While he was speaking, the door was unlocked, and she came in with a small bag of money, which she wanted me to take. I begged her to keep a part of it, at least, to pay for Benny's being sent to the north; but she insisted, while her tears were falling fast, that I should take the whole. "You may be sick among strangers," she said, "and they would send you to the poorhouse to die." Ah, that good grandmother!

For the last time I went up to my nook. Its desolate appearance no longer chilled me, for the light of hope had risen in my soul. Yet, even with the blessed prospect of freedom before me, I felt very sad at leaving forever that old homestead, where I had been sheltered so long by the dear old grandmother; where I had dreamed my first young dream of love; and where, after that had faded away, my children came to twine themselves so closely round my desolate heart. As the hour approached for me to leave, I again descended to the storeroom. My grandmother and Benny were there. She took me by the hand, and said, "Linda, let us pray." We knelt down together, with my child pressed to my heart, and my other arm around the faithful, loving old friend I was about to leave forever. On no other occasion has it been my lot to listen to so fervent a supplication for mercy and protection. It thrilled through my heart, and inspired me with trust in God.

Peter was waiting for me in the street. I was soon by his side, faint in body, but strong in purpose. I did not look back upon the old place, though I felt I should never see it again.

I never could tell how we reached the wharf. My brain was all of a whirl, and my limbs tottered under me. At an appointed place we met my uncle Phillip, who had started before us on a different route, that he might reach the wharf first, and give us timely warning if there was any danger. A rowboat was in readiness. As I was about to step in, I felt something pull me gently, and turning round I saw my son Benny, looking pale and anxious. He whispered in my ear, "I've been peeping into the doctor's window, and he's at home. Goodbye, Mother. Don't cry; I'll come." He hastened away. I clasped the hand of my good uncle, to whom I owed so much, and of Peter, the brave, generous friend who had volunteered to run such terrible risks to secure my safety. To this day I remember how his bright face beamed with joy, when he told me he had discovered a safe method for me to escape. Yet that intelligent, enterprising, noble-hearted man was a chattel! liable, by the laws of a country that calls itself civilized, to be sold with horses and pigs! We parted in silence. Our hearts were all too full for words!

Swiftly the boat glided over the water.

When I entered the vessel the captain came forward to meet me. He was an elderly man, with a pleasant countenance. He showed me to a little box of a cabin, where sat my friend Fanny. She started as if she had seen a spectre. She gazed on me in utter astonishment, and exclaimed, "Linda, can this be *you*? or is it your ghost?" When we were locked in each other's arms, my overwrought feelings could no longer be restrained. My sobs reached the ears of the captain, who came and very kindly reminded us, that for his safety, as well as our own, it would be prudent for us not to attract any attention. He said that when there was a sail in sight he wished us to keep below; but at other times, he had no objection to our being on deck. He assured us that he would keep a good lookout, and if we acted prudently, he thought we should be in no danger. He had represented us as women going to meet our husbands in [the North]. We thanked him, and promised to observe carefully all the directions he gave us.

Fanny and I now talked by ourselves, low and quietly, in our little cabin. She told me of the sufferings she had gone through in making her escape, and of her terrors while she was concealed in her mother's house. Above all, she dwelt on the agony of separation from all her children on that dreadful auction day. She could scarcely credit me, when I told her of the place where I had passed nearly seven years. "We have the same sorrows," said I. "No," replied she, "you are going to see your children soon, and there is no hope that I shall ever even hear from mine."

The vessel was soon under way, but we made slow progress. . . . Ten days after we left land we were approaching Philadelphia. The captain said we should arrive there in the night, but he thought we had better wait till morning, and go on shore in broad daylight, as the best way to avoid suspicion.

I replied, "You know best. But will you stay on board and protect us?"

He saw that I was suspicious, and he said he was sorry, now that he had brought us to the end of our voyage, to find I had so little confidence in him. Ah, if he had ever been a slave, he would have known how difficult it was to trust a white man. He assured us that we might sleep through the night without fear; that he would take care we were not left unprotected. Be it said to the honor of this captain, Southerner as he was, that if Fanny and I had been white ladies, and our passage lawfully engaged, he could not have treated us more respectfully. My intelligent friend, Peter, had rightly estimated the character of the man to whose honor he had entrusted us.

The next morning I was on deck as soon as the day dawned. I called Fanny to see the sun rise, for the first time in our lives, on free soil; for such I *then* believed it to be. We watched the reddening sky, and saw the great orb come up slowly out of the water, as it seemed. Soon the waves began to sparkle, and every thing caught the beautiful glow. Before us lay the city of strangers. We looked at each other, and the eyes of both were moistened with tears. We had escaped from slavery, and we supposed ourselves to be safe from the hunters. But we were alone in the world, and we had left dear ties behind us; ties cruelly sundered by the demon Slavery.

Quick-Witted Mrs. Fisher
Saves Her Husband
from Quantrill's Raiders

(from Reverend H. D. Fisher,
*The Gun and the Gospel: Early Kansas
and Chaplain Fisher,* 1899)

T HE STATE OF KANSAS *was once known as "Bleeding Kansas,"
for it was the battleground—both literal and political—upon
which pro-slavery and abolitionist forces fought. Front and center
in this conflict was the town of Lawrence, populated largely by abolitionists. In 1856 the town was raided and shot up by pro-slavery men on horseback. John Brown came to Lawrence to avenge this raid; indeed his four
sons killed five pro-slavery men in nearby Pottawatomie.*

*In the summer of 1857, twenty-year-old William C. Quantrill quietly
slid into town. He joined the pro-slavery activists and was soon riding
guard escorting captured fugitive slaves back to the South. Gradually
Quantrill came to know the names and addresses of every anti-slavery
activist in town. Within a few years he was pressured to leave town on
suspicion of horse stealing. He left with a chip on his shoulder and hate
in his heart for the abolitionists of Lawrence. In Missouri in 1862, at
the beginning of the Civil War, he assembled and led a group of guerrillas*

who captured the town of Independence. The Confederates commissioned him a captain; in turn the Union Army declared him an outlaw.

Lawrence buzzed with rumors that Quantrill would attack the town during the full moon in early August, 1863. With a small military garrison and armed citizens, the town was ready for him. They would "welcome [him] with bloody hands and hospitable graves." But when the full moon came and went with no sign of Quantrill, the town let down its guard. At dawn on August 21, 1863, well after the full moon, Quantrill and four hundred armed men appeared on horseback and conducted the most brutal, vindictive, ferocious civilian massacre of the Civil War. Name by name, house by house, address by address, the horsemen called forth the marked men from their sleep and shot them, then set fire to their homes. An estimated 200 men and boys were killed, although only 188 could be identified. One hundred eighty-five homes and business buildings were torched, at a loss of two million Civil War–era dollars.

Quantrill spared the women and children—and it was the women who became the heroines of that dawn. Wives tried to stomp out the flames, or pulled furniture and precious possessions from their burning homes. Some women flung their bodies across their wounded, prostrate husbands to protect them from further harm. Still Quantrill's raiders would manage to shoot the men dead. The raid left 85 women widows and 250 children fatherless.

In this selection from his memoir, Gun and the Gospel: Early Kansas and Chaplain Fisher, *the Reverend Fisher, a resident of Lawrence during the raid, tells the story of how his quick-thinking wife saved his life.*

★　★　★

IF I COULD but remove self from the recital of this occurrence, I would freely proclaim that of all the individual incidents of the war none is more deserving of record, none more pregnant with heroism, none more truly illustrative of the bravery of the gentler sex when called upon to face the most exacting trials of life. This is the story of a heroine—my wife—who had faith in herself, faith in her god, and devotion to her husband and family.

I had been ill and was wakeful through the night. About four o'clock in the morning I was awakened by the sound of horses' hoofs directly in front of my dwelling on the northwest corner of the public park in the southern part of the town. Arising hastily I partly dressed and went to the door opening to the east on our upper piazza and saw three horsemen riding rapidly out of town to the south. I felt that some calamity was impending and said to my wife that I was afraid something terrible was going to happen. She replied that I was ill and nervous, that there had been a railroad meeting the night before and that some of the countrymen who had been in attendance were doubtless going out early to their work on their farms. Thus assured I felt easier and lay down again, though troubled in mind and still fearful that the presence of those horsemen and their rapid ride to the southward boded no good. It was so near getting-up time that I did not fully undress but lay on the side of the bed with trousers on.

A half hour later my wife decided to get up, remarking that she had planned to take the older boys and go wild grape gathering that day, and that she believed she would get breakfast and start early that a full day might be put in the woods. She arose, commenced dressing and called the children that it was time to get up. Dawn was just streaking the eastern horizon, and she went to the front windows to raise the curtain to let in the light. As she looked out southeastwardly she was attracted by a body of troops entering the outskirts of the town. She looked attentively for a minute and turning quickly, exclaimed, "Pa, get up!" There is a company of soldiers coming into town. I believe it is Quantrill and his men!"

I bounded to the door just in time to see them shoot down Rev. Mr. Snyder as he sat milking his cow in front of his house, and was confirmed in my wife's fears that Quantrill was upon us. As I watched the raiders for a minute they began to break into squads and fly to different parts of the town, shooting right and left as a man would appear in sight, and calling men to their front doors in their night dresses to kill them at sight.

I did not stop to dress further, except to throw on a shirt and put on my shoes, and thus arrayed I ran downstairs, out of the house to the stable and turned loose on the common back of our lot a blooded horse and a pony we had in the barn, thinking them less likely to be stolen if loose upon the prairie than if tied in the stable.

By this time my boys, William and Edmund, aged respectively twelve and ten years, were dressed, as was also our son Joseph, aged seven. My wife had Frank, six months old, in her arms and Josie by her side, and begged earnestly that with the older boys I should take to Mount Oread lying a quarter of a mile to the West and try to get the bushes beyond it. So we started up the prairie to the foot of the hills, running together, my wife remaining behind with the younger children.

As I ran I felt all the time that I was going away from the only place of safety. I was weak from my illness and knew that I could not run far nor fast. Furthermore, upon glancing up the hill I could see pickets stationed every hundred yards or so, so that it would be impossible for me to get through their line alive. The boys were smaller and could dart through the hazel and sumac bushes skirting the hill, and they ran on while I decided to go back to the house.

Willie fell in with a school fellow named Robbie Martin, an older and larger boy, and they ran together. Robbie's mother had made him a suit of clothing out of his father's old soldier clothes, and as the boys ran together near one of the pickets he was attracted by the uniform and gave them chase, killing young Martin right by my boy's side, his brains and blood spattering in Willie's face, frightening him almost to death and so terrorizing him that he has never fully recovered his nervous vigor.

Edmund got separated from his brother in their flight and caught up with Freddie Leonard, a boy a year or more older than he, the two running together. They succeeded in evading the pickets, though shot at from a distance a number of times, and sought refuge in the town cemetery two and a half miles out. After their first terror had somewhat subsided they became frightened at being in a graveyard and sought a place of hiding in a patch of cotton being grown by an enterprising German farmer a little way from the cemetery. From this they could see the smoke from the burning town and hear the firing, and so terrorized were they that it was well on toward the middle of the afternoon before they dared venture to get a sip of water or to return toward the town.

After leaving my boys, as they ran I made my way back into my yard through a rear gate and down the garden walk into the kitchen and on into the cellar. Our house was a two-story brick, with a one-story stone kitchen built on later. The entrance to the cellar was through the kitchen; consequently I was able to enter it without going through the main part of the house. My wife heard me, however, and asked if it was I who had gone down stairs. I replied in the affirmative, whereupon she expressed her fear that I had done wrong, telling me that the guerrillas were killing everybody they could find to shoot at and that she was afraid they would find and kill me too. I told her of the pickets on the hill and of how weak I found I was as I tried to run, and that under the circumstances there was nothing to do but to come back and take my chances.

"Well, trust in the Lord and pray that he may save you. I will pray also, and do all I can for you," she replied, as she left the cellar way and went to the front part of the house to look after Josie and the baby.

She had hardly got to the front part of the house when four of the murderous villains rode up to the front gate, dismounted and demanded admittance. I was lying just beneath the front hall, parallel with it and near the front door, and could hear every word they said.

Accosting my wife with oaths they inquired, "Is your husband about the house?"

"Do you think," she replied, "that he would be fool enough to stay about the house and you killing everybody you can? No, sir; he left with the little boys when you first came into town."

With an oath one of them contradicted her, and to her astonishment and mine replied, "I know a d——d sight better; he's in the cellar; where is it?"

"It is not very gentlemanly for you to doubt the word of a lady," she said, "and besides, I don't want you to swear in the presence of my children. The cellar is open; if you think he is there go look for yourselves."

The men walked right over where I was lying, through the dining room into the kitchen and to the cellar doorway. There was no other entrance for light and it looked very dark down the steps, so one of them turned to her and remarked, "It is too dark for us to go down there without a light; get us a candle."

"We don't burn candles," she replied.

"What do you burn for a light if you don't burn candles?"

"We burn oil—in a lamp," was her answer.

They demanded a lamp; and my wife, believing the only way to save me was to throw them off the track, freely gave it to them. As the man, after taking it from her, attempted to light it, he turned the wick down into the bowl and turned to her to ask her assistance. She looked at it and told him he had ruined it, that it would take half an hour at least to get it so it would burn.

This diverted them for the time, and they set about ransacking the house, appropriating unto themselves everything they could find of value and many articles that were new to them but which possessed no value. Finally one of them said to her, "Haven't you another lamp in this house?"

"Yes," she replied, "but it is up stairs."

She was ordered to go and get it, but protested that she could not carry the baby and suggested that one of them must go and get the lamp or hold the baby while she went for it.

One of their number took Frank from her arms and walked the floor with him, cooing to him to keep him quiet while his mother went for the lamp, perhaps wondering the while whether the father whose life they were seeking had eyes like the baby's eyes and what would become of the child if they took his life.

I heard my wife come down the front stairs and knew that in her hand she held the lighted lamp with which they were to search for me, and was almost persuaded to save them the trouble, emerging from the cellar and surrendering myself into their hands. Just then, however, I heard the man to whom she handed the lamp say: "Come on, now, cock your revolvers and kill at sight."

This determined my action, and I gave up the thought of surrendering, knowing that it meant certain death. As I reached this conclusion they began to descend the stairway into the cellar and my life hung as by a thread.

The body of our house was twenty by thirty feet in dimension. The cellar was but eight by fourteen feet, occupying the middle part of the space beneath the house. It had been dug just deep enough and large enough to accommodate our immediate necessities, it having been our intention to complete it later. The dirt which had been excavated had been thrown up on the bank between the limits of the cellar and the foundation walls of the house, more on one side than the other. When I entered I crawled upon the bank on that side of the excavation and lay behind the bank of dirt thus carelessly thrown up. I lay flat upon my back, and as my face was deeper than wide I turned my head on the flat also and lay as close to the earth as I possibly could. My left foot shook so that I was compelled to place my right foot upon it to keep it still.

Just as I got as snugly in position as was possible, the scoundrels entered. There were three of them, one having remained behind to guard the house against approach. The ceiling was low, and as the man who held the lamp in one hand, a cocked revolver in the other, stepped to the floor, he was compelled to stoop to keep from striking his head against the joists. In stooping he brought the lighted lamp directly under his face, and the heat and glare caused him to hold it to one side, the side on which I was lying within a few feet of him. This threw the shadow of the bank of dirt over me and they did not see me. My wife had so completely thrown them off of their guard that their search was not thorough, else I would not be here to tell the story. I could see them plainly, could even have reached over and touched the leader on the shoulder. But they did not see me and I was saved.

"The shadow of the Almighty was over me," and under his wings He protected me. My heart stood still. I did not breathe. Every act of my life came before me like a panorama. I lived but did not live. I died but did not die. In God's goodness and mercy the hour of my departure had not yet come. I was naked and helpless before my own conscience and could see eternity as plainly as noonday. "This poor man cried and the Lord heard him and delivered him from all his enemies." Blessed be the name of the Lord; he saved me when salvation seemed impossible, when death was at hand, when deliverance had ceased to be hoped for!

During this fearful ordeal the agony of my wife's soul can readily be imagined. As the guerrillas took the lamp from her and went to the cellar doorway, she passed quickly to the front part of the house, pressed the baby to one ear and her hand to the other to deaden the noise of the fatal shots she now expected to hear and to drown my death groans. Her agony was intense. Her soul was tried to the uttermost. Her heart-strings were almost rended asunder; and especially since she had almost become convinced that her courageous assurance had not misled the villains and that in part upon her pure hands might rest my blood. If it was an awful moment for me, what must it not have been for her? As I calmly consider what she must have passed through during the minutes those murderous men were seeking my life, I am filled with admiration for her courage, her fortitude, her confidence in God. It is one of the grandest exhibitions of womanly devotion and hope of which there is record. Had she swerved in the least degree, had she allowed her emotions to overcome her, had she allowed her fears to be seen, all would have been lost. God never blessed man with a nobler wife than mine, nor one possessed of greater courage and resourcefulness in time of trouble. To God and His servant, my wife, I owe my life, my all.

Finding themselves baffled in their pursuit of the hated pioneer preacher whose life they had so often sought, one of the men said to the others with an oath, "The woman told the truth. The rascal has escaped," and they turned and left the cellar.

When they were gone I found that the suspense had been most awful and that it had left me as one dead. It was a physical effort to return to life, and it was a moment before I fully realized that whether in or out of the body, the Lord had marvelously saved me thus far.

When those cold-hearted villains went up into the dining room my wife's confidence and courage returned, and she took the lamp from one of them, extinguished the flame and said to him: "You will believe me, now, I hope. I told you my husband had gone an hour ago. You needn't suppose that any one is going to be fool enough to remain around and be shot down if he can get away."

He uttered a muttered oath, continued the search for valuables and ordered the house fired, as it was one that was doomed to go.

After the fire had been started up stairs they left one of their number to stand guard, the others riding off to further deviltry.

"Madam," said the one who remained, "if there is anything you wish to save I'll help you save it."

"Turn in and help me put out the fire," she replied, as she struggled to stamp and smother it out in various places.

"It would cost me my life to do that," he replied, "but I can help you save your stuff if you want me to."

"If you can't help me put out the fire," she said, "just get on your horse and ride off, telling them that it was burning when you left and I'll soon put it out myself."

"I will do so," he said, "but it will do you no good, for this is one of the marked houses and is bound to go."

He mounted his horse and rode off, cautioning my wife to save what she could as the house would surely be burned. She thinks he was the one to whom she handed the baby when she went for the lamp and that this confidence in him and the child's cooing had touched his heart.

My wife carried water up stairs and extinguished the flames, and having flooded the floors and beds thoroughly came again to the cellar door.

"Pa," said she, "those men who were hunting you set fire to the house in several places and left, but I have put the fire all out so you have no need of being afraid; I must go now and attend to Frank for he is crying for me. But I am afraid another party may come and find you yet and kill you, and I want to know, if they should, are you ready to die? That knowledge would be better to us than all besides."

I told her how I felt, and she said, "Continue to pray and trust in the Lord, and I'll do all I can to save you; I must go now."

She left me and it seemed like a long time until she returned. Lying on the ground, as I was, I could hear the horses' feet and the roar of the burning town, the noise of the falling houses, the shouts of the human demons and the screams of the dying. It seemed indeed as if pandemonium reigned and that a whirlwind of destruction was sweeping over the city. Imagine, if possible, my relief when I heard the voice of my wife as she came near, talking loudly to the children that I might know it was she.

They had scarcely reached the parlor when three other of the murderers came rushing into the hall inquiring, "Madam, are you a widow?"

"Not unless you men have found my husband outside and have killed him," said she. "He left the house with our little boys when you first came to town. There has been a party of your men here already and they hunted all through the house and in the cellar for him, but thank God, they did not find him."

"I am d——d glad of it," replied the impulsive leader.

They did not visit the cellar; my wife had so completely thrown them off the track. But when they saw the house had been fired by their comrades and that the fire had been extinguished, and having drank whisky freely before coming, they were very angry and swore that the house must be burned, "as it is one that was marked to be destroyed."

This second band broke the window shutters and chairs and bookcase into fuel, made kindling wood of the furniture, and fired the house more effectually than before. Then two of the number left. The other one, now drunk and murderous, remained with revolver in hand and swore he would kill my wife if she attempted to go up stairs and put out the fire. She slammed the door in his face and began drawing water out of the well, filling buckets, tubs and pans. When the fire had driven this fiend out of the hall and into the street she saw that fire from the main building had ignited the kitchen roof, and realizing that through the kitchen was my only way of escape, she climbed upon the cook stove and dished water on the under side of the board roof, then threw a table near outside, set a stand upon that, and putting pans and buckets of water on the roof climbed up and threw the water upon it, thus saving the kitchen.

But she saw another danger. The roof of the main building projected over the kitchen, and the burning cornice was about to fall. So she got down, filled her buckets and pans anew and again climbed to the roof and after dashing a pan of water over her dress to keep the fire from lighting her clothes, stood with the roaring fire in front of her until the flaming cornice fell at her feet. Then she dashed water on it where it was nailed together at the crest, and stamping it apart, tumbled it off the kitchen and threw the rest of the water on the roof.

Then came still a new danger. The small windows in the rear wall of the main building were on fire and might fall outward on the kitchen and yet set it on fire. So she called to Joseph, our seven-year-old boy, to give her a stick of cordwood, and with this she punched the windows into the burning building. She had saved her kitchen, and through it saved me!

The main building was built of brick, which had been saturated by the boys dipping them in tubs of water as the masons laid them in the walls, so the cementing together was perfect. Hence the walls stood when all the lumber was burned out. I was lying on the bank of earth just under the door that led to the kitchen, when the whole upper story of the house fell to the floor immediately over me.

My wife then began pouring water through the kitchen door on the floor beyond, but the heat and flames became so intense that she had to draw the door shut to prevent them from setting fire to the kitchen. The lower floor burned through, fell into the cellar and burned to within a yard or so of where I was lying. I expected to be cremated alive, when suddenly I saw a little stream of water trickling through a knothole in the floor. I then realized what an unconquerable fight my wife was making for my life. Soon a Mrs. Shugro, a neighbor, came to where she was working, close to where I lay, and said to her, "Mrs. Fisher, what are you trying to save that piece of floor for? It won't be worth anything."

"I don't care, I am going to save it if I can for a memento. Bring me more water." Then addressing the woman in a lower tone she said to her, "Mrs. Shugro, I have a secret to tell you. By the Virgin Mary and all the Saints"—she was a Catholic—"will you keep it?"

"I will."

"Mr. Fisher is under that floor."

The woman raised her hands and was about to scream when my wife said to her, "Don't speak a word, for they are all around here watching for him."

"What are you going to do to save him?"

"I'll have him come up the cellar-way and crawl under that piece of carpet, and we will hide him in the garden under yonder little bush, covering it with the carpet."

Then she came down into the cellar and said to me, "You must come out of there or burn alive; I can't keep the fire back any longer. I am afraid they will find you outside and kill you, after all; but stand here till I look outside, and when you come up to the level of the floor, crouch down as low as possible, crawl under the carpet and follow me out into the garden to the little bush overgrown with morning-glory vines, lay flat on the ground under the bush, and I'll throw the carpet over it and you."

She looked out and finding the coast clear told me to follow her. As I came up the stairs she dropped a dress over my head and shoulders. I gathered it about my body, crouched close to the floor, crawled along as close to her and the ground as I could, part of the time tramping on the carpet she was dragging from her shoulders, and followed her to the bush. Here I lay flat upon the ground and wormed myself under the little bush while my wife and Mrs. Shugro threw the carpet over it. When this was done and the women turned away there were four guerrillas by the fence, not eighty feet away, with guns in their hands, standing looking at the women.

"Mrs. Shugro," called my wife, loudly, "let's throw those chairs and things on top of this carpet. What's the use of saving anything from that old burning house and then have them burn up outside?"

We have three of those chairs yet as heirlooms.

They piled the chairs and everything of the kind on the carpet, while the bush kept them from exposing me. I was almost famished for a drink, and at one time as my wife came near I whispered to her that I wanted a drink of water.

Josie, who was close by, heard me and said to his mother, "Pa is here somewhere; I heard him speak."

His mother replied, "Why Josie, your papa went away with the boys when the men first came to town. You go up to the stable and bring me the rake."

When the little fellow had gone she came close, tucked the carpet around the bush and warned me not to speak again for my life. I obeyed and lay there until after eleven o'clock, when the band of murderers had all left town.

When I came out of hiding I was all but dead. I had gone into the cellar before five o'clock and had been under intense mental strain and had been four times in imminent danger of death in those six hours of most terrible and indescribable experience, all of which my wife had passed in agony and heroic effort to save her husband. When I came out from under the carpet and bush our house and all we owned in it were in ashes.

Willie came back after a little while and told of Robbie Martin and his terrible death, of others who were killed in the prairie, of how he ran past the picket after they had killed his little comrade, and joined Mrs. Solomon and her children for safety, and how, bye and bye, another party of the guerrillas had come to them and asked who they were, threatening to kill the boys. When asked whose boy he was he said he was Mrs. Solomon's boy; and he told us how his heart was almost broken at the thought of having denied being my son; but he knew they hated me because I was a chaplain in the army.

Upon recovering our self-control we went down town to find that more than one hundred and eighty of our citizens had been killed and many of them burned until they could not be recognized. The whole business part of our town was in ashes. Eighty-two widows and two hundred and fifty children were in indescribable grief!

Crushed and grief stricken we returned to our own desolation and remained about the ashes of our home until four o'clock. Edmund had not returned, and my wife had become almost frantic by this time, fearing he had been killed and was lying on the prairie uncared for, or perhaps wounded and bleeding to death. She left her babe with a neighbor, and taking an old sheet and table cloth saved from the fire, ran in search of him, calling to everybody she could see, asking for her boy. After traversing nearly a mile she saw him and Freddie Leonard coming toward her, and he, seeing his mother, rushed to her. She joyfully threw away the sheet and table cloth which she had carried to bind up his wounds, and ran to meet her newfound boy. As they came near each other, he called out to her in fright and anguish, "O Ma, is Pa or Willie killed?"

"No, thank God," his mother answered, "we are all alive."

As they came down the garden walk I took the babe in my arms and William and Josie by my side, and we met mother and Edmund in the garden under the shadow of a little peach tree, and there I put my arm around my wife, and we all knelt on the ground and sent up to our Father in Heaven a volume of thanksgiving and praise. None but those who have passed through like dangers and have experienced like deliverance can conceive the gratitude to God that springs up within the heart. We realized that the Angel of the Lord encampeth around about them that fear him and keep his commandments and delivereth them.

The question has often been asked of my wife, "Mrs. Fisher, how could you keep your courage and confidence, and plan and do so much to save your husband?" And always her reply has been, "The Lord helped me. Has he not said, 'Call upon me in the day of trouble; I will deliver thee and thou shalt glorify me'?"

★ 26 ★

Pickett's Charge at Gettysburg

(from General James Longstreet,
From Manassas to Appomattox:
Memoirs of the Civil War in America, 1896)

GENERAL ROBERT E. LEE'S *spectacular triumphs at Fredericksburg (1862) and Chancellorsville (1863) encouraged him to invade the North again. His goal was to demoralize the Union with a smashing victory and achieve a negotiated peace settlement. Advancing into Pennsylvania, Lee's army blundered into contact with the Union forces under General George Meade at Gettysburg—a chance meeting that turned into a crucial three-day battle.*

On the first day of battle, July 1, 1863, the Confederates attacked the northern end of the Union line. On the following day they attacked the southern end. South of the Union line lay Little Round Top. Confederate General James Longstreet believed this was the key to outflank the Union army. Also recognizing the importance of Little Round Top was General Winfield Scott Hancock, commander of the Union Second Corps. He rushed his soldiers to occupy the site as the Confederate men from Alabama clawed their way up the steep slope. The local battle reached its climax as the Twentieth Maine Regiment, under Colonel Joshua Lawrence Chamberlain, was almost out of ammunition. Chamberlain, a minister and professor at Bowdoin College before the war, shouted the command to fix bayonets and drive the Confederates down the hill. The counterattack succeeded, and Little Round Top was held.

The final action at Gettysburg was fought on July 3. To the consternation of Longstreet, Lee ordered a direct assault on the center of the Union line, defended by General Hancock's Second Corps. This charge was to be supported by a Confederate artillery barrage that was meant to obliterate the Union position. The Confederate artillery, commanded by Colonel Porter Alexander, did their thunderous best, using roughly 90 percent of their available ammunition. The Union soldiers crouched behind a stone wall on the forward slope of a rise called Cemetery Hill. The ground between the Union and Confederate positions was open field about three quarters of a mile wide and devoid of shelter.

About five minutes after the end of Alexander's barrage, the Confederate infantry emerged from the woods on Seminary Ridge and drew up in parade-ground order, battle flags flying. General George Pickett's division contained about 4,800 men, organized in three brigades. They outnumbered the Union defenders, who had been seriously depleted by Alexander's shelling, by two to one.

When the Confederate assault commenced there was admiration on both sides at the sight of the Confederate advance. The Virginians came forward in unison with steady steps, sometimes dressing their lines. On one occasion they responded smartly to an order to "By the left, oblique— march!" Their advance was not a charge but a deliberate attempt to maintain their lines until they had reached the stone wall behind which the Union infantry waited. There was no rebel yell traditionally used to demoralize defenders—only silent Confederate troops advancing in near perfect order.

"Pickett's Charge" ranks as a stirring example of collective courage. In this excerpt from his book, From Manassas to Appomattox: Memoirs of the Civil War in America, *General Longstreet gives an account of the action as he saw it, as well as his arguments with Lee concerning the charge—none of which detract from the bravery of the advancing Confederate troops.*

* * *

GENERAL LEE has reported of arrangements for the day, "The general plan was unchanged. Longstreet, reinforced by Pickett's three brigades, which arrived near the battle-field during the afternoon of the 2d [July], was ordered to attack the next morning, and General Ewell was ordered to attack the enemy's right at the same time . . ."

This is disingenuous. He did not give or send me orders for the morning of the third day, nor did he reinforce me by Pickett's brigades for morning attack. As his head-quarters were about four miles from the command, I did not ride over, but sent, to report the work of the second day. In the absence of orders, I had scouting parties out during the night in search of a way by which we might strike the enemy's left, and push it down towards his centre. I found a way that gave some promise of results, and was about to move the command, when he [Lee] rode over after sunrise and gave his orders. His plan was to assault the enemy's left centre by a column to be composed of McLaws's and Hood's divisions reinforced by Pickett's brigades. I thought that it would not do; that the point had been fully tested the day before, by more men, when all were fresh; that the enemy was there looking for us, as we heard him during the night putting up his defences; that the divisions of McLaws and Hood were holding a mile along the right of my line against twenty thousand men, who would follow their withdrawal, strike the flank of the assaulting column, crush it, and get on our rear towards the Potomac River; that thirty thousand men was the minimum of force necessary for the work; that even such force would need close co-operation on other parts of the line; that the column as he proposed to organize it would have only about thirteen thousand men (the divisions having lost a third of their numbers the day before); that the columns would have to march a mile under concentrating battery fire, and a thousand yards under long-range musketry; that the conditions were different from those in the days of Napoleon, when field batteries had a range of six hundred yards and musketry about sixty yards.

He said the distance was not more than fourteen hundred yards. General Meade's estimate was a mile or a mile and a half (Captain

Long, the guide of the field of Gettysburg in 1888, stated that it was a trifle over a mile). He then concluded that the divisions of McLaws and Hood could remain on the defensive line; that he would reinforce by divisions of the Third Corps and Pickett's brigades, and stated the point to which the march should be directed. I asked the strength of the column. He stated fifteen thousand. Opinion was then expressed that the fifteen thousand men who could make successful assault over that field had never been arrayed for battle; but he was impatient of listening, and tired of talking, and nothing was left but to proceed. General Alexander was ordered to arrange the batteries of the front of the First and Third Corps, those of the Second were supposed to be in position; Colonel Walton was ordered to see that the batteries of the First were supplied with ammunition, and to prepare to give the signal-guns for the opening combat. The infantry of the Third Corps to be assigned were Heth's and Pettigrew's divisions and Wilcox's brigade. . . .

The director of artillery was asked to select a position on his line from which he could note the effect of his practice, and to advise General Pickett when the enemy's fire was so disturbed as to call for the assault. General Pickett's was the division of direction, and he was ordered to have a staff-officer or courier with the artillery director to bear notice of the moment to advance.

The little affair between the skirmish lines quieted in a short time, and also the noise on our extreme left. The quiet filing of one or two of our batteries into position emphasized the profound silence that prevailed during our wait for final orders. Strong battle was in the air, and the veterans of both sides swelled their breasts to gather nerve and strength to meet it. Division commanders were asked to go to the crest of the ridge and take a careful view of the field, and to have their officers there to tell their men of it, and to prepare them for the sight that was to burst upon them as they mounted the crest. . . .

The signal-guns broke the silence, the blaze of the second gun mingling in the smoke of the first, and salvoes rolled to the left and repeated themselves, the enemy's fine metal spreading its fire to the converging lines, ploughing the trembling ground, plunging through the line of batteries and clouding the heavy air. The two or three hundred guns seemed proud of their undivided honors and organized confusion. The Confederates had the benefit of converging fire into the enemy's massed position, but the superior metal of the enemy neutralized the advantage of position. The brave and steady work progressed. . . .

General Pickett rode to confer with Alexander, then to the ground upon which I was resting, where he was soon handed a slip of paper. After reading it he handed it to me. It read:

> If you are coming at all, come at once, or I cannot give you proper support, but the enemy's fire has not slackened at all. At least eighteen guns are still firing from the cemetery itself.
>
> ALEXANDER.

Pickett said, "General, shall I advance?"

The effort to speak the order failed, and I could only indicate it by an affirmative bow. He accepted the duty with seeming confidence of success, leaped on his horse, and rode gaily to his command. I mounted and spurred for Alexander's post. He reported that the batteries he had reserved for the charge with the infantry had been spirited away by General Lee's chief of artillery; that the ammunition of the batteries of position was so reduced that he could not use them in proper support of the infantry. He was ordered to stop the march at once and fill up his ammunition-chests. But, alas! There was no more ammunition to be had.

The order was imperative. The Confederate commander had fixed his heart upon the work. Just then a number of the enemy's batteries hitched up and hauled off, which gave a glimpse of unexpected hope. Encouraging messages were sent for the columns to hurry on,—and they were then on elastic springing step. The officers saluted as they passed, their stern smiles expressing confidence. General Pickett, a graceful horseman, sat lightly in the saddle, his brown locks flowing quite over his shoulders. Pettigrew's division spread their steps and quickly rectified the alignment, and the grand march moved bravely on. As soon as the leading columns opened the way, the supports sprang to their alignments. General Trimble mounted, adjusting his seat and reins with an air and grace as if setting out on a pleasant afternoon ride. When aligned to their places solid march was made down the slope and past our batteries of position.

Confederate batteries put their fire over the heads of the men as they moved down the slope, and continued to draw the fire of the enemy until the smoke lifted and drifted to the rear, when every gun was turned upon the infantry columns. The batteries that had been drawn off were replaced by others that were fresh. Soldiers and officers began to fall, some to rise no more, others to find their way to the hospital tents. Single files were cut here and there, then the gaps increased, and an occasional shot tore wider openings, but, closing the gaps as quickly as made, the march moved on. . . .

Colonel Latrobe was sent to General Trimble to have his men fill the line of the broken brigades, and bravely they repaired the damage. The enemy moved out against the supporting brigade in Pickett's rear. Colonel Sorrel was sent to have that move guarded, and Pickett was drawn back to that contention. McLaws was ordered to press his left forward, but the direct line of infantry and cross-fire of artillery was telling fearfully on the front. Colonel Fremantle ran up to offer congratulations on the apparent success, but the big gaps in the ranks grew until the lines were reduced to half their length. I called his attention to the broken, struggling ranks. Trimble mended the battle of the left in handsome style, but on the right the massing of the enemy grew stronger and stronger. Brigadier Garnett was killed, Kemper and Trimble were desperately wounded; Generals. Hancock and Gibbon were wounded. General Lane succeeded Trimble, and with Pettigrew held the battle of the left in steady ranks.

Pickett's lines being nearer, the impact was heaviest upon them. Most of the field officers were killed or wounded. Colonel Whittle, of Armistead's brigade, who had been shot through the right leg at Williamsburg and lost his left arm at Malvern Hill, was shot through the right arm, then brought down by a shot through his left leg.

General Armistead, of the second line, spread his steps to supply the places of fallen comrades. His colors cut down, with a volley against the bristling line of bayonets, he put his cap on his sword to guide the storm. The enemy's massing, enveloping numbers held the struggle until the noble Armistead fell beside the wheels of the enemy's battery. Pettigrew was wounded, but held his command.

General Pickett, finding the battle broken, while the enemy was still reinforcing, called the troops off. There was no indication of panic. The broken files marched back in steady step. The effort was nobly made, and failed from blows that could not be fended. . . .

Looking confidently for advance of the enemy through our open field, I rode to the line of batteries, resolved to hold it until the last gun was lost. As I rode, the shells screaming over my head and plough-ing the ground under my horse, an involuntary appeal went up that one of them might take me from scenes of such awful responsibility; but the storm to be met left no time to think of one's self. The bat-tery officers were prepared to meet the crisis,—no move had been made for leaving the field. . . . Our men passed the batteries in quiet walk, and would rally, I knew, when they reached the ridge from which they started.

General Lee was soon with us, and with staff-officers and others assisted in encouraging the men and getting them together.

⋆ 27 ⋆

Saving the Regimental Colors

(from Henry Cabot Lodge and
Theodore Roosevelt, "The Flag Bearer" in
Hero Tales from American History, 1901)

OLIVER WENDELL HOLMES, Jr., in his youth saw action
during the Civil War. As a justice of the Supreme Court, he
philosophized on combat in an 1884 Memorial Day address:

*The faith is true and adorable which leads a soldier to throw away
his life to a blindly accepted duty, in a cause which he little under-
stands, in a plan of campaign of which he has no notion, of tactics
of which he does not see the use. Through our great good fortune, in
our youth our hearts were touched by fire. It was given to us to learn
at the outset that life is a profound and passionate thing. While we
are permitted to scorn nothing but indifference, and not to pretend
to undervalue the worldly rewards of ambition, we have seen with
our own eyes, beyond and above the gold fields, the snowy heights of
honor, and it is for us to bear the report to those who come after us.*

In the Civil War, regimental colors were carried for all to see during an attack as a guidon for a line of skirmishers. To Confederate and Union soldiers alike, it was a matter of pride for the standard never to fall into the hands of the enemy. Written by Henry Cabot Lodge and Theodore Roosevelt in their Hero Tales from American History, *here are two instances of brave men and boys—from the South and the North— who knowingly risked and gave their lives. Their sole motivation was a sense of duty to preserve the honor of their regiment by savings its colors.*

* * *

THE BATTLE AT GAINES' MILL, Virginia, was General Lee's first victory. Gregg's 1st South Carolina formed part of the attacking force. The resistance was desperate, and the fury of the assault was unsurpassed. At one point it fell upon the lot of this regiment to bear the brunt of carrying a certain strong position. Moving forward at a run the South Carolinians were swept by a fierce and searching fire. Young James Taylor, a lad of sixteen, was carrying the flag, and was killed after being shot down three times, twice rising and struggling onward with the colors. The third time he fell the flag was seized by George Cotchet, and then he, in turn, fell, by Shubrick Hayne. Hayne was also struck down almost immediately, and the fourth lad, for none of them were over twenty years old, grasped the colors, and fell mortally wounded across the body of his friend. The fifth, Gadsden Holmes, was pierced with no less than seven balls. The sixth man, Dominick Spellman, more fortunate, but not less brave, bore the flag throughout the rest of the battle.

Similarly, at the battle of Fredericksburg, half of the Union brigades under Meagher and Caldwell lay on the bloody slope leading up to Confederate entrenchments. Among the assaulting regiments was the 5th New Hampshire, and it lost one hundred and eighty six out of three hundred men who made the charge.

The survivors fell sullenly back behind a fence, within easy range of the Confederate rifle-pits. Just before reaching it the last of the color guard was shot, and the flag fell in the open. A Captain Perry instantly ran out to rescue it, and as soon as he reached it was shot through the heart; another, Captain Murray, made the same attempt and was also killed; and so was a third, Moore. Several private soldiers met a like fate. They were all killed close to the flag, and their dead bodies fell across one another. Taking advantage of this breastwork of corpses, Lieutenant Nettleton crawled from behind the fence to the colors, seized them, and bore back the blood-won trophy.

✶ 28 ✶

"Tell Him He Must Die":
Army Nurse Louisa May Alcott
Comforts a Dying Soldier

(from Louisa May Alcott,
Hospital Sketches and Camp and Fireside Stories, 1892)

LOUISA MAY ALCOTT *wrote the famous books* Little Women *and* Little Men. *But it is often forgotten that during the Civil War she nursed Union soldiers at an army hospital—at a time when army hospitals were often as gruesome and deadly as the field of combat. Later she wrote about her experiences in* Hospital Sketches, *from which the following selection is taken.*

There was little glory for nurses ministering to wards of suffering wounded men. Yet here is a story in which the fortitude of a dying man and the tender care and compassion of his nurse, Miss Alcott, should make both famous. As the passage begins at a hospital in Washington, D.C., an orderly from another ward approaches Miss Alcott and gives her a sorrowful message from one of her patients, a dying West Virginia blacksmith named John.

✶   ✶   ✶

J OHN IS GOING ma'am," said the messenger, "and wants to know if you can come."

"The moment this boy here is asleep," I replied.

"Tell John I'll be there. And let me know if I'm in danger of being too late."

The messenger departed, and while I quieted poor Shaw, I thought of John. He came in a day or two after the others; and one evening, when I entered my "pathetic room," I found a lately emptied bed occupied by a large, fair man, with a fine face, and the serenest eyes I ever met. One of the earlier comers had often spoken of a friend who had remained behind that those apparently worse wounded than himself might reach a shelter first. It seemed a David and Jonathan sort of friendship. The man fretted for his mate, and was never tired of praising John—his courage, sobriety, self denial, and unfailing kindliness of heart; always winding up with: "He's an out an' out fine feller, ma'am; you see if he ain't."

I had some curiosity to behold this piece of excellence, and when he came, watched him for a night or two, before I made friends with him; for, to tell the truth, I was a little afraid of the stately looking man, whose bed had to be lengthened to accommodate his commanding stature; who seldom spoke, uttered no complaint, asked no sympathy, tranquilly observed what went on about him; as he lay high upon his pillows, no picture of a dying statesman or warrior was ever fuller of real dignity than this Virginia blacksmith. A most attractive face he had, framed in brown hair and beard, comely featured and full of vigor, as yet unsubdued by pain; thoughtful and often beautifully mild while watching the afflictions of others, as if entirely forgetful of his own. His mouth was grave and firm, with plenty of will and courage in its lines, but a smile could make it as sweet as any woman's; and his eyes were child's eyes, looking one fairly in the face with a clear, straightforward glance, which promised well for such as placed their faith in him. He seemed to cling to life as if it were rich in duties and delights, and he had learned the secret of content. The only time I saw his composure disturbed was when my surgeon brought another to examine John, who scrutinized their faces with an anxious look asking of the elder: "Do you think I shall pull through, sir?" "I hope so, my man." And, as the two passed on, John's eye still followed them, with an intentness which would have won a clearer answer from them, had they seen it. A momentary shadow flitted over his face; then came the usual serenity, as if, in that brief eclipse, he had acknowledged the existence of some hard possibility, and, asking nothing yet hoping all things, left the issue in God's hands, with that submission which is true piety. The next night, as I went on my rounds with Dr. P., I happened to ask which man in the room probably suffered most; and to my great surprise, he glanced at John.

"Every breath he draws is like a stab; for the ball pierced the left lung, broke a rib, and did no end of damage here and there; so the poor lad can find neither forgetfulness nor ease, because he must lie on his wounded back or suffocate. It will be a hard struggle, and a long one, for he possesses great vitality; but even his temperate life can't save him; I wish it could."

"You don't mean he must die, doctor?"

"Bless you, there's not the slightest hope for him; and you'd better tell him so before long; women have a way of doing such things comfortably, so I leave it to you. He won't last more than a day or two, at furthest."

I could have sat down on the spot and cried heartily, if I had not learned the wisdom of bottling up one's tears for leisure moments. Such an end seemed very hard for such a man, when half a dozen worn-out, worthless bodies round him were gathering up the remnants of wasted lives, to linger on for years, perhaps, burdens to others, daily reproaches to homesick spirits, and make the heavy hours pass easier.

John looked lonely and forsaken just then, as he sat with bent head, hands folded on his knee, and no outward sign of suffering, till, looking nearer, I saw great tears roll down and drop upon the floor. It was a new sight there; for, though I had seen many suffer, some swore, some groaned, most endured silently, but none wept. Yet it did not seem weak, only very touching, and straightway my fear vanished, my heart opened wide and took him in, as gathering the bent head in my arms, as freely as if he had been a little child, I said, "Let me help you bear it, John."

Never, on any human countenance, have I seen so swift and beautiful a look of gratitude, surprise, and comfort, as that which answered me more eloquently than the whispered "Thank you, ma'am; this is right good! this is what I wanted!"

"Then why not ask for it before!"

"I didn't like to be a trouble: you seemed so busy, and I could manage to get on alone."

"You shall not want it any more, John."

Nor did he; for now I understood the wistful look that sometimes followed me, as I went out, after a brief pause beside his bed, or merely a passing nod, while busied with those who seemed to need me more than he, because more urgent in their demands; now I knew that to him, as to so many, I was the poor substitute for mother, wife, or sister, and in his eyes no stranger, but a friend who hitherto had seemed neglectful; for, in his modesty he had never guessed the truth. This was changed now; and, through the tedious operation of probing, bathing, and dressing his wounds, he leaned against me, holding my hand fast, and, if pain wrung further tears from him, no one saw them fall but me.

When he was laid down again, I hovered about him, in a remorseful state of mind that would not let me rest, till I had bathed his face, brushed his "bonny brown hair," set all things smooth about him, and laid a knot of heath and heliotrope on his clean pillow. While doing this, he watched me with the satisfied expression I so liked to see; and when I offered the little nosegay held it carefully in his great hand, smoothed a ruffled leaf or two, surveyed and smelt it with an air of genuine delight, and lay contentedly regarding the glimmer of the sunshine on the green.

Although the manliest man among my forty, he said, "Yes, ma'am," like a little boy; received suggestions for his comfort with the quick smile that brightened his whole face; and now and then, as I stood tidying the table by his bed, I felt him softly touch my gown, as if to assure himself that I was there. Anything more natural and frank I never saw, and found this brave John as bashful as brave, yet full of excellencies and fine aspirations, which, having no power to express themselves in words, seemed to have bloomed into his character and made him what he was.

After that night, an hour of each evening that remained to him was devoted to his ease or pleasure. He could not talk much, for breath was precious, and he spoke in whispers; but from occasional conversations, I gleaned scraps of private history which only added to the affection and respect I felt for him. Once he asked me to write a letter, and as I settled pen and paper, I said, with an irrepressible glimmer of feminine curiosity, "Shall it be addressed to wife or mother, John?"

"Neither, ma'am; I've got no wife, and will write to mother myself when I get better. Did you think I was married because of this?" he asked, touching a plain ring he wore, and often turned thoughtfully on his finger when he lay alone.

"Partly that, but more from a settled sort of look you have, a look which young men seldom get until they marry."

"I don't know that; but I'm not so very young, ma'am, thirty, in May, and have been what you might call settled this ten years; for mother's a widow, I'm the oldest child she has, and it wouldn't do for me to marry until Lizzy has a home of her own, and Laurie's learned his trade; for we're not rich, and I must be father to the children and husband to the dear old woman, if I can."

"No doubt but you are both, John; yet how came you to go to war, if you felt so? Wasn't enlisting as bad as marrying?"

"No, ma'am, not as I see it, for one is helping my neighbor, the other pleasing myself. I went because I couldn't help it. I didn't want the glory or the pay; I wanted the right thing done, and people kept saying the men who were in earnest ought to fight. I was in earnest, the Lord knows! but I held off as long as I could, not knowing which was my duty; mother saw the case, gave me her ring to keep me steady, and said 'Go!' so I went."

A short story and a simple one, but the man and the mother were portrayed better than pages of fine writing could have done it.

"Do you ever regret that you came, when you lie here suffering so much?"

"Never, ma'am; I haven't helped a great deal, but I've shown I was willing to give my life, and perhaps I've got to; but I don't blame any-

body, and if it was to do over again I'd do it. I'm a little sorry I wasn't
wounded in front; it looks cowardly to be hit in the back, but I obeyed
orders, and it don't matter in the end, I know."

Poor John! It did not matter now, except that a shot in front might
have spared the long agony in store for him. He seemed to read the
thoughts that troubled me, as he spoke so hopefully when there was no
hope, for he suddenly added:

"This is my first battle; do they think it's going to be my last?"

"I'm afraid they do, John."

It was the hardest question I had ever been called upon to answer;
doubly hard with those clear eyes fixed on mine, forcing a truthful answer by their own truth. He seemed a little startled at first, pondered
over the fateful fact a moment, then shook his head, with a glance at the
broad chest and muscular limbs stretched out before him:

"I'm not afraid, but it's difficult to believe all at once. I am so strong
it don't seem possible for such a little wound to kill me."

Merry Mercutio's dying words glanced through my memory as he
spoke: "Tis not so deep as a well, nor so wide as a church door, but it
is enough." And John would have said the same could he have seen
the ominous black holes between his shoulders. He never had; and, seeing the ghastly sights about him, could not believe his own more fatal
than these, for all the suffering it caused him.

"Shall I write to your mother now?" I asked, thinking that these
sudden tidings might change all plans and purposes: but they did not;
for the man received the order of the Divine commander to march
with the same unquestioning obedience with which the soldier had received that of the human one, doubtless remembering that the first led
him to life and the last to death.

"No, ma'am; to Laurie. Just the same; he'll break it to her best, and
I'll add a line to her myself when you get done." So I wrote the letter
which he dictated, finding it better than any I had sent; for, though here
and there a little ungrammatical or inelegant, each sentence came to
me briefly worded, but most expressive; full of excellent counsel to the
boy, tenderly bequeathing "Mother and Lizzy" to his care, and bidding
him good-by in words the sadder for their simplicity. He added a few
lines, with steady hand, and, as I sealed it, said, with a patient sort of

sigh, "I hope the answer will come in time for me to see it"; then, turning away his face, laid the flowers against his lips, as if to hide some quiver of emotion at the thought of such a sudden sundering of all the dear home ties.

These things had happened two days before; now John was dying, and the letter had not come. I had been summoned to many death-beds in my life, but to none that made my heart ache as it did then, since my mother called me to watch the departure of a spirit akin to this in its gentleness and patient strength. As I went in, John stretched out both hands:

"I knew you'd come! Guess I'm moving on, ma'am."

He was; and so rapidly that, even while he spoke, over his face I saw the gray veil falling that no human hand can lift. I sat down by him, wiped the drops from his forehead, stirred the air about him with the slow wave of a fan, and waited to help him die. He stood in sore need of help—and I could do so little; for, as the doctor had foretold, the strong body rebelled against death, and fought every inch of the way, forcing him to draw each breath with a spasm, and clench his hands with an imploring look, as if he asked, "How long must I endure this and be still!"

For hours he suffered dumbly, without a moment's respite, or a moment's murmuring; his limbs grew cold, his face damp, his lips white, and again and again he tore the covering of his breast, as if the lightest weight added to his agony; yet through it all his eyes never lost their perfect serenity, and the man's soul seemed to sit therein, undaunted by the ills that vexed his flesh.

One by one the men woke, and round the room appeared a circle of pale faces and watchful eyes, full of awe and pity; for, though a stranger, John was beloved by all. Each man there had wondered at his patience, respected his piety, admired his fortitude, and now lamented his hard death; for the influence of an upright nature had made itself deeply felt, even in one little week. Presently, the Jonathan who so loved this comely David came creeping from his bed for a last look and word. The kind soul was full of trouble, as the choke in his voice, the grasp of his hand, betrayed; but there were no tears, and the farewell of the friends was the more touching for its brevity.

"Old boy, how are you?" faltered the one.

"Most through, thank heaven!" whispered the other.

"Can I say or do anything for you anywheres?"

"Take my things home, and tell them that I did my best."

"I will! I will!"

"Good-by, Ned."

"Good-by, John, good-by!"

They kissed each other, tenderly as women, and so parted, for poor Ned could not stay to see his comrade die.

For a little while, there was no sound in the room but the drip of water from a stump or two and John's distressful gasps, as he slowly breathed his life away. I thought him nearly gone, and had just laid down the fan, believing its help to be no longer needed, when suddenly he rose up in his bed, and cried out with a bitter cry that broke the silence, sharply startling every one with its agonized appeal:

"For God's sake, give me air!"

It was the only cry pain or death had wrung from him, the only boon he had asked; and none of us could grant it, for all the airs that blew were useless now. Dan flung up the window. The first red streak of dawn was warming the gray east, a herald of the coming sun; John saw it, and with the love of light which lingers in us to the end, seemed to read in it a sign of hope of help, for over his whole face there broke that mysterious expression, brighter than any smile, which often comes to eyes that look their last. He laid himself gently down, and stretching out his strong right arm, as if to grasp and bring the blessed air to his lips in a fuller flow, lapsed into a merciful unconsciousness, which assured us that for him suffering was forever past.

He died then; for, though the heavy breaths still tore their way up for a little longer, they were but the waves of an ebbing tide that beat unfelt against the wreck, which an immortal voyager had deserted with a smile. He never spoke again, but to the end held my hand close, so close that when he was asleep at last, I could not draw it away. Dan helped me, warning me, as he did so, that it was unsafe for dead and living flesh to lie so long together; but though my hand was strangely cold and stiff, and four white marks remained across its back, even when warmth and color had returned elsewhere, I could not but be glad that, through its touch, the presence of human sympathy, perhaps, had lightened that hard hour.

When they had made him ready for the grave, John lay in state for half an hour, a thing which seldom happened in that busy place; but a universal sentiment of reverence and affection seemed to fill the hearts of all who had known or heard of him; and when the rumor of his death went through the house, always astir, many came to see him, and I felt a tender sort of pride in my lost patient; for he looked a most heroic figure, lying there stately and still as the statue of some young knight asleep upon his tomb. The lovely expression which so often beautifies dead faces, soon replaced the marks of pain, and I longed for those who loved him best to see him when half an hour's acquaintance with death had made them friends.

As we stood looking at him, the ward master handed me a letter, saying it had been forgotten the night before. It was John's letter, come just an hour too late to gladden the eyes that had longed and looked for it so eagerly. Yet he had it; for, after I had cut some brown locks for his mother, and taken off the ring to send her, telling how well the talisman had done its work, I kissed this good son for her sake, and laid the letter in his hand, still folded as when I drew my own away, feeling that its place was there, and making myself happy with the thought, that even in his solitary place in the "Government Lot," he would not be without some token of the love which makes life beautiful and outlives death. Then I left him, glad to have known so genuine a man, and carrying with me an endearing memory of the brave Virginia blacksmith, as he lay serenely waiting for the dawn of that long day which knows no night.

THE WAYS OF
THE WEST

★ 29 ★

"Portugee" Phillips's
Desperate Ride

(from Paul I. Wellman,
*Death on Horseback: Seventy Years of War
for the American West*)

CAPTAIN WILLIAM FETTERMAN *once blithely boasted he could ride unscathed through the entire Sioux nation with just eighty men. On December 21, 1866, he sallied forth from Fort Phil Kearny, Wyoming, with eighty men to protect a party cutting wood for winter fuel. Indians coaxed him farther and farther from the fort with feigned attacks and retreats. His fire-eating bravado egged Fetterman forward into an ambush. Suddenly two thousand Sioux, Cheyenne, and Arapaho warriors led by Red Cloud and Roman Nose struck and slew every single soldier.*

"*After the fighting the Indians moved about the field killing any soldier who still lived. Then they stripped and mutilated the stiffening bodies as a double form of vengeance, so that the dead men's spirits would be helpless and disfigured. To blind the spirits they tore out the white men's eyes and laid them on the rocks. They cut off noses and ears, chopped off chins, bashed out teeth, tore out entrails and laid then all on rocks besides the bodies. They cut off fingers, hands, feet, took arms out of sockets, scooped out brains. They split skulls up, down and across. They cut muscles out of calves, thighs, stomachs, breasts, arms and cheeks." When the orgy of gore was over, they returned to camp to celebrate.*

Frantic Colonel Carrington in charge of Fort Phil Kearny, collected what recognizable bodies he could, then turned his attention to defending the fort against further attack. The massacre had decimated his ranks. If the Indians stormed the fort, they would overwhelm it. Carrington issued an order: should the Indians fall upon the fort, all women and children were to be placed inside the powder magazine and blown up. Carrington himself was prepared to light the match.

That night, he called for a volunteer to ride for help. John "Portugee" Phillips, who came from the Azores and had a wife and two children at the fort, raised his hand. From Death on Horseback: Seventy Years of War for the American West *by Paul I. Wellman, here is the story of "Portugee" Phillips's desperate ride for help.*

★   ★   ★

THAT NIGHT the threatening sky fulfilled its portent. A terrific blizzard descended. The thermometer fell to thirty degrees below zero. Snow piled up so rapidly against the stockade that details of men had to work constantly to shovel it away lest it pile high enough to allow the Indians to climb over. Sentries could stand the intense cold only twenty minutes at a time. Even with quick reliefs there were many frozen feet, ears, noses and fingers. But for the blizzard the Indians might have followed their advantage by attacking the fort itself. According to their own account this was a part of the plan. To the people at the fort, arrival of cold weather was providential.

Southward, two hundred and thirty-six miles, lay Fort Laramie, with reinforcements, ammunition and supplies. Word must be gotten through. There was no telegraph, so a courier had to take it. Carrington called for volunteers.

Several old plainsmen were in the post and many veteran soldiers, but they shook their heads. That ride, over a broken, snow-covered country, even in times of peace, meant almost certain death by freezing, with the temperature where it was and the blizzard raging so it was hard to see a hundred yards ahead. With the country swarming with hostile Indians the odds were a hundred to one against any man rash enough to attempt it.

But there was one man willing to take the risk. John Phillips, commonly known as "Portugee," was an Indian fighter, trapper and scout. He knew the country and offered to go. Carrington gave him his own horse, a blooded Kentucky runner, the swiftest animal in the post. Wrapping himself in a huge buffalo coat, with a little hardtack for himself and a sack of grain for his horse, he passed out through a side gate into the swirling storm.

Nobody ever got the full details of that ride, but it will always remain one of the epics of the West. At first he walked in the blackness of the night storm. For hours he led his horse, stopping at suspicious noises. He expected to be seen in the first half mile but no Indian yelled. With the howling wind whipping the snow around him, he mounted at last and spurred his horse along, across the Piney and past frozen Lake De Smet. Behind him the lights of the fort grew dim and disappeared.

Gallop—gallop—on through the storm, plunged Portugee Phillips. The miles fell behind him like the snowflakes he shook from his furry shoulders. The Indians were in their teepees, not dreaming that any white man would face the fury of this storm. And Portugee Phillips rode on and on.

Day dawned and still the wind whirled the snow. A short stop to feed his horse and cram a few crackers down his own throat, a handful of snow for a drink, and Portugee Phillips was in the saddle again. How he guided his horse across that wilderness is explained only by the instinct which is sometimes possessed by those perfectly attuned to the wilds. From the Big Horn Mountains the blizzard swept with unslackened fury, piling in drifts from five to twenty feet deep. The storm prevented his seeing any landmarks. The trail itself was covered by the drifts. Yet on he rode, as unerring as a hound on the slot.

Night fell, and still the good steed breasted the snow. In the homes of civilization, happy families gathered around their hearths in the light and warmth of their homes. But alone, a dot in the icy waste, Portugee Phillips was riding for the lives of the women and children at Fort Phil Kearny. Just at dawn he reached Horse Shoe station, forty miles from

Laramie, and one hundred and ninety miles from Phil Kearny. He telegraphed his news to Laramie. Fortunately he did not trust the telegraph. The message never got through. After a brief rest he rode on.

Icicles formed from his beard. His hands, knees and feet were frozen. He looked more like a ghost than a man. But still, with indominitable purpose, he urged his failing horse over the trail.

It was Christmas Eve and they were holding high revel at Fort Laramie. A grand ball was in progress at "Bedlam," the officers' club. Beautiful women, garbed in silks and satins, and gallant officers, in brilliant dress uniforms, made the interior a splendid kaleidoscope of changing color. The sound of violins, the laughter of the ladies, and the gay banter of the brave men who were taking holiday from military cares, created a symphony of cheery sound.

Above this happy noise came suddenly the sharp challenge of a sentry. It was followed by the shouting of men in the fort enclosure and a rush of running steps outside, coupled with a ringing call for the officer of the day. The dancing stopped. Officers and ladies grouped themselves at doors and windows, gazing out at the snow covered parade ground. A horse lay there, gasping its last, fallen from exhaustion. And reeling, swaying like a drunkard, a gigantic, fur-clad figure staggered toward the hall. In through the door he stumbled and stood for a moment, supporting himself on the lintel while his eyes blinked in the unaccustomed light. Then seeing the post commander, he told a story of horror which put a period to the festivities that night—the story of the Fetterman disaster.

As he gasped out his story and appeal for reinforcements, he swayed, then fell to the floor, unconscious from overexposure and exhaustion. Kind hands lifted him and carried him to a bed. Even with his rugged physique it took him weeks to recover from the terrible ordeal. To this day his ride remains unparalleled in American history.

★ 30 ★

Dull Knife's Last Fight

(from Paul I. Wellman,
*Death on Horseback: Seventy Years of War
for the American West*)

I N THE BEGINNING *Dull Knife counseled peace with the whites,
but then, in 1864, Black Kettle's peaceful camp at Sand Creek was
massacred. The fighting parson, Colonel John Chivington, was the
perpetrator of this crime. For Chivington, commander of the vengeful
Third Colorado Volunteers, the best Indians were dead Indians. Before the
massacre he talked of "collecting scalps" and wading in gore. "I have come
to kill Indians, and believe it is right and honorable to use any means
under God's heaven to kill Indians." One morning his militia attacked
Black Kettle's sleeping camp of six hundred Cheyennes. Most warriors were
away hunting buffalo. Two thirds of those remaining were women and
children. When Chivington's mounted men charged the encampment,
Black Kettle stood in front of his tepee under the American flag and a
white flag, calling to his people not to be afraid.*

*Left Hand, with his followers, tried to reach the flag for protection.
When he saw the troops, he stopped, and stood still with his arms folded, because he knew they would not harm him. The mounted men shot him dead.*

Left and right they shot and sabred the huddled masses beneath the flag. Whoever could, fled. Blood-crazed, the militia scalped and obscenely desecrated the Indian bodies. The count: 105 women and children dead; 28 men dead; 7 captured. Dull Knife never forgot.

Dull Knife fought in the Cheyenne-Arapaho War of 1864. His people participated in the battle of the Rosebud (June 17, 1876) and the annihilation of Custer (June 24, 1876). In November 1876, the army attacked his winter camp on the Powder River. He surrendered the next spring and was forced to march south for a hundred days—along with 40 men, 47 women, and 37 children—to Indian Territory—there his people suffered from malnutrition and disease. "Our people died, died, died, kept following one another out of this world."

Openly, Dull Knife declared his intent to return to his homeland. One night in September 1878, Dull Knife's and Little Wolf's bands broke away, heading north to seek asylum on Red Cloud's reservation. Pursued but never caught, Dull Knife finally surrendered at Fort Robinson, Nebraska, thinking he would be permitted to remain. Upon learning of this treachery, Dull Knife and his people escaped from Fort Robinson. After the breakout, the survivors split up; though Dull Knife was concealed by white and Indian friends and lived, most of his people were killed.

From Death on Horseback: Seventy Years of War for the American West, *by Paul I. Wellman, the story begins at Fort Robinson as Dull Knife learns that he has been betrayed. Here is the last cry of a cornered people when their choice was living death or death itself.*

* * *

TREACHERY

WITH THE 1ST OF JANUARY a blizzard covered the ground deep with snow and sent the mercury far below zero. It was weather for staying close indoors. Yet on January 5th [Captain Henry] Wessells received as a reply to his message containing Dull Knife's plea, a peremptory order to march the captives, without delay and with proper escort, to Fort Reno, far to the south, over the same trail they had traveled with such pain coming north.

Wessells saw the terrible mistake. The swivel-chair bureaucrats in the Indian Department could not. But duty was duty. He had the three chiefs, Dull Knife, Wild Hog and Crow brought to him and explained the order. Dead silence greeted his words. Only the wild beast glare in their eyes told the suppressed passion which was making infernos of their hearts. It took Dull Knife minutes to control himself so he could speak with a steady voice. His reply, quiet and cold was: "It is death to us. If the Great Father wishes us to die—very well. We will die where we are. If necessary by our own hands."

But Wessells could only obey orders. He gave his ultimatum: Unless they agreed, he would cut off all their fuel, food and water. In stony silence the chiefs heard their sentence; then went back to their people.

Days passed—five days of bitter cold and hunger in the wooden barracks where shivered the half-clad Cheyennes. Day and night their despairing death songs sounded, with even the little children joining their weak treble voices in the chants. The Indians had made up their minds to die of cold and hunger rather than submit. At last, on January 9th, Wessells sent again for the chiefs. But this time the people would not let Dull Knife go. Strong Left Hand took his place.

For an hour the Cheyennes paced the floor of their barracks, straining their ears. Then they heard a sudden wild, desperate war whoop. It was Wild Hog's voice and it told its own story. Strong Left Hand ran in. The two others had been seized and put in irons. Wild Hog had defied Wessells. And he had stabbed and all but killed a guard before he was overpowered. That wild, ringing cry was his warning and farewell to his people. From the prison barracks rose the answering yells of the Cheyenne men, the cries of women and even the shrieks of little children.

Doors and windows were barricaded. From under the floor were taken the five rifles and the revolvers which had been smuggled in. Floors and iron stoves were broken up to make clubs. Every man who had a gun gave his knife to another who had no weapon. The Cheyennes expected an immediate attack, but none came. The night of January 10th came on, still and frightfully cold.

Just as the last tremulous notes of "Taps" sounded, a shot rang from the barracks, startlingly clear and sharp. A sentry pitched forward in the snow. Three more shots in a rapid rat-tat-tat. Two more guards were down. Then from the doors and windows of the barracks poured the heroic last fragment of the Dull Knife band.

Starved, despairing, they nevertheless acted with coolness and clear judgment. The dead sentries, Corporal Pulver and Privates Hulz and Tommeny, were stripped of their arms. While the few braves formed a rear guard, the Indians ran out of the fort and started across the snow-clad plain.

Out of the barracks poured the troops, half-clad but shooting. Under the heavy fire the gallant Cheyenne rear guard melted fast. But the main body was well on its way to the hills, where a high, precipitous divide separated Soldier Creek from White River, three miles from the fort.

That was a forlorn hope if ever there was one. Within the first half mile of the awful running fight, more than half the Cheyenne fighting men were shot. But as the warriors fell, their weapons were seized by half-grown boys, tottering old men, even women. Often the advance guard of the soldiers and the rear guard of the Indians fought hand-to-hand. The women fell as thickly as the men.

A mile from the fort the troops, many of them badly frozen, were called back to get their clothing and horses. Across the frozen river and up the steep hill toiled the Indians. The cavalry caught up again as the ascent was being made. At the foot of the bluffs the shattered rear guard drew up for a last resistance. The cavalry charged. Back it was hurled. Dull Knife's daughter, known as the "Princess," fighting in the front rank was killed. So were several others. But the precious minutes gained allowed the rest of the people to climb the cliff.

Further pursuit ended for the night. On the way back to the fort the soldiers marked the line of retreat by the huddled bodies in the snow. Buffalo Hump, the chief's son, lay on his back with arms extended and face upturned. In his right hand he held a small knife. The blade was no more than a quarter of an inch wide at the hilt, and yet, the only weapon this magnificent fighter could command in this, his last fight for freedom! As a soldier passed, he rose to a sitting posture and aimed a fierce blow at his leg with his knife, then fell back and lay still . . . dead.

As the soldiers returned to their warm quarters, the surviving

Cheyennes struggled on through the bitter night. For seventeen miles they traveled without a halt. Even well-fed, well-clothed troops would have considered it a wonderful march under the circumstances. Yet it was made by women, children, old men and wounded men, half-clad and weak from five days' starvation.

The limit of even a Cheyenne's endurance finally came. They camped back of a knoll and prepared an ambush—fighters to the very last. In the morning, Captain Vroom's pursuing troop stumbled right into the trap. The spiteful crackle of fire emptied three saddles. The cavalry retreated, dismounted and surrounded the knoll. All that day they fought a long-range battle. As night fell the troops built decoy fires around the knoll and marched back to the warmth of the fort. But Dull Knife's scouts were not "decoyed." They laughed grimly at the white man's transparent trickery and walked over the decoy fires to continue their retreat.

THE FINISH

Thirty-seven Cheyennes were dead and fifty-two, mostly wounded, captured by the night of January 10th. Next day the remnant was brought to bay in a difficult position to attack, far up Soldier Creek. During the fighting that day a troop horse was killed. At night the Indians sneaked out and from the carcass of that horse the poor wretches got the first mouthfuls of food they had eaten in seven days. The troops withdrew, so taking what little flesh was left on the dead horse, the Cheyennes slipped away for six miles more and entrenched themselves in the bluffs, dogged and defiant.

Wessells brought a twelve-pounder Napoleon gun from the fort that day. It arrived at noon and all afternoon its sullen boom was the dominant sound in the snowy wastes. Forty rounds of shells were thrown into the Cheyenne position. The Indians could not reply. Yet Wessells failed to dislodge them. Flattening themselves in the shallow depression they dug in the frozen ground, they endured as well as they could the concussions of the bursting shells.

Toward evening Wessells sent James Rowland, an interpreter, close to the lines, to tell them to surrender. Here was something the Cheyennes could reach with their guns. Rowland was glad to get back to his own lines with his life. No surrender yet.

Wessells was growing worried. The Indians were working toward the cattle country where they could find food and horses. He doubled the guard around their position. But on the morning of the 14th the Cheyennes were gone as usual. Somehow they had slipped through the cordon once more and gone up Hat Creek.

For six days more, it continued. Day after day the Cheyennes fought. Night after night they used their matchless skill to slip away from the encircling lines of soldiers. Each day their numbers grew smaller.

The inevitable came at last. The Cheyennes made their last stand in the Hat Creek Bluffs, forty-four miles southwest of Fort Robinson, on the morning of January 21st, 1879. Worn out, most of them wounded, practically all suffering from frozen hands and feet, they lay in a washout, shoulder-deep, on the edge of the bluffs.

A last summons to surrender. It was answered by three scattering shots from the washout. Those three shots were the last cartridges the Cheyennes had. Forward rushed the soldiers, up the very edge of the washout. Not a shot was fired by the Indians. Into the huddled mass the troops poured a single crashing blast of flame. Without waiting to see the execution done, they leaped back to reload.

And now they saw a strange, uncanny apparition. Over the edge of the washout clambered three awful figures. Smeared with blood they were, their starvation-pinched features looking like living skulls. One carried an empty pistol. Two had worn knives. Tottering on their weak limbs, they poised for a moment on the edge of the grave of their people—the last three warriors of the unconquerable Cheyennes. Then with quavering war cries they madly charged, right into the muzzles of three hundred rifles.

With a shattering roar the fire leaped from those muzzles. The three warriors collapsed, literally shot to bits. They were the last fighters of their people. The Odyssey of the Cheyennes was ended.

Nighttime Stampede

(from Ramon F. Adams,
The Old-Time Cowhand, 1961; James H. Cook,
Fifty Years on the Old Frontier, 1923; and
Philip Ashton Rollins, *The Cowboy*, 1922)

T HE LURE OF CATTLE *ranching in Texas was low overhead and high profits. Maverick cattle were free for the acquiring. Grazing land was the open range. A herd of one thousand head of cattle doubled in size in two years and doubled again in four. In a land of surplus cattle the problem was how to convert a four-dollar longhorn on the hoof in Texas into eight to fifteen dollars cash up north, for in those days there were no railroads in Texas. The answer was to drive the "beeves" to the nearest railroad junction.*

In the heyday of the trail drives, six hundred thousand longhorns were herded each year six to eight hundred miles north to the nearest railroad junction to be sold and shipped east aboard the waiting cattle trains. Later drives stretched up to fifteen hundred miles to reach Wyoming and Montana ranches, the Rocky Mountain mining camps, and government posts supplying food to the Indians. One trail boss with eight to eleven cowboys could move twelve hundred to fifteen hundred longhorns north at the rate of eight to ten miles a day without losing weight and market value.

Before the Civil War the Shawnee Trail was the major cattle route. It ran northeast from Texas to St. Louis, at that time the nearest railroad link to Chicago. Later the railroad extended its tracks to Sedalia, Missouri, then Kansas City, which became the next cattle terminus. The Civil War (1861–1865) interrupted this traffic as Texas cowboys and ranch hands left to join the Confederate Army, while men from Missouri and Kansas mustered under the Union flag.

After the Civil War the Chisholm Trail became the next major route. It ran due north from Texas, crossed seven treacherous rivers, which the cattle had to swim, and cut through Indian Territory (now Oklahoma) to meet the railroad at Abilene, Kansas.

Farmers followed the railroad track westward as it was laid down. They bought up land and fenced it off with newfangled barbed wire for pasture and crops. In order to skirt the advancing "nesters" and the Indians, who by federal law could charge a toll tax per head, the cow trail again shifted west. In 1871 the Western Trail and a western branch of the Chisholm Trail joined the railroad at Dodge City, Kansas.

Danger lurked along the cow trail. Nature sowed locoweed and poisoned water holes with alkaline. Drought could dry up the land and shrivel the grass. Upland rains created flash floods on the Red, Washita, Canadian, North Canadian, and Cimarron Rivers. Quicksand was prevalent. Thunderstorms brought lightning and hail large enough to kill jackrabbits and prairie dogs. Indians and rustlers lay in wait—begging, stealing by stampede, or demanding a toll tax in cattle. And about once a decade a national financial panic could scuttle the dollar value of cattle.

Even the Kansas farmers became the cowboy's nemesis. The impervious herds from Texas carried the dreaded Spanish tick fever, which decimated the cattle on the northern farms. Kansas issued a law imposing a heavy toll tax on passing Texas herds and even gave farmers the right to keep the trail drivers out by the point of a gun.

By 1884 a trail boss complained: "Now there is so much land taken up and fenced in, that the trail for most of the way is little better than a crooked lane, and we have a hard time trying to find enough range to feed on. These fellows from Ohio, Indiana, and other northern states—the 'bone and sinew,' as the politicians call them—have made farms, enclosed pastures, and fenced water holes till you can't rest; and I say damn such bone and sinew!" Such was the slow demise of the long trails "north of 36"—hastened by barbed wire and expanding railroads.

On every trail drive, there was constant danger of thunderstorms setting off stampedes, especially at night. Here is a living, breathing account of a stampede from the writings of Ramon F. Adams, James H. Cook, and Philip Ashton Rollins.

★ ★ ★

WHEN WE REACH the bed-ground most of the cattle's already down, lookin' comfortable. They're bedded in open country, an' things look good for an easy night. It's been mighty hot all day, but there's a little breeze now makin' it right pleasant; but down the west I notice some nasty-lookin' clouds hangin' 'round the new moon that's got one horn hooked over the skyline. The storm's so far off that you can just hear her rumble, but she's walkin' up on us slow, an' I'm hopin' she'll go 'round. The cattle's all layin' quiet an' nice, so me an' Longrope stop to talk awhile.

"They're layin' quiet," says I.

"Too damn quiet," says he. "I like cows to lay still all right, but I want some of the natural noises that goes with a herd this size. I want to hear 'em blowin' off, an' the creakin' of their joints, showin' they're easin' themselves in their beds. Listen, an' if you hear anything I'll eat that rimfire saddle of yours—grass rope an' all."

I didn't notice till then, but when I straighten my ears it's quiet as a grave. An' if it ain't for the lightnin' showin' the herd once in a while, I couldn't a-believed that seventeen hundred head of longhorns lay within forty feet of where I'm sittin' on my hoss. It's gettin' darkers every minute, an' if it wasn't for Longrope's slicker I couldn't a-made him out, though he's so close I could have touched him with my hand. Finally it darkens so I can't see him at all. It's black as a nigger's pocket; you couldn't find your nose with both hands. All of a sudden it got warm and sticky, and there was a thick, muffled feelin' in the air. It wasn't long till the air moved kinda heavy and seemed to be saturated with sulphurous smoke. Then thunder began to mutter beyond the air, a hush as if the world held its breath before a calamity, and the cattle began to grow more restless.

Steadily it growed darker, and I could see two dense clouds were convergin' in heavy ragged columns. The air became oppressive to my lungs. Suddenly a flash of lightnin' licked silently toward the cloud banks. I waited for the thunder, countin' off the seconds till it should strike. Then it burst with a muffled sound and a long rumble. By now the cattle that'd been lyin' down got to their feet and let out an uneasy bawl or two.

Then the sky growed blacker; the slow-gatherin' clouds appeared to be suddenly agitated; they piled and rolled and mushroomed. The storm was upon us with thunder growlin' threats and lightnin' playin' behind the sullen jumble of black clouds. A fork of white lightnin' flashed, and like a boomin' avalanche, thunder followed. A blue-white knotted rope of lightnin' burned down out of the clouds, and instantly a thunderclap cracked, seemin' to shake the foundations of the earth. Then it rolled as if bangin' from cloud to cloud, and boomin' along the peaks, and at last rolled away into silence till the next one.

For a second it'll be like broad day, then darker than the dungeons of hell, an' I notice the little fireballs on my hoss's ears; when I spit there's a streak in the air like strikin' a wet match. These little fireballs is all I can see of my hoss, an' they tell me he's listenin' all ways; his ears are never still.

I tell you, there's something mighty ghostly about sittin' up on a hoss you can't see, with them two little blue sparks out in front of you wigglin' and movin' like a pair of spook eyes, an' it shows me the old night hoss is usin' his listeners pretty plenty. I got my ears cocked, too.

Then when all was panic in the pitchy black, made more terrifyin' by the sizzlin', spittin', snappin' flashes of lightnin', the cattle were suddenly gone.

There was some confusion, some crowdin', here and there a jumble of bodies where a steer had stumbled; but those of us on guard saw nothin' of it, and even while we wheeled our hosses for pursuit, the herd was gone thunderin' in the darkness.

Always the thunder boomed overhead, and by lightnin' flashes I glimpsed the boilin' sea of cattle fleein', with only blind fear crowdin' at their heels. The noise of their hoofs was engulfin'. It sounded like hell migratin' on cartwheels. Their bellowin' was an even higher roar than the thunder of their hoofs, and through all this noise I could hear the clackin' horns and the collidin' of bodies. The rush of horns looked like a movin' thicket of skeleton brush. The earth shook.

Panic-stricken, wild with fright, the cattle ran over bushes and gullies, badlands and prairie-dog holes . . . anythin' and everythin' that came in their way. All the riders were now in their saddles, racin' at top speed through the pitchy blackness of the night, guided only by the sounds of the fleein' animals, and dependin' to a great degree on the eyesight of their horses to keep 'em near the cattle, and to avoid bad gulches into which all might pile.

It had now become so dark that it was impossible for me to see the cattle except durin' the flashes of lightnin' which came with blindin' effect every few seconds. I rode at the top speed of my hoss in order to reach the lead cattle and help my pard turn 'em. Between the flashes of lightnin' the darkness was so intense that I could not even see the hoss I was ridin'.

When the lightnin' struck I could see him ahead racin' neck and neck with the lead cattle, with his hoss in so close to the plungin' mass that he must have felt their hot breath was on his leg and the smell of panic in his nostrils. He was usin' his slicker as a flail, bringin' it down with wide, overhead strokes into the faces of the foremost steers. He was yellin', screamin', cussin' them wild brutes to get their close-packed bodies to yield.

The cattle ran in the direction of the rough ground and the creek channel, where the banks were very high and perpendicular.

A sudden flash of lightnin' lit the surroundin's jes in time to save my life and picture the scene I can never forget.

My companion and his hoss seemed poised in mid-air for a moment far out over the edge of the high bank of the creek! Several head of cattle were leapin' after him to certain death.

My hoss needed a tug at the reins to stop his headlong rush. He braced his forefeet into the earth suddenly and firmly enough to bring 'im to a sudden halt, not more than five or six feet from the edge of the bluff over which my companion had just disappeared. How it happen that the cattle followin' in my rear did not crash against my horse and send up both over the bank, I shall never know. An instant of blindin' light, and then intense inky darkness reigned again.

In the Egyptian blackness I was helpless, so far as goin' to the aid of my pard was concerned. I knew that, because of the darkness of the night, I should hardly be able to find a place to get down into the creek bed to go to his aid.

After every night stampede there was a counting of human noses. This was done with anxiety which always was as tender in spirit as it was flippant in form. The riders, returning one by one during the next day's morning hours, came into camp, and an atmosphere of banter—banter which, in joking phrases and with several participants, ran on one occasion somewhat as follows: "Hulloa, Shorty, where'd you come from? Thought you was dead . . . Where's Baldy? Guess he's gone off to git married . . . No, he ain't. Here he . . .

The banter suddenly ceased, for as soon as Jack had come completely over the top of the hill and into clear view, he had begun to ride rapidly in a small circle. This was one of the equestrian Indians' two signals of important news or of request for strangers to advance for parley, and was often used by whites as a messenger of like import or serious tidings. At the first circle, some one remarked, "Mebbe Jack's playing with a rattler. No, he ain't. There he goes again. He's shore signaling," while some one else added, "Jack wouldn't do that for no cows. It must be Skinny." The camp had risen to its feet and started for the tethered ponies.

Suddenly there floated down the breeze three faint popping sounds evenly spaced. The wind had shifted, and its new course straight from Jack to the camp giving promise that sounds would carry thither, he had used his gun. The camp gasped, "My God, it's Skinny," and then the foreman said, with machine-gun rapidity but icily quiet tone, "Pete, quick, get them two clean shirts that's drying on the wagon tongue. We may need 'em for bandages." Nobody mentioned anything about a shovel, but a collision at the wagon's tailboard and the sound of rasping metal showed that three men instinctively had sought for the sometimes sad utensil, and that it was in hand.

In rapid strides of exaggerated length the punchers approached their horses. One beast shied away, but stopped the instant there rang out with tinny sound, "Damn you, Bronc, quit that," and thereafter the brute crouched and trembled and made no opposition to taking its bit and saddle. Bits were driven into horses' mouths like wedges into split logs. No effort was made to gather in cinches and offside latigos, to lay them atop the saddles, and to place latter gently on the ponies' backs. The saddles, each grasped by the horn and cantle, were waved in air to straighten out the latigos, and were slapped onto cringing backs with a sound like that of a slatting sail on a windy day.

At times like this when men were fierce and in a killing mood, their horses seemed to sense the situation. The most chronic buckers would forgo their pitching avocation, and, squatting low in tremor, would receive their load and never make a single jump.

The camp moved out to waiting Jack, and with it went the two clean shirts, each clutched against the rider's chest.

There were jerky, vertical single nods of heads, Jack supplementing his own nod by one later, slow horizontal turning of his head to right and then to left. A gentle sigh rose from the arriving punchers, two hands impotently opened and let two shirts flutter to the ground. Jack's inquiring look was answered by Ike's slight raising of the handle of the shovel, which thus far he had endeavored to conceal. Then came the first spoken words. Jack commenced the conversation, and in part it ran: "He's up at the end of the big draw, right by the split rock. Went over that high cut bank, him and a mess of cattle. He's lyin under 'em. He never knowed what hit him . . . No, I warn't with him. Just now seen his sign as I was coming acrost. I seen it was headed for the cut bank, so I chasséd over there." The foreman added: "Well, boys, let's get at it."

Then the little funeral cortege, having silently smoked a cigarette or two, fell into jiggling troll and headed for the big draw.

The funerals of the men who died in this way, of many Western men, were deeply affecting from their crude, sincere simplicity. About the open grave, which was at merely "somewhere on the plain," would gather a serious-faced little group. The body, wrapped in a saddle-blanket, would be lowered gently into its resting-place, and then would come a pause. Each attendant strongly wished that some appropriate statement might be made either to God or about the dead; but each man felt himself unequal to the task, and stood nervously wiping his forehead. Perhaps the strain wrung from some one person a sudden ejaculation. If so, the requirement for utterance had been satisfied, and all the mourners felt a buoyant sense of relief. If nobody spoke, some wandering eye fastened on the shovel. Whether by the ending of the spoken words or by the recognition of the spade, the signal for the filling of the grave had come.

When the filled-in earth had been pounded to smoothness and had been overlaid with rocks, as a barrier to marauding animals, it was time to leave. That parting would not be accomplished or even begun until there had terminated the strained, awkward silence under which most American men cloak their deeper feelings. The silence usually was ended by an expression spontaneously emitted from overwrought nerves, and often profane in form though not in intent. Speech broke the tension, horses were remounted, and the world was faced again.

At the foot of one of the noblest peaks in the Rocky Mountains lies a grave. Its occupant died in a stampede. All that was said at the interment came out hesitatingly and as follows: "It's too bad, too bad. Tom, dig a little deeper there. Hell, boys, he was a man," and presently, when the burial had been completed, "Bill, we boys leave you to God and the mountain. Good-by, Bill. Damn it, Jim, look out for your bronc."

32

Desperado with
Two Cocked, Smoking Pistols
Threatens Teddy Roosevelt

(from Theodore Roosevelt,
Theodore Roosevelt—An Autobiography, 1913)

THEODORE ROOSEVELT, *the human cyclone, seemed to be always on the move: hunter, explorer, traveler, governor, speaker, intellectual, and an avid reader (often a book a night), a man with a photographic memory who was equally at ease arranging a box of dinosaur bones into their correct order and shape as analyzing the relative firepower and tactics of man-of-war ships. He authored an estimated eighteen million words during his lifetime, including the* Naval History of the War of 1812 *at age twenty, and some 150,000 letters while serving as governor of New York and president of the United States. Whoever he was with, he "quickened the tempo of life." Henry Cabot Lodge said: "Theodore is one of the most lovable souls, as well as one of the cleverest and most daring men I have ever known."*

Roosevelt expanded our national parks, broke up corporate trusts, created the federal departments of Labor and Commerce, modernized the United States Navy, and sent the Great White Fleet to ports of call around the world—underscoring his phrase "Walk softly, but carry a big stick." He supported the construction of the Panama Canal and won the Noble Peace Prize for negotiating the peace treaty that settled the Russo-Japanese war.

A child of the Civil War, he was often sick from asthma attacks and sought to build up his strength. When he entered Harvard, his father advised him to take care of his morals, health, and grades in that order. He took up boxing. After his father's death he bought a ranch in the Dakotas, raised cattle, and once joined a successful manhunt for horse thieves. When six armed Indians charged him on horseback, he dismounted and coolly stood them off with his rifle.

Born with weak vision, he always wore thick glasses. Out west this initially earned him the jocular sobriquet "Four Eyes." Over time he befriended and earned the respect of settlers and ranch hands. But not everyone was won over by charm alone; from his 1913 autobiography, here is Teddy Roosevelt's tale of an ornery gunslinger who was bent on "makin' the town smoky." Roosevelt prefaces this six-shooter story with a short vignette of western life.

* * *

O F COURSE amusing incidents occur now and then. Usually these took place when I was hunting lost horses, for in hunting lost horses I was ordinarily alone, and occasionally had to travel a hundred or a hundred and fifty miles away from my own country. On one such occasion I reached a little cow town long after dark, stabled my horse in an empty outbuilding, and when I reached the hotel was informed in response to my request for a bed that I could have the last one left, as there was only one other man in it. The room to which I was shown contained two double beds; one contained two men fast asleep, and the other only one man, also asleep. This man proved to be a friend, one of the Bill Joneses whom I have previously mentioned. I undressed according to the fashion of the day and place, that is, I put my trousers, boots, chaps, and gun down beside the bed and turned in. A couple of hours later I was awakened by the door being thrown open and a lantern flashed in my face, the light gleaming on the muzzle of a cocked .45. Another man said to the lantern-bearer: "It ain't him." The next moment my bedfellow was covered with two guns, and addressed:

"Now, Bill, don't make a fuss, but come along quiet." "I'm not thinking of making a fuss," said Bill. "That's right," was the answer; "we're
your friends; we don't want to hurt you; we just want you to come
along, you know why." And Bill pulled on his trousers and boots and
walked out with them.

Up to this time there had not been a sound from the other bed.
Now a match was scratched, a candle lit, and one of the men in the
other bed looked around the room. At this point I committed the
breach of etiquette of asking questions. "I wonder why they took Bill,"
I said. There was no answer, and I repeated, "I wonder why they took
Bill." "Well," said the man with the candle, dryly, "I reckon they
wanted him," and with that he blew out the candle and conversation
ceased.

I later discovered that Bill in a fit of playfulness had held up the
Northern Pacific train at a nearby station by shooting at the feet of the
conductor to make him dance. This was purely a joke on Bill's part, but
the Northern Pacific people possessed a less robust sense of humor, and
in their complaint the United States Marshall was sent after Bill, on the
ground that by delaying the train he had interfered with the mails.

* * *

The only time I ever had serious trouble was at an even more primitive
little hotel than the one in question. It was also on an occasion when I
was out after lost horses. Below the hotel had merely a bar room, a dining room, and a lean-to kitchen; above was a loft with fifteen to twenty
beds in it. It was late in the evening when I reached the place. I heard
one or two shots in the bar room as I came up, and I disliked going in.
But there was nowhere else to go, and it was a cold night. Inside the
room were several men, who, including the bartender, were wearing
the kind of smile worn by men who are making believe to like what
they don't like. A shabby individual in a broad hat with a cocked gun in
each hand was walking up and down the floor talking with strident pro-
fanity. He had evidently been shooting at the clock, which had two or
three holes in its face.

He was not a "bad man" of the really dangerous type, the true man
killer type, but he was an objectionable creature, a would-be bad man, a
bully who for the moment was having things all his own way. As soon

as he saw me, he hailed me as "Four Eyes," in reference to my spectacles, and said, "Four Eyes is going to treat." I joined in the laugh and
got behind the stove and sat down, thinking to escape notice.

He followed me, however, and though I tried to pass it off as a jest
this made him more offensive, and he stood leaning over me with a gun
in each hand, using very foul language.

He was foolish to stand so near, and, moreover, his heels were close
together, so that his position was unstable. Accordingly, in response to
his reiterated command that I should set up the drinks, I said, "Well, if
I've got to, I've got to," and rose, looking past him.

As I rose, I struck quick and hard with my right just to one side of
the point of his jaw, hitting with my left as I straightened out, and then
again with my right. He fired his guns, but I do not know whether this
was merely a convulsive action of his hands or whether he was trying
to shoot at me. When he went down he struck the corner of the bar
with his head. It was not a case in which one could afford to take
chances, and if he had moved I was about to drop on his ribs with my
knees; but he was senseless. I took away his guns, and the other people
in the room, who were now loud in their denunciation of him, hustled
him out and put him in a shed. I got dinner as soon as possible, sitting
in a corner of the dining room away from the windows, and then went
upstairs to bed where it was dark so that there would be no chance of
anyone shooting at me from the outside. However, nothing happened.
When my assailant came to, he went down to the station and left on
a freight.

33

Shoot-out with the Marshal

(from Fred A. Stone,
"Flowers for Charley McDaniels")

THE HEYDAY *of the town-taming marshals was around 1870–
1880. Names like Bat Masterson and Wyatt Earp festoon western
history and legend, making famous such locales as Dodge City;
Tombstone, Arizona; and the O.K. Corral. Indeed, law and order in the
Wild West was established by the seat of one's pants. Shady gunslingers in-
timidated the patrons of saloons, where the fellow with the slower draw
went wobbly-legged and bit the dust. Perhaps there were Doc Hollidays
drinking and occasionally treating the wounded, and the dead were in-
variably put to rest in the local Boot Hill Cemetery. From "Flowers for
Charley McDaniels" by Fred A. Stone—the son of the sheriff in the story—
here is the tale of a thrilling shoot-out between gunman and lawman.*

★ ★ ★

I REMEMBER the day that Charley McDaniels rode into town. I saw
him coming down San Antonio Street. I didn't know who he was

at the time, so I didn't pay him any special mind. To me, just a little old knot-head kid piddling along the dusty, 'dobe-walled street when I should have been home an hour before, the sight of another tough-looking gun-hung rider meant nothing. Along in the 1890's his kind rode in and out of El Paso every day.

But few of his kind, or any other kind, had the sort of horse he rode. That's what caught my eye. I loved fine horses, and this was one of the finest I had ever seen—a big, lanky, stocking-legged sorrel with a white star on his forehead. He was hardly more than a colt, by the looks of him, yet he stepped along under the saddle with all the pride and assurance of a much older horse.

I stood and stared at the beauty of the sorrel and dreamed of the far-off time when I'd be big enough to own such a horse. It wasn't until Dad [Lewis W. Stone] arrived home later in the day that I learned the name of the man who rode the sorrel.

Dad came into the house with his customary long, quick stride, calling to Mother: "Get some dinner on the table as quick as you can, Reb. Got some business downtown that can't wait."

Dad always called Mother "Reb" because her maiden name had been Lee and she was the granddaughter of a general in the Confederate Army. The extra cheerfulness in Dad's voice didn't fool Mother. She waited a while, then asked quietly: "Who is it this time, Rocky?"

Dad's face sobered. "Charley McDaniels," he said, just as quietly, then added, as if to divert her thoughts: "Riding one of the finest sorrel horses I ever saw."

Mother turned to her cooking, and they said no more. But for me they had already said enough.

I knew who Charley McDaniels was. I'd never seen him till he'd ridden past that morning on the star-faced sorrel, but I knew all about him. Kids learn things a lot faster than most grownups realize, and Dad had been United States Deputy Marshal for the southwestern district of Texas too long for me not to know the names and general histories of most of the badmen in our part of the country.

And Charley McDaniels was bad. There was no doubt about that. He was as bad as they came. He was on the wanted list of every law-enforcement officer within the radius of a thousand miles. He was half

Irish and half Mexican. His main specialties were horse-stealing, cattle-rustling, hiring out as a gunman in local range wars and plain murder, for whatever price he could command. He was one of the few real bad-men who never drank: his weakness ran to gambling and women. He loved the game of monte. He had a reputation for never cheating, but a still better one for gunning down any man who tried to cheat him. He preferred Mexican women to white ones, and generally any time he wasn't to be found around a monte table, he'd be down in the red-light district, throwing his money around among the Mexican whores.

I felt a quick surge of excitement as I thought of Charley Mc-Daniels' reputation as a gunman and killer, then recollected the choice Dad always issued to every badman who rode into El Paso: "Get out of town, go to jail or go to Boot Hill."

Dad had made the order stick so far. In one instance I had been on hand to watch him do it. That was the time he put me behind a tele-graph pole with orders to stay there, then walked up to confront a drunken hoodlum who had a reputation for being mighty careless with his guns. Nothing had happened that time. Dad merely talked for a while, and finally the man unbuckled his belt and handed over his guns. But I was betting it wouldn't be that way this time. Not with Charley McDaniels.

Just why the possibility of a gunfight between my father and Charley McDaniels should have stiffed me with a sort of exhilaration in-stead of fear and dread, I'm not sure right now. I was young, but not too young to understand the danger to my father. The only explanation that I can give is the fact that in those days I was so inordinately proud of my father, so sure of his courage and ability to handle any situation, that I may have felt him invincible.

And looking back now I still have that feeling that he was as invinci-ble as any man ever was. I remember following him that day from the kitchen to the back porch, where he went to wash up for dinner. I re-member how he looked bent over the washbasin—the whole six-feet-two-inches-one-hundred-ninety-six pounds of him. He was straight as an arrow, with broad, thick shoulders and a trim gun-hung waist.

He was of Scotch-Irish and Indian origin—two kinds of Indian, Cherokee and Comanche. He looked more Indian than white with his coppery skin, dark eyes and jet black hair. Yet that hair must have been a throwback to some Scotch Gaelic ancestor, for I never knew of a curly headed Indian among either the Cherokee or the Comanches.

I remember how Dad always wound up his face-washings by trying to slick back that unruly hair with his wet hands and never having any luck. And I remember how he failed this time and gave me a solemn wink as he carried the washpan to the edge of the porch and splashed its contents into my mother's flower bed.

We ate. And while Dad did a lot of talking, there was nothing more said about Charley McDaniels. When he rose Dad said, "I won't be gone long, Reb," and left the house, walking as casually as if he'd been going out to shoe a horse.

What happened downtown right after that, I didn't learn about in detail until years later, so many years later in fact, that no doubt some of those details were minimized or exaggerated. Yet with all its many tellings, the main story has never varied much, so that what I tell here can't be far off track.

Dad searched first among the whorehouses, but if the gunman had visited there, the Mexican girls wouldn't admit it. Which didn't surprise Dad. After all McDaniels was young, not hard for a woman to look at and was a free spender. Why should the girls give him away to a peace officer who made a habit of killing or jailing or running out of town some of their very best customers?

It wasn't till Dad entered the Gem Saloon on El Paso Street that he got wind of his man. McDaniels, according to one talkative elbow-bender, had just left, headed for the Ranch Saloon a block or so down the street.

Dad left the Gem through the back door. He hurried down an alley and entered the Ranch Saloon through one of the little wine rooms that were reserved for family drinking, women not being allowed to drink in the main saloons in those days. He walked quietly into a narrow hall that led to the main barroom.

He nudged the door open and took a close look at the customers ringing the gaming tables. His man wasn't there either. He entered the room, then spoke quietly for a moment to Jake Sullivan, the barkeep, then left by the main front door, walking out as unobtrusively as he could. He hadn't fooled anybody, however. Behind him every customer in Jake's place pushed through the swinging doors and stood in the street, watching him. Some followed for a ways, then finally lost interest as Dad turned a corner and went around to Utah Street.

Again he searched the red-light district, combing it carefully as a squaw hunting lice in a buck's hair, and again he had no luck. Then just as he was coming out of the big red brick building known as Tillie Howard's place, his deputy Elmer Wagner came across the street to meet him.

"Been a shooting at the Wigwam Saloon on San Antonio," Elmer reported.

Dad asked quickly: "Who was in it?"

"A gambler and a deputy city marshal," Elmer said.

"Anybody else?"

"Yeah. The fellow what done the shootin'. Didn't get his name. The deputy was Tom Glover. The dead gambler was that big, black Mex monte dealer at the Wigwam."

Together they hurried to the Wigwam. Turning west on San Antonio, they saw a crowd making a rush for the far side of the street, taking cover wherever it was to be found. Across the street on the south side stood a lone man. The man stood hesitant, as if not quite sure where to go next.

"That's our man!" Dad exclaimed to Elmer, then added: "Get to the other side of the street and keep out of this fracas till I'm down or till I invite you to take a hand."

Charley McDaniels caught sight of Elmer crossing the street and burst into sudden laughter. Then he stepped out into the middle of the street, turned his back on Elmer and faced toward Dad, who had also stepped into the clear.

"Marshal," he called to Dad, "I'm coming after my horse. I'm fixing to leave town."

Dad called back to him. "It's too late for that now, Charley. I'm arresting you for murder, and where you're going you won't need a horse."

"That gambler was cheating, Marshal," McDaniels argued. "And I warned that law feller to stay out of the deal, but he went ahead and drawed on me. First!"

"Can you prove that, Charley?"

"I sure can."

"All right then," Dad said. "You got nothing to fear. Just drop your guns, and we'll go talk to the judge. I'll see that you get a fair trial."

Dad didn't expect Charley McDaniels to drop his guns than did the hiding onlookers who peeked from every doorway and window along both sides of the street. But he stood waiting, giving McDaniels a chance. And while he waited he could hear the old-timers calling bets to each other up down and across the street. He took what comfort he could from the fact that the odds offered seemed to make him a favorite to win.

Dad called again. "Drop those irons and lift your hands, Charley. Like I said, I'll see you get a fair trial."

But the killer grinned and shook his head. "Sorry, Marshal," he said. "I can't hear you. Not when you talk like that."

"You better hear me," Dad said. "If you don't, I'm going to have to come and get you, Charley, and you're not going to like that."

McDaniels, as if stalling for time, studied on that for a moment, then tried to make a deal. "Tell you what, Marshal, let's save us both a lot of trouble. You let me get my horse, and I'll leave town—and promise not to come back as long as you are King Pin of the butcher shop here."

Dad shook his head. "You've got me wrong, Charley. I don't make deals with outlaws. You're not getting out of this town until you've settled your bill."

"Well, then," McDaniels said reluctantly, "I reckon you better start walking. I'll be coming to meet you."

There was a span of ninety-six feet between them when they started. I know this because Old Chipmunk, a deputy city marshal, stepped it off the next morning—"Just to keep the books straight." There wasn't a soul in sight between them, but from a hundred different points of cover, there were eyes squinted against the hot glare of the afternoon sun. There was no sound either except their slow, deliberate footsteps, muffled by the powdery dust of the street.

Moving slowly, speaking no word, they closed the gap to sixty feet, to forty, then to thirty.

From that point on, the only thing either man watched was his opponent's eyes. Each knew that the other walked with his hands held level with the gun butts at his belt, but it wasn't hands they watched. It was the eyes that would give the telltale signal.

A listless breeze trailed along the street, picking up a tiny wisp of dust, then dropping it almost before it cleared the ground. The leaves on the big cottonwood overhanging the street trembled slightly and grew still.

Then it came and was over with such shocking suddenness that it was almost a disappointment to the onlookers. There was just one brief instant when the hands of both men were filled, and the guns were bucking and crashing. Then the guns were still again and, through a haze of light bluish smoke that hung in the dead air, the onlookers saw one of the men lower his guns as if he no longer had the strength to hold them. Then as one gun slipped from his hand, he pitched forward, plowing into the dust with his head and shoulder.

He lay there still and quiet, while the second man, bare-headed now, advanced cautiously toward him, still holding a smoking gun in each hand.

Elmer Wagner and Chipmunk were the first to rush out.

"You hurt, Marshal?" Elmer queried, excitedly. "You hit anywhere?"

Dad looked behind him where his black hat lay in the dust. "No," he said, "but I think he ruined a damned good hat for me!"

Chipmunk brought Dad his hat, and Dad poked a finger through one of the jagged holes in the crown and seemed to study his finger for a good long while. Finally, clapping the hat on his head, he said to Elmer: "You and Chipmunk take care of things. I got business at home that can't wait."

I was there in the house when he came through the yard gate. His steps seemed faster and wider apart than ever and there was a wider-than-usual grin on his face. And I remember how Mother was sitting there in the old granny rocking chair, watching him come up the steps, like she was seeing a dream come true.

Dad caught her up out of the chair and kissed her and said, "Hi, Reb; is supper ready?" and winked at me to show that he knew it was way too early for supper yet. Then he headed for the water cooler, where he got himself a big long drink of water.

When he finished Mother asked quietly, "When will the funeral be, Rocky?"

"At ten o'clock in the morning."

Mother nodded. "I'll hunt up my hymn book," she said, "and cut some fresh flowers at daybreak."

Dad said: "Make them something special, Reb. He was a game one; I liked him."

"Then why did you kill him?" she asked. Her tone wasn't accusing; she just wanted to know.

"Why for a couple of reasons, Reb. First he was too old a dog to teach new tricks. Second you're too young and pretty to be left a widow."

Dad grinned at her, pitched his hat onto the couch, hunted up another and left the house headed back for town. Mother picked up the hat, stuck a finger through one of the holes in the crown, then finally went to hang the hat in a closet.

"Now," she said to me, "if he can just get a shirt and a pair of pants, we'll have a whole outfit."

She was smiling at me as she said that, but when I happened to wander into the room a few minutes later, I found her stretched out, face down across the bed, weeping silently, like Dad always said a woman had to do now and then.

The next morning I helped carry the flowers that Mother and Dad took to put on Charley McDaniels' grave, after they buried him and sung over him. But the sorrel horse wasn't anywhere in sight.

I never did find out what happened to him.

★ 34 ★

Saved by Cowboys

(from Philip Rollins,
"A Conversation with Mr. Rollins")

T HE NOBLEST *code of honor ever fashioned in America was the*
cowboy's code.
"One of the first rules of the Code was courage," wrote Ramon
F. Adams in The Old-Time Cowhand:

"Men who followed the life of a cowboy wouldn't tolerate a coward, for
one coward would endanger the whole group. Through the hundreds
of ways of makin' the life of a coward unbearable, he was soon elimi-
nated. If a man had a spark of courage to start with, the life he lived
on the range soon developed it to a high degree. He had to have bones in
his spinal column and know how to die standin' up. His life was full of
dangers such as mad cows, bad hosses rode over a country full of dog
holes at breakneck speed, crossin' swollen rivers, quick sands, and
many other things, not countin' the troubles the early cowman had
with Injuns. If his craw wasn't full of sand and fightin' tallow, he
wouldn't make the grade. . . .

"The cowman laughed in the face of danger, laughed at hardships when laughin' was hard. Tragedy and its possibilities were all 'round 'im, and his cheerfulness was an attempt to offset this. As a man of action he had little time to mourn fatalities. . . . One of the cowman's outstandin' codes was loyalty. He was one class of worker who didn't have to be watched to see that he did his work well. The nature of his work demanded that he be trusted. He took a pride in bein' faithful to his 'brand' and in performin' his job well. He needed no overseer, or advice. . . . He lived up to a law that held the obligation of friendship deeper than all others. Yet, accordin' to the unwritten law, he stood ready to offer friendly service to strangers, or even an enemy, when necessity called for it. The rule required that whoever caught a signal of distress was to render quick assistance. It sometimes happened that a cowboy laid down his own life to save an enemy that he might live up to this code."

Here is the true story of Phillip Rollins in Wyoming, circa 1880. As a boy, he punched cattle on his father's ranch and drove herds up from Texas. At five he studied Latin; at eight, Greek. At college he majored in archaeology. A renaissance man, he was a lawyer, rancher, historian, author, and collector of Americana. As Rollins relates in this archival interview, three different cowboys saved his life on three separate occasions.

* * *

YOU MUST UNDERSTAND, said Phil Rollins with a little smile as he reached for a cigarette, "that I'm sentimental about the cowboy. I have a right to be—I had my life saved three times by cowboys when I was just a kid."

Upon being pressed for details, Rollins said quickly, "You're sure this won't bore you? Well, once when I was riding herd in Montana, my horse went over a steep bank into quicksand—I was twelve then. He began to flounder as he was rapidly sucked down, but before I had time to do anything or to think of doing anything, I was pushed or thrown onto solid ground where the other riders could get a lariat to me and pull me up. That was all I knew at the moment. What had happened was that a cowboy had seen me go over the bank and had instantly spurred his own horse down into the quicksand beside me so that he could throw me with one powerful shove out of the saddle to safety. We never did find his body, though we waited for three days. Years later—I was afraid to say anything before then—I spoke to his brother about it. 'Why, hell,' he said, 'you got no call to worry. Nothing else he could do. He had to do that or leave the range.'

"Another time I was riding a horse that was too much for me. He threw me out of the saddle, but my foot caught in the stirrup, and I was in instant danger of being crushed by the hooves of the excited, bucking horse when I saw a flash of steel: a cowboy dived out of his saddle at my horse, grabbed hold of the stirrup, and with his open knife cut it loose. They told me that horse stamped on his head ten times before it could be stopped. The cowboy had known it was certain death to try to cut off the stirrup, but that didn't stop him. I was twelve then, too.

"The third time was in a blizzard in Montana. A blizzard could cause the loss of a whole valuable herd if it caught them in an unsuitable place, so when a bad storm came up the cattle had to be driven to a place where they would be out of drifts, preferably a low hill where the snow would be blown away so they could get to the grass but protected by higher hills from the full force of the wind. This night the wind was blowing in great wild gusts, driving and whipping the snow, which fell so thick that it was impossible to see more than a foot or so. It was a sudden and dangerous storm, and the cowboy who went out to try to head the lead steer into a safe spot told me not to come with him. I followed him anyway. Presently my horse stumbled, and I was thrown out of the saddle. When they found me next morning, I was lying on top of a steer that had been killed to provide me with warmth, and over me was not only my own bearskin coat but the cowboy's. Beside me was a lump of ice—the cowboy."

THE AMERICAN
CENTURY

* 35 *

Earthquake Pulverizes
San Francisco; Fires Spread;
Banker Struggles to Survive

(from Paul Rink,
A. P. Giannini: Building the Bank of America)

A T 5:13 A.M. *on April 18, 1906, a titanic earthquake shook San Francisco. "There was a deep rumble," reported a police-man on duty, "deep and terrible, and then I could see it actually coming up Washington Street. The whole street was undulating. It was as if the waves of the ocean were coming towards me, billowing as they came." Said another who staggered through the quake: "It was as though the earth was slipping quietly away from under our feet. There was a sickening sway, and we were all flat on our faces."*

"Trolley tracks were twisted, their wires down, wriggling like ser-pents, flashing blue sparks all the time. The street was gashed in any number of places. From some of the holes water was spurting; from others gas."

Earth waves two to three feet high rocked buildings. Brick chimneys toppled and crashed through ceilings. Walls crumbled. Towers and cornices fell. Plaster dust filled the air. Wooden houses heaving and falling sounded like the squeak of nails when a packing crate is pried open. Church bells

*clanged—tolling calamity. "Everywhere there was the noise, like thousands
of violins, all at a discord. The most harrowing sound one could imagine."*

*Rubble was everywhere. Fires broke out. Water mains turned to drib-
bles. As the fires spread for three days, soldiers from the Presidio were summoned to augment the police. The mayor authorized the troops and police
"to KILL any and all persons found engaged in Looting or in the Commission of Any Other Crime." Without water to fight the fires, the firemen
were helpless. Blocks of buildings were dynamited. Eventually the fires
burned from the waterfront (sparing only Telegraph Hill and Russian
Hill) as far west as Van Ness and southwest to the Mission District, and
well below Market Street. Consumed were Union Square and the St. Francis Hotel, the Fairmont and Palace Hotels, and Nob Hill.*

*In this midst of chaos stood Amadeo Peter (A. P.) Giannini, a success-
ful vegetable-commission merchant turned banker. Two years earlier he
had opened the Bank of Italy. On the morning of April 18 two employees
headed for Giannini's small bank to find that it was spared the initial destruction of the quake. But as they soon found out, fires and riotous mobs
presented a greater danger. This passage from* A. P. Giannini: Building
the Bank of America *by Paul Rink, tells the story of how Giannini's quick
thinking both saved his bank and played an instrumental role in helping
San Francisco rebuild from destruction.*

* * *

AFTER PAUSING A MOMENT, Avenali and Pedrini hurried on to
the Bank. They were amazed to find the building still intact. They
pondered a moment, trying to decide what to do. Should they open up
the bank or not?

Already clean-up squads were busy sweeping up the broken glass
from the streets and gathering the tumbled bricks into piles. Businessmen greeted each other and joked about the early morning eye-opener.
Gradually the doors opened; life began to seem once again peaceful and
quiet. The big quake would be something to talk about for a long time;
but right now it was over, and the morning was swiftly returning to
normal.

Avenali and Pedrini looked at each other. The same thought passed through their minds: What would A.P. do? The boss was still far away in San Mateo, presumably enjoying a tranquil breakfast.

"What would A.P. do if he were here?" asked Avenali more of himself than of his companion. The Bank of Italy was still in diapers, but so strong was the spirit and personality of its founder that already everyone connected with it unconsciously tried to mold thought and action after his pattern.

"I think A.P. would say that a little thing like an earthquake shouldn't stop the bank from opening," said Pedrini.

Avenali laughed. "You're right. Let's go."

In a few moments the two had hitched up a bouncy little white mare to a snappy buggy and were rattling through the debris-filled streets to the Crocker National.

The imposing bank was still closed, but the official in charge let them in and passed over three heavy canvas bags filled with $80,000 in gold and silver, which amounted to every penny of the Bank of Italy's hard cash. Avenali and Pedrini quickly counted the money, loaded it under the seat of the buggy, and returned to their own bank. They opened the doors and were ready for business, provided anyone was interested.

They stood in the doorway, thumbs in vest pockets, looking out into the bright morning. Somehow, now, with all the Bank's money in their sole custody, they didn't feel quite so sure of themselves. The morning had taken on a kind of ominous quality. The streets were filling with restless people. There was a nervous, apprehensive tension in the air. Fire engines rumbled continually through the debris, bells clanging, belching smoke. Already a thin brown pall from scattered fires rose into the sky, cut the sunlight, made everything seem a bit unreal. There were ugly rumors, too, of fighting and looting, of roaming gangs of hoodlums.

The two Bank employees gazed behind them, thinking of the stacks of silver and gold behind the teller's wicket. The men were aware of the very dubious protection of the "cracker boxes without tops," and wondered if perhaps they hadn't been too hasty in taking the money out of Crocker's massive steel vaults.

Seventeen miles away in San Mateo, A.P. and his wife took hurried stock of their situation. The big frame house had been badly shaken but had suffered little actual damage. Even at that distance from San Francisco the jolts had been heavy enough to toss them and the children from their beds, break some chinaware and cause chimneys to crumple; but other than these things, the Gianninis were in very good shape. They decided that the place for A.P. at this moment was in San Francisco. Clorinda and the children would be perfectly all right by themselves.

A.P. needed five hours to cover 17 miles. Only occasional trains were running, and these thumped their way at a snail's pace through a countryside jammed with people and filled with rumors of the wildest kind. The closer the train got to San Francisco, the thicker were the mobs. Refugees pouring from the city blocked the way of those who were trying to reach it.

Finally beside himself with the delay, A.P. abandoned the train and started walking, hitching rides on wagons when he could. He arrived at the bank exactly at the stroke of noon. Pedrini and Avenali felt the weight of the world roll from their shoulders as they saw the massive, tall man picking his way through the rubble in Columbus Street.

By now the situation had utterly changed. A dense cloud of dirty brown smoke rose and billowed over the entire stricken city. All the watermains were broken and split, and there was nothing with which to fight the flames except in those few places where engines could pump salt water directly from the bay. Nothing, that is, except dynamite and artillery. Ceaselessly explosions rumbled and thudded as desperate men tried to choke the fires by knocking into rubble whole blocks of buildings.

There was no thought now of business as usual. The streets were boiling with panicky crowds trying to get themselves and a few possessions to safety. Men, women, children, horses, pets, wagons struggled for passage in a confused mass. Gangs of toughs roamed at will, and already martial law had been declared. Squads of soldiers from San Francisco Presidio were deploying with orders to shoot at sight anyone looting or pillaging. They were not yet spread widely enough, however, throughout the doomed city to be much protection.

Only an insane man would open a bank on a day like this; and when

A.P. saw the wide-swinging doors of the Bank of Italy, his first reaction was angry dismay.

"You should have left the money at Crocker," he rumbled in his gravelly voice. "At least, there it would have been safe."

They explained. They'd gotten the money when there had been no fire. The quake was over. Only the best interests of the Bank had prompted them to open. A.P. glanced at them briefly. The justice of what they said cooled him. He cast an anxious glance skyward at the always thickening cloud of smoke.

"What's done is done. Now what do we do?" He closed and locked the doors. "Let's see for ourselves and then make up our minds."

Pedrini was left in charge of the money, with the trusty, $10 six-shooter for protection. A.P. and Avenali started out through the town to see for themselves.

The fire was gaining headway fast. Fanned by brisk winds from the Pacific, it roared and crackled through the matchstick jumble, destroying whole buildings and debris with equal ease. Before it was done, little beside the edges of one of the world's great cities would remain standing. Over 28,000 buildings were to be destroyed, 500 people were to die, and 250,000 were to be left homeless. Property loss was finally to be reckoned at nearly $500,000,000.

By five in the afternoon, A.P. had seen and heard enough. The fires were racing absolutely without hindrance. The Palace Hotel was a roaring mass of flames. The beautiful new eighteen-story *Call* building was a column of fire against the evening sky. His mind was made up. They were getting out.

Quickly he gave his orders. Other employees and anxious stockholders of the bank had arrived and he set them all to work.

Three men were dispatched to the commission district to the warehouse of L. Scatena & Co. "Bring back two heavy fruit trucks," he commanded. As they rushed off, he shouted after them, "Pile on some crates of produce—oranges, apples, tomatoes, anything."

With two other men he started piling the bank's fixtures on the sidewalk. There wasn't much—typewriter, a few chairs, some records. Inside, another man started sweeping the gold and silver coins from the counters back into the bags.

Soon the two wagons were back. Keeping a sharp lookout for hoodlums, who would have lost no time attacking this rich plum had they known about it, A.P. piled the money in the bottom of one of the trucks, along with the records, and everything else that looked as though it had come from a bank. On top he stacked the fruit—crates of oranges and apples.

A.P. looked at the little Bank, then quickly turned his face ahead. There was no use looking back now.

Whips cracked over the heads of the nervous draft horses, who were glad to get moving.

A.P. headed toward the house of Clarence Cuneo, his brother-in-law. Cuneo's house was on the edge of town and might be safe for a while longer.

They needed two hours to cover the few miles. People were clawing madly to get themselves and whatever of their belongings they could salvage out of the city. Night had fallen and the wagons bumped and clattered over the cobbles and bricks and tumbled lumber, with only the lurid glare of the flames for light.

Mrs. Cuneo gave them all a quick supper and then A.P. stripped the house of its furnishings. Rockers, mattresses, bedding, bureaus, chairs—all were piled on the wagons to give the appearance of a refugee caravan.

By eight o'clock they were on their way out of San Francisco headed for San Mateo. The trip was a nightmare. The flames rose higher and higher into the sky, reflecting in weird and frightening patterns from the night fogs. The city and the roads leading from it were choked with people, filled with lawlessness and quick death for the unwary. To avoid as much of the crush as possible, A.P. chose a long, roundabout way out; it was seven in the morning when the weary horses and men plodded into the driveway at Seven Oaks. Mrs. Giannini gave the exhausted "refugees" breakfast, and they fell into bed—all except A.P.

First things first. He had $80,000 of other people's money in three canvas bags. What to do with it? The bags were finally hidden in the ashpit beneath the fireplace in the living room. All the Bank of Italy's cash companionably nestled among the ashes and cinders!

Over Clorinda's protests, A.P. hitched up another horse to a light buggy, headed it toward the city, and gave the mare her head. Then he promptly went to sleep, jogging and bouncing in total weariness on the driver's seat.

In two hours the horse picked her way through the strewn streets of a destroyed and disorganized city. The fire was at its peak. Soldiers everywhere were trying to keep order. Stunned people were camped in the parks, along the beaches, on the sidewalks. The entire business section was gone. The Bank of Italy was a charred mass over which rose threads of smoke. The huge Crocker National was burned to the ground, its fireproof vaults a sizzling hot mass of steel that would need weeks to cool sufficiently to be opened. If A.P. ever looked backwards, surely at this moment he gave thanks that Avenali and Pedrini had removed the cash.

Consider the position of the Bank of Italy at this moment. Giannini had $80,000 in available cash to cover deposits of $846,000. The owners of this money had every right to it; and if they all demanded it at once, which was very likely, it is easy to imagine the catastrophe that could take place. On the other hand, A.P. recognized instantly the tremendous opportunity for the bank to earn money, and its obligation to help rebuild the ruined city.

Before the fires had burned themselves out, San Francisco's bankers were holding meetings, trying to decide what must be done. Every one of them recognized his responsibility. The people of the city must be helped. Money was needed to do the job. Unfortunately, most of the money was in vaults so hot they couldn't be opened.

These staid and conservative gentlemen seemed to be at a loss for ideas. Not one of them came up with any really helpful plan; and in all truth, there was probably very little that could be done. What they did decide upon was useful; but in a way it was negative, rather than truly constructive. A bank holiday was declared; a moratorium on debts was put into effect. Eventually a clearing house in the United States Mint was organized and issued scrip to a small limit per person to cover withdrawals against such time as they could be made. No hard money changed hands, and this scrip did not have the confidence of the masses of the people. It did little actually to help the situation.

Giannini attended a couple of meetings but quickly decided he could do more to help the stricken city by personally looking after his depositors. If the rest of the bankers were dispirited, at loose ends, and shillyshallying, Giannini was not. There was nothing discouraged about A.P. and his plans. He had confidence in himself, in his bank, and in the people of San Francisco.

This confidence was reflected in a circular letter sent out from San Mateo to all the depositors on Sunday, the 22nd, while the city was still burning. It announced that the Bank of Italy was full of life, ready to go, and that offices for the conduct of business would be set up at the office of Dr. Attillio Giannini on Van Ness Street.

A "branch" to facilitate business was also established on a plank laid across two barrels at the Washington Street wharf. Checks would be cashed, loans made, and deposits accepted. The Bank of Italy was in full operation and it was the only bank in San Francisco that was.

Each morning a buggy arrived at the wharf carrying $10,000 in gold from the "vault" in the Giannini fireplace at San Mateo. Back of the plank counter, A.P. radiated confidence and courage. His faith and his enthusiasm were infectious. San Francisco had to be rebuilt, and the Bank of Italy was ready to supply the wherewithal. His distressed and hard-hit customers found they had made no mistake in putting their faith in him and his Bank.

He effectively forestalled any possibility of a run on the $80,000 by voluble good humor and stern insistence that any withdrawals or loans had to be used for the purpose of rebuilding.

If a man requested $5,000, A.P. offered him half that. If another requested $3,000, he talked him down to $1,500, suggesting that elbow grease and determination make up the rest.

"Look," he would say in his deep booming voice, waving a huge sheaf of loan and withdrawal requests in his hand, "we'll supply half of what you want. You'll have to make do with that. If we gave everybody all they want, there wouldn't be enough to go around. Everybody needs a chance."

He worked fast. Not only were most of the other banks without any cash, but they were in most cases hampered by the loss of their records. Giannini didn't need any records. He knew intimately every man who was a customer of his Bank. He knew all about the customer's credit rating, his capacity for work, his reliability, what property he owned. All this information was in his head, and no time was lost when a loan was requested.

The chaotic city was also badly in need of construction materials, and Giannini did his best to alleviate this situation. He roamed the waterfront, collared captains of schooners he had known and with whom he had done business in his produce commission days. He shoved the cash at them, saying, in effect, "Get to sea. Get up north and come back with lumber!" The first shiploads of lumber to arrive in the city came as a result of Giannini's fast thinking and action.

He also immediately sent men into the charred homes of North Beach, and among the Italian refugee groups, prying more hoarded cash out of them. Funds salvaged from ruined homes, hidden in wagons and sewn into the lining of clothes saw the light of day. In this way thousands of extra dollars were deposited in the Bank and became available for the work of reconstruction. Many a hitherto reluctant Italian was at last only too glad to turn his money over to the driving, energetic head of the Bank of Italy and get it out of the barely secure hiding places of the refugee camps. The original $80,000 was thus spread thin and wide and made to do the job of a sum many, many times greater.

Such enthusiasm and courage, coupled with such real practical help, could have but one effect: the North Beach area recovered from the quake and fire far sooner than any other part of San Francisco.

North Beach, and San Francisco as a whole, never forgot the friendly, neighborly help that the Bank of Italy made available to them during the disaster. If the growth of the Bank before the fire had been merely healthy, afterwards it was nothing short of phenomenal. San Franciscans, it seemed, had at long last found out what a *good* bank, a *people's* bank, could accomplish. They backed the bank that had backed them when they needed it.

By the end of 1906, all the other banks were, of course, back in operation. They were doing a volume of business slightly above that of the previous year. The Bank of Italy practically doubled its business by the end of the year. Assets stood at nearly $2,000,000. Deposits had doubled and stood at $1,355,000. The most impressive statistic from the point of view of the Bank's popularity, however, was the number of depositors. The number of savings accounts had risen from 1,023 to 2,644, while commercial checking accounts rose from 280 to 451. Truly the Bank of Italy was on its way . . . to become the Bank of America!

36

Sergeant York—
"The Terminator" in World War I

(from Alvin C. York,
Sergeant York: His Life Story and War Diary, 1928)

SERGEANT ALVIN C. YORK, the mountain man from Tennessee, was awarded the Congressional Medal of Honor, the French Legion of Honor, the Croix de Guerre with palms, the Médaille Militaire, and the Italian War Cross for his exploits during World War I. General "Black Jack" Pershing, U.S. Army, proclaimed York "the outstanding civilian soldier of the war." General Foch, in decorating him, said, "What you did was the greatest thing accomplished by any private soldier of all the armies of Europe."

Sergeant York, for his part, told his life story with great reluctance and modesty:

> *My great-great-grandfather, Coonrod Pile, was the first white man to settle here. He lived in a rock house, a cave, near Wolf River in the Pall Mall Valley in the northeast part of Middle Tennessee. My father was a blacksmith. He ran his shop in the same cave my great-great-grandfather used. We lived in a one-room log cabin, built out of hewn*

logs, hewn with a broad ax, chinked with clay and sticks. My father was fond of hunting and shooting. He'd hunt every day, and if he had blacksmith work he had to catch up with, he'd do that at night. He was a good shot and always won every match. His advice to me was always to be accurate in shooting. . . .

After the war was going on, before America declared war, we were continually reading the papers. We decided long before we received our call that America would be in it. Then I got notice to register at R.C. Pile's store at Pall Mall, the post office [June 5, 1917]. It bothered me a plenty whether the war was right or wrong. I knew if it was right, everything would be all right. And if it was wrong, it would be all wrong. I prayed two whole days and a night on the mountainside. And I received my assurance that it was all right, that I should go, and that I would come back without a scratch. I received this assurance direct from God. I told my little old mother not to worry; that it was all right, and I was coming back. I told my brothers and sisters. I didn't want to go to fight and kill. But I had to answer the call of my country, and I did. I have got no hatred toward the Germans and I never had.

I kept a diary right through the war. And I carried a Testament with me. I read it everywhere. I read it in dugouts, in fox holes, and on the front line. It was my rock to cling to. It and my diary.

York reported for basic training in Atlanta and went overseas with his unit on May 1, 1918. He embarked on an old Scandinavian ship in New York Harbor; it was the first time he had ever seen the ocean. In France, Sergeant York's outfit was moved up to the front line for the American offensive at Chatel-Chehery in the Argonne Forest. There York, with a handful of men, whipped an entire German machine gun battalion, killing 28 and capturing 132. From Sergeant York: His Life Story and War Diary, *here is York's 1928 oral account of those events, with selections from the diary that he kept while at the front.*

* * *

ABOUT 3 A.M. IN THE MORNING, the morning of October 8th, 1918, our Captain, Captain Danforth, come to us and told us we were to move on to Hill 223, which was to be the jumping-off place for our attack, which was to be at daybreak. Our objective was the De-cauville Railroad, which was about three kilometres to the northwest of the hill, and further on almost in the centre of the Argonne Forest. We were to bust that old railroad so as to stop the Germans from sending in their troops and supplies. With the Captain leading, we marched over the Aire River on a little shaky, wooden bridge which the engineers had thrown up for us, on through the town of Chatel Chehery and on up to Hill 223. It was so dark and everything was so mussed up and the going was so rough that it was most awful hard to keep contact and to find the hill. But we done kept on a-going jes the same. We were marching, I might say floundering around, in column of squads. The noise were worse than ever, and everybody was shouting through the dark, and nobody seemed to be able to hear what anybody else said. We should have reached the hill before daybreak. But we didn't. It weren't nobody's fault. The going was too tough. So as soon as they were able to see the German artillery lit into us with a heap of big stuff. One of their shells bust plumb in the middle of one of our squads, and wounded or killed every man. They done laid down the meanest kind of a barrage too, and the air was jes full of gas. But we put on our masks and kept plugging and slipping and sliding, or falling into holes and tripping over all sorts of things and getting up again and stum-bling on for a few yards and then going down again, until we done reached the hill. The First Battalion had takened it the day before, but they hadn't mopped it up. And there were some snipers and German machine guns left there hidden in the brush and in fox holes.

And they sniped at us a whole heap. I guess we must have run over the top of some of them, too, because a little later on we were getting fire from the rear. We were to go over the top at 6:10 A.M. and push on across the ridges to that-there old railroad. The Captain's orders was for two of our platoons to go over the top first and advance as a front wave with the other two platoons in support following about one hun-dred yards behind the front wave. I was in the left supporting platoon.

Hit was the extreme left of our division and was supposed to keep contact with the Twenty-eighth Division, which was on our left, but we never did see anything of them all that morning. I guess they must have run into some awful tough fighting and been held up for a while.

Well, at the zero hour, which was 6:10 A.M., with fixed bayonets, we done went over the top, as ordered.

> October 8th—Argonne Forest, France. And they was to give us a Barrage. So the time came and no Barrage and we had to go with out one. So we started over the top at 6:10 A.M. and the Germans was putting their machine guns to working all over the hill in front of us and on our left and right. So I was in support and I could see my pals getting picked off until it almost looked like there was none left.

I don't know what happened to our artillery support, but we didn't get none nohow, except from a lieutenant from the Third Battalion. He done stood near six-foot-tall. And he come up on top of the hill, dragging what looked like a toy cannon with him. It was a trench mortar. He did the best he could with it, but it didn't help much nohow. The Germans met our charge across the valley with a regular sleet storm of bullets. I'm a-telling you that-there valley was a death trap. It was a triangular-shaped valley with steep ridges covered with brush, and swarming with machine guns on all sides. I guess our two waves got about halfway across and then jes couldn't get no further nohow. The Germans done got us and they done got us right smart. They jes stopped us in our tracks. Their machine guns were up there on the heights overlooking us and well hidden, and we couldn't tell for certain where the terrible heavy fire was coming from. It 'most seemed as though it was coming from everywhere. I'm a-telling you they were shooting straight, and our boys jes done went down like the long grass before the mowing machine at home. Our attacks jes faded out.

We had to lie down flat on our faces and dig in. And there we were out there in the valley all mussed up and unable to get any further with no barrage to help us, and that-there German machine-gun fire and all sorts of big shells and gas cutting us to pieces. There was scarcely none of our front wave left. Lieutenant Stewart, who was leading the platoon in front of where I was lying, went down with a shot through the leg, but got up again and rallied the few men he had left and led them forward until he fell dead with a bullet through the head. I couldn't see Captain Danforth. He was on the other side of the hill, on the right. I could hear shells and machine guns there, too, and I knowed he was getting it jes as bad as we was.

The German machine guns had done stopped our attack. We jes couldn't go on. We could scarcely even lift up our heads as we laid flat on the ground. But all the time we knowed we had to get through to that railroad somehow. We jes had to.

About the time we figured that the worstest machine-gun fire was coming from a ridge over on our left front. We knowed then that them-there machine guns would have to be put out of action before the advance could go on. We also knowed that there was so many of them and they were in such commanding positions that a whole battalion couldn't put them out of action nohow by a frontal attack. I doubt if a whole division could get to them that way. But they had to be takened somehow.

Our platoon sergeant, Harry M. Parsons, from Brooklyn, N.Y., done exposed himself again and again, trying to locate exactly where the machine guns over there on the left front were firing from. He hadn't no chance nohow of getting in touch with the Captain. He had to use his own judgment. He done done it. He ordered the left half of our platoon to crawl back a little and try and work our way down around on the left and then push on through the heavy underbrush and try and jump the machine guns from the rear. He didn't know for sure where they were hid. But he figured it was the only chance. So three squads of us done dropped back and made our way around on the left. Sergeant Bernard Early was in charge and Corporal Murray Savage and Corporal William Cutting and myself each led our squads. The privates under us were: Dymowski, Weiler, Waring, Wins, Swanson, Muzzi, Beardsley, Konotski, Sok, Johnson, Saccina, Donohue, Wills. So you see there were just seventeen of us.

October 8th—Argonne Forest, France. So there was 17 of us
Boys went around on the left flank to see if we couldn't put those
guns out of action.

According to orders, we got around on the left and in single file advanced forward through the brush towards where we could hear the
machine-gun fire. We done went very quietly and quickly. We had to.
We kept well to the left and deep in the brush. At first we didn't see any
Germans and we were not under heavy fire. Jes a few stray bullets.
Without any loss and in right-smart time we done skirted the left side of
the valley and over on the hill somewhere near where the German machine guns were placed. The heavy brush and the hilly nature of the
country hid us from the enemy. We were now nearly three hundred
yards to the left and in front of our own front line. When we figured
that we were right on the ridge that the Germans were on, we done
stopped for a minute and had a little conference. Some of the boys
wanted to attack from the flank. But Early and me and some of the others thought it would be best to keep going until we were well behind
the German lines, and then suddenly swing in and try and jump them
from the rear. We done decided to try and do this. We opened up in
skirmishing order and sorter flitted from brush to brush, using all the
cover we could and pushing on as fast as possible. We had now sorter
encircled the Germans' left end and were going away in deep behind
them without them knowing anything about it.

October 8th—Argonne Forest, France. So when we went a
round and fell in behind those guns we first seen to Germans with a
Red Cross Band on their arm. So we ask them to stop and they did
not so some one of the Boys shot at them and they run Back to our
right. So we all run after them . . .

They jumped out of the brush in front of us and run like two scared
rabbits. We called to them to surrender, and one of our boys done fired
and missed. And they kept on a-going. And we kept on after them. We
wanted to capture them before they gave the alarm. We now knowed by
the sounds of the firing that we were somewhere behind the German

trench and in the rear of the machine guns that were holding up our big advance. We still couldn't see the Germans and they couldn't see us. But we could hear them machine guns shooting something awful. Savage's squad was leading, then mine, and then Cutting's. Sergeant Early was out in front, leading the way.

> October 8th—Argonne Forest, France. . . . And when we jumped across a little stream of water that was there they was a Bout 15 or 20 Germans jumped up an throwed up their hands and said Comrade. So the one in charge of us Boys told us not to shoot they was going to give up any way.

It was headquarters. There were orderlies, stretcherbearers, runners, a major and two officers sitting or standing around a sort of small wooden shack. They seemed to be having a sort of conference. And they done jes had breakfast too. And there was a mess of beefsteaks, jellies, jams, and loaf bread around. They were unarmed. All except the major. And some of them were in their shirt sleeves. By the way they were going on we knowed they never even dreamed that there were any Americans near them.

Of course, we were 'most as surprised as they were, coming on them so sudden. But we kept our heads and jumped on them right smart, and covered them and told them to put up their hands and to keep them up. And they done done it. And we fired a few shots just to sorter impress them. I guess they thought the whole American Army was in their rear. And we didn't stop to tell them any different. Sergeant Early, who was in command of us, told us to hold our fire, as we had them, but to keep them covered and to hurry up and search and line them up. Just as he was turning around from giving this order and we were moving forward to obey, some machine guns up on the hill in front of us and between us and the American lines, suddenly turned around and opened fire on us. Early went down with five bullets through the lower part of his body and one through his arm. Corporal Savage was killed. He must have had over a hundred bullets in his body. His clothes were 'most shot off. And Corporal Cutting was also shot up. Six of the other boys were killed or wounded. That machine-gun burst came sorter sudden and unexpected. And it done got us hard. The moment it begun the German prisoners fell flat on their faces. So did the rest of us American boys who were still standing. You see, while we were capturing headquarters the German machine gunners up there on the hill seed us and done turned their guns around and let us have it.

After the first few bursts a whole heap of other machine guns joined in. There must have been over twenty of them and they kept up a continuous fire. Never letting up. Thousands of bullets kicked up the dust all around us. The undergrowth was cut down like as though they used a scythe. The air was just plumb full of death. Some of our boys done huddled up against the prisoners and so were able to get some protection and at the same time guard the prisoners. Some others crawled under cover, or jumped up and got behind trees. I was caught out in the open, a little bit to the left and in front of the group of prisoners and about twenty-five yards away from the machine guns which were in gun pits and trenches upon the hillside above me. I was now in charge.

October 8th—Argonne Forest, France. So by this time some of the Germans from on the hill was shooting at us. Well I was giving them the Best I had and by this time the Germans had got their machine guns turned around and fired on us so they killed 6 and wounded 3. So that just left 8 and then we got into it right By this time So we had a hard Battle for a little while. . . .

But I hadn't time to give no orders nohow. There was such a noise and racket all around that I would not have been heard even if I had done given them. I had no time nohow to do us nothing but watch them-there German machine gunners and give them the best I had. Every time I seed a German I jes teched him off. At first I was shooting from a prone position; that is lying down jes like we often shoot at the targets in the shooting matches in the mountains of Tennessee; and it was jes about the same distance. But the targets here were bigger. I jes couldn't miss a German's head or body at that distance. And I didn't. Besides, it weren't no time to miss nohow. I knowed that in order to shoot me the Germans would have to get their heads up to see where I was lying. And I knowed that my only chance was to keep their heads down. And I done done it. I covered their positions and let fly every time I seed anything to shoot at. Every time a head come up I done knocked it down.

Then they would sorter stop for a moment and then another head would come up and I would knock it down, too. I was giving them the best I had. I was right out in the open and the machine guns were spitting fire and cutting up all around me something awful. But they didn't seem to be able to hit me. All the time the Germans were shouting orders. You never heard such a racket in all of your life. I still hadn't time or a chance to look around for the other boys. I didn't know where they were now. I didn't know what they were doing. I didn't even know if they were still living. Later on they done said that in the thick of the fight they didn't fire a shot.

Of course, all of this only took a few minutes. As soon as I was able I stood up and begun to shoot offhand, which is my favourite position. I was still sharpshooting with that-there old army rifle. I used up several clips. The barrel was getting hot and my rifle ammunition was running low, or was where it was hard for me to get at it quickly. But I had to keep on shooting jes the same.

In the middle of the fight a German officer and five men done jumped out of a trench and charged me with fixed bayonets. They had about twenty-five yards to come and they were coming right smart. I only had about half a clip left in my rifle; but I had my pistol ready. I done flipped it out fast and teched them off, too.

I teched off the sixth man first; then the fifth; then the fourth; then the third; and so on. That's the way we shoot wild turkeys at home. You see we don't want the front ones to know that we're getting the back ones, and then they keep on coming until we get them all. Of course, I hadn't time to think of that. I guess I jes naturally did it. I knowed, too, that if the front ones wavered, or if I stopped them the rear ones would drop down and pump a volley into me and get me.

Then I returned to the rifle, and kept right on after those machine guns. I knowed now that if I done kept my head and didn't run out of ammunition I had them. So I done hollered to them to come down and give up. I didn't want to kill any more'n I had to. I would tech a couple of them off and holler again. But I guess they couldn't understand my language, or else they couldn't hear me in the awful racket that was going on all around. Over twenty Germans were killed by this time.

October 8th—Argonne Forest, France. . . . and I got hold of a German major and he told me if I wouldn't kill any more of them he would make them quit firing. So I told him alright if he would do it now. So he blew a little whistle and they quit shooting and come down and give up.

I think he had done been firing at me while I was fighting the machine guns—I examined his pistol later and sure enough hit was empty. Jes the same, he hadn't pestered me nohow. After he seed me stop the six Germans who charged with fixed bayonets he got up off the ground and walked over to me and yelled, "English?"

I said, "No, not English."

He said, "What?"

I said, "American."

He said, "Good Lord!" Then he said, "If you won't shoot any more I will make them give up."

I told him he had better. I covered him with my automatic and told him if he didn't make them stop firing I would take his head next. And he knowed I meaned it. So he blowed a little whistle and they come down out of the trench and throwed down their guns and equipment and held up their hands and begun to gather around. I guess, though, one of them thought he could get me. He had his hands up all right. But he done had a little hand grenade concealed, and as he come up to me he throwed it right at my head. But it missed me and wounded one of the prisoners. I had to tech him off. The rest surrendered without any more trouble. There must have been about fifty of them.

October 8th—Argonne Forest, France. So we had about 80 or 90 Germans there disarmed and had another line of Germans to go through to get out. So I called for my men and one of them answered from behind a big oak tree and the others were on my right in the brush so I said let's get these Germans out of here. So one of my men said it is impossible so I said no lets get them out. So when

my men said that this German major said how many have you got
and I said I have got a plenty and pointed my pistol at him all the
time—in this battle I was using a rifle or a 45 Colts automatic pistol.
So I lined the Germans up in a line of twos and got between the
ones in front and I had the German major before me. So I marched
them straight into those other machine guns and I got them.

The German major could speak English as well as I could. Before
the war he used to work in Chicago. When the prisoners in the first
trench surrendered I yelled out to my men to let's get them out. And
one of my men said it was impossible to get so many prisoners back to
the American lines. And I told him to shut up and to let's get them out.
Then the German major became suspicious and wanted to know how
many men I had. And I told him I had a-plenty. And I told him to keep
his hands up and to line up his men in a column of two and to do it in
double time. And he did it. And I lined up my men that were left on either side of the column and I told one to guard the rear.

Sergeant Early and Corporal Cutting then come up towards me.
Corporal Cutting said: "I am hit and hit bad." He was wounded in the
arm. He done had all the buttons shot off his uniform and there was a
great big "X" shot in his helmet. Sergeant Early said: "York, I am
shot and shot bad. What shall I do?" I knowed by the look of him that
he was very badly wounded. He was dazed and in most awful pain. I
done told them they could come out in the rear of our column with the
other boys.

I ordered the prisoners to pick up and carry our wounded. I wasn't
a-goin' to leave any good American boys lying out there to die. So I
made the Germans carry them. And they did. And I takened the major
and placed him at the head of the column and I got behind him and
used him as a screen. I poked the Colt in his back and told him to hike.
And he hiked. I guess I had him bluffed. It was pretty hard to tell in the
brush and with all the noise and confusion around which way to go.
The major done suggested we go down the gully. Then I knowed that
was the wrong way. And I told him were not going down any gully. We
were going straight through the German front-line trenches back to the
American lines. It was their second line that I had captured. We sure did

get a long way behind the German trenches. And so I done marched them straight at that old German front-line trench. And some more machine guns swung around to fire. I told the major to blow his whistle and they all done surrendered. All except one. I made the major order him to surrender twice. But he wouldn't. And I had to tech him off. I hated to do it. I've been doing a tol'able lot of thinking about it since. He was probably a brave soldier boy. But I couldn't afford to take any chance, and so I had to let him have it. There was considerably over a hundred prisoners now. It was a problem to get them back safely to our own lines. There was so many of them there was danger of our own artillery mistaking us for a German counterattack and opening up on us. I sure was relieved when we run into relief squads that had been sent forward through the brush to help us.

October 8th—Argonne Forest, France. So when I got back to my majors P.C. I had 132 prisoners.

We marched those German prisoners on back into the American lines to the Battalion P.C. and there we came to the Intelligence Department and Lieutenant Woods come out and counted them and counted 132. We were ordered to take them out to Regimental Headquarters at Chatel Chehery; and from there all the way back to Division Headquarters and turn them over to the Military Police. We had such a mess of German prisoners that nobody seemed to want to take them over. So we had to take them back a right-far piece ourselves.

On the way back we were constantly under heavy shell fire and I had to double-time them to get them through safely. There was nothing to be gained by having any more of them wounded or killed. They done surrendered to me and it was up to me to look after them. And so I done done it. I had orders to report to Brigadier General Lindsay, our brigadier commander, and he said to me, "Well, York, I hear you have captured the whole damned German army." And I told him I only had 132.

Five Aviators Die Trying
to Cross the Atlantic Ocean—
Then Came Charles Lindbergh

(from Charles A. Lindbergh, *We*, 1927)

I N 1919 French restaurateur-hotel proprietor Raymond Orteig offered a $25,000 prize for the first continuous solo flight between New York and Paris across the Atlantic. In 1920 René Fonck crashed on takeoff from New York's Roosevelt Field. Two American naval officers were subsequently killed in a trial flight. Two Frenchmen, Charles Nungesser and François Coli, were lost over the Atlantic in the difficult east-to-west crossing. Charles Lindbergh then stepped up to the plate.

Backed by a group of St. Louis businessmen, Lindbergh supervised the construction of a Ryan monoplane, christened the Spirit of Saint Louis. Propelled by a 225-horsepower Wright Whirlwind motor, it weighed 5,135 pounds, with a wingspan of 46 feet.

Lindbergh flew it east from St. Louis reporting no problems until the Allegheny Mountains, where "the sky was overcast and some of the mountain tops were in low hanging clouds, and I followed the passes." Nungesser and Coli had disappeared shortly before he landed at Curtiss Field, Long Island.

Lindbergh was twenty-five years old, handsome, clean-cut, and modest with a farm-boy demeanor. Myron Herrick, the American ambassador to France, later captured his essence, the "phenomenon of Lindbergh": "He started with no purpose but to arrive. . . . No flaw marked any act or word, and he stood forth amidst the crowds as the very embodiment of a fearless, kindly, cultivated American youth—unspoiled and unspoilable. A nation which breeds such boys need never fear for its future." Written soon after, here is Lindbergh's own account of his famous 1927 flight.

* * *

A T NEW YORK we checked over the plane, engine and instruments, which required several short flights over the field.

When the plane was completely inspected and ready for the transatlantic flight, there were dense fogs reported along the coast and over Nova Scotia and Newfoundland, in addition to a storm area over the North Atlantic.

On the morning of May 19th, 1927, a light rain was falling and the sky was overcast. Weather reports from land stations and ships along the great circle course were unfavorable and there was apparently no prospect of taking off for Paris for several days at least. In the morning I visited the Wright plant at Paterson, New Jersey, and had planned to attend a theater performance in New York that evening. But at about six o'clock I received a special report from the New York Weather Bureau. A high-pressure area was over the entire North Atlantic, and the low pressure over Nova Scotia and Newfoundland was receding. It was apparent that the prospects of the fog clearing up were as good as I might expect for some time to come. The North Atlantic should be clear with only local storms on the coast of Europe. The moon had just passed full and the percentage of days with fog over Newfoundland and the Grand Banks was increasing so that there seemed to be no advantage in waiting longer.

We went to Curtiss Field as quickly as possible and made arrangements for the barograph to be sealed and installed, and for the plane to be serviced and checked.

We decided partially to fill the fuel tanks in the hangar before towing the ship on a truck to Roosevelt Field, which adjoins Curtiss on the east, where the servicing would be completed.

I left the responsibility for conditioning the plane in the hands of the men on the field while I went into the hotel for about two and one-half hours of rest; but at the hotel there were several more details which had to be completed, and I was unable to get any sleep that night.

I returned to the field before daybreak on the morning of the twentieth. A light rain was falling which continued until almost dawn; consequently we did not move the ship to Roosevelt Field until much later than we had planned, and the take-off was delayed from daybreak until nearly eight o'clock.

At dawn the shower had passed, although the sky was overcast, and occasionally there would be some slight precipitation. The tail of the plane was lashed to a truck and escorted by a number of motorcycle police. The slow trip from Curtiss to Roosevelt was begun.

The ship was placed at the extreme west end of the field heading along the east and west runway, and the final fueling commenced. About 7:40 A.M. the motor was started, and at 7:52 I took off on the flight for Paris.

The field was a little soft due to the rain during the night, and the heavily loaded plane gathered speed very slowly. After passing the halfway mark, however, it was apparent that I would be able to clear the obstructions at the end. I passed over a tractor by about fifteen feet and a telephone line by about twenty, with a fair reserve of flying speed. I believe that the ship would have taken off from a hard field with at least five hundred pounds more weight.

I turned slightly to the right to avoid some high trees on a hill directly ahead, but by the time I had gone a few hundred yards I had sufficient altitude to clear all obstructions and throttled the engine down to 1750 R.P.M. I took up a compass course at once and soon reached Long Island Sound where the Curtiss Oriole with its photographer, which had been escorting me, turned back.

The haze soon cleared and from Cape Cod through the southern half of Nova Scotia, the weather and visibility were excellent. I was flying very low, sometimes as close as ten feet from the trees and water. On the three hundred mile stretch of water between Cape Cod and Nova Scotia I passed within view of numerous fishing vessels.

The northern part of Nova Scotia contained a number of storm areas, and several times I flew through cloudbursts. As I neared the northern coast, snow appeared in patches on the ground and far to the eastward, the coastline was covered with fog. For many miles between Nova Scotia and Newfoundland, the ocean was covered with caked ice, but as I approached the coast, the ice disappeared entirely and I saw several ships in this area.

I had taken up a course for St. Johns, which is south of the great Circle from New York to Paris so that there would be no question of the fact that I had passed Newfoundland, in case I was forced down in the north Atlantic. I passed over numerous icebergs after leaving St. Johns, but saw no ships except near the coast. Darkness set in about 8:15 New York time and a thin, low fog formed through which the white bergs showed up with surprising clearness. This fog became thicker and increased in height until within two hours I was just skimming the top of storm clouds at about ten thousand feet. Even at this altitude there was a thick haze through which only the stars directly overhead could be seen.

There was no moon, and it was very dark. The tops of some of the storm clouds were several thousand feet above me and at one time, when I attempted to fly through one of the larger clouds, sleet started to collect on the plane, and I was forced to turn around and get back into clear air immediately and then fly around any clouds which I could not get over.

The moon appeared on the horizon after about two hours of darkness; then the flying was much less complicated. Dawn came at about 1 A.M. New York time, and the temperature had risen until there was practically no remaining danger of sleet. Shortly after sunrise the clouds became more broken, although some of them were far above me, and it was often necessary to fly through them, navigating by instruments only.

As the sun became higher, holes appeared in the fog. Through one, the open water was visible, and I dropped down until less than a hundred feet above the waves. There was a strong wind blowing from the northwest, and the ocean was covered with white caps. After a few miles of fairly clear weather, the ceiling lowered to zero, and for nearly two hours I flew entirely blind through the fog at an altitude of about 1500 feet. Then the fog raised and the water was visible again.

On several occasions it was necessary to fly by instrument for short periods; then the fog broke up into patches. These patches took on forms of every description. Numerous shorelines appeared, with trees perfectly outlined against the horizon. In fact, the mirages were so natural that, had I not been in mid-Atlantic and known that no land existed along my route, I would have taken them to be actual islands.

As the fog cleared I dropped down closer to the water, sometimes flying within ten feet of the waves and seldom higher than two hundred. There is a cushion of air close to the ground or water through which a plane flies with less effort than when at higher altitude, and for hours at a time I took advantage of this factor.

Also, it was less difficult to determine the wind drift near the water. During the entire flight the wind was strong enough to produce white caps on the waves. When one of these formed, the foam would be blown off, showing the wind's direction and approximate velocity. This foam remained on the water long enough for me to obtain a general idea of my drift.

During the day I saw a number of porpoises and a few birds but no ships, although I understand that two different boats reported me passing over.

The first indication of my approach to the European Coast was a small fishing boat which I first noticed a few miles ahead and slightly to the south of my course. There were several of these fishing boats grouped within a few miles of each other. I flew over the first boat without seeing any signs of life. As I circled over the second, however, a man's face appeared, looking out of the cabin window.

I have carried on short conversations with people on the ground by flying low with throttled engine, shouting a question, and receiving the answer by some signal. When I saw this fisherman I decided to try to get him to point towards land. I had no sooner made the decision than the futility of the effort became apparent. In all likelihood he could not speak English, and even if he could he would undoubtedly be far too astounded to answer. However, I circled again and, closing the throttle as the plane passed within a few feet of the boat, I shouted, "Which way is Ireland?" Of course the attempt was useless and I continued on my course.

Less than an hour later, a rugged and semi-mountainous coastline appeared to the northeast. I was flying less than two hundred feet from the water when I sighted it. The shore was fairly distinct and not over ten or fifteen miles away. A light haze coupled with numerous local storm areas had prevented my seeing it from a long distance.

The coastline came down from the north, curved over towards the east. I had very little doubt that it was the southwestern end of Ireland, but in order to make sure, I changed my course towards the nearest point of land. I located Cape Valentia and Dingle Bay, then resumed my compass course towards Paris.

After leaving Ireland I passed a number of steamers and was seldom out of sight of a ship. In a little over two hours the coast of England appeared. My course passed over Southern England and a little south of Plymouth; then across the English Channel, striking France over Cherbourg. The English farms were very impressive from the air, in contrast to ours in America. They appeared extremely small and unusually neat and tidy with their stone and hedge fences.

I was flying at about a 1500-foot altitude over England, and as I crossed the Channel and passed over Cherbourg, France, I had probably seen more of that part of Europe than many native Europeans. The visibility was good, and the country could be seen for miles around. People who have taken their first flight often remark that no one knows what the locality he lives in is like until he has seen it from above. Countries take on different characteristics from the air.

The sun went down shortly after passing Cherbourg, and soon the beacons along the Paris-London airway became visible.

I first saw the lights of Paris a little before ten P.M., or five P.M. New York time, and a few minutes later I was circling the Eiffel Tower at an altitude of about four thousand feet.

The lights of Le Bourget were plainly visible, but appeared to be very close to Paris. I had understood that the field was farther from the city, so continued out to the northeast into the country for four or five miles to make sure that there was not another field farther out which might be Le Bourget. Then I returned and spiralled down closer to the lights. Presently I could make out long lines of hangars, and the roads appeared to be jammed with cars.

I flew low over the field once, then circled around into the wind and landed.

After the plane stopped rolling I turned it around and started to taxi back to the lights. The entire field ahead, however, was covered with thousands of people all running towards my ship. When the first few arrived, I attempted to get them to hold the rest of the crowd back, away from the plane, but apparently no one could understand, or would have been able to conform to my request if he had.

I cut the switch to keep the propeller from killing some one, and attempted to organize an impromptu guard for the plane. The impossibility of any immediate organization became apparent, and when parts of the ship began to crack from the pressure of the multitude I decided to climb out of the cockpit in order to draw the crowd away.

Speaking was impossible; no words could be heard in the uproar and nobody apparently cared to hear any. I started to climb out of the cockpit, but as soon as one foot appeared through the door I was dragged the rest of the way without assistance on my part.

For nearly half an hour I was unable to touch the ground, during which time I was ardently carried around in what seemed to be a very small area, and in every position it is possible to be in. Everyone had the best of intentions but no one seemed to know just what they were.

The French military flyers very resourcefully took the situation in hand. A number of them mingled with the crowd; then, at a given signal, they placed my helmet on an American correspondent and cried: "Here is Lindbergh." That helmet on an American was sufficient evidence. The correspondent immediately became the center of attraction, and while he was being taken protestingly to the Reception Committee via a rather devious route, I managed to get inside one of the hangars.

Jimmy Doolittle's Daylight
Raid Over Tokyo

(from Carroll V. Glines, *The Doolittle Raid:*
America's Daring First Strike Against Japan)

F OR THE FIRST *months following the Japanese attack on Pearl*
Harbor in December 1941, the news from the Pacific front was di-
sastrous. Singapore surrendered February 15, 1942. Nine days later
the British withdrew from Rangoon in Burma. After taking Borneo, the
Celebes, and Timor, the Japanese landed at Lae and Salamaua in New
Guinea. By March 9 their conquest of Java was complete. In the Philip-
pines fifteen thousand Americans and sixty-five thousand Philippine
troops were captured and forced to walk the Bataan Death March.

Franklin D. Roosevelt kept asking his military chiefs, "How can we
strike back at Japan?"

The answer, concocted by the U.S. Navy's forward-thinking Captain
Francis Low and Admiral Ernest King, became the top mission of the day.
Low and King proposed placing long-range bombers aboard the navy's
newest aircraft carrier, the Hornet. *Heavy bombers aboard a carrier*
could extend the navy's bombing range from three hundred to one thou-
sand miles, barely within reach of Tokyo. However, it would be a one-way

mission for the pilots and crew of the bombers, which would not have enough fuel to return to the carrier—and where they could not physically land anyway. Low and King's plan called for the bombers to fly over Japan to inland China, where Chiang Kai-shek was holding out against the Japanese. The aviators would have to hitchhike home.

Ace flyer Jimmy Doolittle—MIT Ph.D., speed record holder, the first to fly the outside loop, and confidant of the top military brass—was chosen to train and lead this adventure. Under perfect conditions Doolittle thought there might be a 50/50 chance of success, but unforeseen variables made the odds much longer. Amazingly, however, the gamble was a success: the first American attack on the Japanese mainland took place on April 18, 1942—just four months after Pearl Harbor.

"In my opinion," wrote Admiral "Bull" Halsey, "their flight was one of the most courageous deeds in military history." Eighty men and sixteen B-25 bombers flew over Japan. All planes were lost; three died in crash landings and eleven were captured, including three who were tortured and executed. Opening on the deck of the Hornet, *this is the story of the raid narrated in part by Doolittle's copilot, Lieutenant Richard Cole, as told in Carroll V. Glines's* The Doolittle Raid: America's Daring First Strike Against Japan.

*   *   *

DOOLITTLE WENT from plane to plane, questioned the mechanics, and inspected each B-25 from nose wheel to the broomstick "guns" in the tail. On the afternoon of the seventeenth, he called the flying crews together for a final briefing.

"The time's getting short," he said. "By now every one of you knows exactly what he should do if the alarm is sounded. We were originally supposed to take off on the nineteenth but it looks like it will be tomorrow, the eighteenth, instead. This is your final briefing. Be ready to go at any time.

"We should have plenty of warning if we're intercepted. If all goes as planned, I'll take off tomorrow afternoon so as to arrive over Tokyo at dusk. I'll drop incendiaries. The rest of you will take off later and can use my fires as a homing beacon."

Doolittle repeated what he had been saying since the first meeting, that any man could drop out if he wished. Again, no one took him up on the offer. He cautioned the rear gunners about not dropping the five-gallon gas cans overboard after they were emptied because they might float long enough to leave a trail back to the task force.

There was one question that lurked in the minds of most of the crewmen but no one had yet dared to ask it. Finally, one pilot raised his hand and asked, "Colonel Doolittle, what should we do if we lose an engine or get hit by ack-ack fire and crash-land in Japan?"

Doolittle's answer was quick and firm. "Each pilot is in command of his own plane when we leave the carrier," he said. "He is responsible for the decision he makes for his own plane and his own crew. If you're separated, each one of you will have to decide for yourself what you will do. Personally, I know exactly what I'm going to do."

The room was silent. Doolittle didn't go any further so one of the group asked, "Sir, what *will* you do?"

"I don't intend to be taken prisoner," he answered. "If my plane is crippled beyond any possibility of fighting or escaping, I'm going to bail my crew out and then drive it, full throttle, into any target I can find where the crash will do the most damage. I'm forty-five years old and have lived a full life. Most of you are in your twenties and if I were you, I'm not sure I would make the same decision. In the final analysis, it's up to each pilot and, in turn, each man to decide what he will do." Doolittle's final caution was to get rid of any letters, diaries, photos, and identification that would link them with the *Hornet,* their former units in the States, or their training.

The weather was turning sour. Moderately rough during the night, the wind increased and low clouds hung ominously over the area. Rain squalls smashed across the decks and the sea began to swell into thirty-foot waves. The wind sliced off the tops of the waves and drenched the deck crews.

At 5:58, Lt. O. B. Wiseman, one of the SBD pilots, sighted a small fishing vessel. He jotted down the following message on his knee pad:

"Enemy surface ship—latitude 36-04N, Long. 153-10E, bearing 276 degrees true—42 miles. Believed seen by enemy."

Wiseman passed the paper to the gunner in the rear seat, making a throwing motion with his hand. The gunner pulled a small bean bag from his pocket, stuffed the message inside and peered over the side as Wiseman headed for the Big E.

When the SBD was directly over the carrier, the gunner threw the bag on the deck, where it was scooped up by a sailor and rushed to Halsey on the bridge. Halsey immediately ordered all ships to turn left to a course of 220 degrees. Had Wiseman's plane been seen? It wasn't likely at forty-two miles, but at 7:38 another patrol vessel was sighted by a lookout on the *Hornet* only twenty thousand yards away. If the vessel could be seen by the *Hornet*, it had to be assumed that the task force had been sighted and that it had radioed the sighting to Japan.

The sighting became a certainty when the *Hornet*'s radio operator intercepted a message in Japanese that had originated close by. At 7:45, Ens. J. Q. Roberts sighted the vessel, now only twelve thousand yards away.

Halsey had no option but to order the *Nashville* to sink the enemy boat. He then flashed a message to Mitscher:

LAUNCH PLANES X TO COL DOOLITTLE AND GALLANT
COMMAND GOOD LUCK AND GOD BLESS YOU

Doolittle, on the bridge when the order came, shook hands with Mitscher, leaped down the ladder to his cabin, shouting to everybody he saw, "OK fellas, this is it. Let's go!" At the same time, the blood-chilling klaxon horn sounded, followed by the announcement: "Army pilots, man your planes!"

Doc White hurriedly passed out two pints of rye to each man as they rushed past. Lt. Dick Knobloch ran from plane to plane with bags of sandwiches he had gotten from the galley. There was confusion as army and navy men ran back and forth on their respective missions. Mechanics ripped off engine covers and stuffed them up into the rear hatches. Tie-down ropes were unfastened and wheel chocks pulled away. A navy "donkey" attached a tow bar to nose wheels and pushed and pulled the planes into takeoff position. Gas tanks were topped off and the crews rocked the planes back and forth to get rid of any air bubbles in the tanks that would prevent a few more gallons of precious fuel from being pumped in. Sailors filled the five-gallon cans with fuel and passed them hand-to-hand to the rear gunner in each B-25.

On the bridge, Mitscher ordered the *Hornet* to full speed into the wind and her bow plunged into towering waves that smashed across the deck. The *Hornet*'s air officer on the bridge brought out a large blackboard and noted the carrier's compass heading and the wind speed so the pilots would have some idea how much airspeed they had to gain for takeoff. Hank Miller rushed from plane to plane to shake hands and wish the crews good luck. "I'll be on the right side holding up a blackboard to give you any last-minute instructions before you go," he shouted. "Look at me just before you release your brakes."

Doolittle, in the lead plane, started his engines and warmed them up. Near the bow on the left side, Lt. Edgar G. Osborne, the signal officer, stood by holding a checkered flag. When Doolittle was satisfied that his engine instruments were "in the green," the checklist complete, and crew ready, he gave a "thumbs up" to Osborne. Osborne responded by swinging the flag in a circle as a signal for Doolittle to ease the throttles forward. Osborne swung the flag in faster and faster circles, keeping one eye on the bow. At the instant the deck was beginning its upward movement, chocks were pulled from under Doolittle's wheels and Osborne gave him the "go" signal. Doolittle released the brakes and the B-25 inched forward, slowly at first, then faster. As the plane passed the ship's island, the nose wheel rose first, followed by the main wheels, and Doolittle was airborne with plenty of deck to spare.

All the remaining pilots, now getting ready to be jockeyed into position, had watched Doolittle's plane apprehensively. They knew that if he had had trouble and didn't make it, they couldn't. They breathed sighs of relief as Doolittle brought up his gear and flaps, circled to the left, came back over the deck to check his compass against the carrier's course and faded off into the distance.

The log of the *Hornet* noted that Doolittle was airborne at 8:20 ship time. Instead of following three hours later as originally planned, Lt. Travis Hoover was maneuvered into takeoff position, started his engines, and took off five minutes after Doolittle.

Lt. Richard E. Cole, Doolittle's co-pilot, recalled:

After takeoff and when everything was squared away, the boss and I took turns at flying. When I wasn't flying, Hank Potter, Braemer, Leonard, and I were continually checking the gas or other things about the ship. No one slept or got sick. Everyone prayed but did so in an inward way. I guess we all wondered more than anything—trying to imagine what was in store for us. If anyone was scared it didn't show. I believe I can honestly say that no one was really scared. I don't say this in a bragging way, it's just that at least we had never faced danger and didn't have sense enough to be scared.

One thing I remember clearly is that the tune "Wabash Cannonball" kept running through my mind. One time I was singing and stamping my foot with such gusto that the boss looked at me in a very questioning manner like he thought I was going batty.

We flew low and kept a sharp lookout for surface ships and other aircraft. We veered once or twice to miss some ships and flew directly under a Japanese flying boat, which didn't see us. Aside from this our trip from the *Hornet* to Japan was uneventful.

Since we had a load of incendiaries, our target was the populated areas of the west and northwest parts of Tokyo. Over the target I kept Paul Leonard advised of enemy aircraft and at one time counted more than eighty. We were not bothered by fighters; however, flak shook us up a little and left some holes in the tail. We made landfall on the Chiba Peninsula east and northeast of Tokyo. Japan looked very pretty and picturesque from what I could see. We flew at treetop level until our target area then pulled up to twelve hundred feet, dropped our bombs, and lowered to treetop level again. People on the ground waved to us. It was about 12:15 Tokyo time, the weather was clear but a little hazy, which limited forward vision. We could see the moat, the Imperial Palace, and downtown Tokyo. Hoover flew on our wing practically all the way to the target, then he turned off and headed for his target, which was an electrical plant. I saw his bombs hit and explode, throwing much debris into the air.

Hank Potter did a fine job of navigating. After we left the target area we headed for open sea, taking a southwest course to the southernmost tip of Japan. As we headed out over the China Sea,

Hank estimated we would run out of gas 135 miles from the Chinese coast. Because of this we began making preparations for ditching. Without our knowledge the good Lord had fixed us up with a brisk tailwind. We flew at low level and occasionally could see sharks basking in the sun—which made the ditching very unappealing.

We made landfall on the Chinese coast about 8:45 p.m. as it was just getting dark. Shortly after we climbed to eight thousand feet and we all bailed out when the fuel warning light came on. I dove out head first facing the rear of the ship. This caused me to scrape or drag on the sides of the hatch. Fortunately, it didn't affect the operation of the chute. I remember I had my flashlight in my right hand and after bailing out changed it to my left so I could pull the ripcord. The descent seemed like ages. The clouds, rain, and fog were so thick nothing could be seen, so I just waited. Suddenly a tree limb brushed my feet and I came to a stop. My chute had drifted over the top of a thirty-foot pine tree. I couldn't have landed easier if I had planned it. Except for a black eye, I was all in one scared piece and I do mean scared.

I climbed to the top of the tree and untangled my chute, then got down for a look around. I had landed on the top of a very steep mountain and from what I could see with my flashlight, it looked treacherous. I decided to make a hammock from my chute and spend the night in the tree. This I did. It was quite comfortable and kept me dry but I didn't sleep except for short dozes.

My only visitor was a cottontail rabbit, which I could see with my flashlight. Daylight came about 5:30 so I gathered up my chute and started walking. Using my compass I walked due west keeping to the ridges and avoiding traveled footpaths. I ran across several wood gatherers, farmers, and even one hunter. They paid no attention to me nor I to them.

Since most of the walking was up and down, I figure I walked only ten or fifteen miles. About sundown I came to a well-traveled path which circled a high peak. I could not avoid this path so I started walking it. Shortly, I ran into an Oriental gentleman who was too nosy to suit me, so I pulled my .45 and chased him away. As I walked, he followed me at a good safe distance. At the top of the mountains below my path I could see a small settlement or compound. It looked peaceful enough so I decided to try my hand at meeting the Chinese. As I neared the buildings I could see a Chinese Nationalist flag flying from one. Approaching this, a small boy ran out to meet me, yelling something in Chinese. A Chinese soldier appeared and beckoned me to come inside. He showed me some drawings of an airplane with five chutes drifting down. After a time he and his fellow soldiers understood that I wanted to be taken to the place where the artist had drawn the pictures and the artist was the old man I had seen previously. He turned out to be a loyal Chinese who later served as our guide and stayed with us until we passed out of occupied territory.

Shortly after this I was taken to the place where the boss was located. He appeared none the worse for his experience except that he had landed in the middle of a rice paddy and was still damp. Later, Potter, Leonard, and Braemer were brought in. They had been picked up by a roving band of renegade guerrillas who robbed them and tied them up. This band was fortunately interrupted by a band of friendly guerrillas who rescued the boys and returned their belongings.

We were holed up in occupied territory at a place called Tien Mu Shen which is between fifty and one hundred miles southwest of Hangchow. This was our base of operations while the boss visited the wreck of our ship. After they decided to move us, we walked, rode small horses, and were even carried in seat chairs to a secret place where we were kept until dark. At about 9:00 p.m. we boarded a Chinese riverboat. The scheme was to move us down the river to a point where another river joined, thence up the second river and out of occupied territory. We got underway about midnight, and as we moved down the river we could see the searchlights of Japanese patrol boats. Fortunately, we were not stopped and completed the journey without difficulty. We arrived at Chosin where we were greeted by all who arrived before us.

WANTED: An Elegant
Female Spy to Bribe or Seduce
Top Officials at Nazi-Controlled,
Vichy French Embassy

(from H. Montgomery Hyde, *Cynthia*)

T O THE INTELLIGENCE AGENCIES *of the U.S.A. and Great Britain the choice was obvious. In early 1941, "Cynthia" (her code name) had already delivered to MI6 the cipher books of the Italian Navy, which helped the Royal Navy defeat a superior Italian fleet in Cape Matapan, Greece. Further, she had inveigled a Polish foreign-affairs officer to show her a Nazi map of Adolf Hitler's plans to dismember Czechoslovakia.*

Cynthia was born Amy Elizabeth "Betty" Thorpe, the daughter of a decorated major in the U.S. Marines. Growing up in the social swing of Washington, she was advanced for her age. "The usual fourteen year old games and playmates," she wrote, "seemed tame and banal. They were never fast enough or hard enough or frenzied enough to suit me. Everything had to be headlong for me. Yet all those early years I had to curtsy, to mind my manners, to go out for organized school sports, to live by the codes and mores of my family. Just think, I had been seduced [at fourteen]*! I had known the Grand Passion, and I still had boarding school ahead of me. Ridiculous! No?"*

As an adult she was a well-bred, elegant beauty with blond curls. Drawn to adventure and liaisons, she had a "light, quicksilver wit, a sharp intelligence, and a soft, soothing voice that somehow inspired trust and confidence." Intensely patriotic, her overarching trademark was her allure. Here's how one male colleague described her charm: "She had a force, or magnetism, to a terrifying degree. It leapt like light from the whole of her, not just from her green eyes or wide smile. Many a man, I think, read this force as warmth; as a concentrated and passionate interest in himself. The trick of making a man feel he is her entire universe is an old feminine wile, but 'Cynthia' had it to the nth degree. I felt the impact at once."

In March 1942, Cynthia received an urgent call from her intelligence handler in New York, known as Johnny. They met at the Ritz-Carlton Hotel. Johnny immediately asked her to secure the Vichy French naval ciphers. Unknown to Cynthia at the time, the Americans were planning to land on the coast of North Africa (Operation Torch). The French posed a threat. They still manned their fleet of warships, and controlled French ports in Morocco and Algeria. The nefarious Nazis watched their every move, while the odious and obsequious Pierre Laval, Vichy's puppet prime minister, obeyed the Nazis like a trained dog. In this selection from H. Montgomery Hyde's biography, Cynthia, we follow Cynthia and Johnny's daring, sultry gambit to steal the French ciphers.

* * *

CYNTHIA NOW TOLD JOHNNY in New York that in her opinion there was no hope of achieving their objective by means of an inside job in the code room. "We shall have to do it ourselves in a direct manner," she said.

"What have you got in mind?" asked Johnny.

"Burglary," she replied simply.

"How would you propose going about it?" he went on, with a characteristic twinkle in his eyes.

"The ciphers are kept in a safe in the code room," Cynthia explained. "This is on the ground floor, with a window overlooking a small stretch of tree-shaded lawn. If I could find out the combination of the safe, I could get into the office through the window with the help of a ladder. I could then pass the cipher books out of the window to our people and hide inside until they had photographed and returned them. On a dark night it would be easy!"

Johnny seemed to think this idea rather crude. Nevertheless he said he would think it over and see what could be made of it. Meanwhile Cynthia was to get Charles Brousse [her lover and Vichy French military attaché] to make a floor plan of the embassy chancery and bring it to New York as soon as possible.

Cynthia carried out these instructions faithfully, and at their next meeting she was able to produce an excellent map of the interior of the embassy that Charles had prepared. Johnny then introduced her to a gentleman whom he called "Mr. Hunter" and who, he told her, was to be her on-the-spot American liaison for operational purposes.

By this time the United States had been in the war for some months and the British Secret Service was working closely with the Office of Strategic Services (OSS), the American wartime intelligence agency headed by General William "Wild Bill" Donovan. Mr. Hunter belonged to the latter organization.

It was agreed that Cynthia's room in the Wardman Park Hotel in Washington should become their tactical headquarters. But first of all she gathered that she was to have a visit from another employee of the OSS, who was to look the room over and see that it was completely secure for their purpose.

The following afternoon there was a knock at her door. She opened it to find a man standing outside. "I am from the exterminating company," he announced.

"Come right inside," said Cynthia.

The visitor immediately got down on his hands and knees, crawled under the bed, disappeared behind the curtains and then into her clothes closet, then gave the furniture, carpet, and walls a most thorough going-over. Finally, he delivered his verdict: "Everything is OK, ma'am. You got no bugs!"

Cynthia thanked the exterminator for this welcome reassurance that there were no microphones or other voice-recording gadgets concealed in the room, and that it would be safe to go ahead with her planning.

Following this visit, she spent many hours with Mr. Hunter and Charles, looking at the projected operation from every angle. Eventually they decided to discard her proposal to enter the embassy by the code room window in favor of a more conventional and simpler entry through the front door of the embassy building. For this purpose Charles undertook to fix the night watchman.

Her lover [Brousse] then proceeded to take the night watchman into his confidence. He explained that he had a girl friend, that the Washington hotels were crowded, that in any case he dared not take her to one, as his wife was already suspicious, and finally that as a member of the embassy he must be discreet. The night watchman said he quite understood, and any lingering doubts he may have had were removed by the offer of a generous tip.

A series of nocturnal visits to the embassy now began. Charles and Cynthia would arrive after dark, let themselves in with his key and after exchanging a few words with the night watchman, settle down on the divan in the hall, which they were allowed to use for the ostensible purpose of making love. They would leave about one or two o'clock in the morning.

When several nights had passed in this way and the watchman had become accustomed to their comings and goings, Cynthia decided that the time had come to move into the next phase of the operation. The detailed plan which she had worked out with the others involved drugging the watchman—this was Mr. Hunter's idea—admitting an expert locksmith, who would open the safe. Cynthia would then extract the cipher books and hand them over to another of Stephenson's [head of the British Secret Intelligence Service in the Western hemisphere] men who would be waiting outside the window to take them away to photograph.

If they were interrupted for any reason, she was to escape by the window with the locksmith, who was known as the Georgia Cracker. "You must know the rules, Cynthia," said Johnny at her final briefing.

"If anything goes wrong, don't involve us. You and the Georgia Cracker may be picked up and even go to jail for a while, but that's all in the game. From now on, you're on your own. Good luck!"

* * *

Charles and Cynthia arrived at the embassy as usual shortly after dark on the appointed night. They brought several bottles of champagne with them as well as a certain white powder which was hidden in her handbag and which she was told was used for women in childbirth to promote twilight sleep. In fact it was Nembutal.

They told the night watchman that they wished to have a little celebration, as it was the anniversary of their first meeting, and they invited him to join them in a glass. He willingly accepted, and they opened the champagne in his room in the basement. While the watchman's attention was distracted a moment, Cynthia quickly slipped the sleeping draught into his glass.

They had several drinks together and then Cynthia hinted that it was time for her to get ready for the purpose of their visit. With this amorous excuse, she shyly withdrew to the divan in the hall, leaving Charles behind with the watchman.

After what seemed an eternity of waiting in the hall, Charles returned and told her that the watchman had dropped off into a deep sleep. She opened the front door and gave the prearranged signal to the car that was waiting in the shadows.

In a few moments the Georgia Cracker appeared and bounded up the embassy steps as quickly and quietly as a cat. Cynthia took him straight to the door of the code room, and he started working on its rather complicated lock. As he worked, she held a muffled flashlight in front of him, since they dared not turn on the electric light for fear of attracting attention outside.

The Georgia Cracker knew his job, and soon the door yielded to his expert touch. They then went directly to the safe and sat down on the floor in front of it. Cynthia shone the torch on its face while her companion manipulated the dial.

The safe was an antiquated affair and its cracking proved much longer and more difficult than they had thought. Several hours went by. From time to time Charles would leave his vigil in the hall to come and see how they were getting on. At long last, the Georgia Cracker leaned toward Cynthia and whispered, "Now I've got it!"

Slowly the door of the safe swung open, and there, right in front of them, were the cipher books. Cynthia looked at her wristwatch, and saw to her horror that it was past two o'clock in the morning. There could be no question of removing the books and photographing them in the remaining time available, since the operation had to be finished by 4 A.M. So she contented herself with caressing them with the tips of her fingers and registering a silent vow that she would have them in her hands yet.

Her safe-cracking companion then closed the safe door, adjusted the numbers on the dial to their original position, and wrote down the combination on a piece of paper which he handed to her. They got up and stretched their numbed legs and then crept out of the office and into the hallway, where some further minutes passed while Cynthia noted how the lock on the door was fixed into place.

She asked the Georgia Cracker to report to New York what had happened and to tell Johnny that she now had the combination of the safe, and that she proposed to make an attempt on her own the following night. "To tease him," she added, "tell him from me that I have never in my life laid eyes or fingers on such tantalizing reading material!"

She and Charles then returned to the hotel, and arranged to meet at noon so that he could let her know whether everything was all right in the embassy. Meanwhile, she revived herself under a cold shower and waited to hear from Johnny, which she did quite soon and with the answer she wanted. He agreed that the same dispositions could be made on the next night, but without the assistance of the safe cracker.

A little later, Charles arrived to say that all was well at the chancery. The guard was apparently his usual self and the naval attaché and the other members of the staff were going about their business as if nothing had happened. Cynthia breathed a sigh of relief.

In breaking the news to Charles that there was to be a repeat performance that night, she told him that she thought it would be too risky to drug the watchman a second time. Anyhow it could look rather odd if they invented a second anniversary to celebrate with champagne so soon after the first.

"That's all very fine," said Charles. "But supposing he appears while you are in the code room?"

Cynthia was quite prepared for such an eventuality. "If he does that," she told her lover, "and if it does not offend your sense of decorum, tell him that I am in the toilet. Then, if he has the indelicacy to look for me there, he will find me back with you on the divan in the hall, be ashamed of himself and go away."

Again at nightfall, they took the familiar walk to the chancery and let themselves in. The watchman was in the hall, this time with a large Alsatian dog, and Cynthia made some casual remark about what a splendid animal he was. This aroused his enthusiasm and he launched out into a long description of the dog's merits, which included police training, instantaneous obedience, seizing and holding any intruder, and a particularly loud bark. All this was necessary, he said, "because one never knows."

Cynthia allowed half an hour for the watchman and his dog to settle down in their quarters. Then, when everything was quiet, she tiptoed across the hall and began picking the lock of the office door. It opened without any trouble and she immediately got to the safe.

The first thing she did was to make a note of the position of the numbers on the dial, which she saw were different from those of the night before. This suggested that the safe had been opened and the ciphers used since her previous visit.

She quickly moved the figures round to make the required combination, which she now knew by heart, and pulled the door towards her. *Nothing whatever happened.*

She tried again, slowly and carefully, but with the same disappointing result. The door refused to move.

Thinking that she might have slipped up somehow with the combination, she had a look at the piece of paper the Georgia Cracker had given her. But there was no mistake.

Again and again she twirled the dial, with the same movements of the fingers that she had watched the professional safe cracker make. But always in vain, although she must have done this a hundred times. Finally, she gave it up in despair.

With a heavy heart she reset the dial, wiped off any possible fingerprints, relocked the door of the office, and went out to signal the man who was waiting for the cipher books.

"What took you so long?" he asked.

"The damned thing won't open!" Cynthia replied.

★   ★   ★

After a few hours sleep, Cynthia rang Johnny in New York and told him what had happened, or rather what she suspected he already knew had *not* happened.

"Don't worry," he reassured her. "I understand the article you are dealing with is very temperamental and is apt to behave unpredictably." Meanwhile, she was to take things easy and fly up to New York next day to meet him.

Soon after eight o'clock the following morning, Cynthia picked up Johnny at his apartment and they took a cab downtown. At one of the Broadway intersections he told the driver to stop, and then turning to her, said: "Hop into that black car standing by the curbside, and come back to the apartment before you catch the Washington plane."

She did as she was bidden, and to her surprise found herself sitting beside none other than her old friend the Georgia Cracker.

"I've never been so glad to see anyone in my life," she said with some feeling. "How I wish you had been with me the night before last!"

"To tell you the truth," he replied, "I don't like that piece of junk myself. Why do you suppose they don't get themselves a new one?"

Cynthia made some remark about French thrift and added, "In any case, why should they get themselves a new one as it would only make things easier for the likes of us?"

Her friend agreed, and they drove on for a while in silence. She was feeling tired with strain and must have dozed off, because the next thing she remembered was seeing the sun high in the sky and a long stretch of sand and water in front of her.

She recognized the popular bathing resort known as Jones Beach. But Cynthia and her companion had not come there to swim.

Pulling up at an isolated spot on the beach, the Georgia Cracker removed the back seat of the car and told her to move in. He then unwrapped a large object on the floor, which turned out to be a safe.

They both lay down on the floor and covered their heads with newspapers. "Now," he said, "do exactly what you did the other night—and I mean exactly!"

She proceeded to repeat the same combination of numbers and manipulations as she had used in the embassy chancery. This time the door of the safe opened quite easily.

The Georgia Cracker was nothing if not thorough and he put Cynthia through this exercise innumerable times. He also set her to work on other combinations of his own devising.

At last he pronounced himself satisfied, and jokingly said that if she ever got tired of her present job he would take her on as his assistant.

It was late in the afternoon when they got back to Johnny's apartment in New York. Her instructor reported on the excellent progress she had made and recommended that she should persevere with the embassy safe on her own.

Cynthia objected to this on the ground that, in spite of her increased proficiency in the art of safe-cracking, there was no guarantee that the safe would yield to her next attempt. Several more attempts might prove necessary. She pointed out she was afraid that the night watchman's suspicions would be aroused, if indeed they had not been aroused already.

It was eventually agreed that the Georgia Cracker should be available the following evening, when they would try again. Cynthia then returned to Washington and let Charles know that he must be prepared for another night of feminine caprice.

She found him quite resigned. "Never a dull moment with you!" he remarked. "I am probably the only man alive who spends both his days and his nights at his office in order to satisfy his lady love."

When they reached the embassy the next night, Cynthia had an uneasy feeling that something was wrong. On their way she had spotted a parked car, which she guessed contained a couple of FBI men, who were obviously keeping a watch on the building. She reckoned the Federal agents must have known that the OSS, not to mention the British, were in on this job. And she feared that for reasons of departmental jealousy the G-men might suddenly find it necessary to enter the embassy and wreck all their carefully laid plans.

Nor was the night watchman in the hall of the chancery when she and Charles took up their accustomed places on the divan and settled down to an uneasy wait. Cynthia could feel her heart beating furiously. She knew it must be now or never.

Then she made a sudden decision. She stood up and pulled her dress over her shoulders, tossing it onto the floor in the middle of the hall. Then she took off her slip and threw it in the same direction. Her bra, panties, girdle and stockings followed. She was now quite naked except for a string of pearls and her high-heeled shoes.

Charles watched her in speechless amazement. At last he managed to ask in an anguished whisper, "You haven't gone mad?"

"I don't think so," replied Cynthia. "But we shall see."

"But it's not done!" her poor lover went on. "You know that! Suppose someone should come in! What are you thinking of?"

"I am thinking of just that," she said coolly. "Supposing someone *does* come in!"

There was a note of asperity in her voice as she looked down at him and added, "What are we here for? We are here to make love. Yes? All right. Whoever heard of making love with clothes on if they can be taken off? I am not suggesting that we actually make love, God help us, only that we give that impression. If you wish to help me, you will get up and start undressing yourself too!"

Still looking bewildered, Charles slowly rose to his feet and began to do as his mistress had told him. He had barely time to take off his jacket, when suddenly the door behind them opened. Cynthia turned round quickly and her heart missed several beats. A powerful flashlight shone in her direction. Its ray went over every inch of her from head to foot.

Then the light was turned aside and she recognized the wielder of the torch. It was the night watchman.

As she snatched up her slip from the floor to cover her nakedness, the man was profuse in apologies. "I beg your pardon a thousand times, madame. I thought . . . didn't rightly know . . . ." His voice trailed away in confusion, as he beat a hasty retreat from the room.

"So you see," Cynthia remarked, after the night watchman had disappeared. "There was method in my madness. And now let's hope we shan't have any more interruptions."

But she was determined to take no chances. "All the same," she said, as she got into her slip, "I shan't put on anything more, for as the night watchman pointed out the other evening, one never knows!"

With that she gave Charles a kiss and signaled "all clear" to the Georgia Cracker after the FBI car had driven off. In a matter of minutes they were in the code room together sitting opposite the safe. To shade the light from her torch, Cynthia kept it under her slip. Her companion's deft fingers were soon at work on the combination.

Almost immediately she heard the welcome sound of the tumblers falling into place, and the door swung open to reveal the cipher books and their priceless secrets. "Thank you" was all she could whisper to the Georgia Cracker. The words came from the bottom of her heart as she carried away the books to the other confederate who was waiting outside.

Then began an agonizingly long wait with Charles on the divan, since each page in the books, amounting to some hundreds, had to be taken out, photographed and carefully replaced in its proper order, before the books themselves could be safely returned.

For a time Cynthia heard the night watchman's radio playing in the basement. It was around two o'clock, when the radio was switched off, and she waited expectantly for the night watchman to reappear. But nothing happened, and this she took to be a good omen. She guessed the watchman was having a nap.

For nearly two more hours she sweat it out on the divan, comforting herself with the reflection that the boys in the front line could hardly be having a worse time than this.

Then, as the appointed hour of 4 A.M. approached, she got up and put on the rest of her clothes and took up her post at the front door.

Promptly on the stroke of four, a figure appeared out of the darkness, carrying something large, and dashed up the steps.

Moments later the cipher books were in her hands and she was back beside the safe. She held up each book in front of her and kissed it reverently before returning it to its corner in the safe. Finally, having made certain that everything was in order, she closed and locked the safe door, office door, and returned to the divan.

Then she took Charles by the hand, and in silence together they went quietly down the embassy steps for the last time.

A few hours later she was lying on her bed in the hotel, too tense to sleep and too exhausted almost to move, when she heard the door open and looked up to see Mr. Hunter smiling at her. But it was not the Mr. Hunter she had known, for he was now wearing the immaculate summer uniform of the United States Army, and there were silver eagles on his shoulder tabs.

Cynthia immediately got up and waited for him to break the silence. He did so after several moments.

"Colonel Ellery Huntington is at your command, Cynthia!"

"And I am at yours, sir," she smiled.

"In that case we are at each other's, so now you come along with me as there is someone downstairs who wants to see you."

Cynthia followed the colonel to the opposite end of the hotel, where he led her into a room, which was full of photographic equipment of various kinds and crowded with people. Suddenly Johnny emerged. He too was smiling as he waved his hand in a gesture that took in the whole room, where every available piece of furniture was covered with photographic prints.

"Does that mean anything to you, Cynthia?" Before she had time to reply, he added quickly: "Good work. You are a credit to us!"

Cynthia looked at the fine, clear prints of the pages of the Vichy French naval ciphers, and then she appreciated the full significance of his words. Altogether it was the proudest moment of her life.

One morning several months afterwards Cynthia happened to be taking the train from Washington to New York. The date was November 8, 1942. As she was getting on board she saw Colonel Huntington, who saluted and suggested that they should sit together during the journey.

Cynthia sat down beside him in his drawing room, and as the train got under way he took the morning papers out of his briefcase and asked her if she had seen them. She replied that she had not.

"We have reached a turning point in the war," he said, pointing to the headlines. "American and British troops have landed in North

Africa, and have met with practically no enemy resistance. The reason there has been no resistance is a military secret. But I think that *you* should know that it is due to your ciphers. They have changed the whole course of the war."

"That's wonderful news," she answered, her voice shaking with pleasure.

Émigré Physicist Enrico Fermi
Tests the Precursor to the Atomic Bomb
in a Chicago Squash Court

(from Richard Rhodes,
The Making of the Atomic Bomb)

HITLER'S RISE *to power forced many important scientists to flee to American shores during the 1930s. Among them were Albert Einstein; John von Neumann, who conceived of using zeroes and ones as the language for computers; and physicists Niels Bohr, Leo Szilard, Edward Teller, and Eugene Winger.*

Italian physicist Enrico Fermi won the Nobel Prize in 1938; after receiving the prize in Sweden, he never returned to Italy, which was then under Mussolini's fascist dictatorship. Concerned for the safety of his Jewish wife, he fled to the United States, where he took a faculty position at Columbia University and later at the University of Chicago. Fermi possessed an extraordinarily creative analytical mind. He told his physics students that if you conducted an experiment, and the results match an existing theory, then you have made a measurement. On the other hand, if the results do not conform to an existing theory, then you have made a discovery. And discover he did. Oscillating between theoretical and experi-

mental physics, Fermi proved man can control nuclear fission for power plants and release it in the atomic bomb.

At Princeton, Szilard and Winger conferred with fellow émigré Albert Einstein about the import of current experiments at Columbia. In August 1939 the three prepared a letter addressed to President Franklin D. Roosevelt. The letter read, in part, "Some recent work by E. Fermi and L. Szilard, which has been communicated to me by manuscript, leads me to expect that the element uranium may be turned into a new and important source of energy in the immediate future. This new phenomenon would also lead to the construction of bombs, and it is conceivable—though much less certain—that extremely powerful bombs of a new type may thus be constructed." From this letter sprang the Manhattan Project to develop the atomic bomb, which culminated in the destruction of Hiroshima and Nagasaki, the surrender of Japan, and the end of the war in the Pacific.

Fermi explained his concept, which built on the German work of Otto Hahn, Fritz Strassman, and Lise Meitner, this way: "It takes one neutron to split one atom of uranium. We must first produce then use up that one neutron. Let's assume however that my hypothesis is correct, and that an atom of uranium undergoing fission emits two neutrons. There would now be two neutrons available without the need of producing them. It is conceivable that they might hit two more atoms of uranium, split them, and make them emit two neutrons each. At the end of this second process of fission we would have four neutrons, which would split four atoms. After one more step, eight neutrons would be available and could split eight more atoms of uranium. In other words starting with only a few man-produced neutrons to bombard a certain amount of uranium, we would be able to produce a set of reactions that would continue spontaneously until all uranium atoms were split."

This was the basic theoretical idea of a self-sustained chain reaction. Fermi next moved to prove it in a University of Chicago squash court, acutely aware that the outcome was unknown and potentially catastrophic. From Richard Rhodes's The Making of the Atomic Bomb, *the following passage tells the story of the first sustained nuclear reaction.*

★ ★ ★

A NDERSON'S CREW assembled this final configuration on the night of December 1:

> That night the construction proceeded as usual, with all cad-
> mium covered wood in place. When the 57th layer was completed,
> I called a halt to the work, in accordance with the agreement we
> had reached in the meeting with Fermi that afternoon. All the cad-
> mium rods but one were removed and the neutron count taken
> following the standard procedure which had been followed on the
> previous days. It was clear from the count that once the only re-
> maining cadmium rod was removed, the pile would go critical. I re-
> sisted great temptation to pull the final cadmium strip and be the
> first to make a pile chain react. However, Fermi had foreseen this
> temptation and extracted a promise from me to make the measure-
> ment, record the result, insert all cadmium rods, and lock them all
> in place.

Which Anderson dutifully did, and closed up the squash court and
went home to bed.

The pile as it waited in the dark cold of Chicago winter to be released to the breeding of neutrons and plutonium contained 771,000
pounds of graphite, 80,590 pounds of uranium oxide and 12,400
pounds of uranium metal. It cost about $1 million to produce and
build. Its only visible moving parts were its various control rods. If
Fermi had planned it for power production he would have shielded it
behind concrete or steel and pumped away the heat of fission with he-
lium or water or bismuth to drive turbines to generate electricity. But
CP-1 was simply and entirely a physics experiment designed to prove
the chain reaction, unshielded and uncooled, and Fermi intended, as-
suming he could control it, to run it no hotter than half a watt, hardly
enough energy to light a flashlight bulb. He had controlled it day by
day for the seventeen days of its building as its k approached 1.0, match-
ing its responses with his estimates, and he was confident he could
control it when its chain reaction finally diverged. What would he do if
he was wrong? one of his young colleagues asked him. He thought of

the damping effect of delayed neutrons. "I will walk away—leisurely," he answered.

"The next morning," Leona Woods remembers—the beginning of the fateful day, December 2, 1942—"it was terribly cold—below zero. Fermi and I crunched over to the stands in creaking, blue-shadowed snow and repeated Herb's flux measurement with the standard boron trifluoride counter." Fermi had plotted a graph of his countdown numbers; the new data point fell exactly on the line he had extrapolated from previous measurements, a little shy of layer 57.

Fermi discussed a schedule for the day with Zinn and Volney Wilson, Woods continues; "then a sleepy Herb Anderson showed up . . . Herb, Fermi and I went over to the apartment I shared with my sister (it was close to the stands) for something to eat. I made pancakes, mixing the batter so fast that there were bubbles of dry flour in it. When fried, these were somewhat crunchy between the teeth, and Herb thought I had put nuts in the batter."

Outside was raw wind. On the second day of gasoline rationing Chicagoans jammed streetcars and elevated trains, leaving almost half their usual traffic of automobiles at home. The State Department had announced that morning that two million Jews had perished in Europe and five million more were in danger. The Germans were preparing a counterattack in North Africa; American marines and Japanese soldiers struggled in the hell of Guadalcanal.

Back we mushed through the cold, creaking snow . . . Fifty-seventh Street was strangely empty. Inside the hall of the west stands, it was as cold as outside. We put on the usual gray (now black with graphite) laboratory coats and entered the doubles squash court containing the looming pile enclosed in the dirty, grayish-black balloon cloth and then went up on the spectators' balcony. The balcony was originally meant for people to watch squash players, but now it was filled with control equipment and read-out circuits glowing and winking and radiating some gratefully received heat.

The instrumentation included redundant boron trifluoride counters for lower neutron intensities and ionization chambers for higher. A wooden pier extending out from the face of the pile supported automatic control rods operated by small electric motors that would stand idle that day. ZIP, a weighted safety rod Zinn had designed, rode the same scaffolding. A solenoid-actuated catch controlled by an ionization chamber held ZIP in position withdrawn from the pile; if neutron intensity exceeded the chamber setting the solenoid would trip and gravity would pull the rod into position to stop the chain reaction. Another ZIP-like rod had been tied to the balcony railing with a length of rope; one of the physicists, feeling foolish, would stand by to chop the rope with an ax if all else failed. Allison had even insisted on a suicide squad, three young physicists installed with jugs of cadmium-sulfate solution near the ceiling on the elevator they had used to lift graphite bricks; "several of us," Wattenberg complained, "were very upset with this since an accidental breakage of the jugs near the pile could have destroyed the usefulness of the material." George Weil, a young veteran of the Columbia days, took up position on the floor of the squash court to operate one of the cadmium control rods by hand at Fermi's order. Fermi had scalers that counted off boron trifluoride readings with loud clicks and a cylindrical pen recorder that performed a similar function silently, graphing pile intensities in ink on a roll of slowly rotating graph paper. For calculations he relied on his own trusted six-inch slide rule, the pocket calculator of its day.

Around midmorning Fermi began the crucial experiment. First he ordered all but the last cadmium rod removed and checked to see if the neutron intensity matched the measurement Anderson had made the night before. With that first comparison Volney Wilson's team working on the balcony took time to adjust its monitors. Fermi had calculated in advance the intensity he expected the pile to reach at each step of the way as George Weil withdrew the last thirteen-foot cadmium rod by measured increments.

When Wilson's team was ready, writes Wattenberg, "Fermi instructed Weil to move the cadmium rod to a position which was about half-way out. [The adjustment brought the pile to] well below critical

condition. The intensity rose, the scalers increased their rates of click-
ing for a short while, and then the rate became steady, as it was supposed to." Fermi busied himself at his slide rule, calculating the rate of
increase, and noted the numbers on the back. He called to Weil to move
the rod out another six inches. "Again the neutron intensity increased
and leveled off. The pile was still subcritical. Fermi had again been busy
with his little slide rule and seemed very pleased with the results of his
calculations. Every time the intensity leveled off, it was at the values he
had anticipated for the position of the control rod."

The slow, careful checking continued through the morning. A
crowd began to gather on the balcony. Szilard arrived, Wigner, Allison, Spedding whose metal eggs had flattened the pile. Twenty-five or
thirty people accumulated on the balcony watching, most of them
the young physicists who had done the work. No one photographed
the scene but most of the spectators probably wore suits and ties in the
genteel tradition of prewar physics and since it was cold in the squash
court, near zero, they would have kept warm in coats and hats, scarves
and gloves. The room was dingy with graphite dust. Fermi was calm.
The pile rising before them, faced with raw 4-by-6-inch pine timbers
up to its equator, domed bare graphite above, looked like an ominous black beehive in a bright box. Neutrons were its bees, dancing
and hot.

Fermi called for another six-inch withdrawal. Weil reached up to
comply. The neutron intensity leveled off at a rate outside the range of
some of the instruments. Time passed, says Wattenberg, the watchers
abiding in the cold, while Wilson's team again adjusted the electronics:

> After the instrumentation was reset, Fermi told Weil to remove
> the rod another six inches. The pile was still subcritical. The inten-
> sity was increasing slowly—when suddenly there was a very loud
> crash! The safety rod, ZIP, had been automatically released. Its
> relay had been activated by an ionization chamber because the in-
> tensity had exceeded the arbitrary level at which it had been set. It
> was 11:30 a.m., and Fermi said, "I'm hungry. Let's go to lunch."
> The other rods were put into the pile and locked.

At two in the afternoon they prepared to continue the experiment. Compton [MIT] joined them. He brought along Crawford Greenewalt, the tall handsome engineer who was the leader of the Du Pont contingent in Chicago. Forty-two people now occupied the squash court, most of them crowded onto the balcony.

Fermi ordered all but one of the cadmium rods again unlocked and removed. He asked Weil to set the last rod at one of the earlier morning settings and compared pile intensity to the earlier reading. When the measurements checked he directed Weil to remove the rod to the last setting before lunch, about seven feet out.

The closer k approached 1.0, the slower the rate of change of pile intensity. Fermi made another calculation. The pile was nearly critical. He asked that ZIP be slid in. That adjustment brought the neutron count down. "This time," he told Weil, "take the control rod out twelve inches." Weil withdrew the cadmium rod. Fermi nodded and ZIP was winched out as well. "This is going to do it," Fermi told Compton. The director of the plutonium project had found a place for himself at Fermi's side. "Now it will become self-sustaining. The trace [on the recorder] will climb and continue to climb; it will not level off."

Herbert Anderson was an eyewitness:

At first you could hear the sound of the neutron counter, clickety-clack, clickety-clack. Then the clicks came more and more rapidly, and after a while they began to merge into a roar; the counter couldn't follow anymore. That was the moment to switch to the chart recorder. But when the switch was made, everyone watched in the sudden silence the mounting deflection of the recorder's pen. It was an awesome silence. Everyone realized the significance of that switch; we were in the high intensity regime and the counters were unable to cope with the situation anymore. Again and again, the scale of the recorder had to be changed to accommodate the neutron intensity which was increasing more and more rapidly. Suddenly Fermi raised his hand. "The pile has gone critical," he announced. No one present had any doubt about it.

Fermi allowed himself a grin. He would tell the technical council the next day that the pile achieved a k of 1.0006. Its neutron intensity was then doubling every two minutes. Left uncontrolled for an hour and a half, that rate of increase would have carried it to a million kilowatts. Long before so extreme a runaway it would have killed anyone left in the room and melted down.

"Then everyone began to wonder why he didn't shut the pile off," Anderson continues. "But Fermi was completely calm. He waited another minute, then another, and then when it seemed that the anxiety was too much to bear, he ordered 'ZIP in!' " It was 3:53 p.m. Fermi had run the pile for 4.5 minutes at one-half watt and brought to fruition all the years of discovery and experiment. Men had controlled the release of energy from the atomic nucleus.

★ 41 ★

D-Day: World War II

(from Cornelius Ryan,
The Longest Day—June 6, 1944)

B Y JUNE 1944, *World War II had been going on for almost five years. In Eastern Europe the Nazis were retreating, but they still controlled Estonia, Latvia, Lithuania, Poland, Hungary, Rumania, Bulgaria, and Greece to the east, and Norway, Denmark, Belgium, the Netherlands, and France to the west. In the south, Operation Torch, the American invasion of North Africa, had, after a difficult start, evicted General Erwin Rommel, "the Desert Fox," commander of Germany's Afrika Korps. This was followed by the invasion of Sicily and then the Italian boot.*

England became the staging area for the next invasion target—Nazi-occupied France, the heart of the matter. Winston Churchill had named this long-planned invasion Operation Overlord; it would be known to history as D-Day, the largest invasion ever. General Dwight Eisenhower, as commander in chief, was charged with coordinating the Allies and making the ultimate decisions of where and when to land. The German coastal defense, now under Rommel's control, went hell-for-leather to increase the coastal defenses to a depth of five to six kilometers from Denmark to Brittany. The coast under the breaking waves was mined, and underwater obstructions were put in place. On shore were tank obstructions, minefields, barbed wire, reinforced pillboxes harboring artillery and machine guns, and connecting trenches zigzagged across the headlands. Guns were calibrated to destroy the landing craft and enfilade the troops as they reached the beaches. Rommel kept mobile reserves in the rear to smash any landing in its initial stages. He believed that any toehold landing had to be counterattacked and destroyed within twenty-four hours, otherwise the landing forces would overpower the defenders. Rommel thought the main landings would be between the Somme and the Seine Rivers, and at the Pas-de-Calais. Eventually he chose Normandy as the probable main landing area.

And he was right. In early June 1944, thirty-seven divisions lay in wait in southern England to take part in the largest amphibious landing ever. England's shores were lashed by a storm, which the meteorologists predicted would abate. General Eisenhower alone was responsible for the go-no-go decision. When the weather forecast called for a break in the storm, Ike said simply: "Okay, we'll go."

On June 6, 1944—D-Day—the Allies concentrated on a sixty-mile stretch of Normandy coast, from the mouth of the Orne to the beaches near Sainte-Mère-Église on the Cotentin Peninsula. Four thousand invasion craft carried 176,000 troops protected by six hundred warships, while overhead eleven thousand planes provided air cover for the massive assault. Parachute troops were dropped inland.

From The Longest Day *by war reporter Cornelius Ryan, here is the definitive account of the Allied experience on D-Day.*

* * *

B Y NOW THE LONG, bobbing lines of assault craft were less than a mile from Omaha and Utah beaches. For the three thousand Americans in the first wave, H Hour was just fifteen minutes away.

The noise was deafening as the boats, long white wakes streaming out behind them, churned steadily for the shore. In the slopping, bouncing craft the men had to shout to be heard over the roar of the diesels. Overhead, like a great steel umbrella, the shells of the fleet still thundered. And rolling out from the coast came the booming explosions of the Allied air forces' carpet bombing. Strangely, the guns of the Atlantic Wall were silent. Troops saw the coastline stretching ahead and wondered about the absence of enemy fire. Maybe, many thought, it would be an easy landing after all.

The great square-faced ramps of the assault craft butted into every wave, and chilling, frothing green water sloshed over everyone. There were no heroes in these boats—just cold, miserable, anxious men, so jam-packed together, so weighed down by equipment that often there was no place to be seasick except over one another. *Newsweek*'s Kenneth Crawford, in the first Utah wave, saw a young 4th Division soldier, covered in his own vomit, slowly shaking his head in abject misery and disgust. "That guy Higgins," he said, "ain't got nothin' to be proud of about inventin' this goddamned boat."

Some men had no time to think about their miseries—they were bailing for their lives. Almost from the moment the assault craft left the mother ships, many boats had begun to fill with water. At first the men had paid little attention to the sea slopping about their legs; it was just another misery to be endured. Lieutenant George Kerchner of the Rangers watched the water slowly rise in his craft and wondered if it was serious. He had been told that the LCA was unsinkable. But then over the radio Kerchner's soldiers heard a call for help: "This is LCA 860! . . . LCA 860! . . . We're sinking! . . . We're sinking!" There was a final exclamation: "My God, we're sunk!" Immediately Kerchner and his men began bailing.

Directly behind Kerchner's boat, Sergeant Regis McCloskey, also of the Rangers, had his own troubles. McCloskey and his men had been bailing for more than an hour. Their boat carried ammunition for the Pointe du Hoc attack and all of the Rangers' packs. The boat was so waterlogged McCloskey was sure it would sink. His only hope lay in lightening the wallowing craft. McCloskey ordered his men to toss all unnecessary equipment overboard. Rations, extra clothing and packs went over the side. McCloskey heaved them all into the swells. In one pack was $1,200 which Private Chuck Vella had won in a crap game; in another was First Sergeant Charles Frederick's false teeth.

Landing craft began to sink in both the Omaha and Utah areas—ten off Omaha, seven off Utah. Some men were picked up by rescue boats coming up behind, others would float around for hours before being rescued. And some soldiers, their yells and screams unheard, were dragged down by their equipment and ammunition. They drowned within sight of the beaches, without having fired a shot.

In an instant the war had become personal. Troops heading for Utah Beach saw a control boat leading one of the waves suddenly rear up out of the water and explode. Seconds later heads bobbed up and survivors tried to save themselves by clinging to the wreckage. Another explosion followed almost immediately. The crew of a landing barge trying to launch four of the thirty-two amphibious tanks bound for Utah had dropped the ramp right onto a submerged sea mine. The front of the craft shot up and Sergeant Orris Johnson on a nearby LCT watched in frozen horror as a tank "soared more than a hundred feet into the air, tumbled slowly end over end, plunged back into the water and disappeared." Among the many dead, Johnson learned later, was his buddy, Tanker Don Neill.

Scores of Utah-bound men saw the dead bodies and heard the yells and screams of the drowning. One man, Lieutenant (j.g.) Francis X. Riley of the Coast Guard, remembers the scene vividly. The twenty-four-year-old officer, commanding an LCI, could only listen "to the anguished cries for help from wounded and shocked soldiers and sailors as they pleaded with us to pull them out of the water." But Riley's orders were to "disembark the troops on time regardless of casualties." Trying to close his mind to the screams, Riley ordered his craft on past the drowning men. There was nothing else he could do. The assault waves sped by, and as one boat carrying Lieutenant Colonel James Batte and the 4th Division's 8th Infantry Regiment troops threaded its way through the dead bodies, Batte heard one of his gray-faced men say, "Them lucky bastards—they ain't seasick no more."

The sight of the bodies in the water, the strain of the long trip in from the transport ships and now the ominous nearness of the flat sands and the dunes of Utah Beach jerked men out of their lethargy. Corporal Lee Cason, who had just turned twenty, suddenly found himself "cursing to high heaven against Hitler and Mussolini for getting us into this mess." His companions were startled at his vehemence—Cason had never before been known to swear. In many boats now soldiers nervously checked and rechecked their weapons. Men became so possessive of their ammunition that Colonel Eugene Caffey could not get a single man in his boat to give him a clip of bullets for his rifle. Caffey, who was not supposed to land until 9:00 A.M., had smuggled himself aboard an 8th Infantry craft in an effort to catch up with his veteran 1st Engineer Brigade. He had no equipment and although all the men in the boat were overloaded with ammunition, they were "hanging onto it for dear life." Caffey was finally able to load the rifle by taking up a collection of one bullet from each of eight men.

In the waters off Omaha Beach there had been a disaster. Nearly half of the amphibious tank force scheduled to support the assault troops had foundered. The plan was for sixty-four of these tanks to be launched two to three miles offshore. From there they were to swim in to the beach. Thirty-two of them had been allotted to the 1st Division's area—Easy Red, Fox Green and Fox Red. The landing barges carrying them reached their positions, the ramps were dropped and twenty-nine tanks were launched into the heaving swells. The weird-looking amphibious vehicles, their great balloonlike canvas skirts supporting them in the water, began breasting the waves, driving toward the shore. Then tragedy overtook the men of the 741st Tank Battalion. Under the pounding of the waves the canvas water wings ripped, supports broke, engines were flooded—and, one after another, twenty-seven tanks foundered and sank. Men came clawing up out of the hatches, inflating their life belts, plunging into the sea. Some succeeded in launching survival rafts. Others went down in the steel coffins.

Two tanks, battered and almost awash, were still heading for the shore. The crews of three others had the good fortune to be on a landing barge whose ramp jammed. They were put ashore later. The remaining thirty-two tanks—for the 29th Division's half of the beach—were safe. Officers in charge of the craft carrying them, overwhelmed by the disaster they had seen, wisely decided to take their force directly onto the beach. But the loss of the 1st Division tanks would cost hundreds of casualties within the next few minutes.

From two miles out the assault troops began to see the living and the dead in the water. The dead floated gently, moving with the tide toward the beach, as though determined to join their fellow Americans. The living bobbed up and down in the swells, savagely pleading for the help the assault boats could not tender. Sergeant Regis McCloskey, his ammunition boat again safely under way, saw the screaming men in the water, "yelling for help, begging us to stop—and we couldn't. Not for anything or anyone." Gritting his teeth, McCloskey looked away as his boat sped past, and then, seconds later, he vomited over the side. Captain Robert Cunningham and his men saw survivors struggling, too. Instinctively their Navy crew swung the boat toward the men in the water. A fast launch cut them off. Over its loudspeaker came the grim words, "You are not a rescue ship! Get on shore!" In another boat nearby, Sergeant Noel Dube of an engineer battalion said the Act of Contrition.

Now the deadly martial music of the bombardment seemed to grow and swell as the thin wavy lines of assault craft closed in on Omaha Beach. Landing ships lying about one thousand yards offshore joined in the shelling; and then thousands of flashing rockets whooshed over the heads of the men. To the troops it seemed inconceivable that anything could survive the massive weight of fire power that flayed the German defenses. The beach was wreathed in haze, and plumes of smoke from grass fires drifted lazily down from the bluffs. Still the German guns remained silent. The boats bored in: In the thrashing surf and running back up the beach men could now see the lethal jungles of steel-and-concrete obstacles. They were strewn everywhere, draped with barbed wire and capped with mines. They were as cruel and ugly as the men had expected. Back of the defenses the beach itself was deserted; nothing and no one moved upon it. Closer and closer the boats pressed in . . . 500 yards . . . 450 yards. Still no enemy fire. Through waves that were four to five feet high the assault craft surged forward, and now the great bombardment began to lift, shifting to targets farther inland. The first boats were barely 400 yards from the shore when the German guns—the guns that few believed could have survived the raging Allied air and sea bombardment—opened up.

Through the din and clamor one sound was nearer, deadlier than all the rest—the sound of machine-gun bullets clanging across the steel, snoutlike noses of the boats. Artillery roared. Mortar shells rained down. All along the four miles of Omaha Beach German guns flayed the assault craft.

It was H Hour.

They came ashore on Omaha Beach, the slogging, unglamorous men that no one envied. No battle ensigns flew for them, no horns or bugles sounded. But they had history on their side. They came from regiments that had bivouacked at places like Valley Forge, Stoney Creek, Antietam, Gettysburg, that had fought in the Argonne. They had crossed the beaches of North Africa, Sicily and Salerno. Now they had one more beach to cross. They would call this one "Bloody Omaha."

The most intense fire came from the cliffs and high bluffs at either end of the crescent-shaped beach—in the 29th Division's Dog Green area to the west and the 1st Division's Fox Green sector to the east. Here the Germans had concentrated their heaviest defenses to hold two of the principal exits leading off the beach at Vierville and toward Colleville. Everywhere along the beach men encountered heavy fire as their boats came in, but the troops landing at Dog Green and Fox Green hadn't a chance. German gunners on the cliffs looked almost directly down on the waterlogged assault craft that heaved and pitched toward these sectors of the beach. Awkward and slow, the assault boats were nearly stationary in the water. They were sitting ducks. Coxswains at the tillers, trying desperately to maneuver their unwieldly craft through the forest of mined obstacles, now had to run the gauntlet of fire from the cliffs.

Some boats, unable to find a way through the maze of obstacles and the withering cliff fire, were driven off and wandered aimlessly along the beach seeking a less heavily defended spot to land. Others, doggedly trying to come in at their assigned sectors, were shelled so badly that men plunged over the sides into deep water, where they were immediately picked off by machine-gun fire. Some landing craft were blown apart as they came in. Second Lieutenant Edward Gearing's assault boat, filled with thirty men of the 29th Division, disintegrated in one blinding moment three hundred yards from the Vierville exit at Dog Green. Gearing and his men were blown out of the boat and strewn over the water. Shocked and half drowned, the nineteen-year-old lieutenant came to the surface yards away from where his boat had gone down. Other survivors began to bob up, too. Their weapons, helmets and equipment were gone. The coxswain had disappeared and nearby one of Gearing's men, struggling beneath the weight of a heavy radio set strapped to his back, screamed out, "For God's sake, I'm drowning!" Nobody could get to the radioman before he went under. For Gearing and the remnants of his section the ordeal was just beginning. It would be three hours before they got on the beach. Then Gearing would learn that he was the only surviving officer of his company. The others were dead or seriously wounded.

All along Omaha Beach the dropping of the ramps seemed to be the signal for renewed, more concentrated machine-gun fire, and again the most murderous fire was in the Dog Green and Fox Green sectors. Boats of the 29th Division, coming into Dog Green, grounded on the sand bars. The ramps came down and men stepped out into water three to six feet deep. They had but one object in mind—to get through the water, cross two hundred yards of the obstacle-strewn sand, climb the gradually rising shingle and then take cover in the doubtful shelter of a sea wall. But weighed down by their equipment, unable to run in the deep water and without cover of any kind, men were caught in criss-crossing machine-gun and small-arms fire.

Seasick men, already exhausted by the long hours spent on the transports and in the assault boats, found themselves fighting for their lives in water which was often over their heads. Private David Silva saw the men in front of him being mowed down as they stepped off the ramp. When his turn came, he jumped into chest-high water and, bogged down by his equipment, watched spellbound as bullets flicked the surface all around him. Within seconds, machine-gun fire had riddled his pack, his clothing and his canteen. Silva felt like a "pigeon at a trap shoot." He thought he spotted the German machine gunner who was firing at him, but he could not fire back. His rifle was clogged with sand. Silva waded on, determined to make the sands ahead. He finally pulled himself up on the beach and dashed for the shelter of the sea wall, completely unaware that he had been wounded twice—once in the back, and once in the right leg.

Men fell all along the water's edge. Some were killed instantly, others called pitifully for the medics as the incoming tide slowly engulfed them. Among the dead was Captain Sherman Burroughs. His friend Captain Charles Cawthon saw the body washing back and forth in the surf. Cawthon wondered if Burroughs had recited "The Shooting of Dan McGrew" to his men on the run-in as he had planned. And when Captain Carroll Smith passed by, he could not help but think that Burroughs "would no longer suffer from his constant migraine headaches." Burroughs had been shot through the head.

Within the first few minutes of the carnage at Dog Green one entire company was put out of action. Less than a third of the men survived the bloody walk from the boats to the edge of the beach. Their officers were killed, severely wounded or missing, and the men, weaponless and shocked, huddled at the base of the cliffs all day. Another company in the same sector suffered even higher casualties. Company C of the 2nd Ranger Battalion had been ordered to knock out enemy strongpoints at Point de la Percée, slightly west of Vierville. The Rangers landed in two assault craft with the first wave on Dog Green. They were decimated. The lead craft was sunk almost immediately by artillery fire, and twelve men were killed outright. The moment the ramp of the second craft dropped down, machine-gun fire sprayed the debarking Rangers, killing and wounding fifteen. The remainder set out for the cliffs. Men fell one after another. Private First Class Nelson Noyes, staggering under the weight of a bazooka, made a hundred yards before he was forced to hit the ground. A few moments later he got up and ran forward again. When he reached the shingle he was machine-gunned in the leg. As he lay there Noyes saw the two Germans who had fired looking down on him from the cliff. Propping himself on his elbows he opened up with his Tommy gun and brought both of them down. By the time Captain Ralph E. Goranson, the company commander, reached the base of the cliff, he had only thirty-five Rangers left out of his seventy-man team. By nightfall these thirty-five would be cut down to twelve.

Misfortune piled upon misfortune for the men of Omaha Beach. Soldiers now discovered that they had been landed in the wrong sectors. Some came in almost two miles away from their original landing

areas. Boat sections from the 29th Division found themselves inter-
mingled with men of the 1st Division. For example, units scheduled to
land on Easy Green and fight toward an exit at Les Moulins discovered
themselves at the eastern end of the beach in the hell of Fox Green.
Nearly all the landing craft came in slightly east of their touch-down
points. A control boat drifting off station, a strong current running
eastward along the beach, the haze and smoke from grass fires which
obscured landmarks—all these contributed to the mislandings. Companies that had been trained to capture certain objectives never got near
them. Small groups found themselves pinned down by German fire
and isolated in unrecognizable terrain, often without officers or communications.

The special Army-Navy demolition engineers who had the job of
blowing paths through the beach obstacles were not only widely scattered, they were brought in crucial minutes behind schedule. These
frustrated men set to work wherever they found themselves. But they
fought a losing battle. In the few minutes they had before the following
waves of troops bore down on the beaches, the engineers cleared only
five and a half paths instead of the sixteen planned. Working with desperate haste, the demolition parties were impeded at every turn—
infantrymen waded in among them, soldiers took shelter behind the
obstacles they were about to blow and landing craft, buffeted by the
swells, came in almost on top of them. Sergeant Barton A. Davis of
the 299th Engineer Combat Battalion saw an assault boat bearing
down on him. It was filled with 1st Division men and was coming
straight in through the obstacles. There was a tremendous explosion
and the boat disintegrated. It seemed to Davis that everyone in it was
thrown into the air all at once. Bodies and parts of bodies landed all
around the flaming wreckage. "I saw black dots of men trying to swim
through the gasoline that had spread on the water and as we wondered
what to do a headless torso flew a good fifty feet through the air
and landed with a sickening thud near us." Davis did not see how anyone could have lived through the explosion, but two men did. They
were pulled out of the water, badly burned but alive.

But the disaster that Davis had seen was no greater than that which
had overtaken the heroic men of his own unit, the Army-Navy Special

Engineer Task Force. The landing boats carrying their explosives had been shelled, and the hulks of these craft lay blazing at the edge of the beach. Engineers with small rubber boats laded with plastic charges and detonators were blown apart in the water when enemy fire touched off the explosives. The Germans, seeing the engineers working among the obstacles, seemed to single them out for special attention. As the teams tied on their charges, snipers took careful aim at the mines on the obstacles. At other times they seemed to wait until the engineers had prepared whole lines of steel trestles and tetrahedra obstacles for blowing. Then the Germans themselves would detonate the obstacles with mortar fire—before the engineers could get out of the area. By the end of the day casualties would be almost fifty percent. Sergeant Davis himself would be one. Nightfall would find him aboard a hospital ship with a wounded leg, heading back for England.

It was 7:00 A.M. The second wave of troops arrived on the shambles that was Omaha Beach. Men splashed ashore under the saturating fire of the enemy. Landing craft joined the ever growing graveyard of wrecked, blazing hulks. Each wave of boats gave up its own bloody contribution to the incoming tide, and all along the crescent-shaped strip of beach dead Americans gently nudged each other in the water.

Piling up along the shore was the flotsam and jetsam of the invasion. Heavy equipment and supplies, boxes of ammunition, smashed radios, field telephones, gas masks, entrenching tools, canteens, steel helmets and life preservers were strewn everywhere. Great reels of wire, ropes, ration boxes, mine detectors and scores of weapons, from broken rifles to stove-in bazookas, littered the sand. The twisted wrecks of landing craft canted up crazily out of the water. Burning tanks threw great spirals of black smoke into the air. Bulldozers lay on their sides among the obstacles. Off Easy Red, floating in and out among all the cast-off materials of war, men saw a guitar.

Small islands of wounded men dotted the sand. Passing troops noticed that those who could sat bolt upright as though now immune to any further hurt. They were quiet men, seemingly oblivious to the sights and sounds around them. Staff Sergeant Alfred Eigenberg, a medic attached to the 6th Engineers Special Brigade, remembers "a terrible politeness among the more seriously injured." In his first few minutes on the beach, Eigenberg found so many wounded that he did not know "where to start or with whom." On Dog Red he came across a young soldier sitting in the sand with his leg "laid open from the knee to the pelvis as neatly as though a surgeon had done it with a scalpel." The wound was so deep that Eigenberg could clearly see the femoral artery pulsing. The soldier was in deep shock. Calmly he informed Eigenberg, "I've taken my sulfa pills and I've shaken all my sulfa powder into the wound. I'll be all right, won't I?" The nineteen-year-old Eigenberg didn't quite know what to say. He gave the soldier a shot of morphine and told him, "Sure, you'll be all right." Then, folding the neatly sliced halves of the man's leg together, Eigenberg did the only thing he could think of—he carefully closed the wound with safety pins.

Into the chaos, confusion and death on the beach poured the men of the third wave—and stopped. Minutes later the fourth wave came in—and they stopped. Men lay shoulder to shoulder on the sands, stones and shale. They crouched down behind obstacles, they sheltered among the bodies of the dead. Pinned down by the enemy fire which they had expected to be neutralized, confused by their landings in the wrong sectors, bewildered by the absence of the sheltering craters they had expected from the Air Force bombing, and shocked by the devastation and death all around them, the men froze on the beaches. They seemed in the grip of a strange paralysis. Overwhelmed by it all, some men believed the day was lost. Technical Sergeant William McClintock of the 741st Tank Battalion came upon a man sitting at the edge of the water, seemingly unaware of the machine-gun fire which rippled all over the area. He sat there "throwing stones into the water and softly crying as if his heart would break."

The shock would not last long. Even now a few men here and there, realizing that to stay on the beach meant certain death, were on their feet and moving.

Sniper Fight on Okinawa

(from William Manchester,
Goodbye, Darkness—A Memoir of the Pacific War)

THE ROLLBACK *of the Japanese conquests in the Pacific be-gan in August 1942, when the U.S. Marines fought a bloody six-month battle to capture Guadalcanal. Thereafter continuous island-hopping invasions in the Central Pacific were mingled with fierce and successful naval battles which eroded Japan's sea and air power. The "up the ladder," leapfrogging amphibious landings on island chains started in the Solomon and moved to the Gilberts, the Marshall, the Mari-ana and Bonin Islands. Better remembered are the blood-soaked battles named after the conquered islands. In 1943: Bougainville, Tarawa, and Makin. In 1944: Kwajalein, Eniwetok, Siapan, Guam, Tinian, Peleliu, and Leyte in the Philippines. Followed in 1945 by Luzon, Iwo Jima, and Okinawa.*

Okinawa, in the Ryukyu chain, was the last island invaded (April 1945) by the U.S. Army and Marines. A natural air base for launching round-the-clock bombing raids against Japan, it was also within easy reach of southern Kyushu—the obvious first target for the invasion of

Japan proper. The strategy predated President Harry S. Truman's authorization of the use of the newly developed atomic bomb. Upon the atomic destruction of Hiroshima and Nagasaki, Japan surrendered unconditionally. The uncommon casualty rate experienced on Okinawa and other islands, where the entrenched Japanese fought to the death, helped convince the American command that the atomic bomb was an acceptable option—indeed it has been estimated that the Japanese surrender saved roughly two million casualties.

From his memoir Goodbye, Darkness, *here is William Manchester's account of his encounter with a Japanese sniper. His Marine Corps regiment landed 3,512 men on Okinawa, including rear-echelon troops; of these, 2,812 fell—an 80 percent casualty rate.*

* * *

THERE WAS just one moment in the war when I saved my own life, and it came right after my soggy nap in that defective cave. Back on our own little amphitheater of war, still soaked to the skin, I started a routine tour of the line companies that afternoon, covering it much as a mailman covers his route, except that I had company, because, if possible, we always moved in pairs. My buddy that day was Chet Przyastawaki, the Colgate athlete with the shrill voice. We followed the embankment as far as it went and then moved from one local feature to another: the Long Square, the Blue Icicle, Grable's Tit, the X, the Iron Claw, Thurston's Trick, and the V, also known as the Hairless Pussy. This was a time when the Japanese were constantly challenging us, trying to infiltrate every night and sometimes, brazenly, by day. If their purpose was to keep us off balance, they were succeeding. This surging back and forth quickened the pulses of the Raggedy Asses. People like us, moving from one command post to another, could get caught by occasional Nips [Niponese] who were testing us, penetrating as deeply as they could and then, when found, trying to slip back.

Chet and I had covered the companies, Fox to Easy to Dog, as smoothly as Tinker to Evers to Chance. Positions around Sugar Loaf were in constant flux—at one time or another nine Marine battalions fought on the hill—and we had been told to skirt enemy lines on our way back, scouting every dip, crease, cranny, and rut in the ground that might be useful in combined attacks. The last leg of our journey, before we reached the lee side of the railroad embankment, took us past the crevice called McGee's Closet and down Windy Alley, a rock gulch which, like Sugar Loaf itself, had changed hands repeatedly. We arrived there at the worst possible time. The Japs had launched a reconnaissance in force; no sooner had we entered the lower throat of the alley than we heard the unmistakable sounds of an enemy patrol sealing it off behind us, closing our option of retracing our steps. Then we heard a familiar, husky sob in the air, directly overhead. We hit the deck, and a mortar shell burst a hundred feet away, followed by another, and then another. Silence followed. Chet crossed himself. Another shell burst. The stupid Japs were falling short of their targets, our lines, mortaring us in. When mortared, you are supposed to flee in almost any direction, but, as we were about to discover, it is not always that easy. As we rose cautiously, we heard jabbering on the opposite slopes of both sides of Windy Alley. So much for our flanks. We darted ahead, toward the embankment, and that was when the pneumatic whuff of the first bullet from that direction sang between us. It wasn't from an M1; it had that unmistakable Arisaka whine. We hit the deck again and rolled rightward together, toward the protection of a huge boulder, a rough slab of rock. Two more bullets whuffed past before we made it. Our problem now, and I cannot begin to tell you how much it discouraged me, was that a Nip sniper was in position at the alley's upper throat, behind another boulder, blocking the maze of intersecting paths there, cutting us off at the pass. We were trapped, the nightmare of every foot soldier. All I had going for me was sheer desperation. *Warning: this animal is vicious; when attacked, it defends itself.*

Lying in tandem, Chet and I exchanged wide-eyed glances. The coral had cut both his hands, but I was in no mood to comfort him. I felt a wave of self-pity. For several seconds I was completely mindless. Fear is the relinquishment of reason; we yield to it or fight it, but there are no halfway points. Then I struggled and shook off the panic. It was one of Napoleon's maxims that in war you must never do what the enemy wants you to do. This Jap expected us to stay put. So we wouldn't. Each of us had two grenades hooked on his harness. I hunched up and reached for one. Chet shook his head. "Too far," he whispered. If the range was too great for a Colgate halfback, a scrawny sergeant didn't have a chance, but I already knew the distance was too great; reaching the Nip with a pitch wasn't what I had in mind. I didn't tell Chet now what was there, because as I unlooped the grenade I had to think about a weapon which would reach our man. I was carrying a carbine and a .45, both useless in a sniper's duel. Chet had an M1. I asked, "Did you qualify?" He said, "Sharpshooter. Under three hundred." I shook my head. It wasn't good enough. For once I was going to do what the Marine Corps had taught me to do best. I said to Chet, "Give me your weapon and an extra clip."

My problems were complicated. I knew nothing, for example, of the Japs' timetable. If this was a quick in-and-out operation, the sniper might disappear, running back to his hole in Sugar Loaf. But that wasn't the way their snipers worked; if they had quarry, they usually hung around until they flushed it. And this one now confirmed his personal interest in us in a thin, falsetto, singsong chant, a kind of liquid gloating: "One, two, three—you can't catch me!" Chet muttered in an even higher register, "No, but he can catch us." I was looking up at the sky. The light was clouded. Soon waves of darkness would envelop us, and conceivably it could come to the knife. I couldn't even think about that. Instead, I asked Chet, "Is your piece at true zero? He said, "It throws low and a little to the right." I took it, leaving him the carbine, and said, "His piece must throw high, and he probably doesn't know it. He had three clear shots at us and drew Maggie's drawers every time." Chet said, "But from where he is . . ." I nodded grimly. That was the worst of it. An invisible line lay between his position and ours. It was diagonal. The azimuth of his lair was about 45 degrees west; mine was 135 degrees east. On a clock this would put him at eight minutes before the hour and me at twenty-three minutes past—northwest for him, southeast to me. Since both our slabs of rock were set dead against the alley's walls, I couldn't use my weapon and my right arm without stepping clear of my boulder, exposing myself completely. All he needed to show was an arm and an eye, unless, by some great stroke of luck, he was left-handed. I had to find that out right now.

Peering out with my left eye I caught a glimpse of him—mustard colored, with a turkeylike movement of his head. He was right-handed, all right; he snapped off a shot. But he wore no harness, and I had been right about his rifle. It wasn't true; the bullet hummed overhead and hit the gorge wall, chipping it. So much for the marksmanship of the Thirty-second Manchurian Army. My job was to beat it. Luckily Windy Alley was calm just now. I checked the cartridge in the chamber and the five in the magazine. Now came the harnessing. The full sling I had perfected during my Parris Island apprenticeship involved loops, keepers, hooks, feed ends, and buckles. It took forever, which I didn't have just then, so I made a hasty sling instead, loosening the strap to fit around and steady my upper arm. My options were narrowing with each fading moment of daylight, so I didn't have time to give Chet an explanation. I handed him the grenade now and said, "Pitch it at him, as far as you can throw. I'm going to draw him out." He just stared at me. What I loved about the Raggedy Ass Marines was the way my crispest commands were unquestioningly obeyed. He started to protest: "But I don't understa—" "You don't have to," I said. "Just do it." I started shaking. I punched myself in the throat. I said, *"Now."*

I turned away; he pulled the pin and threw the grenade—an amazing distance—some forty yards. I darted out as it exploded and rolled over on the deck, into the prone position, the M1 butt tight against my shoulder, the strap taut above my left elbow, and my left hand gripped on the front hand guard, just behind the stacking swivel.

Load and lock
Ready on the left   Ready on the right   Ready on the firing line
Stand by to commence firing

My right finger was on the trigger, ready to squeeze. But when I first looked through my sights I saw dim prospects. Then, just as I was training the front sight above and to the left of his rocky refuge, trying unsuccessfully to feel at one with the weapon, the way a professional assassin feels, the air parted overhead with a shredding rustle and a mortar shell exploded in my field of fire. Momentarily I was stunned, but I wasn't hit, and when my wits returned I felt, surprisingly, sharper. Except for Chet's heavy breathing, a cathedral hush seemed to have enveloped the gorge. I could almost hear the friction of the earth turning on its axis. I had literally taken leave of my senses. There remained only a trace of normal anxiety, the roughage of mental diet that sharpens awareness. Everything I saw over my sights had cameolike clarity, as keen and well-defined as a line by Van Eyck. Dr. Johnson said that "when a man knows he is to be hanged in a fortnight, it concentrates his mind wonderfully." So does that immediate prospect of a sniper bullet. The Jap's slab of rock had my undivided attention. I breathed as little as possible—unlike Chet, who was panting—because I hoped to be holding my breath, for stability, when my target appeared. I felt nothing, not even the soppiness of my uniform. I looked at the boulder and looked at it and looked at it, thinking about nothing else, seeing only the jagged edge of rock from which he had to make his move.

I had taken a deep breath, let a little of it out, and was absolutely steady when the tip of his helmet appeared, his rifle muzzle just below it. If he thought he could draw fire with that little, he must be new on the Marine front. Pressure was building up in my lungs, but I thought I would see more of him soon, and I did; an eye, peering in the direction of my boulder, my last whereabouts. I was in plain view, but lying flat, head-on, provides the lowest possible profile, and his vision was tunneled to my right. Now I saw a throat, half a face, a second eye—and that was enough. I squeezed off a shot. The M1 still threw a few inches low, but since I had been aiming at his forehead I hit him anyway, in the cheek. I heard his sharp whine of pain. Simultaneously he saw me and shot back, about an inch over my head, as I had expected. He got off one more, lower, denting my helmet. By then, however, I was emptying my magazine into his upper chest. He took one halting step to the right, where I could see all of him. His arms fell and his Arisaka toppled to the deck. Then his right knee turned in on him like a flamingo's and he collapsed.

Other Nips might be near. I knifed another clip into the M1, keeping my eyes on the Jap corpse, and crept back to the boulder, where Chet, still breathing hard, leaned against me. I turned toward him and stifled a scream. He had no face, just juicy shapeless red pulp. In all likelihood he had been peering out curiously when that last mortar shell burst. Death must have been instantaneous. I had been alone. Nobody had been breathing here but me. My shoulder was all over blood. Now I could feel it soaking through to my upper arm. I shrank away, sickened, and the thing he had become fell over on its side. Suddenly I could take no more. I jumped out and dodged, stumbling, up the pitted, pocked alley. I braked to a halt when I came to the body of the dead sniper. To my astonishment, and then to my rage, I saw that his uniform was dry. All these weeks I had been suffering in the rain, night and day, this bastard had been holed up in some waterproof cave. It was the only instant in the war when I felt hatred for a Jap.

The Perils of Civil Rights for Nine
Little Rock Students

(from Henry Hampton and Steve Fayer
with Sarah Flynn,
*Voices of Freedom: An Oral History of the Civil
Rights Movement from the 1950s through the 1980s*)

B ETWEEN RECONSTRUCTION *and the 1950s the effort to ex-
pand civil rights for African Americans stagnated and in fact
had regressed in much of the South, where segregation remained
entrenched. In Alabama, Arkansas, Florida, Georgia, Kentucky, Louisiana, Mississippi, Missouri, North Carolina, Oklahoma, South Carolina,
Texas, and Virginia, laws prohibited black and white children from attending the same public schools.*

*In the early 1950s this inequality became the focus of the National As-
sociation for the Advancement of Colored People (NAACP). At first the
United States Supreme Court had taken the position on segregation that if
two schools (one all black, the other all white) were "separate but equal,"
then segregation was acceptable. The NAACP quickly proved there was no
equality between such schools. On May 17, 1954, in the landmark case*
Brown v. Board of Education of Topeka, Kansas, *the Supreme Court declared the racial separation of schools unconstitutional. Chief Justice
Earl Warren read the unanimous decision of the Supreme Court:*

We come to the question presented: Does segregation of children in public schools solely on the basis of race, even though physical facilities and other "tangible" factors may be equal, deprive the children of the minority group of equal educational opportunities? We believe it does. . . . We conclude that in the field of public education the doctrine of "separate but equal" has no place. Therefore, we hold that the plaintiffs. . . are, by reason of the segregation complained of, deprived of the equal protection of the laws guaranteed by the Fourteenth Amendment.

While most states accommodated the new ruling, some populations in the Deep South resisted. In Arkansas, most famously, the Little Rock School Board agreed to comply with the Supreme Court's decision, starting with gradual integration at the high school level. Unfortunately, to many the transition was unwelcome, and on the night before the 1957 school year was set to begin, Arkansas governor Orval Faubus ordered the local National Guard to surround the school and prevent black students from entering. Later that month, however, a federal judge granted an injunction against the use of National Guard troops and they were withdrawn on September 20. Whereupon President Eisenhower ordered one thousand U.S. Airborne troops to the school to protect the black students.

In the spring of 1957 there were 517 black students living in the Central High School district who were eligible to attend. Seventeen were selected as pioneers for integration. Eight withdrew, leaving "the Little Rock Nine." In this selection from Voices of Freedom: An Oral History of the Civil Rights Movement, *the nine Little Rock students face taunts, threats, and physical danger as we follow several of their lives during this integration crisis.*

* * *

ERNEST GREEN (STUDENT)

IN EARLY AUGUST, the newspapers ran the names of the nine of us who were going to Central. And I'll never forget what happened when I went to work the next day. This young guy, he was about my age, his folks were members of the Jewish country club where I worked

as a towel boy, and he came up to me and said, "How could you do it?"
I said, "What do you mean, how could I do it?" He said, "You seem like
such a nice fellow. Why is it you want to go to Central? Why do you
want to destroy our relationship?" For the first time it began to hit me
that going there was not going to be as simple as I had thought when I
signed up. I was still committed to go, but it made me know at that
time that it was going to mean a lot to a lot of people in that city. Particularly to white folks. From then on, events started to cascade.

There hadn't been any trouble expected, given the fact that there
had been other schools in Arkansas that had been integrated—Fort
Smith, Arkansas, and some others. The buses in Little Rock had been
desegregated without any problem. The library was integrated, the
medical school, and the law school at the University had admitted some
blacks. So there was an expectation that there would be minimal problems, but nothing major that would put Little Rock on the map. The
first inclination that I had of it was the night before we were to go to
school, the Labor Day Monday night. Governor Orval Faubus came on
TV and indicated that he was calling out the National Guard to prevent
our entrance into Central because of what he thought were threats to
our lives. He was doing it for our own "protection." Even at that time
that was his line. He said that the troops would be out in front of the
school and they would bar our entrance to Central—for our protection
as well as for the protection and tranquility of the city. So it was only
that Monday night that I knew that I wasn't going to be able to go to
school the next morning.

MELBA PATTILLO BEALS (STUDENT)

I wanted to go to Central High School because they had more privi-
leges. They had more equipment, they had five floors of opportunities.
I understood education before I understood anything else. From the
time I was two, my mother said, "You will go to college. Education is
your key to survival," and I understood that. It was a kind of curiosity,
not an overwhelming desire to go to this school and integrate this
school and change history. Oh no, there was none of that. I just
thought it'd be fun to go to this school I ride by every day. I want to

know what's in there. I don't necessarily want to be with those people; I assumed that being with those people would be no different than being with people I was already with. My getting into Central High School was somewhat of an accident. I simply raised my hand one day when they said, "Who of you lives in the area of Central High School?" That was two years before, in 1955. And they said, Who had good grades? and I had excellent grades. It was an accident of fate.

In late August, I was sitting in Cincinnati, Ohio, with my mother on a couch, and Walter Cronkite came on television and said that Central High School was going to be integrated in Little Rock, Arkansas, that they were already beginning to have difficulty with the white Citizens' Council and the Ku Klux Klan, and that these were the children who were going, and he mispronounced my name. My mother said, "What did he say?" And that was it, my mother started making phone calls back home. Then we came back to Little Rock and I began to be involved in the preparation that the NAACP was making for us to go to Central High School. But before that I had no real consciousness that I was going to go.

ERNEST GREEN

The morning that we went to school, Daisy [Bates, president of the Arkansas NAACP] had called us all up to meet at her house. And eight of us showed up. Elizabeth [Eckford] had missed the call—she didn't have a phone, I think—so she wasn't there. At the Bates' house, there were a number of ministers that had been involved in trying to lay a groundwork to have the integration of the schools reasonably accepted by the people in the city. So that morning, we went by car to Central. We got to school. We were at one end of the school, Fourteenth Street, and Elizabeth was at the other end, Sixteenth Street, neither group knowing where the other was. Because it's a big place. Two blocks separating it. And we just made a cursory kind of attempt to enter school, but we were denied access. Elizabeth attempted to go through the guards and have the mobs behind her. It had to be the most frightening thing, because she had a crowd of a hundred, two hundred, white people threatening to kill her. She had nobody. I mean, there was not a black face in sight anywhere. Nobody that she could turn to as a friend except this white woman, Grace Lorch, came out of a crowd and guided her through the mob and onto the bus and got her home safely. None of us knew that until we met at Daisy's house. Elizabeth was there; she was in tears. The rest of us had not experienced anything like that.

*

THE MOB SCENES AT CENTRAL HIGH *attract the national press. On September 14 Governor Faubus visits President Dwight Eisenhower and asks him to help defy the court order. Eisenhower refuses. A week later Faubus announces the removal of the National Guard surrounding the school. The Little Rock Nine still have not taken their classroom seats. They try again.*

Melba Pattillo Beals

The first day [September 25] I was able to enter Central High School, what I felt inside was terrible, wrenching, awful fear. On the car radio I could hear that there was a mob. I knew what a mob meant and I knew that the sounds that came from the crowd were very angry. So we entered the side of the building, very, very fast. Even as we entered there were people running after us, people tripping other people. Once we got into the school, it was very dark; it was like a deep, dark castle. And my eyesight had to adjust to the fact that there were people all around me. We were met by school officials and very quickly dispersed our separate ways. There has never been in my life any stark terror or any fear akin to that.

I'd only been in the school a couple of hours and by that time it was apparent that the mob was just overrunning the school. Policemen were throwing down their badges and the mob was getting past the wooden sawhorses because the police would no longer fight their own in order to protect us. So we were all called into the principal's office, and there was great fear that we would not get out of this building. We were trapped. And I thought, Okay, so I'm going to die here, in school. And I remember thinking back to what I'd been told, to understand the realities of where you are and pray. Even the adults, the school officials, were panicked, feeling like there was no protection. A couple of kids, the black kids, that were with me were crying, and someone made a suggestion that if they allowed the mob to hang one kid, they could then get the rest out. And a gentleman, who I believed to be the police chief, said, "Unh-uh, how are you going to choose? You're going to let them draw straws?" He said, "I'll get them out." And we were taken to the basement of this place. And we were put into two cars, grayish blue Fords. And the man instructed the drivers, he said, "Once you start driving, do not stop." And he told us to put our heads down. This guy revved up his engine and he came up out of the bowels of this building, and as he came up, I could just see hands reaching across this car, I could hear the yelling, I could see guns, and he was told not to stop. "If you hit somebody, you keep rolling, 'cause the kids are dead." And he did just that, and he didn't hit anybody, but he certainly was forceful and aggressive in the way he exited this driveway, because people tried to stop him and he didn't stop. He dropped me off at home. And I remember saying, "Thank you for the ride," and I should've said, "Thank you for my life."

*

W ITH THE ARKANSAS GUARD GONE, *the mayor of Little Rock appeals to Washington for U.S. troop protection. Eisenhower federalizes the Arkansas National Guard, and dispatches a thousand 101st Airborne troops to protect the Little Rock Nine.*

MELBA PATTILLO BEALS

I went in not through the side doors, but up the front stairs, and there was a feeling of pride and hope that yes, this is the United States; yes, there is a reason I salute the flag; and it's going to be okay.

The troops were wonderful. There was some fear that they were dating the girls in high school, but I don't care what they were doing; they were wonderful, they were disciplined, they were attentive, they were caring. They didn't baby us, but they were there. So for the first time I began to feel like there is this slight buffer zone between me and this hell on the other side of this wall. They couldn't be with us everywhere. They couldn't be with us, for example, in the ladies' bathroom, they couldn't be with us in gym. We'd be showering in gym and someone would turn your shower into scalding. You'd be walking out to the volleyball court and someone would break a bottle and trip you on the bottle. I have scars on my right knee from that. After a while, I started saying to myself, Am I less than human? Why did they do this to me? What's wrong with me? And so you go through stages even as a child. First you're in pain, then you're angry, then you try to fight back, and then you just don't care. You just, you can't care; you hope you do die. You hope that there's an end. And then you just mellow out and you just realize that survival is day to day and you start to grasp your own spirit, you start to grasp the depth of the human spirit and you start to understand your own ability to cope no matter what. That is the greatest lesson I learned.

ERNEST GREEN

For a couple of weeks there had been a number of white kids following us, continuously calling us niggers. "Nigger, nigger, nigger," one right after the other. Minniejean Brown was in the lunch line with me. I was in front of Minnie, and there was this white kid, a fellow who was much shorter than Minnie. Minnie was about five foot ten. This fellow couldn't have been more than five five, five four. He reminded me of a small dog, yelping at somebody's leg. Minnie had just picked up her chili, out of this line. The help in the whole cafeteria was black, all black. And before I could even say, "Minnie, why don't you tell him to shut up," Minnie had taken this chili, dumped it on this dude's head. There was just absolute silence in the place. And then the help, all black, broke into applause. And the other white kids there didn't know what to do. I mean it was the first time that anybody, I'm sure, had seen somebody black retaliate in that sense. It was a good feeling to see that happen, to be able to let them know that we were capable of taking care of ourselves. With that the school board suspended Minnie. Part of it was the attitude at that time, which was somehow we were supposed to be so stoic that we weren't to retaliate to any of this. Finally, after the suspension, they moved to remove her from school, and Minnie went to school in New York, finished up the other semester outside of Little Rock.

ERNEST GREEN

Graduation was the end of May. I had been there nine months and had thought that all I needed to do was to graduate, just get out of there, so that it would be impossible for white people to say that nobody black had ever graduated from Central High School. I was having difficulty with one course, it was a physics course, and almost up to the last minute I didn't know whether I was going to complete it successfully so that I would get out of there. But as things were, I got a fairly decent grade out of it.

The interesting thing about graduation was, being the only senior, I'd given up all the graduation activity that had gone on in the black high school—the school play and the prom and all of those kinds of things. Sometimes because of not having that activity, I would really feel isolated, because I wasn't going to Central High School's prom, and I wasn't going to be invited to be in the school play at Central. But all of the black students at Horace Mann [in Little Rock], which was the school that I would have graduated from, invited me to all the activities, included me in all of it, really made me feel a super part of it. So that I had the best of both worlds. I had cracked this white institution and still had all of my friends who were super supportive of what I was trying to do.

At the graduation ceremony, one of the guests was Martin Luther King. He was speaking in Pine Bluff, Arkansas, at the black college there. And he came up to sit with my mother and Mrs. Bates and a couple of other friends in the audience. I figured all I had to do was walk across that big huge stage, which looked the length of a football field. I'm sure it was very small, but that night before I had to walk up and receive my diploma, it looked very imposing. I kept telling myself I just can't trip, with all those cameras watching me. But I knew that once I got as far as that principal and received that diploma, that I had cracked the wall.

There were a lot of claps for the students. They talked about who had received scholarships, who was an honor student, and all that as they called the names off. When they called my name there was nothing, just the name, and there was this eerie silence. Nobody clapped. But I figured they didn't have to. Because after I got that diploma, that was it. I had accomplished what I had come there for.

★ 44 ★

Roy Benavidez,
Vietnam Superman

(from Roy Benavidez,
*Medal of Honor: One Man's Journey from
Poverty and Prejudice*)

R OY BENAVIDEZ *is an American proud of his heritage. His
father was Mexican, and when he was a soldier in Vietnam, Roy's
radio call name, affectionately given him by his brothers in
arms, was "Tango Mike/Mike," bemusedly signifying "That Mean Mexican." His mother was Yaqui Indian. The Yaqui were implacable warriors. For 350 years they fought all interlopers, be they Spanish, French,
Mexican, or American; hidden in their mountain fastness, invisible in
their barren deserts, the Yaqui were feared by even the Apaches. Such a
bloodline would serve Master Sergeant Benavidez well in Vietnam.*

*President Ronald Reagan pinned the Congressional Medal of Honor
on Benavidez's jacket for his exceptional courage during a firefight in
1968. During his first tour of duty in Vietnam, Roy had stepped on a land
mine and miraculously recovered; he returned to Vietnam for service as a
member of the elite special forces, the Green Berets. On May 2, 1968, twelve
soldiers, including three of Benavidez's Green Beret friends, were dropped
into a small jungle clearing west of Loc Ninh, inside the Cambodian bor-*

der, on a secret reconnaissance mission authorized by special presidential orders. A North Vietnamese regiment quickly surrounded the twelve-man team, whose leader carried highly confidential papers and radio equipment. Three helicopter attempts were made to evacuate the Green Beret team; at the time Roy Benavidez was safely back at the base. As soon as he heard the news, however, he boarded the next helicopter and flew into the fighting to save his friends. Benevidez's account of his remarkable, almost superhuman performance in combat is taken from his autobiography, Medal of Honor: One Man's Journey from Poverty and Prejudice.

*   *   *

I WAS AT A CHURCH SERVICE. A chaplain was using the hood of a jeep as the altar. The first I knew that anyone was in trouble, I heard the clattering of weapons over the radio and a voice begging for help.

I ran for the airstrip, knowing they would need all the help they could get. Everyone was gathered around the radio, listening for news. We learned that one of the choppers, piloted by Warrant Officer Curry, had gone down, but that a second pilot had stopped to pick up the crew and they were headed back.

One chopper returned. It was badly shot up, but no one seemed to be injured. The second chopper to come in, though, was a whole different story. The pilots flew in, landing as fast as they could with their beat-up chopper. For a moment I stood there, staring at the chopper. I didn't see how it could still fly.

That's when I saw Michael Craig, the door gunner for that chopper. He had taken a couple of hits, and I knew that he was going to die. He was only nineteen years old. We had celebrated his birthday just two months earlier.

I helped them take Michael out of the helicopter; then I sat with him on the ground. I put my arms around him and called for help. His pilot was Roger Waggie and he joined me. Michael was still conscious and in great pain, gasping for breath.

Michael was like our son or little brother. We all loved him. "Oh, my God, my mother and father . . ." he said as I held him. Then he died, right there in my arms, his parents' only child. I lowered Craig's body and turned to the co-pilot of the chopper. "Who's in trouble down there?"

Waggie told me it was Wright's team, and I felt my heart sink. Those were my brothers, and there wasn't much anyone could do to help them. My mind seemed to explode.

No one was giving up. After changing out a few parts, one of the pilots, Larry McKibben, announced he was going back in. While they were working on the chopper, members of the different crews compared notes about what they had seen. Each of them claimed there were more NVA [North Vietnamese Army] down there than the man before him had.

I had to go with McKibben. When I heard his chopper start, I jumped in and buckled up. "You're going to need a bellyman," I told him. "I'm it."

Midway there, I wondered what I was really doing. I hadn't really thought my actions through before I got on the chopper. But once I could hear the cracking of guns below me, I began to think. I needed a plan.

"I don't think I can get down there," McKibben said. "It's just too hot."

That's when I really made up my mind. I couldn't leave them down there. We had to do something. Everyone had been trying and trying hard, of course, but there had to be a way. I just couldn't sit there and listen to my buddies die on the radio. "I'll get down there," I promised McKibben. "Just get me as close as you can." My fear was gone. I can't explain what happened inside me. The best way to express my actions is "autopilot." It seemed that all I had been taught in my entire lifetime just kicked in and my body went on autopilot.

McKibben flew straight into the gunfire, zigzagging the chopper and making every attempt to dodge the bullets that were being fired at the aircraft. I crossed myself one last time, threw a bag of medical supplies out the doorway, and rolled out with nothing but my buddies on my mind.

Gunships above us were diving and firing in a desperate effort to draw enemy fire away from us. I managed to get safely to a treeline, but I hadn't been on the ground more than a few seconds when the first bullet hit my leg. To be honest, I thought it was a thorn until I took a good look at it. That's how pumped up I was. The gunships overhead were now out of ammo and were almost out of fuel. They headed back to Loc Ninh to rearm and refuel.

I found Mousseau first, and even though I knew the team was in trouble, I was shocked by what I saw. Mousseau had taken a round in the eye and in the shoulder. His right eye had been blown out of its socket, and his eyeball was hanging down on his cheek. He had dragged himself to a tree and propped himself up against it, running out of energy. But he was a good soldier, and he could still fire his weapon. He was determined to keep going. The CIDG's [Civilian Irregular Defense Group] were in what seemed to be a pool of blood, but everyone seemed to be patched up as well as could be expected.

I used Mousseau's radio to call McKibben. "You better come get us fast," I said. "We're in real bad shape."

The firing had died down some. I couldn't see any of the enemy, and I figured that the gunship strikes might have slowed them down. But I did see O'Connor, and he indicated that two of them were still alive.

I told O'Connor that we were going to get out. "We're going to live. We don't have permission to die yet. Not here." He and the other survivor, his interpreter, half dragged themselves toward us, but suddenly the firing started up again, and I motioned them back.

That's when I took another round, in my thigh. I wondered how I was going to be able to walk back to the chopper, but I sent green smoke up to signal McKibben anyway, and yelled for everyone to run for the chopper.

Everyone who could make it got in. The crew inside dragged the men into the chopper, but O'Connor and the interpreter were still out there. I ran along the treeline, spraying it with an AK-47 until I reached O'Connor. McKibben and the chopper were right behind me.

"What does Wright still have on him?" I asked O'Connor. He told me Wright had been carrying the Standard Operating Instructions (SOI), some maps, and the intelligence-gathering device. I knew the documents were classified, and if I left them on his body, they would fall into enemy hands. I would have to get them. There was no choice.

I tried to get the interpreter to his feet, but he couldn't make it. He begged me not to leave him, and I promised I wouldn't. I told him to crawl toward O'Connor, and for both of them to get to the chopper. Then I went looking for the SOI.

I needed the documents, but I also needed Wright. I had no intention of leaving him there like that. But as I was crying and dragging him toward the chopper, a third shot caught me square in the back. I dropped my friend's body and fell forward.

I guess I was knocked unconscious. When I woke up, I rolled onto my stomach and got to my knees. I had a hard time breathing and I was soaked in blood. I knew I was going to have to leave Wright. I didn't have the strength to carry him. But when I turned to run to the chopper, I saw that it was nothing more than a smoking mess. It had crashed to the ground just before I had passed out.

McKibben was dead, I knew that much. The co-pilot, Fernan, ran from around the nose. He had a blood-covered tree branch sticking out of his ear. He was waving a gun . . . dazed and in pain.

O'Connor and the interpreter were lying about ten feet from the crash. They hadn't made it all the way there. A CIDG, who seemed to be only mildly wounded, also lay on the ground. I sent him to get O'Connor's radio, certain he was dead, but I was mistaken. He called that he was okay.

Five men, including Mousseau, had survived the crash. They were hanging out of the chopper's tail, returning enemy fire. I knew I had to get them out of there. The NVA could have easily blown up the whole chopper with them inside. When we got the men out, I shot out the radio so it could no longer transmit.

We tried to set up a perimeter around a small clump of trees. We divided into two groups, and I followed Mousseau's team. I called for heavy air support, and when it came, I dispensed morphine shots. One of the CIDGs who was badly wounded pleaded with me to kill him. The poor guy's guts were hanging out, and with the sun and wind, they were drying up. Man, that's a tough thing to take.

Our air force forward air controller was Lieutenant Robin Tornow, who was now overhead. He had located two F-100s, with ordnance on board, in the area being flown by Captains Howard "Howie" Hanson and Robert Knopoka. He was calling them as the ground battle kept getting worse.

Tornow called out, "This is a Daniel Boone tactical emergency. I say again. This is a Daniel Boone tactical emergency."

Captains Hanson and Knopoka had taken off from Phan Rang Airbase, Republic of South Vietnam, on a preplanned strike mission targeted somewhere north of Saigon. Their call signs were "Bobcat" followed by two numerical digits.

Their mission was uneventful until they were about to drop their ordnance on the preplanned target. Just before they received clearance to drop, they heard Tornow on the UHF "guard channel" requesting immediate assistance for "U.S. troops in heavy contact." That was the highest priority request and always brought U.S. fighters to those in contact.

"Howie" Hanson, as flight lead, contacted the forward air controller and was told to vector north into an area where they were generally not permitted to fly. That area was Cambodia.

With FAC clearance they "screamed" across the border from South Vietnam into Cambodia and were the first fighters on the scene. Tornow, at great personal risk, "hung tight" and vectored the F-100s to the target.

The following minutes belonged to TAC AIR and gunship strike after strike after strike. They were pouring it on the PZ and back into the woodlines and the clearing in front of us that intersected with the small road.

Branches, slivers of wood, metal, dirt and body parts were stinging us from the percussion caused by the bombing. We could feel the tremendous heat of the afterburners of the F-100s. That's how low they were flying.

Gunships were diving and diving between the passes of the jets. The air support was like a swarm of killer bees attacking us. It later reminded me of that passage of scripture from the Book of Revelations about the sky turning black with locusts.

Through the middle of this moment of hell came a lone slick that touched down about twenty to thirty meters away. We knew that this was our last hope to leave alive. We loaded the last of our ammunition. This was it. Now or never.

I got to O'Connor and gave him his third shot of morphine. I also took another shot in the leg. We were under heavy fire again, and I wasn't sure what was going to happen to us, even though I tried to reassure O'Connor. He must've thought I was losing it because I don't think any of us really thought we were going to get out of there.

We were surrounded. There was no way we could fire back at the NVA because it was impossible to tell where their shots were coming from. They seemed to be coming from everywhere. We had no way of knowing until later that our LZ was surrounded by over 350 NVA and thirty crew-served weapons (machine guns).

The air attack managed to stop the assault for a few moments, but it was long enough for that single chopper to lower right in front of us, and a Special Forces medic, Sergeant Sammons, ran to us from the aircraft. Roger Waggie and his newly formed crew of volunteers, WO Bill Darling as crew chief and WO Smith as door gunner, came to our rescue. Everyone had come to the rescue. What I saw was the American fighting man at his best.

The two of us carried or dragged as many of the men as we could. But the NVA were firing directly at the chopper, shooting the men as they were lifted aboard. Two of the men were shot in the back as they tried to crawl to safety inside the chopper. I could barely see through the matted blood in my eyes due to shrapnel wounds on my face and head. Waggie's chopper was badly shot up. He and his co-pilot were shooting through their front windshield with their thirty-eight pistols, while Darling and the door gunner and Smith were firing the M-60s at separate groups of NVA charging from the sides. Darling and Smith had volunteered to man a gun because they knew we were running out of men, and as officers they didn't have to volunteer for this situation. All I know is that because they did, soldiers would live.

I made another trip to find Mousseau. He was lying in the grass. I tried to carry him to the chopper. I didn't even notice when one of the NVA soldiers, lying on the ground, got to his feet. I also didn't notice when he slammed his rifle butt into the back of my head. I turned to look at him. Both of us were surprised, I because I hadn't seen him, and he, because I had turned around after he had delivered the blow, but he reacted quickly and hit me again. I fell, my head swimming in pain.

I now had only one weapon with me, my Special Forces knife. I reached for it, and when I did, he pointed his bayonet at the front of my belly. Fortunately, he hesitated, and it gave me enough time to get to my feet. He sliced my left arm with the bayonet, and I shouted to O'Connor to shoot him. But he was too drugged to move, so I did the only thing I could. I stabbed him with every bit of strength I had left, and when he died, I left my SF knife in him. The last round in my stomach had exposed my intestines, and I was trying to hold them in my hands. I could see Mousseau lying on the floor, staring at me with his one good eye. I reached down and clasped his hand and prayed that he would make it until we reached Saigon, where the medics could help him. Sadly, he would be among the approximately two hundred men who died on both sides during that battle.

I hoped that LeRoy was with us, that at least his body was going home to his family. I had loaded some bodies on the chopper, and I prayed that his was among them. The problem was that I couldn't always see what I was doing because I was bleeding profusely, and the blood obscured my vision.

How Waggie flew that chopper is a miracle itself. No instruments were left, badly shot up, the cabin floor ankle-deep in blood, and we were headed in the wrong direction. Some air force jets showed up and turned us around for home.

Later I learned that LeRoy did make it out of the jungle. Sergeant Rodolfo "Banzai" Montalvo led a platoon of Chinese Nung mercenaries into the area the next day on a body recovery mission. He located LeRoy and the other dead CIDGs.

Banzai told me that the NVA had been "waiting" for us that day. He said that he counted approximately thirty foxholes with crew-served weapons around the LZ and more dead NVAs than he had time to count. As they were attacked by NVAs and had to leave the area, he observed that the entire area was a carnage of dead bodies.

My next semiconscious memory was that of lying on the ground outside the chopper. I couldn't move or speak. I was in deep shock, but

I knew that the medics were placing me in a body bag. They thought I was dead, and I couldn't respond. To this day I can still hear the sound of the snaps being closed on that green bag.

My cycs were blinded. My jaws were broken. I had over thirty-seven puncture wounds. My intestines were exposed. Jerry Cottingham recognized my face in the body bag before it was closed. I remember Jerry screaming, "That's Benavidez. Get a doc!" When the doctor placed his hand on my chest to feel for a heartbeat, I spat into his face. He quickly reversed my condition from dead to "He won't make it, but we'll try."

I was truly once again totally in God's hands.

⋆ 45 ⋆

Astronauts Rocket
to the Moon

(from Buzz Aldrin and Malcolm McConnell,
Men from Earth)

T*HE FIRST MAN IN orbital flight around the earth was a Russian, Yuri Gagarin, in April 1961. President John F. Kennedy responded within weeks to this Russian challenge, promising that the USA would place a man on the moon and return him safely "within this decade." Kennedy's proposal was highly ambitious by any account, but on July 20, 1969, Neil Armstrong became the first man to walk on the moon, with his now famous words: "That's one small step for man, one giant leap for mankind."*

We may simply think of astronauts as well-trained airplane pilots, but in fact, only the "best of the best" are selected. In the race to the moon each Apollo astronaut was a combination of test pilot, engineer, computer guru, celestial navigator, emergency M.D., and wise improviser. Each had natural leadership, a sense of humor, profound knowledge, and the ability to think swiftly. In sum, the astronauts were personable, cool, courageous, and calculating risk-takers.

All astronauts know they may die, either in training or in space. In fact, three died from lack of oxygen in a fire during a routine ground test as they lay in the command module attached to the gantry. Four pilots died in NASA aircraft accidents. Apollo 13 almost ran out of electricity and oxygen in 1970 as it approached the moon. Even Neil Armstrong had a close call while flying a simulator lunar landing training vehicle (LLTV). As he started to land, a sudden gust of wind spun the LLTV out of control. Armstrong ejected to parachute to earth, and his LLTV crashed and burned. Every mission had its brushes with death.

For all astronauts, knowledge and training insured their survival and success. The pilots and copilots had the responsibilities of millions of integrated systems; an incalculable number of variables fell on their shoulders to understand, operate, and at times remedy. These men and women not only knew the risks, they understood the complexity of those risks and embraced them to conquer them. It was not a matter of daring without knowledge as in the days of Christopher Columbus. It was a matter of accepted responsibility for the people, systems, and goals of manned space flight.

From Men from Earth, *published on the twentieth anniversary of the* Apollo 11 *mission, we turn now to Buzz Aldrin's firsthand account as copilot of the first landing on the moon—where temperatures range from minus 250 degrees to 200 degrees Fahrenheit, where there is no air to breathe, where gravity is one sixth that of Earth, and where space radiation and hazardous micrometeorites shower down.*

* * *

NEIL AND I had moved into the LM [Lunar Module] in preparation for undocking from *Columbia*. Mike told us to be patient while he worked through his preseparation checklist. Mike had to replace the drogue and probe carefully before sealing off the command module and separating from the LM. We were all conscious of the fragile docking mechanism. In 24 hours, we would be needing that tunnel again. When Mike finally finished we were on the far side of the moon again, in the middle of our thirteenth orbit.

Back on the moon's near side, we contacted Houston, so that Mission Control could monitor the stream of data from the LM and CSM

[Command Service Module]. The hatches were sealed; now the LM was truly the *Eagle* and the command module was *Columbia.* "How's the czar over there?" Mike asked Neil.

Neil watched the numbers blinking on our DSKY [Display and Keyboard], counting down for the separation maneuver. "Just hanging on and punching buttons," Neil answered. We exchanged long blocks of data with Mike and with Houston. The numbers seemed endless.

Houston rewarded us with a terse, "You are go for separation, *Columbia.*"

Mike backed the command module away with a snapping thump. Then the moonscape seemed to rotate slowly past my window as the LM turned, until it hung above my head. "The *Eagle* has wings," Neil called.

Neil and I stood almost shoulder to shoulder in our full pressure suits and bubble helmets, tethered to the deck of the LM by elastic cords. Now we were the ones who were engrossed with long checklists. But I felt a sharp urgency as I flipped each switch and tapped the data updates into the DSKY. When Mike thrust away from us in *Columbia,* he simply said, "Okay, *Eagle,* you guys take care."

"See you later," was all Neil replied. It sounded as if they were heading home after an easy afternoon in the simulator room.

Just before Neil and I looped around the back of the moon for the second time in the LM, Charlie Duke, who was now capcom, told us, "*Eagle,* Houston. You are go for DOI [Descent Orbit Insertion]."

"Descent orbit insertion" was a 29.8-second burn of our descent engine that would drop the perilune, the lowest point in our orbit, to eight miles above the surface. If everything still looked good at that point, Houston would approve Powered Descent Initiation (PDI). Twelve minutes later, Neil and I would either be on the moon or would have aborted the landing attempt.

★   ★   ★

The LM flew backward, with our two cabin windows parallel to the gray surface of the moon. The DOI burn was so smooth that I didn't even feel a vibration through my boots, only a slow sagging in my knees as the deceleration mounted when we throttled up from 10 percent to 100 percent thrust. Before the throttle-up was finished, I could tell from the landing radar data that our orbit was already bending. Neil turned a page in the flight plan and grinned at me through his helmet.

The moon rolled by silently outside my window. The craters were slowly becoming more distinct as we descended. There wasn't much to do except monitor the instruments and wait for AOS (acquisition of signal). As we got closer, the moon's color changed from beige to bleached gray. The hissing crackle of Houston's signal returned to our earphones. "*Eagle,* Houston," Charlie Duke called through the static. "If you read, you're go for powered descent. Over."

Neil nodded, his tired eyes warm with anticipation. I was grinning like a kid. We were going to land on the moon. . . .

LUNAR MODULE *EAGLE,* JULY 20, 1969

We were just 700 feet above the surface when Charlie gave us the final "go," just as another 12 02 alarm flashed. Neil and I confirmed with each other that the landing radar was giving us good data, and he punched PROCEED into the keyboard. All these alarms had kept us from studying our landing zone. If this had been a simulation back at the Cape, we probably would have aborted. Neil finally looked away from the DSKY screen and out his triangular window. He was definitely not satisfied with the ground beneath us. We were too low to identify the landmark craters we'd studied from the *Apollo 10* photographs. We just had to find a smooth place to land. The computer, however, was taking us to a boulder field surrounding a 40-foot-wide crater.

Neil rocked his hand controller in his fist, changing over to manual command. He slowed our descent from 20 feet per second to only nine. Then, at 300 feet, we were descending at only three and a half feet per second. As *Eagle* slowly dropped, we continued skimming forward.

Neil still wasn't satisfied with the terrain. All I could do was give him the altimeter callouts and our horizontal speed. He stroked the hand controller and descent-rate switch like a motorist fine-tuning his cruise control. We scooted across the boulders. At two hundred feet our hover slid toward a faster descent rate.

"Eleven forward, coming down nicely," I called, my eyes scanning the instruments. "Two hundred feet, four and a half down. Five and a half down. One sixty. . . ." The low-fuel light blinked on the caution-and-warning panel, ". . . quantity light."

At 200 feet, Neil slowed the descent again. The horizon of the moon was at eye level. We were almost out of fuel.

"Sixty seconds," Charlie warned.

The ascent engine fuel tanks were full, but completely separate from the descent engine. We had 60 seconds of fuel remaining in the descent stage before we had to land or abort. Neil searched the ground below.

"Down two and a half," I called. The LM moved forward like a helicopter flaring out for landing. We were in the so-called dead man's zone, and we couldn't remain there long. If we ran out of fuel at this altitude, we would crash into the surface before the ascent engine could lift us back toward orbit. "Forward. Forward. Good. Forty feet. Down two and a half. Picking up some dust. Thirty feet. . . ."

Thirty feet below the LM's gangly legs, dust that had lain undisturbed for a billion years blasted sideways in the plume of our engine.

"Thirty seconds," Charlie announced solemnly, but still Neil slowed our rate.

The descent engine roared silently, sucking up the last of its fuel supply. I turned my eye to the ABORT STAGE button. "Drifting right," I called, watching the shadow of a footpad probe lightly touching the surface. "Contact light." The horizon seemed to rock gently and then steadied. Our altimeter stopped blinking. We were on the moon. We had about 20 seconds of fuel remaining in the descent stage. Immediately I prepared for a sudden abort, in case the landing had damaged the *Eagle* or the surface was not strong enough to support our weight.

"Okay, engine stop," I told Neil, reciting from the checklist. "ACA out of detent."

"Got it," Neil answered, disengaging the hand control system. Both of us were still tingling with the excitement of the final moments before touchdown.

"Mode controls, both auto," I continued, aware that I was chanting the readouts. "Descent engine command override, off. Engine arm off. . . ."

"We copy you down, *Eagle*," Charlie Duke interrupted from Houston.

I stared out at the rocks and shadows of the moon. It was as stark as I'd ever imagined it. A mile away, the horizon curved into blackness.

"Houston," Neil called, "Tranquillity Base here. The *Eagle* has landed."

It was strange to be suddenly stationary. Spaceflight had always meant movement to me, but here we were rock-solid still, as if the LM had been standing here since the beginning of time. We'd been told to expect the remaining fuel in the descent stage to slosh back and forth after we touched down, but there simply wasn't enough reserve fuel remaining to do this. Neil had flown the landing to the very edge.

"Roger. Tranquillity," Charlie said, "we copy you on the ground. You've got a bunch of guys about to turn blue. We're breathing again. Thanks a lot."

I reached across and shook Neil's hand, hard. We had pulled it off. Five months and 10 days before the end of the decade, two Americans had landed on the moon.

⋆ 46 ⋆

September 11, 2001:
The Passengers Counterattack the
Hijackers on United Flight 93

(from Jere Longman,
Among the Heroes: United Flight 93
and the Passengers and Crew Who Fought Back)

I*N HIS TORA BORA redoubt in Afghanistan Osama bin Laden,
the al-Qaeda leader, sat listening to Khalid Shaikh Mohammed, the
alleged mastermind of the September 11 attacks. While in the Philippines in 1994–95, Mohammed had participated in a plan to blow up
twelve Western airliners simultaneously. That plot was foiled by the arrest
of its two ringleaders. Now in 1996 Mohammed sought bin Laden's support and financial aid to enact the same plan in the United States. His
concept was to simultaneously hijack five airplanes on the East Coast and
hit targets in New York and Washington, D.C., and hijack five airplanes
on the West Coast, headed for Asia, and blow these up over the Pacific. Bin
Laden bought the idea that a large, transcontinental airplane, fully
loaded with fuel and piloted by a pilot bent on suicide, was a made-to-
order flying missile of great precision. In 1998 Mohammed received bin
Laden's blessing to begin plotting the September 11 attacks, which would
kill nearly three thousand civilians on American soil.*

In 1999 Bin Laden offered Mohammed four operators; they trained in Afghanistan in commando tactics and how to blend in to American society, which they did—even taking lessons on how to fly commercial aircraft. The "muscle men" had to be selected and trained too. In the spring of 2000, Bin Laden canceled the idea of further hijackings in eastern Asia to concentrate on the United States. By September 11, 2001, the men were in place and armed with box cutters. The timeline of that tragic day:

7:59 A.M. *American Airlines Flight 11, a Boeing 767 carrying 81 passengers and 11 crew, departs from Boston bound for Los Angeles. It is hijacked fourteen minutes later and at 8:46 A.M. crashes into the North Tower of the World Trade Center between the ninety-fourth and ninety-eighth floors at a speed of 490 miles per hour.*

8:14 A.M. *United Airlines Flight 175, a full-fueled Boeing 767 with 65 passengers and 9 crew members, takes off from Boston for Los Angeles. The hijackers seize the plane at 8:42 A.M. and slam it into the South Tower of the World Trade Center at 9:03 A.M. at 590 miles per hour. About 2,600 occupants die in the two towers.*

8:20 A.M. *American Flight 77, a Boeing 757 with 58 passengers and 6 crew, departs from Virginia's Washington-Dulles Airport for Los Angeles. At 9:37 American Flight 77 crashes into the Pentagon, where 125 military are killed.*

8:42 A.M. *United Airlines Flight 93, a Boeing 757, takes off from Newark, New Jersey, after a forty-minute delay, bound for San Francisco with 37 passengers and 7 crew. At 9:28 it is hijacked, and at 10:03 A.M. it crashes.*

From New York Times *reporter Jere Longman's 2002 account,* Among the Heroes: United Flight 93 and the Passengers and Crew Who Fought Back, *here is the full story of Flight 93, whose passengers rallied against the terrorists and, at the cost of their own lives, saved the country from another horrific bombing.*

* * *

T HE SKY ON SEPTEMBER 11 dawned cerulean blue—rinsed, cloudless, apparently cleansed of tumult. It was just after Labor Day. School was in session, and autumn had arrived in New York City.

Dressed in his navy-blue uniform, Capt. Jason Dahl, 43, entered United Airlines' flight operations center at Newark International Airport at about 7 A.M. He logged on to a computer and verified his schedule. Flight 93 was scheduled to depart at one minute after eight. Dahl signed a release for the plane, a Boeing 757, placing it in his control. Then he met LeRoy Homer, Jr., the first officer on Flight 93. The two men had not flown together before but they had one thing in common: this was the only job they ever really wanted.

Boarding the plane, Dahl checked the cockpit, ensured that the flight data recorder and cockpit voice recorder were functioning, and examined the engine instrument indicators. After entering his destination into the computerized flight management system, Dahl met with Deborah Welsh, the flight attendant in charge, also known as the purser. The two spoke about security. Up to an altitude of 10,000 feet, the cockpit was to remain sterile—no one could enter. Dahl and Welsh also established the secret knock sequence she would use before entering the cockpit.

In the event of a hijacking, pilots and flight attendants had been taught passive compliance. The United flight attendants' manual advised: "Be persuasive to stay alive. Delay. Let the hijackers select a liaison. Do not challenge their power. Use eye contact to calm and reduce anxiety." This advice was based on old rules that would soon no longer apply. Rules that were mortally inadequate. Rules that did not anticipate the use of planes as suicide missiles. Advice to remain unthreatening would not work against a knife at the throat and an intent at martyrdom.

In a taxi on his way to the airport, Tom Burnett left a voicemail for his boss. There was room on United Flight 93 to San Francisco, he said, so he would be leaving at 8 A.M. instead of 9:20, on Flight 91. He would get home early to see his wife, Deena, and their three young daughters in San Ramon, Calif. Tom was chief operating officer of

Thoratec Corporation, a leading manufacturer of heart pumps for patients awaiting transplants.

At 7:20 A.M., a United agent at Gate 17 made the first boarding call for Flight 93. Thirty-eight-year-old Lauren Grandcolas, a marketing executive, called her husband, Jack, in San Rafael, Calif. With the three-hour time difference, he was still in bed, so she left a message. Her car service had arrived early. "Just want to let you know I'm on the 8:00 instead of the 9:20," she said.

At 7:33, as he waited in the boarding area, Todd Beamer of Cranbury, N.J., got a call on his cell phone. It was his colleague Jonathan Oomrigar, a vice president at Oracle software, where Todd was a top account manager. Todd had generated $33 million worth of business the last fiscal year, blowing out all the numbers. Six months earlier, he had put together Oracle's largest deal ever with Sony's semiconductor division. He and Oomrigar had an important meeting today at headquarters in Redwood Shores, Calif. A top Sony executive was flying in from Japan to discuss a possible new deal.

Flight attendants Lorraine Bay and Wanda Green were standing inside the doorway at row eight, greeting passengers as they boarded. The ten passengers traveling in first class were guided down the aisle to their left. The 27 traveling in coach were ushered down the aisle to the right.

Deborah Welsh now began making her way through the forward cabin, asking if she could hang up suit coats and jackets. Four Middle Eastern men were among those in first class. Ziad Jarrah took seat 1B, first-row aisle, close to the cockpit. Ahmed al-Haznawi, Saeed al-Ghamdi and Ahmed al-Nami sat in 3C, 3D and 6B, which was in the last row of first class.

At six feet tall, Debbie Welsh could be an assertive personality. In her Hell's Kitchen neighborhood in New York City, she had become an activist for pedestrian rights after a neighbor's mother had been struck by a bicyclist and died of complications from a broken hip.

Mark Bingham was the last passenger to board Flight 93. He had been driven to the airport by his friend Matt Hall. Mark ran a public relations firm that had an office in San Francisco and another in New York City. He was flying to the West Coast for a business meeting and a weekend wedding. Mark sat in seat 4D, in the same row as Tom Burnett.

Soon everyone was seated, and the door closed and sealed. Only 37 passengers were on the plane. Captain Dahl now asked for authorization to depart the gate. It was about 8 A.M.

* * *

American Airlines Flight 11, meanwhile, was leaving from Boston's Logan Airport for a flight to L.A. The Boeing 767 was instructed to climb to 35,000 feet, but the plane climbed to only 29,000 feet and then halted radio contact.

At 8:24, a voice thought to be that of the terrorist Mohamed Atta, who apparently believed he was speaking to the passengers, was overheard by air traffic controllers: "We have some planes. Just stay quiet and you will be okay. We are returning to the airport. Nobody move, everything will be okay. If you try to make any moves, you'll endanger yourselves and the airplane."

The Boston air control tower alerted air traffic centers that Flight 11 had been hijacked. Several minutes later, the Boeing 767 made a turn that took the shape of a shark's fin and headed south for Manhattan. At 8:34, a hijacker spoke again: "Nobody move, please; we are going back to the airport. Don't try to make any stupid moves."

The pilots, flight attendants and passengers on United Flight 93 were unaware of the trouble aboard American Flight 11. They were also unaware that the four Middle Eastern men sitting in first class were confederates of Mohamed Atta's.

On a videotape made perhaps six months earlier, a man identified as Ahmed al-Haznawi said, "We left our families to send a message that has the color of blood. This message says, 'Oh, Allah, take from our blood today until you are satisfied. The time of humiliation and subjugation is over.' It is time to kill Americans in their homeland, among their sons, near their forces and intelligence."

By September 11, the four Islamic men were to have showered, shaved and splashed themselves with cologne. They should have blessed their bodies by reading the Koran. They should have also blessed their luggage, clothes, knives, passports and papers. They were to have remembered that "this is a battle for the sake of God." When the airplane took off, they were to pray for victory over the infidels and say, "May the ground shake under their feet."

When the confrontation came, they were to clench their teeth and "strike like champions who do not want to go back to this world." They had been told, "Strike for God's sake. Take prisoners and kill them."

The terrorists intending to hijack four flights this morning had done their homework. They had apparently taken rehearsal trips and armed themselves with low-tech weapons that would not be detected or confiscated. The hijackers on Flight 93 had at least one box cutter—legal to carry aboard—and another cutting device that seemed homemade, a piece of metal wrapped in tape.

The Monday rush of businessmen and tourists was over. Tuesday was a light travel day. There were fewer passengers to confront and maximum fuel to detonate on a scheduled cross-country flight. It was Tuesday, September eleventh. 9/11. 9-1-1. National Emergency Day.

Flight 93 fell into a line of about a dozen planes taxiing toward the runway. When he reached the front for takeoff, Captain Dahl was instructed by the Newark control tower, "United 93, you are cleared to position, hold on runway four left."

"Roger, position hold, four left."

And finally: "United 93, you're cleared for takeoff, runway four left."

The flight attendants were seated. Deborah Welsh took a jump seat in first class, while Lorraine Bay and Wanda Green took the jump seats at the door between first class and coach. The other two attendants, CeeCee Lyles and Sandra Bradshaw, were sitting in the rear galley.

With the 36,600-pound thrust of its twin Pratt & Whitney engines, Flight 93 roared down the runway, the nose wheels lifting and the rest of the plane leaving the ground with a swooping weightlessness. It was 8:42 A.M. The plane went northeast on a 40-degree heading, turned another 20 degrees to the right and followed this path for four miles toward Manhattan. It held to an altitude of 2500 feet and then banked gracefully, nearly due west. To the right, the towers of the World Trade Center were visible in the metallic shimmer of early morning.

Five minutes later, American Flight 11 rammed into the North Tower of the World Trade Center at nearly 500 miles an hour. Not long after, at 9:03 A.M., United Flight 175 sliced into the South Tower, a deadly scythe, and sent up a mushrooming explosion.

*   *   *

United Flight 93 now climbed past 23,000 feet. The Boeing 757 soon reached a cruising altitude of 35,000 feet, its flight path to San Francisco appearing as a magenta line on a cockpit computer screen. Captain Dahl trimmed the plane, stabilizing it along all three axes, and turned on the autopilot.

Once it became evident that Flight 175 had been hijacked, the United flight operations center began alerting all of its flights. The dispatchers began firing off messages: "Beware cockpit intrusion." "Confirm operations are normal." The alert was sent to United Flight 93 via a cockpit computer device called ACARS, the Aircraft Communications Addressing and Reporting System. The warning arrived as a kind of e-mail, making a chiming sound.

"Confirmed," United 93 answered, the one-word response typed on a computer-screen keypad.

As Flight 93 approached the Cleveland center—a regional air traffic center that guided long-range, high-altitude flights—one of the pilots reported in with a chipper "Good morning." While pilots on other flights asked in a puzzled way about problems in New York, Flight 93 did not. Then came an interruption, an indeterminate rush in the cockpit, a screaming of "Hey" and violent non-words, high-pitched and muffled exertion, the rustling of surprise and ominous resolve.

An air traffic controller was startled by what he heard. "Did somebody call Cleveland?" he asked.

Silence followed, and then either Captain Dahl or First Officer Homer had the presence of mind to hit an audio button. The cockpit scuffle played desperately over the air traffic control frequency. More yelling, an American voice in a bloodcurdling scream, "Get out of here." Then the same scream again, this time sounding wounded and pleading. And then "Get out of here" again, an angry, unheeded order.

The controller at Cleveland center sounded alarmed and asked Flight 93 to verify its altitude. No reply. Another call to verify. More silence, the plane heading westward into a threatening unknown.

"United 93, Cleveland," the controller said, raising his voice. "United 93, if you hear Cleveland, ident please."

The Cleveland center called to another aircraft in the area, United Flight 1523: "Did you hear interference on the frequency, screaming?"

"Yes, I did," the pilot replied.

"Okay," Cleveland said. "United 93, if you hear the center, ident."

Then, from American 1060: "Ditto on the other transmission."

Cleveland: "American 1060, you heard that also?"

"Yes, sir, twice."

"Roger, thanks," Cleveland said. "I just wanted to confirm it wasn't some interference."

It was 9:32 A.M. The hijackers had control of Flight 93 now and were out of breath from subduing the pilots. "Ladies and gentlemen here, it's the captain," one of the terrorists said, apparently believing he was speaking to the passengers but broadcasting instead over the air traffic control frequency. "Please sit down. We have a bomb aboard."

The voice had a panting formality, an odd pleasantness. "Please sit down," the man asked again. This was believed to be the voice of Ziad Jarrah, a 26-year-old from Lebanon. He had entered the United States in June 2000 and immersed himself into transient, touristy, racially diverse South Florida so thoroughly that he seemed no more out of place than the humidity. His skin was so light, his appearance so blandly handsome, that some thought him European instead of Arabic.

In the weeks before September 11, Jarrah had lived in Florida with Ahmed al-Haznawi, another suspected terrorist aboard United Flight 93. Earlier in the summer, all four of the hijackers on the flight opened Florida SunTrust bank accounts with cash deposits.

As did terrorists on the other suicide flights, Jarrah traveled to Las Vegas over the summer and studied self-defense. He lived near other hijackers in South Florida, training at nearby flight schools. But because al Qaeda cells operated with murkiness, the overlapping contact was flimsy and difficult to detect. The terrorists knew they were participating in a "martyrdom operation," but they did not know its precise nature until shortly before boarding the planes, according to a tape that was later released by the Defense Department.

Flight 93 now turned directly toward Washington, perhaps toward the U.S. Capitol, its neoclassical dome standing nearly 300 feet above the ground. The hijacker had made a bomb threat. Commercial pilots on Jarrah's frequency, along with the air traffic controllers directing them from Cleveland, could not believe the chilling words they heard.

Cleveland center: "You're unreadable. Say again, slowly."

Jarrah spoke once more. "Hi, this is the captain. We'd like you all to remain seated. There is a bomb aboard. And we are going to turn back to the airport. And they have our demands, so please remain quiet."

Cleveland began ordering other jets to turn away from Flight 93.

"United 93, do you hear Cleveland center?" asked Cleveland.

There was no answer. The plane's transponder had been shut off, so neither the air traffic center in Cleveland nor United's operations center in Chicago could determine Flight 93's altitude.

Cleveland asked the pilot of another plane, Executive Jet 956, if he could change course and attempt to visually spot Flight 93. The pilot saw it, lost it, and saw it again. Then it was headed right for him, causing him to make an evasive turn.

"United 93, do you still hear the center?" asked Cleveland. "United 93, do you hear Cleveland?"

Twenty more times the controller would call Flight 93. And twenty times he would get no response.

* * *

In San Ramon, Calif., Deena Burnett awoke to get her three daughters ready for school. Deena went downstairs and turned on the television to check the weather. Every channel was carrying urgent news about the World Trade Center being hit by an airplane.

What about Tom? Deena thought. He was on his way home from New York. As she watched, a second plane rammed the World Trade Center. Then the phone rang. It was Tom's mother, Beverly, calling from Bloomington, Minn. As they spoke, the call waiting on Deena's phone beeped. It was her husband, calling from his cell phone.

"Tom," she said. "Are you okay?"

"No," he replied. "I'm on United Flight 93 from Newark. The plane has been hijacked. They already knifed a guy. One of them has a gun. They're saying there is a bomb on board. Please call the authorities." And he hung up.

Deena scribbled down what he'd said and noted the time: 6:27, 9:27 in the East. Tom had spoken quietly, quickly. A guy had been knifed, he said. Deena assumed Tom meant a passenger, and she had asked him before he hung up. He confirmed that, yes, it was a passenger.

Sheer terror now coursed through Deena's body. *What do I do? Who do I call for a hijacking? Dial 911. Maybe they'll know who to call.*

She dialed and was transferred to the police and then to the FBI. She was telling an agent her husband's flight number and destination when her call waiting interrupted again. It was Tom. Again, Deena noted the time: 6:34, 9:34 in the East.

"They're in the cockpit," Tom said.

The man who had been knifed was dead. Tom had tried to help but felt no pulse. Deena told him what she knew, that planes were hitting the World Trade Center. Terrorists seemed to be hitting designated targets. Immediately Tom pieced things together. "Oh, my God," he said. "It's a suicide mission."

Deena heard Tom relaying the information to someone else. Were commercial airlines being hijacked? Tom asked her. How many planes? Who was involved? Deena gave him what little information she had. His plane seemed to be turning east, Tom reported. Then he said, "Wait, wait . . . We're going south."

What could he see? Deena asked. It was a rural area, just fields. "I've got to go," he said. Deena called the FBI again. *Things would work out. We have a perfect life. A good job, great kids, health. Nothing bad ever happens to us.* Then the television reported that the Pentagon had been hit. *It must be Tom's plane.* Deena sat down and started wailing, a keening despair strange and full of loss.

The phone rang again. It was Tom a third time. It was 6:45, 9:45 in the East. For a fleeting second Deena thought Tom had miraculously survived the crash into the Pentagon.

"Tom, you're okay?" she asked.

"No, I'm not," he said.

A third plane had hit the Pentagon, she told him. He repeated this to others. The planes seemed to be commercial airliners originating in the East, Deena said. Had she called the authorities? Yes, Deena said. "They didn't seem to know anything about your plane." The hijackers, Tom said, were talking about crashing the plane into the ground. "We have to do something." He and others were making a plan. "A group of us. Don't worry," he told Deena, "I'll call you back."

Tom had not spoken elaborately in his phone calls. He wasn't whispering sweet nothings of farewell. He was making a plan to get home safely to his wife and three children. Deena couldn't accept that he was going to die. *We are the golden couple. Everything good was showered on us. Nothing bad ever happened.*

Tom then called a fourth time. It was 6:54, 9:54 in the East. He asked about their daughters. They wanted to talk to him, Deena said. Tom said he would talk to them later. He and others had come up with a plan to regain control of the plane over a rural area. "We have to do something," he said. There was no time to wait for the authorities. "It's up to us. I think we can do it . . . Pray, Deena, just pray."

"I love you," Deena said.

"Don't worry," Tom said. Then, "We're going to do something."

★ ★ ★

If anyone could formulate a plan, organize a team of people, it was Lauren Grandcolas, seated in row 11. She had spent a career in marketing and advertising, most recently for *Good Housekeeping*. In her spare time she volunteered at AIDS walks and adopt-a-kid programs. She was also a certified emergency medical technician.

When her husband, Jack, awoke on September 11, he looked out the window and felt a kind of oddness. The clouds seemed to have strange shapes. He turned the television to ESPN and then switched to the news. He sat there horrified. Planes had flown into the World Trade Center. When he saw that other planes had been grounded, he felt certain Lauren would be safe. Her flight was not due to take off until 9:20. Then Lauren's sister, Vaughn, called him. "Have you heard from Lauren?" she asked. "We need to find out where she is." Lauren had taken an earlier flight, Vaughn told him.

"You're kidding me," Jack said.

He went downstairs to the kitchen and saw two messages on the machine. The first said she would be home early. In the second message, Lauren seemed calm and hopeful, yet there was urgency in her voice. "Honey, are you there? Jack, pick up, sweetie," Lauren said from Flight 93. "Okay, well, I just wanted to tell you I love you. We're having a little problem on the plane. I love you more than anything, just know that. I'm comfortable and I'm okay for now. I'll—I—just a little problem. I love you. Please tell my family I love them too. Bye, honey."

Jack was overwhelmed and could barely speak. He dropped to his knees. "No, my God, no."

Mark Bingham called his mother, Alice Hogian, and told her that he loved her. It was not unusual for Mark to call Alice to express his love, but it was unusual for him to do it at 6:44 in the morning. His voice sounded both controlled and rattled. "I'm on a flight from Newark to San Francisco," Mark told her. "There are three guys aboard who say they have a bomb."

"Who are these guys, Mark?"

A long pause. Mark said he was calling from an Airfone. He was probably in first class, Alice thought, and the hijackers were probably up there. She worried that he was drawing attention to himself, making himself a target. Then the line went dead. Alice saw the television and understood. She felt that Mark knew what he was up against, that the situation was dire and he was calling to say goodbye.

Alice dialed Mark's cell phone number. Later, she would retrieve her message from the phone company. "Mark, this is your mom," she said. "The news is that [the plane has] been hijacked by terrorists. I would say, Go ahead and do everything you can to overpower them, because they're hell-bent. Okay, I love you, sweetie. Goodbye."

In Catonsville, Md., Esther Heymann was speaking to her husband, Ben Wainio, vice president of First Union Bank in nearby Columbia. Anxious calls had been coming in full of worry and uncertainty. The call-waiting signal clicked and Heymann put her husband on hold. Her stepdaughter, Elizabeth Wainio, was on the other line. It was about 9:50.

"Hello, Mom," Elizabeth said. "We're being hijacked. I'm calling to say goodbye." Esther knew her stepdaughter was flying. They had spoken before the plane had left Newark. If she heard Elizabeth's voice again this morning, Esther knew what it would mean.

"Do you know what's going on?" the younger woman asked.

"No," Esther said. Her first thought was to comfort her daughter, not alarm her. If Elizabeth wanted to talk about what was happening aboard the plane, that was her choice.

This "really nice person" sitting next to her, perhaps Lauren Grandcolas, had given her the phone to call her family, Elizabeth said. Elizabeth spoke calmly, but her breathing was shallow.

"Elizabeth, I've got my arms around you. I'm holding you and I love you," Esther told her daughter.

"I can feel your arms around me," Elizabeth said. "And I love you too."

Esther looked out the window in her bedroom. She told her daughter to hold the hand of the nice person beside her. Elizabeth spoke about each person in her family and said how much she loved them. She worried about how her older brother, Tom, and her younger sister, Sarah, would handle this terrible news.

"Let's just be here in the present," Esther said. "Let's look out at the beautiful blue sky and take a few deep breaths." With that, Elizabeth's breathing seemed to grow deeper and more relaxed.

The hijackers apparently did little to prevent the passengers and flight attendants from making phone calls. People spoke nervously but freely. Perhaps, with so few hijackers trying to control so many passengers, the terrorists considered it too risky to intervene. And perhaps the passengers in the rear of the plane were being only loosely watched or left unattended.

Still, none of the calls mentioned one critical element. If the passengers were able to overpower the hijackers and regain control of the plane, who would fly it? Had the pilot and copilot been killed by the hijackers? Were they still alive? There was no way to know conclusively.

Unlike the other hijacked planes, Flight 93's navigational system was apparently reprogrammed from its original destination to Reagan National Airport, providing the Boeing 757 with steering coordinates toward Washington. Yet Flight 93 had descended to less than 10,000 feet, not even two miles above ground. Either it was trying to fly below radar, as investigators theorized, or it was navigating clumsily due to inadequately trained hijacker pilots.

At 9:45, Todd Beamer reached an Airfone operator in Oak Brook, Ill. The operator took the call, but the news of a hijacking apparently traumatized her, so she handed off the call to Lisa D. Jefferson, a supervisor with 17 years of experience and a soft, reassuring voice. "I understand this plane is being hijacked," Lisa Jefferson said to the caller. "Please give me detailed information as to what's going on."

Todd Beamer introduced himself. Speaking in a calm voice, he said that three people had hijacked the plane. Two with knives went into the cockpit and locked the door. The third person stood in first class with what appeared to be a bomb strapped to his waist. He ordered everyone to sit down; then he closed the curtain between first class and coach. Ten people were in first class, 27 were in coach, and there were five flight attendants, Todd told her.

Two people were lying on the floor in first class, Todd said. He did not know if they were still alive. Lisa Jefferson overheard a flight attendant tell Todd that the men on the floor were the captain and co-captain. She seemed certain, and Todd repeated this information. If he felt his life was threatened, Jefferson said, he could lay the phone down. Just don't hang up, she said to him. Keep the line open. Todd said he was fine, free to talk.

"Do you know what they want?" Todd asked her. "Money or ransom or what?" He seemed confused.

"I don't know," Jefferson said.

Then Todd's voice rose a bit. "We're going down, we're going down. No, wait, we're coming back up. We're turning around. I think we're going north."

It was disorienting; he didn't know where they were going. "Oh, Jesus, please help us," Todd said. He asked Jefferson to say the Lord's Prayer with him. They did, and then Todd began the 23rd Psalm: "The Lord is my shepherd; I shall not want . . ."

The plane seemed to take another dive, and nervousness came back into Todd's voice. "Oh, God," he said. "Lisa."

The operator thought this was odd. She had introduced herself as Mrs. Jefferson and had not given Todd her first name. "Yes?" she said.

"That's my wife's name."

"Oh, that's my name too," Lisa Jefferson said.

"Oh, my God," Todd said of the coincidence.

He told her about his family, his two young sons, David and Andrew, and his wife, who was expecting a third baby. He had thought about calling Lisa but did not want to upset her if he didn't have to. "If I don't make it out of this, would you please call my family and let them know how much I love them?" Todd asked Jefferson. Of course, she said.

The plane moved erratically now, and Todd thought he'd lost contact with the operator. "Lisa, Lisa," he hollered into the phone.

"I'm still here, Todd," she said. "I'll be here as long as you will."

He said that he and a few passengers were going to "jump" the hijacker with the bomb and try to regain control of the plane.

"I stand behind you," Jefferson told him.

Then, in the background, Jefferson heard an "awful commotion," men's voices raised and hollering and women screaming, "Oh, my God," "God help us," and "Help us, Jesus."

Afterward Todd seemed to turn away from the phone to speak with someone else. "You ready?" he said to someone. "Okay. Let's roll."

* * *

Flight 93 descended to the southeast. Rodney Peterson and Brandon Leventry, auto mechanics in Boswell, Pa., were crossing Main Street in this former mining town at about 10 A.M. when they saw a jetliner lumbering through the sky at about 2000 feet.

Peterson had worked previously at an airport and was familiar with flight patterns. He knew that jetliners generally approached nearby Johnstown airport at a much higher altitude. "Check that plane out," he said to Leventry.

Then the plane did something odd. It dipped its wings sharply to the left, then to the right. "Something ain't right," Peterson said.

The wings leveled off but the plane was headed southward. Peterson broke into a run, trying to follow the plane up Main Street. But the jetliner disappeared over a line of trees and houses. "If they were fighting with the hijackers, I guarantee it happened right here," Peterson said later. It dipped left and dipped right. No plane that big flies like that."

Much of what happened in the final minutes of the flight falls into conjecture, officials say. No clear determination was provided by the voice recorder, which operated on a 30-minute loop and taped remarks using microphones in the pilots' headsets and in the cockpit ceiling. Still, family members later said they were provided an encouraging scenario when they heard the voice recorder tape: Federal prosecutors in the upcoming trial of Zacarias Moussaoui, said to be the intended 20th hijacker, proposed that the passengers used a food cart as a battering ram to enter the cockpit, even if they were ultimately unable to save a plane that was flying too low and fast and turning upside down.

The final loop on the voice recorder tape began at 9:31. Near the beginning, an accented voice in English ordered someone to sit down. A voice implored in English, "Don't, don't." A woman pleaded not to be hurt or killed, saying, "Please, please."

After the plane was hijacked, at least one flight attendant pressed a code on an Airfone and reached a United office in San Francisco, airline officials said. She reported that one hijacker was holding the crew at knifepoint. Evidence that at least one flight attendant was bound by the hands would turn up at the World Trade Center; the same method of restraint was suspected on Flight 93.

Patrick Welsh, husband of purser Deborah Welsh, said he was told by United that one flight attendant was stabbed early in the takeover. Presumably, this was learned from a call to United. It was "strongly implied," he said, that his wife had been a victim, given her position in first class. "Knowing Debbie, she would have resisted," Patrick said.

An alarm sounded when the autopilot was disconnected. An alarm also would have sounded because the plane was traveling at 575 miles an hour in the final minutes, far exceeding the design limits of 425 miles an hour below 20,000 feet and the regulated limit of 287 miles an hour below 10,000 feet. It could have even broken the sound barrier for a while, according to Hank Krakowski, head of United's flight operations control in Chicago on September 11. The apparent maneuvering of hydraulics could also be heard, along with the rushing of wind close to the ground.

The fate of the pilots, Jason Dahl and LeRoy Homer, Jr., could not be clearly determined. About midway through the tape, one hijacker said to another, "Let the guys in now," apparently referring to other terrorists entering the cockpit. A vague instruction was given to bring the pilot back in. What this meant is not known. Was one of the United pilots needed to shut off the autopilot's alarm or to set a new course? Was the body of one of the pilots to be brought into the cockpit?

Flight 93 continued in trouble as it flew over U.S. Highway 30, now 80 miles southeast of Pittsburgh. The morning fog was just burning off as Terry Buder worked among the metal carcasses at Stoystown Auto Wreckers. When Butler heard a loud rumbling sound, he looked toward the mountains. Then he turned and saw the United jet flying above a house. It seemed to be only 500 feet above the ground now.

No big plane flies that low around here, he thought. *It will hit a tree.*

The plane skimmed over a ridge, made a sharp right turn and began to roll over on its side. Several miles away, truck driver Rob Kimmel saw the jetliner fly overhead, banking hard to the right. It was only 100, 200 feet off the ground as it crested a hill. "I saw the top of the plane, not the bottom," Kimmel said.

Lee Purbaugh didn't hear the plane until it was nearly on top of him. He was working at the Rollock scrap metal company, standing on a bluff overlooking a reclaimed strip mine. The Boeing 757 flew over his head, 40 or 50 feet above him, he estimated, so close that the bottom of the plane seemed a tan color as it reflected the fields below.

The plane was hurtling along at nearly 600 miles an hour. According to investigators, the jetliner rolled onto its back. Then it made a fatal, sharp tilt and dived, one wing and the nose of the plane hitting with an awkward crumpling. The plane seemed swallowed in flames, there was an explosion, and a dark cloud mushroomed. It was just after 10:00.

* * *

Twenty minutes longer, and Flight 93 would have reached Washington in a finale of suicidal fireworks.

* * *

Six days after the crash, families of the passengers and crew members gathered on a bluff above the soft, cratered soil where Flight 93 had been entombed. They cried and prayed and left remembrances of their loved ones, flowers, photographs.

In his State of the Union address on January 29, 2002, President George W. Bush said, "None of us would ever wish the evil that was done on September the eleventh. Yet after America was attacked, it was as if our entire country looked into a mirror and saw our better selves. We were reminded that we are citizens, with obligations to each other, to our country and to history. We began to think less of the goods we can accumulate and more about the good we can do. For too long our culture has said, 'If it feels good, do it.' Now America is embracing a new ethic and a new creed: 'Let's roll.' "

Jack Grandcolas, the husband of Lauren Grandcolas, said of the passengers: "They were the ultimate patriots. They did the most democratic thing they could do. They gathered information, they voted to do something. They knew there's a ninety-eight percent chance we're not going to make it, but let's save others. That's what Americans are all about. Lauren's bravery has given me hope. All their bravery has given me hope."

Acknowledgments

I wish to thank these friends who helped create this book: Peter Riva, my literary agent, and his wife, Sandra, whose advice, enthusiasm and connections brought this book to print. Henry Ferris, executive editor at William Morrow, who believes that history can inspire as well as inform, and considered *American Courage* a worthy expression especially when told by participants. Peter Hubbard, editorial assistant, who organized and edited the chapters with diplomacy and good taste. Mary L. Douglas, who started the ball rolling with her interest in an old manuscript of mine, introduced me to Connie and Pete Wyrick, thereby rekindling my yen to publish after a long hiatus. Julia vanderElst, my mission control, skillfully produced and juggled over eighty chapters in the original manuscript with lightening speed and fidelity. Ellen Bates for her historical research done with depth and dispatch. Helene Steinhauer for her intrepid editorial counsel. Keith and Frannie Moffat for the introduction to Pickett's Charge. Harry Webster for leading me to the spy story. And Roland T. Ely, Harvard

Ph.D. for his valuable insights and wise suggestions on reading the manuscript.

As with any endeavor that spans years, these kind people each contributed a building block to this book: Dotsie and Jack Adams, Bob Aquilina (USMC Historic Center), Jean Becker, Amber Bowman, David Bryant and staff (New Canaan Library), James Byrne, Lee Drake, Nick Fellner, Jack Fitch, Karl Gridley, Alexandra Hatcher, Fritz Kraker, Pat Kruger, Gerry Kunutz, William Larsen (NASA), Carol Mann, Ada Osborn, Susan Peck, Gerry and Maria Phillips, Elise Pickney, William Reese, Charles Reis, Dennis Shaub, Herb Taylor, Bert Warden, Nancy Warden, Phoebe Welsh, Tom White, Sue Yonce, Richard Williams, and Barbara Zimmerman. My thanks to each of you.

—*HWW III*

Bibliography

Adams, Ramon F. *The Old-Time Cowhand*. New York: Macmillan, 1961.

Alcott, Louisa May. *Hospital Sketches and Camp and Fireside Stories*. Boston: Roberts Brothers, 1892.

Aldrin, Buzz, and Malcolm McConnell. *Men from Earth*. New York: Bantam Books, 1989.

Allen, Ethan. *A Narrative of Colonel Ethan Allen's Captivity from the Time of His Being Taken by the British, Near Montreal, on the 25th Day of September, in the Year 1775 to the Time of His Exchange, on the 6th Day of May, 1778*. 1779. Reprint, Boston: Draper and Folsom, 1779.

Benavidez, Roy, with John R. Craig. *Medal of Honor: One Man's Journey from Poverty and Prejudice*. Washington: Brassey's, 1999.

Boone, Daniel. "The Adventures of Col. Daniel Boone, One of the First Settlers, Comprehending Every Important Occurrence in the Political History of That Provence." In *The Discovery, Settlement, and Present State of Kentucke*, by John Filson. Wilmington: James Adams, 1784.

Brown, George R. T. "Spirit of Seventy-Six." In *Yankee Life by Those Who Lived It*. Edited by June Barrows Mussey. New York: Alfred A. Knopf, 1947.

Cartwright, Peter. *Autobiography of Peter Cartwright, the Backwoods Preacher*. New York: Carlton & Porter, 1857.

Congressional Globe. 46 vols. Washington, D.C., 1834–73.

Cook, James H. *Fifty Years on the Old Frontier.* New Haven: Yale University Press, 1923.

Cooper, William. *A Guide in the Wilderness: Or the History of the First Settlement in the Western Counties of New York.* Dublin: Gilbert & Hodges, 1810. Reprint, Rochester, N.Y.: G. P. Humphrey, 1879.

Crockett, Davey. *Col. Crockett's Exploits and Adventures in Texas.* Cincinnati: U. P. James, 1839.

Erskine, Gladys Shaw. *Broncho Charlie—A Saga of the Saddle.* New York: Thomas Y. Crowell, 1934.

Fisher, Rev. H. D. *The Gun and the Gospel: Early Kansas and Chaplain Fisher.* 2d ed. Chicago and New York: Medical Century, 1899.

Franklin, Benjamin. *The Autobiography of Benjamin Franklin.* New York and London: G. P. Putnam's Sons, 1889.

Glines, Carroll V. *The Doolittle Raid: America's Daring First Strike Against Japan.* New York: Orion Books/Crown Publishers, 1988.

Goodrich, Rev. Charles A. *Lives of the Signers of the Declaration of Independence.* New York: Thomas Mather, 1832.

Hampton, Henry, and Steve Fayer, with Sarah Flynn. *Voices of Freedom: An Oral History of the Civil Rights Movement from the 1950s through the 1980s.* New York: Bantam Books, 1990.

Havighurst, Walter. *George Rogers Clark: Soldier in the West.* New York: McGraw-Hill Book Company, 1952.

Houston, General Sam. *Speech of General Sam Houston, of Texas, Refuting Calumnies Produced and Circulated Against His Character as Commander-in-Chief of the Army of Texas; Delivered in The Senate of the United States,* February 28, 1859. Washington: Congressional Globe Office.

Hyde, H. Montgomery. *Cynthia.* New York: Farrar, Straus and Giroux, 1965.

Inglis, Rewey Belle, John Gehlmann, Mary Rives Bowman & Norman Forseter. *Adventures in American Literature.* New York: Harcourt, Brace, 1945.

Jacobs, Harriet, "for the author." *Incidents in the Life of a Slave Girl.* Boston: 1861.

Jones, U. J. *History of the Early Settlement of the Juniata Valley.* 1855. Reprint, Historical Society of Pennsylvania, 1889.

Lindbergh, Charles A. *We.* New York: G. P. Putnam's Sons, 1927.

Lodge, Henry Cabot. *George Washington. American Statesmen,* vol. 1. Boston and New York: Houghton, Mifflin and Riverside Press, 1890.

Lodge, Henry Cabot, and Theodore Roosevelt, "The Flag Bearer." In *Hero Tales from American History.* New York: Century, 1901.

Longman, Jere. "Let's Roll: The Untold Story of Flight 93." *Reader's Digest,* September 2002. Reprinted from *Among the Heroes: United Flight 93 and the Passengers and Crew Who Fought Back.* New York: HarperCollins, 2002.

Longstreet, James. *From Manassas to Appomattox: Memoirs of the Civil War in America.* Philadelphia: J. B. Lippincott, 1896.

Manchester, William. *Goodbye, Darkness: A Memoir of the Pacific War.* Boston: Little, Brown, 1980.

M'Clung, John A. *Sketches of Western Adventure; Containing an Account of the Most Interesting Incident Connected with the Settlement of the West from 1755–1794.* Philadelphia: Grigg and Elliot, 1832.

Morison, Samuel Eliot. *Of Plymouth Plantation 1620–1647 by William Bradford, Sometime Governor Thereof.* New York: Alfred A. Knopf, 1952.

Parton, James. *General Jackson.* New York: D. Appleton, 1892.

Rhodes, Richard. *The Making of the Atomic Bomb.* New York: Simon & Schuster, 1986.

Rink, Paul. *A. P. Giannini: Building the Bank of America.* Chicago: Encyclopedia Britannica Press, 1963.

Rollins, Philip Ashton. *The Cowboy—His Characteristics, His Equipment, and His Part in the Development of the West.* New York: Charles Scribner's Sons, 1922.

Roosevelt, Theodore. *Theodore Roosevelt: An Autobiography.* New York: Macmillan, 1913.

Rowlandson, Mary White. *The Soveraignty & Goodness of God, together with the Faithfulness of His Promises Displayed; Being a Narrative of the Captivity and Restauration of Mrs. Mary Rowlandson. Commended By Her to all that Desires to Know the Lords Doing to, and Dealings with Her. Especially to Her Dear Children and Relations. The Second Addition* [sic] *Corrected and Amended. Written by Her Own Hand for Her Private use, and Now Made Publick at the Earnest Desire of Some Friends, and for the Benefit of the Afflicted.* Cambridge, Mass.: Samuel Green, 1682.

Ruxton, George Frederick Augustus. *Adventures in Mexico and the Rocky Mountains.* London: J. Murray, 1847.

Ryan, Cornelius. *The Longest Day—June 6, 1944.* New York: Simon & Schuster, 1994.

Stone, Fred A. "Flowers for Charley McDaniels." In *The Best of True West.* Edited by Joe Austell Small. New York: Julian Messner, 1964.

Washington, George. *The Journal of Major George Washington: Sent By the Hon. Robert Dinwiddie, Esq., His Majesty's Lieutenant-Governor, and Commander in Chief of Virginia, to the Commandant of the French Forces on [the] Ohio, to which are Added, the Governor's Letter, and a Translation of the French Officer's Answer.* Williamsburg: William Hunter, 1754.

Wellman, Paul I. *Death on Horseback: Seventy Years of War for the American West.* Philadelphia: J. B. Lippincott, 1947.

Whipple, A. B. C. *Tall Ships and Great Captains.* New York: Harper Brothers, 1953.

Yoakum, Henderson. *History of Texas from Its First Settlement in 1685 to Its Annexation to the United States in 1846.* New York: Redfield, 1856.

York, Alvin C. *Sergeant York: His Life Story and War Diary.* Edited by Tom Skeyhill. Garden City, N.Y.: Doubleday Duran, 1928.

"A Conversation with Mr. Rollins." In *Princeton University Library Chronicle 9,* no. 4 (June 1948). Reprinted in *A Vanished Society: Essays in American History*. Edited by Esther Felt Bentley. Princeton: Princeton University Library, 1962.

"Letter from J. M. Nevins to Russell Nevins in Wisconsin, Sacramento City, Dec. 2, 1849." In David Boring, *Nobility in the Rough*. New York: Daniel Ryerson, 1938.

Permissions

Grateful acknowledgment is made to reprint excerpts from the following:

Chapters 1 and 2: "The Pilgrims' Farewell" and "The Decimation and Survival of Plymouth Colony" by William Bradford. From *Of Plymouth Plantation 1620–1647 by William Bradford*, edited by Samuel Eliot Morison, copyright 1952 by Samuel Eliot Morison and renewed 1980 by Emily M. Beck. Used by permission of Alfred A. Knopf, a division of Random House Inc.

Chapter 15: "American Privateer and British Man-of-War Clash" by A. B. C. Whipple. Pages 128–141 from "VII—Privateer—The Prince de Neufchâtel" from *Tall Ships and Great Captains* by A. B. C. Whipple and illustrations by G. A. Little. Copyright 1951, 1956, 1960 by A. B. C. Whipple. Reprinted by permission of Harper-Collins Publishers, Inc. Reprinted by permission of the William Morris Agency, Inc., on behalf of the author.

Chapters 29 and 30: " 'Portugee' Phillips's Desperate Ride, 1866" and "Dull Knife's Last Fight, 1878" by Paul I. Wellman. From *Death on Horseback: Seventy Years of War for the American West* by Paul I. Wellman. Copyright © 1934, 1935, 1947 by Paul I. Wellman. Copyright renewed © 1974 by Laura M. Wellman. Reprinted by permission of Paul I. Wellman, Jr.

Chapter 31: "Nighttime Stampede" by Ramon F. Adams, James H. Cook, and

Philip Ashton Rollins. Pages 289–290 from "Stampedes" by Ramon F. Adams. Reprinted with the permission of Scribner, an imprint of Simon & Schuster Adult Publishing Group, from *The Old-Time Cowhand* by Ramon F. Adams. Copyright © 1948, 1949, 1954, 1959, 1960, 1961 by Ramon F. Adams.

Chapter 34: The author's introduction to "Saved by Cowboys" by Philip Rollins, pages 53–55, from "The Cowman's Code of Ethics" by Ramon F. Adams. Reprinted with the permission of Scribner, an imprint of Simon & Schuster Adult Publishing Group. From *The Old-Time Cowhand* by Ramon F. Adams. Copyright © 1948, 1949, 1954, 1959, 1960, 1961 by Ramon F. Adams.

Chapter 35: "Earthquake Pulverizes San Francisco, 1906; Fires Spread; Banker Struggles to Survive" by Paul Rink. From *A. P. Giannini: Building the Bank of America* by Paul Rink. Copyright © 1963 by Encyclopaedia Britannica, Inc. Reprinted by permission of Encyclopaedia Britannica, Inc.

Chapter 37: "Five Aviators Die Trying to Cross the Atlantic Ocean—Then Came Charles Lindbergh" by Charles A. Lindbergh. From *We* by Charles A. Lindbergh. Copyright 1927, renewed © 1955 by Charles A. Lindbergh. Used by permission of G. P. Putnam's Sons, a division of Penguin Group (USA) Inc. Reprinted by permission of Yale University.

Chapter 38: "Jimmy Doolittle's Daylight Raid Over Tokyo—April 18, 1942" by Carroll V. Glines. From *The Doolittle Raid: America's Daring First Strike Against Japan* by Carroll V. Glines. Copyright © 1988, 1991 by Carroll V. Glines. Reprinted by permission of the author.

Chapter 39: "WANTED: An Elegant Female Spy to Bribe or Seduce Top Officials at the Nazi-Controlled, Vichy French Embassy" by H. Montgomery Hyde. From "Assault on an embassy" from *Cynthia* by H. Montgomery Hyde. Copyright © 1965 by Cynmont Productions Ltd. Reprinted by permission of Farrar, Straus and Giroux, LLC. Copyright © 1965 by H. Montgomery Hyde. Reprinted by permission of SLL/Sterling Lord Literistic, Inc.

Chapter 40: "Émigré Physicist Enrico Fermi Tests the Precursor to the Atomic Bomb in a Chicago Squash Court" by Richard Rhodes. From *The Making of The Atomic Bomb* by Richard Rhodes. Copyright © 1986 by Richard Rhodes. Reprinted with the permission of Simon & Schuster Adult Publishing Group. Reprinted with the permission of JCA Literary Agency, Inc., on behalf of the author.

Chapter 41: "D-Day: World War II" by Cornelius Ryan. From *The Longest Day—June 6, 1944* by Cornelius Ryan. Copyright © 1959 by Cornelius Ryan; copyright renewed 1987 by Kathryn Morgan Ryan, Victoria Ryan Rida and Geoffrey J. M. Ryan. Reprinted with the permission of Simon & Schuster Adult Publishing Group. Reprinted with the permission of McIntosh and Otis, Inc.

Chapter 42: "Sniper Fight on Okinawa" by William Manchester. From *Goodbye, Darkness—A Memoir of the Pacific War* by William Manchester. Copyright © 1979, 1980 by William Manchester. Reprinted by permission of Don Congdon Associates, Inc.

Chapter 43: "The Perils of Civil Rights for Nine Little Rock Students" by Henry Hampton and Steve Fayer with Sarah Flynn. From *Voices of Freedom: An Oral History of the Civil Rights Movement from the 1950s through the 1980s* by Henry Hampton and Steve Fayer with Sarah Flynn. Copyright © 1990 by Blackside, Inc. Used by permission of Bantam Books, a division of Random House, Inc. Reprinted with permission by Blackside, Inc.

Chapter 44: "Roy Benavidez, Vietnam Superman" by Roy Benavidez with John R. Craig. From *Medal of Honor: One Man's Journey from Poverty and Prejudice* by Roy Benavidez with John R. Craig. Copyright © 1995 by Roy Perez Benavidez and John R. Craig. Reprinted by permission of Potomac Books Inc.

Chapter 45: "Astronauts Rocket to the Moon" by Buzz Aldrin and Malcolm McConnell. From *Men From Earth* by Buzz Aldrin and Malcolm McConnell. Copyright © 1989 by Buzz Aldrin and Malcolm McConnell. Reprinted by permission of William Morris Agency, Inc., on behalf of the Authors.

Chapter 46: "September 11, 2001: The Passengers Counterattack the Hijackers on United Flight 93" by Jere Longman. From *Among the Heroes: United Flight 93 and the Passengers and Crew Who Fought Back* by Jere Longman. Copyright © 2002, 2003 by Jere Longman. Reprinted by permission of HarperCollins Publishers Inc. Adapted from the September '02 issue of *Reader's Digest*.